Stephen Russell Mallory

ALSO BY RODMAN L. UNDERWOOD
AND FROM McFARLAND

Waters of Discord: The Union Blockade of Texas During the Civil War (2003; paperback 2008)

Stephen Russell Mallory

*A Biography of the
Confederate Navy Secretary
and United States Senator*

RODMAN L. UNDERWOOD

McFarland & Company, Inc., Publishers
Jefferson, North Carolina, and London

> The present work is a reprint of the illustrated case bound edition of Stephen Russell Mallory: A Biography of the Confederate Navy Secretary and United States Senator, first published in 2005 by McFarland.

LIBRARY OF CONGRESS CATALOGUING-IN-PUBLICATION DATA

Underwood, Rodman L., 1930–
Stephen Russell Mallory : a biography of the Confederate Navy secretary and United States senator / Rodman L. Underwood.
    p.   cm.
Includes bibliographical references and index.

ISBN 978-0-7864-4927-9
softcover : 50# alkaline paper ∞

1. Mallory, Stephen R. (Stephen Russell), 1813–1873.
2. Confederate States of America. Navy — Biography.
3. Cabinet officers — Confederate States of America — Biography.
4. Legislators — United States — Biography.
5. United States — History — Civil War, 1861–1865 — Naval operations, Confederate.
6. Confederate States of America. Navy — History.
7. United States. Congress. Senate — Biography.   I. Title.
E664.M25U53 2010   973.7'57092 — dc22   2005024681

British Library cataloguing data are available

©2005 Rodman L. Underwood. All rights reserved

No part of this book may be reproduced or transmitted in any form or by any means, electronic or mechanical, including photocopying or recording, or by any information storage and retrieval system, without permission in writing from the publisher.

On the cover: *Monitor* and *Virginia*, March 9, 1862, by Raymond Bayless (Naval Historical Center, NH 84512 KN, and U.S. Navy Art Collection, donation of Raymond Bayless, 1975); Stephen Russell Mallory (Library of Congress)

Manufactured in the United States of America

McFarland & Company, Inc., Publishers
Box 611, Jefferson, North Carolina 28640
www.mcfarlandpub.com

Acknowledgments

First and foremost, I must express my gratitude to Dean B. Mahin, who is a friend and fellow author as well as an energetic and intelligent man. He gave this manuscript's first draft exacting scrutiny and developed a host of constructive criticisms that improved the finished product. I am beholden to him for his interest and help.

My quest for primary documents took me to four university libraries and four historical societies in three states—Florida, North Carolina, and Virginia. In Florida, the Pensacola Historical Society's Mallory collection focuses on the family's activities in that city. The curator, Dan Scott, went out of his way for me. The University of West Florida's John C. Pace Library, Special Collections Department, also is in Pensacola. Much of the Mallory documentation found there—some of which is unique and not found elsewhere—was a gift from Cora Mallory, Stephen Mallory's granddaughter. Ms. Katrina King was prompt and efficient in pulling documents for my perusal. Another rich source of Mallory documentation is the University of Florida at Gainesville where, in the George A. Smathers Library, there are abundant resources that concentrate upon Florida history. Dr. James Cusick guided me through the intricacies of a large university library system and was always responsive to my questions before, during, and after my on-site visit. Important letters from Mallory to Florida governor John Milton, as well as papers and books pertaining to general Florida history, are found at the Florida Historical Society, Alma Clyde Field Library of Florida History, in Cocoa, Florida. The society's executive director, Dr. Nick Wynne, and his wife, Debra, the library archivist, were of great assistance.

In North Carolina, a mother lode of Mallory documents is found in the Southern Historical Collection at the University of North Carolina, Chapel Hill. The most important of these documents are "Stephen R. Mallory Papers" (#1186), and "Stephen R. Mallory Diary and Reminiscences" (two volumes, #2229). The staff was cordial, attentive to my needs, and efficient.

Virginia also has extensive primary documents relating to Stephen Mallory. The University of Virginia, Albert and Shirley Small Special Collections Library, at Charlottesville houses 697 items found in the Samuel Barron Papers (#10134) that are important for increased understanding of Mallory's role as navy secretary. The staff here was helpful, as were the people at the Virginia Historical Society in Richmond, where I reviewed numerous documents. The Museum of the Confederacy also is located in Richmond and it is a first-class resource for everything "Confederate." Ms. Heather W. Milne was especially helpful in providing me with a reproduction of a rarely seen Stephen Mallory portrait.

Rodman L. Underwood
Port Orange, Florida

Contents

Acknowledgments — v
Preface — 1

PART I. ORIGINS

1. Key West: The Early Years — 5
2. Key West: The Maturing Years — 16

PART II. UNITED STATES SENATOR

3. A Potpourri of Issues — 29
4. Strengthening the Navy — 51
5. Secession and Fort Pickens — 62

PART III. CONFEDERATE NAVY CHIEF

6. Initial Moves — 77
7. Ironclad Victories and Defeats — 94
8. Commerce Raiders — 114
9. Southern-Built Defensive Ironclads — 127
10. Foreign-Built Offensive Ironclads — 140
11. Technically Advanced Weapons — 148
12. The Beginning of the End — 155

13. Southern Strategies and Outcomes 167
14. Confederate Collapse and Prison 174

PART IV. THE LATER YEARS

15. Stephen and Angela 187
16. The Declining Years and Quietus 202

Chapter Notes 215
Bibliography 233
Index 243

Preface

For many people the name "Mallory" is associated with Mallory Square, a tourist magnet at Key West, Florida. However, Stephen Russell Mallory's chief claim to fame is his public service. For 10 years he was a senator in service to the United States of America and for four years he was navy secretary in service to the Confederate States of America.

In American Civil War literature, most attention has been focused on massive land battles; less has been directed to naval activities. There has been little examination of navy leadership in Richmond, especially that of Confederate navy chief Stephen Russell Mallory. He is an important historical figure because he accomplished so much with so little. He faced daunting problems: political interference, nautical activities in a region lacking seafaring traditions, great difficulty in obtaining supplies and resources needed to build a navy, and an inadequate rail transport system. But Mallory built a strong navy fleet from scratch.

Prior to his appointment to serve the Confederate States of America, Mallory ably served the United States of America as a Florida senator. Upon entering the Senate, his national political and legislative experiences were insignificant, but he quickly developed skills and brought useful knowledge to the Senate Committee on Naval Affairs. He became chairman of that committee, making important contributions toward improving the strength and efficiency of the Federal navy.

It is strange that literature is meager in its coverage of Stephen Mallory, given the importance of the two positions he held. In 1930, Professor Kathleen Bruce, at the College of William and Mary, recognized his worth when she wrote in her book *Virginia Iron Manufacture in the Slave Era* that he was "a man of wide horizon, of quick grasp of the important idea and tireless in his endeavor to make it concrete." Nine years later another book appeared, Burton J. Hendrick's *Statesmen of the Lost Cause: Jefferson Davis and His Cabinet*. Hendrick wrote, "Mallory figures little in Confederate histories and has been neglected by biographers. Yet all contemporary witnesses testify to his industry and spirit."

The first Mallory biography was Joseph T. Durkin's *Stephen R. Mallory: Confederate Navy Chief*, published by the University of North Carolina Press in 1954 and reprinted by the University of South Carolina Press in 1987 under the title *Confederate Navy Chief: Stephen R. Mallory*. Both the initial edition and reprint are out of print but are readily available in major libraries. It should be noted that considerable scholarship about Mallory and the Confederate navy, that was unavailable to Durkin, has emerged in the past half-century.

Predating the Durkin biography was a body of outstanding scholarship written by Miss Occie Clubbs who was a teacher in Pensacola, Florida, for 48 years. In 1936 she wrote her in-depth examination of Mallory for her master's thesis at the University of Florida. In 1947 she wrote a three-part article that appeared in the *Florida Historical Quarterly*, which expanded upon her thesis material.

This biography surveys the life of Stephen Russell Mallory. It is intended to be a careful evaluation of his character and experiences, especially between 1851 and 1865 when he reached the zenith of his public service career as senator and navy secretary. Attention is directed to his formative years in Key West when he acquired his capacity for future greatness. His deep relationship with his wife and children is explored. Additionally, new material is added and previously published erroneous information is corrected.

Earlier Mallory studies have provided rich accounts of his operation of the Confederate Navy Department but have provided little examination of underlying strategic concepts. This book emphasizes strategies and tactics that Mallory developed as Confederate navy chief and examines the Confederate navy infrastructure.

Any reliable analysis of Stephen R. Mallory must draw heavily upon his extensive autobiographical documents. When studying these, it must be remembered that he was writing for his family and their descendents as well as others in future generations. Such information would enable them to understand and appreciate Mallory's perception of his essential being. His two diaries were written while he was imprisoned and he intended to leave a positive record of his time on earth. Generally he did not identify his shortcomings, or his most intimate and darkest secrets. Mallory stressed how he wanted to be remembered.

All this is not to minimize the importance of the diaries for they are basic to understanding this man. However, they must be read with the caveat that they tell the truth about Stephen Russell Mallory as he perceived it. Mallory's Senate speeches and documents located in the Navy and Army Official Records of the War of the Rebellion likewise are invaluable sources for any researcher. Also of interest are observations of Mallory and his family by his contemporaries.

Unfortunately, heirs and others have destroyed a number of potentially important historical documents pertaining to the Mallory family to protect their privacy. Specifically, the majority of letters from Angela Mallory to her husband have been lost or destroyed, and one can only surmise their content from Stephen's written responses. Many valuable records of the Confederate Navy Department were partially destroyed when the building housing it was burned during the evacuation of Richmond on April 2, 1865. Other navy archives got as far as the Navy Yard in Charlotte, North Carolina, where they were almost totally destroyed because of fear they would be used in prosecuting southern naval personnel. Mallory himself says that these records were destroyed "upon and soon after the evacuation of Richmond."

Fortunately, secondary sources are available. These are always important in portraying the subject under scrutiny as long as biases and prejudices of the author(s) of that material are acknowledged. All written history builds upon the contributions of others. Consequently, a historian pens very little that is truly original in thought or concept, instead synthesizing and interpreting that which has been done earlier. Hence, the biographer constructs upon the foundations built by his predecessors and he is always indebted to them.

Part I

Origins

1

Key West: The Early Years

Stephen Russell Mallory is identified as a Floridian but his roots go back to the Redding and Bridgeport, Connecticut, area because that is where his father was born; he was a "Connecticut Yankee." The author Mark Twain is reputed to have been a cousin of the Mallory clan. He lived in Redding for a while and mentioned the area in *A Connecticut Yankee in King Arthur's Court*. In his story the Connecticut Yankee went back in time to the days of King Arthur's court and a mailed knight of the court seized him. The two of them began a journey. The Yankee pondered: "At the end of an hour we saw a far-away town sleeping in a valley by a winding river; and beyond it on a hill, a vast gray fortress, with towers and turrets, the first I had ever seen out of a picture. 'Bridgeport?' said I, pointing. 'Camelot,' said he."[1]

In later years Mallory and his family returned frequently to the Bridgeport area.

It is fitting that the future chairman of the United States Senate Committee on Naval Affairs and secretary of the Confederate States of America Navy Department was born and reared near the sea. Stephen Russell Mallory came into this world on the island country of Trinidad in the West Indies and was raised on the Florida peninsula, on the most westerly of keys extending into the Caribbean — Key West. He remained there as a young adult but during the last half of his life he resided in the seaport of Pensacola, Florida, on the Gulf of Mexico.

Mallory's mother, Ellen Russell, was born in 1792 at Carrick-on-Suir, County Waterford, in southeast Ireland. In 1805 she was sent to live with two maternal uncles who had migrated to Trinidad and had established a sugar plantation. Ellen married Stephen's father around 1808 when she was nearly 16. She gave birth to two sons: John about 1811 and Stephen around 1812 or 1813. The marriage date and children's birth dates cannot be established because no records were maintained in Trinidad before 1848.[2]

Biographer Joseph T. Durkin wrote that Mallory's birth date "was certainly 1810 or 1811."[3] On July 10, 2003, I viewed his headstone at the Mallory family burial plot at St. Michael Cemetery in Pensacola, Florida. Mallory's birth date is stated to be 1812.[4] Several reference sources give birth dates ranging from 1811 to 1814.[5] The consensus is that he was born around 1813.

In addition to confusion around his birth date, debate exists in regard to his correct paternal lineage. Scholar Occie Clubbs has identified Stephen's father as Charles Mallory both in her master's thesis and in an article in the *Florida Historical Quarterly*. In the article, she adds that in Trinidad, Charles was "a building superintendent and contractor...."[6] Historian J. Thomas Scharf confirms the information supplied by Clubbs by writing that "He [Stephen] was the second son of Charles Mallory, and Ellen his wife.... Charles Mallory was ... a civil engineer by profession...." Kathleen Bruce in the *Dictionary of American Biography* also identifies Charles Mallory as the father of Stephen Mallory, as does Burton J. Hendrick in *Statesmen of the Lost Cause*.[7] *Appleton's Cyclopaedia of American Biography* similarly lists Charles Mallory as the father of Stephen and states that he was from Redding (not "Reading" as some sources claim), Connecticut.[8] The Todd history of the "Mallory Family" in Redding, Connecticut, states,

> Samuel and Charles Mallory were born April 6, 1780. The names of the parents are not given. Charles Mallory was the father of Stephen Mallory, United States Senator from Florida, and later Secretary of the Confederate Navy.[9]

Cora S. Mallory was the granddaughter of Stephen Mallory. On February 6 and 12, 1959, she exchanged correspondence with L. B. Atwood of Salinas, California, regarding the lineage of Stephen's father. This correspondence confirms that Charles Mallory of Redding, Connecticut, who was born April 6, 1780, was the father of Stephen.[10]

The "Family Origins" Web site states that Charles Mallory, who was married to Ellen Russell, died in Key West, Florida, around 1922 [*sic*: 1822] and his son was Stephen Russell Mallory.[11] The Genealogy.com Web site hosts a genealogy forum and the Mallory Family Forum contains a posting dated May 9, 2003, by Mallory Smith (ID# 3674). It says that Stephen R. Mallory's father was Charles Mallory, born in Redding, Connecticut, on April 6, 1780, along with his twin brother, Samuel. Stephen's mother is listed as Ellen Russell. His father, Charles, is said to have been "a civil engineer working in the West Indies when Stephen was born."[12] This information is confirmed further by *The Barbour Collection of Connecticut Town Vital Records*, which states that Charles Mallory was born in Redding on April 6, 1780, as was his twin, Samuel.[13]

Contrarily, Stephen R. Wise states that Stephen Mallory was "the son of John Mallory, an engineer, and Ellen Russell." He is joined in this assessment by biographer Joseph T. Durkin who writes that Ellen Russell was "Sent as a child to the island of Trinidad to live with her two planter uncles [and] she had there eventually married John Mallory, a construction engineer from Connecticut."[14] Raimondo Luraghi in his book, *A History of the Confederate Navy*, also identifies John Mallory as Stephen's father.[15] Both Luraghi and Durkin infer that their authority for naming John Mallory as father of Stephen rises from a letter written by Mallory to his son "Buddy" on September 27, 1865, found in the Mallory "Diary and Reminiscences." However, I reviewed the transcript of the letter and could not confirm this as fact.

To summarize, J. Thomas Scharf gave the first reference to Charles as Stephen's father in 1886 and he had ample contact with Mallory's relatives that were of value to him in verifying this information. Thereafter, relatives and most scholars continued to identify Charles as Stephen's father. The first reference to John as Mallory's father was in the 1954 publication of Durkin's biography. Subsequently Wise, Luraghi, and others repeated this information. All the conflicting data creates uncertainty. However, the weight of evidence, coupled with an evaluation of the probative value of various documentations, can only lead to one conclusion: Stephen Russell Mallory was born around

1813 in Trinidad, West Indies, and his father was Charles Mallory, who was born in 1780 in Redding, Connecticut.

Stephen Mallory tells us that his father "had been regularly trained as a carpenter in all its branches, but in the years when I knew him, did no work himself, but took contracts and superintended work."[16] Twenty-eight-year-old Charles Mallory probably arrived in Trinidad in mid–1808 as the result of a tragedy that occurred in that British colony on the evening of March 24, 1808. Fire consumed over half the houses in the capital, Port of Spain, leaving more than 3,000 people homeless. The town council immediately decided to rebuild the city, and word quickly spread that skilled carpenters were needed immediately, at a good wage, to commence reconstruction.[17] Considering Stephen's diary entry, we can safely assume that his father responded to the call and was in a supervisory position over carpenters rebuilding the town of Port of Spain. There he met and married Ellen Russell and their first son, John, was born sometime around 1811; Stephen followed one or two years later.[18] Both Charles and his son John died in Key West about 1822.[19]

Ellen Russell's birth has never been verified. After independent genealogist Dana Leslie Hughes of Clearwater, Florida, determined that no records existed in the United States to verify this data, she had a search conducted in Ireland. That investigation revealed there were no surviving birth records for Ellen Russell, but strong circumstantial evidence disclosed that her father was Stephen Russell. Also, her parents gave birth to a son in 1811 named Stephen Russell[, Jr.?].[20] Finally, Stephen Mallory, the elder, once chastised his son for signing a letter "Stephen Mallory," and not "Stephen R. Mallory." The father asked him, "Why do you ignore the 'R'? Unless you have some sufficient reason, — and I cannot think of any, — you must retain it; just because it is a part of your name, and next, out of respect to your *Irish Grandfather Stephen Russell* [emphasis added]...."[21] All of this strongly suggests the basis for Mallory's first and middle names. Evidently Ellen Russell Mallory felt it important to keep her father's lineage alive in her second son.

Around 1814, the Mallory family sailed from Trinidad, probably landing at either New York or Bridgeport. Their arrival in the United States coincided with the end of the War of 1812 between Great Britain and America; an "Era of Good Feelings" followed.[22] The United States continued the quest for new territory, as its thirst had not been quenched by the Louisiana Purchase of 1803. Following this event, there was increasing friction between American settlers and Seminole Indians in Florida, because Indians allegedly were harboring runaway slaves from southern plantations. Antagonism persisted and Andrew Jackson was ordered to control Indians in United States territory. However, Jackson did not confine himself to U.S. territory; he made an unauthorized excursion across the border into Spanish territory. In Pensacola he demanded that Spain surrender its fort there, as well as territory in West Florida, in order to end the illicit supply of arms to Indians. The Spanish surrendered Pensacola in May 1818.[23] Jackson's activities to control Indian uprisings, along with Spain's weakened position due to Napoleon's invasion of that country, stimulated Spain to consider ceding Florida to the United States. The American government declared Spain to be incompetent in policing its own territory. Since Madrid could not strenuously deny that claim, she decided to sell the land before it was seized. The treaty of February 1819 between the United States and Spain ceded all Spain's lands east of the Mississippi to the United States and opened that territory for settlement. This activity stimulated westward migration and cotton production flourished in the new Gulf States. Alabama became a state in 1819, and large tracts of land were cleared in the Mobile area to attract settlers. Florida was organized as a territory on March 30, 1822, and American settlers began arriving in large numbers that same year.

Around 1820 Charles and Ellen Mallory and their two children appeared in Mobile, apparently attracted by low-priced land and the opportunity to make a new start in virgin territory. After their arrival, a particularly virulent yellow fever epidemic erupted in Mobile and the Mallory family decided to relocate in Key West.[24] While in Mobile, they may have met John W. Simonton, a Mobile merchant from New Jersey who originally had settled in Key West before moving to Mobile. He had purchased Key West for $2,000 in 1822 and as one interested in the town's development may have influenced the decision of the Mallory clan to move to that small community.[25]

In Key West the family found a small, low island over three miles long and one mile wide, the last of a succession of keys (cays or islands) extending about a hundred miles from the tip of the Florida peninsula. Because its location is the most westerly of the island chain extending from the peninsula, it eventually came to be known as Key West.[26]

A high ridgeline existed along the portions of the key fronting on the deep-water ocean and gulf sides and from there the land gently sloped back to ponds and lagoons. Early construction was restricted to the ridgeline; lower land was filled later and developed. The superior deep harbor, with its convenient location and good shelter, attracted shipping. It was a refuge for commercial fisherman who supplied the market in Havana, only about 100 miles distant. Since the 16th century, ships entering and leaving the Gulf of Mexico had wrecked on nearby coral reefs that are partially or wholly submerged in the ocean. The wrecking and salvage industry in Key West rose from this happenstance and this enterprise, plus fishing, were chief sources of income for inhabitants. In March 1819 a territorial government was established for Florida. This marked the beginning of settlement of Key West and 10 years later it had been surveyed and mapped.[27]

One of the early Key West settlers was John Whitehead, who himself had fallen victim to a shipwreck in 1818 on the Bahama Banks. He eventually reached Key West, where he sensed potential for profit. Whitehead entered into a commercial partnership (possibly with John W. Simonton) for settlement of the town.[28] It is quite possible that Whitehead, or one of his agents, was at Mobile when Charles Mallory arrived and encouraged the family to relocate to Key West. Whitehead's younger brother, William, came to the island late in 1828 to assist his older brother in this enterprise. He was about Stephen's age and they became close friends. William A. Whitehead surveyed and mapped Key West in 1829.

When Ellen Mallory arrived with her husband and children, she was the only white woman in this small community.[29] A leading citizen of Key West, Walter Maloney, recalled that "an enumeration of the inhabitants was taken in 1835, which gave the total resident population as 582, including black, white and all other colors, lame, lazy and blind."[30] After their arrival, Charles Mallory purchased a lot and built a house.[31]

Around 1822 Charles and Ellen decided to send Stephen to a private school in the Mobile area because there were no schools in Key West until 12 years later. Charles prevailed upon a friend to take his son to Mobile and enroll him in a school located at "The Village," at the site of present-day Daphne, Alabama, on the east shore of Mobile Bay.[32]

Stephen was at The Village private school for a year or so. He recalled that his learning was limited to reading. He added that the teacher was "a man of fair attainments, good practice with the hickory, and fondness for whiskey." The boy learned to ride a horse, shoot a gun, engaged in hunting, and shared in sports with the rest of the boys, who were all bigger than he. One day they were in the piney woods with a single-barreled shotgun. When it was Stephen's turn to use the gun, he saw an animal crawling up a tree with a dog chasing it. He took aim and fired at the animal; it was a wildcat that fell down and it got in a fierce fight with the dog. All the bigger boys fled, but Stephen stayed and with a club helped the dog subdue and kill the wild animal. The other boys thereafter admired Stephen and he developed self-reliance and self-esteem. On another occasion, Stephen and the boys were on an outing in a schooner in the Bay off Mobile Point when he fell overboard. This created a stir because Stephen could not swim. The mate of the boat recovered him and then taught him to swim.[33] Stephen got very little formal education from this school, but he learned many important life lessons outside school that would serve him well in his future adult activities.

In 1822 while Stephen was at The Village, his father died of tuberculosis and his brother died sometime later.[34] Ellen Mallory ran the principal boarding house in the town as a means of supporting her and Stephen. Ellen later needed Stephen home to help her and she prevailed upon local officials to have a U.S. Revenue cutter pick him up in Mobile and bring him home.[35]

By 1826 Mrs. Mallory decided to enroll Stephen in another private school. She chose the "Boarding School for Young Gentlemen" at Nazareth, Pennsylvania.[36] This prestigious boys' school had been founded in 1759 by a group of Moravians, a German Protestant sect that had been hired to run the institution.[37]

Mrs. Mallory and Stephen were both Roman Catholics. Why would Ellen Mallory choose a Protestant school for her son's education? She never gave her reasons, but it is likely she desired the finest education possible for her son and this institution had the reputation as one of the most outstanding schools of its kind in the country.[38] It adhered to the principles of Bishop John Amos Comenius who developed "a philosophy, pansophism, which stressed political unity, religious reconciliation, and educational cooperation. This philosophy of pansophism related education to everyday life and advocated systematizing all knowledge...." This educational style introduced new science studies into the school, the school was free of sectarian bigotry, and instruction was tailored to the needs of an individual child.[39]

Stephen Mallory recalled later that the school (there were 112 students) was admirably managed, teachers were conscientious, and he was happy there. In his three years at this school he had attained "proficiency in writing ... [and] learned much arithmetic, bookkeeping, geography, grammar, astronomy, ancient and modern history...." Additionally, he could recite distinctly, express himself well both orally and in writing, and could play the piano. Stephen recalled that at Nazareth "we were the happiest set of boys I ever met."[40] His mother need not have worried about Stephen remaining true to his faith. Years later he wrote, "To pray & bless myself was a habit; and I can never forget how boldly I could confront real or imaginary danger, that others frequently shrunk from, after blessing myself, & invoking Heaven's protection."[41] However, Ellen Mallory would have to remove him from school when she no longer could afford the tuition.[42]

Stephen wrote, "My mother was one of the most affectionate humane, kind, charitable & unselfish natures I have ever known, & was ready ever to make any sacrifice for my happiness or advancement, loving me dearly."[43] But years later Stephen remembered, "She was passionate, & punished me severely & unreasonably at times; & this, from my peculiarly sensitive appreciation of wrong, rankled & festered in my heart, & was never entirely rooted out until after her death."[44]

Some of Ellen Mallory's adult contemporaries recorded their opinions about her. Judge William Marvin wrote that Ellen Mallory was "intelligent, possessed of ready Irish wit, was kind, gentle, charitable, sympathetic and considerate of the wants of the sick and the poor." Jefferson Browne scribed this: "She nursed [me] through an attack of yellow fever and was always as good to [me] as [my] own mother could have been."[45] Walter C. Maloney was poetic: "Me thinks I hear her musical voice today, as she was wont to speak, standing at the bedside of the sick and dying, in days gone by. Catholic by rites of baptism, oh! How truly catholic, in the better and non-sectarian use of that term, was her life, devoted as it was to acts of kindness.... Next to her God, her devotion centered in her son, Stephen R. Mallory...."[46]

By this stage in his life, Stephen had developed a sense of respect, not only for his mother, but also for women in general. He honored females and took action should they be wronged. At school he had an episode of puppy love with "Arabella," an overweight Dutch girl of Nazareth. A classmate made reference to Arabella being fat; to defend her honor Stephen fought the boy. His sense of courtesy extended to all kinds of women. He wrote that he would be as respectful to the washerwoman as to the first lady of the land, and that he would hold an umbrella over the head of a laundress or would get her shawl should it fall in the street. When he spoke to a lady in the street, he would keep his cap off until she departed or suggested he replace it. Stephen wrote his son that women have a great deal to do with man's place in society, and reminded him that chivalry is characterized by gallantry toward women.[47]

The youngster who returned to Key West in 1829 was no longer a boy; he was entering manhood. For three years he had been well educated in a fine institution, had close associations with a broad variety of people, his mind had been stimulated by all that he had been exposed to, and he had developed good study habits.

Although he had concluded his formal education, Stephen engaged in self-instruction and he did so with gusto. He began to isolate himself in his room and read everything available, always taking notes. This broad sweep of classic and not so classic literature plus reference material was to serve him well in his adult life.

When the young man returned, he began helping his mother in all ways possible. He made purchases, ran errands, took care of correspondence, and did minor household repairs. While he continued to help his mother with the boarding house operation, he confined himself to his room as much as possible to read, write, and study. During this period he made a vow "to study law, become a lawyer and at some day to go to Congress." In order to prepare for attaining this goal, he studied "law trials, lectures & Congressional debates."[48]

A developing personal characteristic was his perseverance that enabled him to focus upon a clear objective, and then pursue it tenaciously in spite of obstacles he might encounter. This trait would emerge many times in his later life. Furthermore, Stephen was undergoing a period of self-examination and concluded he was too opinionated and likely to reject the views of others without giving them a fair hearing. The young man felt this was a very negative quality in his character that he needed to change. He feared he was depriving himself of knowledge from others and giving the impression he was an egotist. Stephen learned it was to his advantage to become a good listener and to respect the views of others. He became convinced that good manners and courtesy would always serve him well.

From self-study Stephen learned to read and speak acceptable French and Spanish.

There were numerous opportunities to use his new language skills with both the Spanish settlers in Key West and with passengers and crews of ships frequenting the harbor. After his three-year absence, he had returned to a cosmopolitan town full of all kinds of diverse people: travelers from the southeast United States and the Gulf region, shipwrecked sailors, personnel from navy ships, discharged military men, Bahama wreckers and personnel on fast ships traveling to and from the sailing center of Mystic, Connecticut, and vagabonds wandering through town on the way to their next adventure. He learned from all these people and further enriched his life.

During this time, Stephen devoted most of his energies to continuing his self-education, but he managed to find time to be a young man enjoying life. He probably accepted invitations to afternoon teas aboard navy ships in the harbor and enjoyed dancing on deck afterward. He may have attended the primary social event of the year, the Masonic Ball.[49] Charles Walker, a visitor to Key West in 1838, observed the social activities in the town of about 300 people. He related that many residents participated in dinner and evening parties of the kind found in large cities. Good books and publications were abundant. Walker added that in the winter there were weekly parties and "the ladies dress, dance and waltz with great skill & taste, especially the descendants of the Spaniards.... [S]o passionately fond of this amusement are the ladies, & I suppose I may add gentlemen, that the music ceases not near the first grey of the morning."[50] Another observer said of Key West, "Many of the leading merchants are from New England. The society of the place is excellent. The people are very social and hospitable. The ladies are intelligent, accomplished and refined...."[51] The citizens were said to dress in good taste: "Perfectly laundered white linen duck suits were worn by the gentlemen in the summer, while on Sundays frock coats and silk hats were general."[52]

Mallory loved ships and often went sailing in boats he had built. Years later his widow remarked that he had been "a born sailor and loved the sea. He knew all about the construction of vessels and how to man them, having had experience in the management of his own yachts."[53] On occasion Stephen sailed to nearby Cuba for brief visits and he cruised in waters surrounding the keys. Mallory explored the islands near Key West, went hunting, and sometimes explored the east coast of Florida. On one occasion he went to New River in east Florida with a Colonel Fitzpatrick to help him develop a plantation. While there, he became enamored with the woods and outdoors and learned about woodcraft from Indians in the area.[54] He also made time to learn to fence, box, and play the flute.[55]

Judge William Marvin wrote this about Stephen and his friends:

> Among the young men about town are to be named Amos and Asa Tift, Stephen R. Mallory, Joseph B. Browne ... I do not know that these young fellows ever "painted the town red," for they were a well behaved and orderly set of young gentlemen; but they, or some of them, were known to be in the streets very often in the small hours of the morning, serenading some one or more of the young ladies of the town.... Nothing pleased Mallory better than to take his flute and get one or two friends, and Roberts, a colored man with his fiddle, to join him and go out into the beautiful moonlight nights and serenade some lady or ladies. Among the married ladies [serenaded was] Mrs. Ellen Mallory.[56]

As he matured, Stephen became less individualistic and redirected his interests and activities toward community affairs and responsibilities. In 1832 the citizens selected P.B. Prior as the town marshal, but he did not qualify and Mallory was chosen instead. It was his first public office. This was a modest entry into the public sector and the duties were minimal. At 9:30 P.M. the town bell tolled to let citizens know it was time "for the cessation of nocturnal business and pleasures...." The marshal's job was to apprehend "any Negroes, bond or free, appearing upon the street without authority...." Extra punishment would be forthcoming if that man had also been "merrymaking by fiddle, drum, or any other kind of noise."[57]

On February 22, 1832, he made his first political utterance of a national character at a banquet celebrating the centenary of George Washington's birth. There were many toasts, including one by Stephen Mallory: "Daniel Webster. Changeless as the Northern Star of whose true, fixed and resting quality there is no fellow in the firmament."[58] This toast was more embellished than those preceding it, and the crowd may have questioned the relevancy of Daniel Webster. Through his self-study, Stephen probably was aware of Webster's backing of a high tariff bill on manufactured goods in 1828, and South Carolinian John C. Calhoun's angry reaction to it. Calhoun had condemned the tariff and argued that the state had the right to nullify the law and, if necessary, secede from the Union. In an 1830 Senate debate Webster defended the Union and said, "Liberty and Union, now and forever, one and inseparable!"[59] Mallory supported the concept of the permanence of the Union, especially since the Florida territory expected to be granted statehood in the future. His stance would change over time as the issue of slavery created increasing sectional divisiveness.

Religion and worship were important to Stephen and he displayed flexibility in meeting these needs. Both Ellen Mallory and her son were Catholics, but apparently the diocese of Savannah, Georgia, had little interest in establishing a church in Key West until the early 1840s. Nevertheless, there was a strong desire by the population to establish a church in town. The protestant Episcopal Church displayed interest in meeting these religious needs. This led a committee to write a letter to the bishop of this denomination in New York City pledging $1,000 for the first year of a pastor's services. A priest was hired; he conducted the first service on Christmas Day 1832 in what would become St. Paul's Episcopal Church. After the service, "Mr. Stephen R. Mallory" was among 30 men enrolled in the first congregation, as was his lifelong friend Asa Tift. Mallory demonstrated flexibility in his spiritual faith by transcending the bounds of his chosen religion so that he might participate in group worship through this Protestant church.[60]

Occasionally there were no Sunday services during the period when one clergyman had departed and the church awaited his replacement. Stephen always had been aware of his community obligations so he considered a suggestion by a visiting Baptist minister from Mobile who said it might be appropriate, in the absence of an ordained minister, to hold religious services conducted by lay people using the Common Prayer Book. Stephen and others agreed this was a respectable way of spending Sunday, whereupon Mallory, Judge William Marvin, and William H. Wall (a leading businessman) acted upon the suggestion. They sent notices announcing that a service would be conducted the following Sunday. On that day, a good crowd attended and the men divided portions of the service among the three of them: Marvin read the prayers, Wall read the Scripture lessons, and Mallory read the sermon. The trio continued these prayer services for a total of three weeks, at which time a new minister arrived.[61]

Stephen's next civil venture occurred in 1834 when the first fire department was organized. It was called the Lafayette Fire Department (probably because of the recent death of the French hero) and Mallory and his friend Asa Tift were on the election committee. A few months later the fire department failed to extinguish a blaze and Mallory reorganized the department. Later, a hand engine was purchased to fight future fires, but it was improperly maintained and failed to function properly in a warehouse conflagration. Key West citizens apparently were unhappy with Mallory's leadership and the improper maintenance of the fire engine. Thereafter his name no longer appeared in association with the Lafayette Fire Department.[62]

Stephen also labored as a volunteer in his community. In 1831 the city council passed a resolution giving citizens the right to clear land alongside Eaton Street but this had not been completed by 1836. The street outside the main business area remained covered with trees, underbrush, vines, and cacti. Various citizens, along with 50 United States sailors, cleared most of the area in one day of hard work. Among those participating were Mallory and his friends Asa Tift and Judge William Marvin.[63]

Stephen Mallory became interested in writing and editing, trying his hand at newspaper journalism several times in his life. In October 1834 he became associated with the *Enquirer* in Key West as an editorial writer and correspondent. The name of this paper was changed to the *Inquirer* in December 1835 and was published continuously until late in 1836. One authority said that these newspapers were well edited and their ideals were high. As a stringer for the popular *New York Herald*, Mallory contributed an article on the hurricane of 1835. His journalistic talents can be judged by examining a few lines from this article:

> One of the schooners was driven by a gale upon a bank, which, when the wind had somewhat abated, was left high and dry, but her persevering master with eleven men actually cut a canal two hundred yards long, and in twenty-four hours after it commenced the ship was again at sea and obtained a cargo.[64]

In the 1830s nearly all money earned in Key West was connected with wrecking and salvage. The "city of wrecking" arose from an accident of nature. The island where Key West is located gained importance because of its geographical location adjacent to the Straits of Florida that run between Florida and Cuba. Fishermen, explorers, and traders were present in this area, as were pirates in the sixteenth and seventeenth centuries, who haunted the straits to intercept ships bound for Spain laden with treasure. Because of adverse winds and currents, this passage was favored over the other main passage between Cuba and the Yucatan peninsula.

The Florida Keys are a chain of low islands that extend from the tip of the Florida peninsula in a flat crescent arc to the west for about 140 miles. Skirting the keys facing the Straits of Florida is the "Great Reef." This reef runs parallel to the keys and is four to six miles away from these islands. It is composed of sand, rocks, and coral lying from one to 20 feet below the surface. Between the Great Reef and the keys is Hawk Channel and one must stay in this passage to avoid wrecking. This can be difficult due to heavy currents and eddies and the channel's curved shape that requires continuous changes of direction.

These hazards, coupled with lack of adequate charts and lights to aid navigation, caused ships to ground on reefs where they were in danger of breaking up due to surf or storms. Such wrecks attracted those who would salvage ship, crew, and cargo for compensation. The Key West harbor was deep, protected, and easily accessible; it was the anchorage nearest to areas where ships usually wrecked. Thus, the wrecking-salvage industry flourished in Key West and by the mid–1830s produced a per-capita income superior to any other location in Florida.[65]

One writer has described the arrival of the salvagers after a ship had wrecked on the reefs:

> Just at day-light ... the white cotton sails of some twenty beautiful sloops & schooners are hoisted, and each to its utmost presses ahead.... [E]ach [vessel is] manned with from ten to fourteen men. Each vessel has a diver, who will go in the cabin of a ship, or to the bottom of the sea, if not over six fathoms deep and bring up goods sunk, & each has also spare anchors & cables....[66]

The first person to board a wreck had undisputed control over her until the claim to the damaged vessel and cargo was delivered to a court of competent jurisdiction. The court then decided who was to receive what share of the proceeds. Before Florida became United States territory, all wrecked goods and vessels were taken to Nassau where the British admiralty court adjudicated the salvage claim. After Florida became a U.S. territory in 1821, speculators began pressing for Key West to become the site to determine salvage litigation. In March 1822 the United States vessel *Shark* anchored in the harbor and claimed the key to be U.S. property. United States Navy surveyors had judged that Key West, with its location and good harbor, was a suitable spot from which to suppress piracy in the Gulf of Mexico. Subsequently a U.S. Navy squadron was stationed there for that purpose. Key West, at the end of 1822, was made a port of entry for the southern part of Florida and a customs office was established to collect revenue. By 1825 legislation specified that all salvaged goods taken within the jurisdiction of the United States must be taken to an American port of entry for adjudication.

Litigation could be complicated because of the huge sums of money involved and the complex factors that needed to be examined in each wrecking and salvage operation. One source claimed that the value of salvaged property brought into Key West from "December, 1824, to December, 1825, [was] $293,353.00."[67] The judicial proceeding required evaluation of the division of shares of prize money by assessing these factors: to what extent did the first arriving salvager require assistance from other salvagers, to what extent did time lost saving passengers' lives (always a first priority) diminish the salvager's ability to recover cargo, what degree of danger and hardship was involved, what was the legality of contracts made by a salvager with his fellow salvagers, what sum should be awarded underwriters, and what commission should go to the auctioneer who sold the cargo?

In 1828 Congress established a superior court at Key West and it was given territorial jurisdiction in south Florida, as well as admiralty jurisdiction and authority to license wreckers. James Webb was appointed the first judge of this court and William Marvin succeeded him in 1839.[68] The presence of this court resulted in a need for lawyers and customs workers in Key West. In 1831 Stephen R. Mallory found he was in the right place at the right time.[69]

Stephen's friend William Whitehead was appointed collector of customs in 1830 and the next year he appointed Mallory as inspector of customs. This was the first full-time job for the young man and it launched his career in the public sector.[70] He applied his talents and learned the intricacies of the customs service. In his spare time he continued his self-study and read law. In his legal study, he placed himself under the tutelage of William Marvin, who not only was his mentor, but also something of a father figure. Marvin was an excellent lawyer and later would enjoy worldwide renown because of a book he wrote on the law of wreck and salvage.[71] Mallory ultimately was admitted to the bar and gained a solid reputation as a skillful lawyer. He had an extensive practice in Key West and in 1837 he was elected judge for Monroe County in which capacity he served until 1845.[72] President Polk appointed Mallory collector of the customs effective July 17, 1845, where he served until September 30, 1849.[73]

Mallory was inspector at the customs service in 1836 when an opportunity arose that appealed to his adventurous spirit. He was able to secure a leave of absence to take a job as a guide. Stephen was sought for this position because of his knowledge of the keys and surrounding waters, but he was not to be an ordinary pathfinder. At the time the United States government was in the midst of the Second Seminole War, one of a series of prolonged attempts to relocate Seminole Indians to reservations in Oklahoma territory. The previous year the commander of the navy's West India Squadron based at Pensacola had been instructed to aid Brig. Gen. Duncan L. Clinch with his task of rounding up and relocating renegade Seminole Indians. According to one scholar, George Buker, "The army was the first to realize the importance of naval forces working close to shore and in harmony with the land forces."[74]

In October 1836, Lt. Levin M. Powell was part of a task force that was ordered to intercept around 200 Indians in the vicinity of Cape Florida or New River. Buker wrote, "Powell had the services of Mr. Stephen R. Mallory, 20, a resident of Key West, who had experience sailing the waters of the keys." This group departed Key West on October 13 and sailed in the vicinity of the nearby keys, the Miami River, and Cape Florida. Lieutenant Powell methodically scoured the area, sending "Stephen Mallory to explore along Little River and Arch Creek, but with no positive results." The force then conducted a fruitless search of the Everglades interior, found no Indians, and returned to Key West in early December.[75]

Lieutenant Powell led another naval expedition that was combined with an army force in December 1837. The combined army-navy force departed for south Florida on December 26, 1837, toward the St. Lucie and Jupiter rivers. On January 15, 1838, at the headwaters of the Jupiter River, the military group was involved in a fierce engagement with the Indians, and the United States expedition was badly beaten. Later, the force advanced into the Everglades and south Florida coastal areas. In April 1838 Powell returned to Pensacola with his sailors.[76]

Of these expeditions, Stephen Mallory remarks, "I had a very pleasant & somewhat independent position assigned to me, with the command of a fine body of seamen & my own superb long, center board, schooner rigged, whale boat.... The campaign was to me a most agreeable one. In the fall of the following year I again found Capt. Powell in a similar service, over the same ground, with a larger force ... & though I never killed or wounded an Indian, I enjoyed capital health, good spirits, and reaped much useful experience, self reliances & benifit [sic] generally from my service."[77]

Mallory presented these expeditions as something of an exciting adventure, but in reality he was engaged in unpleasant, backbreaking work wading through the Everglades and pulling boats across half-submerged islands. He also stretched the truth a bit by saying the sailors were under his command. He undoubtedly directed them in the operation of his whaleboat, but they remained under the military command of Powell.

Stephen Mallory had engaged in an adventure that he would talk about for years. He was about to engage in an even more intense endeavor that would last for a lifetime.

2

Key West: The Maturing Years

Angela Sylvania Moreno was a 15-year-old Spanish girl who came into 17-year-old Stephen Russell Mallory's life on a spring morning in 1830. Thirty years later, in a letter to his eldest son, Stephen remembered the details of this important event in his life:

> Sitting upon a wharf at Key West, dressed, I remember, all in white, & with a white round jacket, I first saw your mother, then just from Pensacola, & with two other young ladies, on her way to Bridgeport [Connecticut] to school. She spent a day at Key West; & my attention was very strongly attracted by her; so strongly that I never forgot her, but on the contrary thought of her much & often.[1]

Although he visited young ladies in this period, he avoided becoming involved in extended relationships because he would allow nothing to interfere with his self-instruction. This was the period just after his return from the boarding school in Pennsylvania when he began his intense study of hundreds of books and learned to speak French and Spanish. But Angela was frequently in his thoughts.

Angela Moreno also remembered that day and 68 years later in a newspaper interview she said, "I remember that he was the only well dressed young gentleman I saw, and he was very handsome. But no thought of him and the future entered my mind then."[2]

Angela was the eldest daughter of a respected and successful businessman who was also the Spanish vice consul in Pensacola. Her paternal grandfather had been a surgeon with the Spanish army when it occupied that town.[3] She remained in school in Bridgeport for two years where she studied English. Upon returning to her family, she was presented to society. Pensacola was a naval station and summer resort and the young lady was active in many social events. There was an abundance of parties and naval escorts. Angela met numerous young gentlemen and had her share of admirers, one of whom was Stephen Mallory who came to Pensacola in 1834.[4]

His appearance in Pensacola ostensibly was to visit his cousin, Mrs. Lydia McIntosh, and her husband, James, the Pensacola Navy Yard commandant. However, the true reason for Stephen's arrival was to call upon Angela Moreno with Mrs. McIntosh playing the role of intermediary. Stephen and Angela visited one another in the McIntosh home; following some initial contacts Stephen decided that Angela was the woman he would marry. He had developed a standard of excellence for a wife: she would be a Catholic, would speak French, Spanish, and English, and would be musical. Mallory wrote, "Such were my demands; but she [Angela] excelled all my ideals; she had what I regarded as a sine qua non, & a great deal besides."[5] An unusual courtship ensued.

After more visits with Angela, Stephen was determined to let his feelings for her be known before he left Pensacola. One evening Stephen was visiting her in the McIntosh home when Mrs. McIntosh and the children rose to retire. Stephen wrote to his eldest son about what happened next:

> I requested Miss Moreno to remain, said that it was early, & I would read to her.... After reading a brief time I laid the book aside, & began very nervously & formally the story of my love, & my "ideal." She listened not very long, but rose with apparent feeling, almost anger, & with a very demonstrative manner, picked up her candle stick, told me that she would not have remained with me had she known my purpose, that I had misled her....

Stephen related that he was indignant because he had thought of her and no one else since he first saw her; she was his ideal, and she dismissed him in what he perceived as a "heartless & contemptuous air of superiority." The house was shut up and the parlor door was the only open exit. Angela started to leave the room; Stephen wrote that he "jumped to the door, closed, locked it, & put the key in my pocket — there she stood, looking at me in mute surprise, & finding retreat cut off, looked as if about to hurl the candlestick at my head."[6] He explained to Angela that he had said things to her that he had never said to another human, and added that his soul was upon his lips. He continued in a respectful manner urging her to hear him out. Angela replied, "Well Sir I will hear you." The suitor then explained to the girl the intensity of his feelings for her and his long devotion to her. He closed by telling her he wanted no answer to his entreaty at the present "but that in two years time I would renew this suit, & would marry no other woman than her. — To all of which, when I unlocked the door, she simply said, 'you need never renew your offer, for I will never listen to it again....'"[7]

Of this visit Angela said, "After the presentation I must have shown by my eyes, which always speak the truth, that I did not like his looks." Regarding his stated intent to propose marriage in two years, Angela said she replied, "Neither then nor thereafter will you have a favorable answer."[8]

Stephen Mallory returned to Key West and in October 1836 joined Lieutenant Powell on his first expedition to search for Seminole Indians. Two months later he returned to Key West from that foray and as promised wrote a letter to Angela renewing his marriage offer. Her response was polite, with no air of superiority or scorn, but she rejected his advance for a second time. Angela said that Stephen's letter indicated that if she gave him no hope, he would go and fight Indians; she replied that he should go and do so.

During 1837 the rejected lover continued to stay in contact by letter with Lydia McIntosh in Pensacola, letting her know of his unceasing love for Miss Moreno. He told his cousin that he had named his race boat for Angela. Perhaps this constituted a continuation of his romanticism coupled with a dash of melancholy. Undoubtedly, he expected his cousin to pass on these sentiments to her friend. Angela reported that during this period "his fidelity and devotion touched my heart and as the years went on I began to relent."[9] Meanwhile, Stephen labored as an inspector at the customhouse,

Key West, 1838. This William A. Whitehead pencil sketch depicts the business district of Key West, Florida, in June 1838. The view from the cupola of the Tift & Co. warehouse is looking north toward the harbor. Stephen Mallory and Angela Moreno were married that summer; the newlywed couple took residency in Key West in July 1838. COURTESY OF MONROE COUNTY HISTORIAN THOMAS L. HAMBRIGHT AND MONROE COUNTY LIBRARY, KEY WEST.

checking inventories and similar tasks, while at the same time continuing to gain expertise in the legal profession by copying briefs in Judge Marvin's office.

During the winter of 1837–1838 Mallory participated in the second Powell expedition into the Everglades. The naval force concluded its activities in April 1838 and Lieutenant Powell took his sailors to the navy yard at Pensacola. Mallory elected to remain with the coterie so that he might see Miss Moreno. Mallory reported that he landed there at daybreak and he walked with a few officers from the wharf on Palafox Street to the Collins hotel where they cleaned up and had breakfast.

Stephen and Angela later engaged in an impromptu elaborate masquerade suggestive of a primitive mating dance. Mallory and Lieutenant Powell went to the piazza of the Collins hotel to prepare horses they had ordered to ride to the navy yard to visit Commander and Mrs. McIntosh's home. Not by coincidence, the hotel piazza could be observed from the Moreno home across the street. Angela saw Stephen arranging the stirrups on his horse, but he pretended not to see her. Consequently she had her sister play her guitar and sing a favorite song of Stephen's as something of a restrained welcome. He was quite aware of what was ensuing and managed to consume a great deal of time fixing the stirrups. Then he rode off without looking at her and called upon Mrs. McIntosh. Stephen told his cousin that he had come to see Angela but would not call upon her unless his chances with her had improved. Mrs. McIntosh told him he had better go and judge for himself. Mallory took this to be a favorable indicator. He rode quickly back to the Moreno home and was looking at a picture on the wall, when he "heard a voice at my very heart say 'So sir, you have come at last have you? After not even looking at me this morning.'" Stephen was overpowered with emotion and asked Angela to walk outside with him so he might have a private talk with her. She put on her bonnet and once on the street she said in an off-hand manner, "What in the world has brought you here?"

Stephen responded, "You have, I came to see you alone — Refuse me & I go back at once; but not to give you up, for I am determined to marry you...." Angela said, "I had determined to accept your offer if you ever renewed it." Her acceptance of his proposal concluded the mating dance.[10]

What is remarkable about this entire episode is Stephen's dogged pursuit of his goal through an eight-year period, and Angela's reluctance to enter into the contract. Stephen did not know her well but obviously was attracted to her. Angela's early reluctance to marry him is more complex. She was the eldest daughter in a large, financially secure and highly respected family living in a cosmopolitan city. Perhaps she did not wish to leave the bosom of her family, and a comfortable life, to venture into the strangeness of a small town in a relatively unsettled section of south Florida, risking marriage to this relatively unknown young man. However, it may have been her age that moved her toward marrying Stephen. In an era when most brides were in their teens, Angela was 23 years old when they exchanged vows. Possibly, Angela and her family feared she was facing a lifetime of spinsterhood.

A priest named S. Y. Guinard married Stephen Russell Mallory and Angela Sylvania Moreno on July 19, 1838, at St. Michael Catholic Church in Pensacola, Florida.[11] The couple arrived in Key West shortly thereafter and took up housekeeping in a rented dwelling. The next year Don Francisco Moreno paid his daughter and son-in-law a visit in Key West. Mr. Moreno was an astute businessman and he must have recognized Stephen's sound judgment because he offered to advance a sum of money for purchasing a house. Stephen and Angela accepted the offer.[12]

Stephen was admitted to the bar in 1839 or 1840, and he began expanding his practice. He soon developed a reputation as a hard-working and effective barrister. Mallory gained much practical experience in the courtroom in Key West. As judge of the United States District Court, Southern District of Florida, William Marvin presided over numerous salvage cases arising from the wrecking business. Mallory appeared in his friend's court from time to time as counsel for one side or another. The young lawyer refined his legal skills through these court appearances. Judge Marvin was scrupulous in considering only the facts of a case and reaching the best possible decision through careful consideration of those facts. Personal friendship never entered into the judicial process and Mallory expected no favoritism. As he honed his skills in court, Stephen gained a reputation as one of the most skilled young lawyers in Florida.

By 1848 Stephen Mallory's talent as a lawyer was noticed at the national level. He was selected by a resolution of the United States Congress to arbitrate a conflict of property rights between the Federal government and the Catholic church of St. Augustine, Florida. This was an important and delicate matter and it was the mark of a maturing lawyer that he should be selected for this work. In spite of his being a Catholic, the Congress evidently believed he could be fair and impartial in arbitrating the matter.

This dispute centered on ownership of the St. Francis monastery and other buildings erected by the Order of Franciscans in St. Augustine under the sponsorship of the Spanish government in the early 1600s. By a treaty of 1763, Spain ceded Florida to Great Britain and the monastery was used as a barracks for English troops. Twenty years later Florida was returned to Spain and the Franciscan Order petitioned to regain this property. The request was denied on the ground that there was only a small Spanish population in town at that time. On July 10, 1821, Florida became a United States territory and in 1832 Congress declared the barracks to be a Federal military reservation.

In 1848 the Order of Franciscans sent a petition to the U.S. Congress claiming that this property belonged to the Catholic church and Congress submitted the matter for arbitration.

The arbitrator, Stephen Mallory, studied the matter carefully and determined that the Catholic church had not taken appropriate and timely action to establish just title to the property. His decision rested on three points: (1) When Spain surrendered Florida to the United States, it took no action to safeguard the property; (2) in 1783 Spain took possession of the monastery, used it to house its soldiers, and made no effort to compensate the friars for depriving them of their domicile; (3) the friars never requested compensation.[13] Thus Stephen Mallory established a presence and reputation in north Florida and nationally. This was an important precursor to his future in a prominent political career.

After 1846 Mallory had become a well-known political figure in Key West. He had been elected a circuit court judge and later was a probate judge for Monroe County. Stephen became active in the Democratic Party, but there were instances in which the Whig leaders supported him. Jackson Morton, a Whig opponent, said that Mallory conducted his office as collector of customs with "honesty, capacity, and fidelity in an eminent degree." Morton added that Mallory was apolitical in conducting customs affairs. The U.S. Treasury Department regarded him as a "prompt, vigilant, and efficient officer." Few Whigs in Key West were opposed to him because they feared any candidate of their own would suffer in comparison with Mallory.[14]

In addition to developing his political acumen, he also was gaining some modest wealth in his business activities. He held power of attorney for some business leaders, and he was joint owner of some land with his friend Asa Tift. A significant part of his legal practice came from representing business leaders in tax and civil suits.[15]

Florida was admitted as a state on March 3, 1845, and, as a slave state, became involved in the national debate on bondage. This issue had always been a divisive force in the United States of America and a series of agreements had been struck to avoid war. The Missouri Compromise of 1820 was the first of a series of legislative concessions between slavery and free-soil proponents that would serve to delay onset of war. The Mexican War concluded with signing of the 1848 Treaty of Guadalupe Hidalgo, under which Mexico ceded vast new western lands to the United States. Southerners were eager to expand slavery into the newly acquired territory. The question of the day was whether the new territory would be slave or free, and debate on slavery was intense. Once again, war was averted only through a series of bills that collectively formed the Compromise of 1850. This legislative activity was meant to please everyone, but in fact it pleased no one. It sowed seeds of discord, but averted secession for another decade.

Against this backdrop of turmoil and dissension, the new state of Florida became embroiled in the national debate. Florida as a slave state had a vested interest in the outcome of the slavery issue. The stake was significant because "39,000 of the state's 87,000 inhabitants were slaves."[16]

In Monroe County (Key West), Stephen Mallory was politically active as a Democrat, but he refused to run for any public office.[17] However, he made clear his early political proclivities when he wrote, "I was conservative, and though I believed in secession as a right from the history and theory of Government, I deemed it hazardous as a remedy and was thus held to be a 'Union' man."[18] Mallory was a complex character. He was the kind of man who could be persistent and stubborn as demonstrated by his pursuit of Angela; but he also was a flexible individual who could support the dichotomous positions of union and disunion. As a political matter, he would characterize himself as a "Union man" because he supported Florida as a new entity in the union of states, while at the same time favoring disunion by supporting secession to protect states' rights. Stephen saw himself as maintaining flexibility during these difficult times. His detractors would accuse him of waffling. His personal characteristics of persistence, stubbornness, and flexibility would become both strengths and weaknesses in his future trials. Stephen Mallory experienced divided loyalties over what route to follow in response to the cataclysmic events that were erupting in the United States of America. He was not unique in this respect — restlessness and divisiveness were the national norm.

When Florida attained statehood, the congressional delegation consisted of three men: Senators David Levy Yulee and Jackson Morton and Representative Edward Carrington Cabell. Of the three, David Yulee, the senior senator from Florida, was the most prominent figure. He was a Democrat who became an associate and admirer of South Carolina's Senator John C. Calhoun, and he strongly supported slavery. He viewed various northern actions as a menace to southern rights. Jackson Morton was a Whig from Pensacola. He was less experienced politically than Yulee and frequently followed his lead. Representative Cabell, also a Whig, was from the Tallahassee area. Cabell supported states' rights and expansion of slavery westward, but he was more agreeable than Yulee to compromise with the North.[19]

In 1849 a convention of representatives of southern states was held in Mississippi at the urging of John C. Calhoun. The purpose of the gathering was to exhort all slaveholding states to send delegates to a meeting in Nashville, Tennessee. The meeting's objective was to establish a united front against perceived northern intrusions upon slavery and the rights of these states to maintain the "peculiar institution."[20] Yulee, Morton, and Cabell signed a letter on February 6, 1850, to Florida governor Thomas Brown requesting that he name delegates to attend this "Nashville Convention." The gist of this letter was that northern interests had become hostile toward the South's social structure and were attempting to cripple the growth and progress of slaveholding states. To resist this menace, it was necessary for southern states to organize and stand firm against these forces. The Florida governor wrote that he did not have the authority to appoint delegates. Further, he added that the Nashville Convention was revolutionary in spirit, and Florida's Constitution prohibited the state from entering into any confederation. Also, he pointed out that the North had committed no specific act of aggression against the South.[21]

Members of Florida's political parties reacted by holding local meetings for selection of representatives to district assemblages that would appoint delegates to the Nashville Convention. Bird M. Pearson was named as a delegate from east and south Florida. He asked Mallory to act as his alternate and travel with him to Nashville. Mallory declined in a letter to Pearson saying he had "important preengagements." He apparently was fearful that the Nashville Convention would become a secession forum, and he was unready for such a radical step at this time.[22] Mallory staked out his position when he wrote this to Pearson: "In union is our safety. In union let us prescribe the limits of our forbearance, and in union let us preserve them. Constitutional rights are secondary in importance to the question of our united action."[23]

While some southern extremists might have hoped the Nashville Convention would result in secession, forces in Washington were moving to minimize the risk of this occurring. On January 29, 1850, Henry Clay presented a series of resolutions in the Senate designed to end the controversy over slavery in the territories. These constituted the Compromise of 1850. The Nashville Convention met during June 3–12, 1850, and it became obvious that Clay's efforts had served to enervate the influence of extremists. Secession was not an option, and the delegates passed a series of 28 resolutions condemning Clay's Compromise. In the end, the Nashville Convention was all sound and fury, accomplishing little.[24]

As the year 1850 began, political alignments forming in Florida mirrored those found within the nation. The Whig Party was conservative in nature, and most Florida planters allied themselves with this party. Affluent individuals usually were allied with the Whigs and the status quo because they had the most to lose from the disruptions of slavery and the southern social structure. Democrats, members of the other major party in Florida, included both radicals and moderates. Radicals wanted no compromise on slavery, and insisted that abolitionists and those from the North not disturb this "peculiar institution." If the North should refuse to leave the state alone, radicals considered secession as the only appropriate response. Senator David Yulee was strongly allied with these radicals and with their national leader, Calhoun. The moderate wing of the Democratic Party desired to avoid secession and felt it wise to work within the Union to deal with problems of slavery. They supported the peacemaking efforts of Henry Clay.

Stephen Mallory, a lifelong Democrat, was a pragmatic man who supported secession in theory, but also found it advantageous in this decade to work within the Union to correct perceived wrongdoings being threatened against Floridians. Mallory clearly dreaded secession because he thought it to be a dangerous step. He regarded separation from the Union as a revolution that could be justified only as a last resort from intolerable oppression.[25] He was sufficiently flexible that he could shift back and forth between the camps of the radicals and moderates without offending either or compromising himself.

Over the past 15 years, Stephen Mallory had demonstrated his developing intellectual talents and skills as a public servant in Key West. Now he was moving from this small stage toward the national scene. As an adolescent, Mallory had expressed a desire to go to Congress. That opportunity was about to open to him, albeit through the route of contested elections for senator both in the Florida Legislature and the United States Senate.

In the congressional election of October 1850, the Democratic Party gained control of the Florida Legislature, which it had lost two years earlier. David L. Yulee's six-year term as U.S. senator from Florida was to expire in March 1851 and it would be the responsibility of the Florida Legislature to select a senator for the next term.[26] Yulee was a candidate for reelection, but elements both inside and outside of the Democratic Party opposed him for a second term. Some were disenchanted because of his vociferous attacks against the Compromise of 1850, but local issues pertaining to railroads were equally important. Yulee had worked long and hard to promote railroads in Florida in order to open the state to economic development. He proposed that a railroad be built from Fernandina on the Atlantic Ocean in northeast Florida to Cedar Key on the Gulf of Mexico on Florida's west coast. The new road was incorporated in 1849 and came to be known as the Atlantic and Gulf Railroad. A competing group, which was promoting a railroad from Jacksonville to Pensacola, tried to influence legislators to vote against Yulee. Key West commercial groups, believing that interests in north Florida were ignoring them, concluded that any northern transstate railroad would siphon business away from south Florida.

David Yulee controlled the Democratic caucus in Florida's legislature by a slim majority of 16 to 15. Two of these members determined they could not vote for him for senator. A total of 30 votes was required to be selected as senator. Before the Florida Legislature convened, Yulee forces could count only 28 Democratic votes plus one Whig vote—a total of 29 votes. It was taken for granted that those who would not vote for Yulee were hostile to his election. Yulee's supporters canvassed both parties in December 1850 to secure one more vote.[27]

On January 13, 1851, a joint session of the Florida Legislature convened to select a senator. The only name placed in nomination was that of David Levy Yulee. Twenty-nine voice votes were recorded for Yulee and 29 blank ballots were cast. The president of the joint session, R. J. Floyd, declared there was no election. A second vote was taken with the same results. In a third vote, 28 ballots were cast for Yulee and 30 blank ballots were cast. These three votes ensured that any candidate who was nominated by the anti–Yulee forces would win the election. The joint session adjourned and set a later meeting date to elect a senator.[28]

Among those considered for nomination was Stephen Russell Mallory. When Mallory first heard his name was being considered for candidacy, he responded in a way that was a surprise to many. He appealed to the Democratic Party to unite in support of Yulee or some other suitable candidate who could be relied upon to support the rights of Florida. He did not, however, decline to serve should he be nominated. Mallory had always been a staunch supporter of Yulee on states' rights issues, but he did not believe it was desirable to strongly support secession as suggested by Yulee. Also, he was concerned about being unknown throughout the state, thereby causing a schism within the Democratic Party (he was personally known to only seven members of the legislature). Mallory made these views clear on December 7, 1850, in a letter to J. T. Archer, Esq.:

> The effect of [my nomination] *may* [italics in original] be to distract and divide the members of the democratic party, and to impair those kindly and generous feelings which ought to exist among them.... I do not desire, nor am I willing to occupy the attitude of an aspirant for political distinction, at the expense of the harmony of the democratic party.... If I were the choice of the party, I would not feel at liberty to decline serving the State in that or in other official capacity, but I cannot consent to the use of my name if discord is to result when a thorough union is so manifestly important.[29]

The name of Stephen Russell Mallory was placed in nomination for senator. Most legislators probably felt he was a safe candidate who was not burdened with the baggage carried by Yulee, and was one who could be relied upon to continue the work of Yulee in protecting Florida's rights.

On January 15, 1851, the fourth ballot was taken by the Florida Legislature. Mallory gained the votes of those representing Key West and the southeast coast along with some Whig support. The vote count was 31 for Mallory to 23 for Yulee, plus four blank ballots. Stephen Russell Mallory was duly elected United States senator.[30]

The prominent Tallahassee newspaper, the *Floridian & Journal*, wrote this about the new senator from Florida:

> While we do not disguise our deep regret at the failure of the Legislature to return Mr. Yulee.... we rejoice that one every way qualified to succeed him has been selected in the person of Mr. Mallory. He has again and again given to the

course of his predecessor (Mr. Yulee) his most explicit and unequivocal commendation, and expressed his strong desire to see that gentleman re-elected. Going to Washington, he will take the place vacated by Mr. Yulee; in the noble band of Southern patriots ... to resist Northern injustice ... to do battle for Southern laborers rights and the Constitution ... and in him his co-laborers will find not only a willing but also an able auxiliary. We feel that we may congratulate our Southern friends at home and abroad on the selection of one entirely worthy of their confidence.[31]

Yulee and his supporters contested the election of Mallory on disputed grounds regarding voted ballots versus the four blank ballots and how those ballots were considered in defining a quorum. The contest would largely be played out in the United States Senate, but in the meantime Mallory prepared to go to Washington. He felt he had fairly won the seat and he did not intend to relinquish it.

Sometime after the election, the senator-elect met with Henry Clay in Havana, Cuba, to let him know that he supported Clay's Compromise of 1850. Senator Clay may have suggested to Mallory that he could be helpful to him in the Senate with respect to the contested seat.[32] Clay probably thought Mallory was preferable to Yulee since Yulee was much more inclined toward disunion than Mallory. In fact, the aged Clay did appear in Mallory's behalf in December 1851, and made his last speech in the Senate.[33]

Drama revolving around the contested election of Stephen Russell Mallory commenced in the Senate chambers when Congress convened on December 1, 1851. Florida senator Jackson Morton presented the Florida governor's certification of Mallory's election to the Senate effective March 4, 1851. He also presented a copy of the Florida joint legislative session record that pertained to the contested seat. A motion was made by Senator Bright (Indiana) to refer these documents to a select committee of five, whereupon Henry Clay (Kentucky) objected. Senator Clay contended that Mallory had arrived with proper credentials that produced prima facie evidence of his right to the Senate seat that he claimed. Discussion of the motion followed, and Senator Clay opposed referring the matter to the committee prior to seating Mallory. He argued that it would be proper for Yulee to contest the Senate seat after Mallory was seated. Bright withdrew his motion and Clay moved that Mallory be sworn in. The motion was agreed to and the oath was administered to Stephen Mallory on December 1, 1851.[34]

The first appearance before the Senate Select Committee by David Yulee, who was represented by Edwin M. Stanton, was on June 10, 1852. Stanton provided his definition of a quorum:

> The General Assembly consists of forty Representatives and nineteen Senators ... [and] ten Senators and twenty-one Representatives being a majority, constitute a quorum of each House: and that number being present ... business may be transacted by a major part of them; so that, a quorum being present, six Senators and eleven Representatives may transact business ... and may choose a Senator.

He went on to explain that those who had cast a blank ballot supported the choice of their colleagues, and consequently Mr. Yulee had been elected unanimously on the first ballot.[35]

Stephen Mallory interpreted the meaning of the blank ballots in an entirely different way:

> If the twenty-nine members who voted blank be considered absent, or as not participating in the election, then there was not a quorum present, and the attempt of the other twenty-nine to do anything but to adjourn, or to enforce the presence of absent members, was void. But if they were present, then the contestant did not get a majority of those present.

Mallory explained that the blank ballots were the only way that members of the state legislature could assert dissent. He insisted, "Theirs was not a vote of assent, but of dissent; and the blank vote, there being no other person in nomination, was their true and only means of expressing dissent." He closed by saying that Florida proceeded in accordance with her statutes and the Senate could not reverse Florida's election of a senator "without trespassing on the sovereign rights of the state."[36]

Other arguments centering on these issues followed, but on August 27, 1852, a Senate resolution was presented in response to a report by the Senate Select Committee: "Resolved, that the Hon. Stephen R. Mallory was duly elected a member of the Senate of the United States from the third day of March 1851." The resolution reported by the committee was adopted unanimously.[37] Nearly nine months after he was sworn into office, Stephen Russell Mallory was confirmed as a United States senator.

The new senator had already received some positive notice in a popular periodical of the day, the January 1852 issue of *Hunt's Merchants' Magazine*:

> Senator Mallory is ... a man of mark. Self-educated, and self-made, he has by industry, perseverance, and an indomitable energy of character, risen to his present high position, which it is not doubted he will maintain, with honor to himself and dignity and advantage to the State. He is a man of great industry, and said to be possessed of unusual powers of memory.[38]

PART II

UNITED STATES SENATOR

3

A Potpourri of Issues

During his service as a United States senator, Stephen Russell Mallory spoke on diverse issues of the day. Some of these were of prime national importance, while others were less urgent matters associated with interests of his constituents. Mallory's expertise in naval matters was acknowledged in spring 1853 when he was named chairman of the Senate Naval Affairs Committee.[1] From this position, Senator Mallory worked continuously to strengthen the United States Navy. This undoubtedly was his most significant contribution to the nation and the next chapter concentrates upon this pursuit. This section is devoted to reviewing his other Senate activities.

Eleven days after he was sworn in, Stephen Mallory made one of his first forays into debate regarding an unlikely subject for a resident of Key West, who it could be assumed might have a somewhat parochial outlook. On December 12, 1851, the Senate was debating a joint resolution to welcome Louis Kossuth to the United States. Louis (Lajos) Kossuth was a Hungarian revolutionary hero whose republic had fallen to invading Russian troops in 1849. After liberation from a Turkish prison, he was invited by President Millard Fillmore to visit the United States. The purpose of the pending resolution was to welcome him as a champion of liberty.[2]

Senator Badger (North Carolina) had the floor and yielded his time to Mallory because "on account of the state of his [Mallory's] health, he may not be able to remain within the Chamber so as to be able to submit his views...."[3] As befitting a new senator, Mallory opened his remarks by saying he had listened carefully to what other senators had said about the resolution. He spoke in support of it saying, "I regard him [Kossuth] as the impersonation,[4] the imbodiment [sic] of the principles of civil and religious liberty among the millions of Europe. I am prepared to honor this man."

The senator from Florida then addressed the concerns of others who contended that honoring Kossuth might lead "to intervention and entangling alliances in the affairs of Europe." Mallory said if that were the case, he could never vote to support the resolution. He added, "But it is impossible to regard this simple resolution as intervention.... I do not see intervention in this proposition, and shall therefore vote for it." The joint resolution to welcome Kossuth to the United States passed by a vote of 33 to 6.[5] Louis Kossuth arrived in New York as a guest of the nation and was given a warm welcome.[6]

On January 5, 1852, he was introduced to the Senate and was received in the upper chamber.[7]

Senator Mallory further displayed his interest in world affairs in the spring of 1858 when he spoke in favor of promoting trade with Paraguay. Five years earlier the United States had entered into discussions with this young republic for the purpose of establishing trade agreements. Misunderstandings arose and violence erupted. The United States steamer *Water Witch* was engaged in a survey on a branch of the La Palata River when a fort on the Paraguay side of the river fired upon her. This caused one sailor's death and damage to the vessel. The Senate was discussing what action should be taken in response to this provocation. Many indignant senators wanted to use force to punish the government of Paraguay. Mallory desired an appropriate reaction to the offense, but preferred to use negotiation, not vengeance. He wished to support trade with that South American republic. Eventually a compromise was reached.[8]

Mallory did not forget where he came from and who his friends were; pork barreling was an accepted practice for all congressmen. On December 23, 1851, he submitted a resolution "that the Committee on Naval Affairs be instructed to inquire into and report on the expediency of establishing a Naval Depot at Key West, in the State of Florida."[9] The Senate supported the resolution. A navy depot had been established at Key West in 1822. However, claims were made in 1825 of an unhealthy climate and lack of potable water in Key West, and the navy depot and a shipyard were authorized for construction at Pensacola, Florida. Mallory was a member of the committee to whom the resolution was referred.

On February 13, 1852, there came before the Senate a claim arising from the government's occupation of Key West. John W. Simonton, one of the leading businessmen in Key West (and Mallory's friend), had made a claim on behalf of himself and others for damages resulting from the government's use of their property. Mallory supported these private claims although opposition was expressed by a number of senators. He explained how individual citizens were affected by the arrival of the army and navy during the period 1823–1826: they were deprived of property without receiving just compensation, were restricted in placing certain buildings on their property, had to abandon their livestock, and were subjected to martial law. Congress had considered a similar claim in previous years and there were sound arguments pro and con. No decision was reached and on April 2, 1852, the matter was postponed indefinitely.[10] The new senator was not always successful in helping his friends, but that would not stop him from trying.

On February 24, 1852, Senator Mallory presented petitions on behalf of individuals to whom money was due for past services. They were the district attorney and district judge for the northern district of Florida and the heirs of a Revolutionary War soldier.[11] On August 21, 1852, he offered an amendment to a river and harbors bill that entailed spending $15,000 for improvement of the harbor at Apalachicola Bay, just south of Tallahassee. In spite of his logical argument, the amendment was rejected.[12] On August 23, 1852. he offered another amendment to the same bill providing that a space behind the seawall at St. Augustine, Florida, be filled at a cost of $3,000. This amendment was approved.[13]

In another debate, Senator Mallory displayed his extensive knowledge of lighthouses. The discussion occurred in the upper chamber on August 30, 1852. Mallory first presented his credentials: "I have had some practical knowledge of light-houses. I have had the control and charge of them. I have procured their oil and appointed their keepers, and have made a practical examination of them for years, and therefore know something of the importance of the subject." The debate previously had centered on the high cost of the Fresnel lens purchased in France, but Mallory argued that this cost consideration should be secondary to the matter of safe navigation. Then he added, "It is a common thing to hear even American ship-masters classify our first-class lights with the first-class lights of England and France." Mallory asserted that one of the best lighthouses in America was located on the Tortugas off the coast of Florida and "Its light can be seen as far as the curvature of the earth will permit."[14] Obviously this broad knowledge base was accumulated during his work with the customs service and with related maritime duties, as well as his reading detailed reports both in Key West and Washington.

The next day Senator Mallory moved to amend an appropriation for completion of a lighthouse on Sand Key, Florida. His amendment provided that an engineer by the name of Lewis, who previously had charge of that construction, be named to oversee its completion. However, other senators railed at this suggestion; they believed the law required that the project be under the direction of an Army engineer, not a civilian. Mallory developed strong arguments relating to why Mr. Lewis was best qualified to complete the project, stressing that he had done all the original drawings and specifications. In the end, Mallory had to compromise by revising his amendment to provide that an army officer would superintend the work. In this revised form, the amendment passed.[15] Senator Mallory had sound reasons for Mr. Lewis doing this work, but he also recognized the necessity of compromise in order to get the badly needed lighthouse built. Stephen Mallory was a persistent man but he was a pragmatist who recognized that concessions occasionally were necessary to accomplish an objective. This character trait would be evident throughout his life.

Slavery was one of the most contentious issues facing Senator Stephen Russell Mallory throughout his service in the United States Senate. The controversy around involuntary servitude had first arisen as the American colonies struggled with drafting the Declaration of Independence in 1776. Some members of the Continental Congress wanted to prohibit slavery, but yielded on this point to ensure ratification of the document. However, the founding fathers did insert the phrase that all men are created equal. This ideal was compromised by the silence about slavery, but such action was necessary then. Opposition to slavery was expressed later when the Northwest Ordinance of 1787 banned slavery in that vast territory and again in 1807 when the African slave trade was prohibited. But compromise would be necessary later to delay an eruption of civil war.

The 1803 Louisiana Purchase opened 2 million square miles west of the Mississippi for settlement. Would it be free or slave? After Louisiana attained statehood in 1812 as a slave state, thousands of slave owners migrated into the upper Louisiana Territory where they sought statehood for Missouri as a slave state. Northerners felt the balance of power was being tipped toward the South, southerners proclaimed their right to carry their property into Missouri, and Congress was split on the issue of involuntary servitude. Into the breach stepped Senator Henry Clay who engineered legislation in 1820–1821 that came to be known as the Missouri Compromise. It allowed Maine to enter the Union as a free state. In order to maintain a balance between free and slave states, the mutual concessions also provided for Missouri to be admitted as a slave state with the proviso that bondage was to be prohibited in the rest of the Louisiana Territory located north of the southern boundary of Missouri (36°30" north latitude). All western territories north of 36°30" were to be free soil.

The next major congressional compromise on slavery occurred in 1850. Texas had been admitted as a slave state in 1845 and the Mexican War was concluded in 1848 with the signing of the Treaty of Guadalupe Hidalgo. Through this treaty the United States gained vast new lands, and there was urgency to expand slavery west of Texas. Again there was sound and fury over whether or not this territory would be free or slave. The congressional debate was intense and lengthy. Threat of secession erupted. Once again the peacemaker, Senator Henry Clay, proposed a series of proposals he hoped would reduce anxiety and avoid civil war. Some of the more important proposals:

1. California would be admitted as a free state.
2. The people in the territories of Utah and New Mexico would decide for themselves as to whether they wished slavery.
3. A more strict fugitive slave law would be adopted.

Much of 1850 was consumed with extensive congressional debate over these and related proposals. In September 1850 proposals were passed that formed the Compromise of 1850. Once more the Union had been preserved through conciliation.

The fugitive slave law had not been debated extensively, but it caused much dissension because of its vigorous enforcement by President Franklin Pierce's administration. These stringent efforts to return runaway slaves to their southern masters produced a reaction in northern states that consisted of passage of state personal liberty laws designed to enervate the federal legislation.

On June 28, 1854, the proposed repeal of the fugitive slave law was debated in the United States Senate.[16] In response to a question as to whether he would honor the Constitution should the fugitive slave law be repealed, Senator Charles Sumner (Massachusetts) replied, "I said I recognized no obligation in the Constitution of the United States to bind me to help to reduce a man to slavery."[17] But others in the Senate alleged they heard him say that he "never would surrender a fugitive slave."[18]

The debate become more heated and Senator Mallory, referring to Senator Sumner, interjected:

> When that honorable Senator here in the face of the country, in the presence of this Senate, within these hallowed walls, which have so often responded to the eloquence and patriotism of his own State — when he at the foot of this altar, upon which he pledged his fidelity to his country, upon which he called upon God to witness that he would defend and sustain her Constitution — when he rises in his place and tells the American Senate that he does not recognize the obligation of that Constitution, what does he expect at the hands of the Senator?

Sumner in response to Mallory said, "The Senator places in my mouth words and sentiments which have never fallen from me." Mallory's retort followed: "I should be unwilling to place in the mouth of a dog sentiments which were unbecoming to him, and will therefore ask the Senator, with all proper respect, to state what he did say; for that, I presume, is the understanding of the Senate."

The debate continued:

> Mr. Sumner. I stated that I would never render any personal assistance in returning or reducing a fellow man to slavery.
>
> Mr. President —

> Mr. Clay [C.C. Clay, Alabama]. When I hear the Senator from Massachusetts, with unblushing presumption and insolence, (Order!) without shame, without contrition or repentance, contumaciously repeating that he had said only that he would not reduce a fellow man to bondage—
>
> Mr. Sumner. Return.
>
> Mr. Clay. Return a fellow man to bondage—
>
> Mr. Sumner. Or reduce, which is the same thing.
>
> Mr. Mallory. ... I was interrupted by the Senator, who said I had put words into his mouth which he did not utter. Sir, I deny it! ... Sir, I heard the honorable Senator say, in open Senate, "I recognize no such obligation." Whether that appears in the report or not, I have not examined.
>
> Mr. Sumner. It is there, and I repeat it now.
>
> Mr. Mallory. Sir, if the Senator will examine theConstitution, he will find it there written that a fugitive from service or labor "*shall* [emphasis in original] be delivered up." If he recognizes no such obligation, I leave it to himself to explain the consistency between the oath which he has taken and the sentiments which he avows. Sir, can he rise in his place and say here that a Senator shall be permitted to make mental reservations? Is that the explanation? That he is at liberty to exempt himself from those obligations which bind the humblest citizen?[19]

The invectives of Mallory, Sumner, and others demonstrate two points. First, Stephen Mallory could become adamant and castigating when he felt strongly and was emotionally involved in a subject. He would not be bullied. Second, slavery had become such a divisive and heated issue that normal decorum found in the upper chamber was breaking down, thus forecasting the direction in which the country was heading.

Following the Compromise of 1850, tension in the United States over slavery had been reduced. It was the calm before the storm that erupted when Senator Stephen A. Douglas presented a bill in January 1854 to organize the Territory of Nebraska in such a fashion that he might gain the rights to run a transcontinental railroad from Chicago to San Francisco. But to get the bill passed, he needed the support of southern senators so he baited the bill with the notion that people of the new territory would decide for themselves if they would become a slave state or a free state. However, "popular sovereignty" was not sufficient inducement for southern senators to vote for the bill and they demanded an explicit right to bring slaves into the Territory of Nebraska. Since Nebraska Territory was located north of the Missouri Compromise line of 36° 30," slavery would have been prohibited there. Douglas knew that if he could not sidestep the issue of explicit support of slavery with the concept of popular sovereignty, then "a hell of a storm" would be raised in the North.[20] Nevertheless he finally took the dangerous step and added to his bill the repeal of the ban on slavery north of the Missouri Compromise line. The revised bill additionally provided for establishment of the states of Nebraska west of Iowa and Kansas west of Missouri. It was assumed that pro-slavery people from the neighboring slave state of Missouri would migrate into Kansas, ensuring it would become a slave state, and that Nebraska would attract free-soil farmers. Indeed this action did provoke "a hell of a storm" and three months of ensuing congressional debate hardened the positions of both sides. Northern senators demanded that the Nebraska Territory be maintained as free soil as agreed to in the Missouri Compromise.

The other side argued that its citizens had a "southern right" to bring slaves with them into frontier territories.

Appearing in the Senate on May 25, 1854, Stephen Mallory allied himself solidly with the southern block in his support of the bill. In referring to earlier statements made by Senator Seward (New York) he said:

> He, and others of his peculiar stamp, have repeatedly spoken of the aggressive power of slavery. The aggressive power of slavery! And this in face of the fact that slavery has been gradually but steadily pushed from State to State, and would doubtless have been, even now, extinct in Virginia, had not the bold and defiant attack upon southern rights by northern men compelled the South to rally, and stand firm upon the institution.... Sir, the South seeks not, in this bill, never has sought, to obtain any advantage of the North; nothing but that equality which is guaranteed by the Constitution, which they cannot tamely surrender without incurring the contempt of all honorable minds, and without which their place in this Union would be odious.[21]

Mallory was representing himself as a strong supporter of slavery and was encompassing the southern concept of states' rights. He was following the same path that had been endorsed by his radical predecessor, David Yulee, and was portraying himself as a true Southron. Just three years earlier he appeared to be much more of a moderate when he supported Henry Clay's activities associated with the compromises of 1850 that marked attempts to avoid disunion. How could Mallory lean toward supporting the Union in 1850 while, in 1854, supporting slavery and states' rights? How could he suggest that if these institutions were continuously and destructively verbally attacked by the North, it would be odious for southern states to remain in the Union? He had seemed to change from endorsing oneness to approval of separation.

This enigma has always been of concern to scholars and confusing to both his supporters and detractors. In 1850 it appeared to Mallory and his constituents that preserving the Union was possible, but four years later the earlier compromise began falling apart and disunion became a viable alternative. Times were changing rapidly, and Mallory with them. Consequently, Mallory, the moderate whose politics were flexible and pragmatic, inched toward separation. The senator from Florida avoided extremes. He never adopted the objectives of unionists, who would avoid disunion at any cost, or secessionists, who would withdraw from the Union at first hint of attack on southern institutions. Mallory was a centrist who could switch without difficulty to the left or right as his conscience and the will of his constituency dictated. In the Kansas-Nebraska territorial matter, he undoubtedly gauged the support of Floridians for the bill and had no trouble philosophically with supporting the will of the people.

On May 25, 1854 the Kansas-Nebraska Bill passed the Senate and was signed by President Franklin Pierce. Historian Gorrell Prim, Jr., labels Mallory as one of the more radical southerners on the slavery issue due to his stance on the Kansas-Nebraska Act.[22] McPherson states that "...this law may have been the most important single event pushing the nation toward civil war."[23]

In accordance with the provisions of the Kansas-Nebraska Act, a series of events took place in Kansas regarding whether that territory would be admitted as a slave state or a free-soil state. Rigged elections and fraudulent voting followed, and in September 1857 proslavery delegates won all the seats to a constitutional convention at Lecompton, Kansas. Emerging from this convention was the so-called Lecompton Constitution that legalized slavery in Kansas. Furthermore, a referendum for approval of the constitution by the voters was rejected, to assure it would not be altered; the document, accompanied by a petition for statehood, was sent to Congress. President James Buchanan endorsed this action and sent the Lecompton Constitution to Congress on February 2, 1858, recommending that Kansas be admitted as the 16th slave state.[24]

On March 15, 1858, debate commenced shortly after noon on the issue of whether or not slavery would be extended into Kansas. Discussions, often acrimonious, carried on through the day and night and the Senate adjourned at 6:05 A.M. on March 16, 1858.[25] That afternoon Senator King (New York) addressed the gathering saying, "The question is not that of admission of Kansas ... it is the monstrous proposition to impose upon the people of the Territory of Kansas a constitution and form of government known to be obnoxious to a very large majority of that people." King continued, "For the purpose of extending slavery into Kansas, a great wrong has been committed against the principles of republican government, and against the rights of the people of that Territory." He added, "The People of Kansas will never consent to have slavery established among them...." Senator King explained that the Democratic Party was "responsible for the long series of outrage, and for the great wrong which the bill before us proposes to consummate," but he hailed all those "honest Democrats, who, all over the country, at this moment are renouncing the long-cherished party name of Democrat because it has become tainted with treason to the rights of the people." Senator King warned, "The organization of the Democratic party has fallen irretrievably under the control of nullifiers and slave propagandists [and] when it becomes faithless to the rights and liberties of the people its organization must be dissolved."[26]

Senator Stephen R. Mallory rose in response. During the previous night and early morning hours, he had listened to speeches of his fellow senators and came into this session tired and emotionally drained due to the length and content of the debates. Adding to his distress were family problems: his two-year-old daughter, Nellie, had died two months earlier and his beloved 11-year-old son, Francis "Frankie," had died just five days before. Furthermore, by the standard of the day he was not, at 45 years of age, a young man anymore. Additionally, there was the matter of his health. On this day, he apparently was suffering from another, and more frequently occurring, gout attack. The condition was painful and was causing him to limp occasionally.[27]

On this afternoon, other senators noted Mallory's health problems. Midway into his address he was interrupted by Senator William H. Seward (New York) who, without rancor or sarcasm, asked, "Will the honorable Senator allow me, as an act of kindness to himself, to say that his speech is a very interesting one, and I am listening to him with great pleasure; but I am sure he speaks so low that he is not doing justice to himself. If he will raise his voice a little louder, he will be heard more distinctly across the Chamber." Mallory replied, "Thank you, sir. I cannot be expected to overcome any noise that may be made in the Chamber, but I will endeavor to make myself heard." The presiding officer, Mr. Stuart, stated, "The Chair will endeavor to preserve as good order as can be maintained in the Chamber; and he submits to Senators that it is important, on account of the evident condition of health of the Senator from Florida."[28]

Mallory's health is a significant matter because it may have affected the quality of his remarks, at least from his viewpoint. Following his speech and upon reflection, Senator Mallory evidently was less satisfied with his address than he had been with most of his previous Senate speeches. Evidence of this is seen in comparing his remarks made in the Senate with the revised speech that was published later. Senators could revise their oral remarks in the published version of their speeches. Mallory always took care to see that his published addresses were free of grammatical errors. However, with this speech, revisions in the published version were more extensive than normally was the case. He not only corrected grammatical errors, but also syntax; words were substituted to clarify and add emphasis. More importantly, he edited text that provided substantive changes to his meaning.[29]

For example, in the second paragraph of his Senate speech, Mallory made a significant revision for the printed version. In the Senate he explained:

> Some little pains are being taken by persons in my own State to misrepresent me there, and to say that I, with other Democrats, was going off on this question in Kansas.

In the written version he took a different slant by indicating:

> Some little pains have been taken to misrepresent my views upon the subject to friends in my own State, for whose generous support and unfailing confidence I shall ever feel deeply grateful.

In the published version he had clarified the issue and switched from focusing on his enemies to expressing his gratitude to his supporters.

Mallory then moved directly to the King speech and in the published version he said of it:

> The feature which struck me as most offensive ... was the cold and unpromising future of the whole production, the want of light and life throughout. It came over my senses like cold northern blasts, telling of an icy origin. Like a treacherous guide, it takes us over a barren waste, and after pointing out all the horrors of the road, leaves us without a ray of light to govern our future steps ... and he tells us, in effect, that if we submit to our fate gracefully, our death may be without terrors; but submission or not, die we must!

This phrasing had been altered from the Senate speech to heighten the sense of drama.

In the upper chamber speech, Mallory continued:

> In my judgment his extraordinary speech is not a work of statesmanship, but approaches the confines of special pleading; and I may freely say of it, that whatever there be in it which is true, is not new; and whatever it contains which is new, is not true. The Senator's political vision is limited by a geographical line, and he speaks, not to his country, but to his party.

Mallory next reviewed the Kansas-Nebraska issue from a southern perspective:

> A great national wrong has been done to the southern portion of this Confederacy by the act of admitting Missouri into the Union [because of the] prohibition of involuntary servitude ... from all that portion of the territory acquired by our treaty with France in 1803, which lay north of 36° 30". [The South] did demand, as a recognition of the political equality of the States, the right to go with her property into the common domain of the Confederacy ... and the offensive statute was wiped from the statute book. The meaning of the [Kansas-Nebraska] bill [was] not to legislate slavery into any State or Territory, nor to exclude it there-

from; but to leave the people thereof perfectly free to form their domestic institutions in their own way, subject only to the Constitution of the United States.

He related that delegates were legally elected to form a state constitution and after a popular vote, people of Kansas accepted a constitution with the slavery clause. In tracing the progress of the Lecompton Constitution, Mallory adhered to dogma of the Democratic Party and southern states by ignoring alleged voting irregularities and focusing on legal votes. He explained:

> I have equally ignored all alleged violations of election laws and acts of border ruffianism [because] no great political change, under popular forms of government, will, probably, ever be perfected without similar violations of law to some extent; and if the lawful acts of the legal people were thereby to be annulled, anarchy would necessarily be the result.

Senator Mallory then shifted his sights:

> The constitutional rights of the South, Mr. President, never have depended, and I trust they never will depend, on an equality of slave and free States in this Confederacy. Therefore, in my judgment, we must look inevitably to a preponderance of free States in this Confederacy. If I believed the rights of the South were dependent upon an equilibrium of free and slave States, I would use every human effort of which I am capable to induce the South to go out of the Union tomorrow.

This segment of his remarks was not spoken in the Senate; it was added to the published version. This is somewhat broader thinking than many southerners had adopted. The focus previously had been on balancing the number of slave and free states and Mallory had abandoned this principle. His point was that the constitutional rights of the South must be protected.

In reply to the argument that the proposed Kansas constitution should be submitted to a popular vote, Mallory provided the results of a survey to show that most state constitutions did not require ratification. Also, he dealt with the northern arguments that domestic slavery debased and brutalized the individual. Mallory recited the traditional southern arguments: the slave is treated well by his master, he is more civilized than his African descendents, he has been Christianized, servitude is not degrading for the individual because he is better off in all respects than he was in Africa, and the slave is among the best-fed, best-clothed and cared for among all laboring classes.

Senator Mallory then concluded his remarks:

> With exultant tone we are told that she [the South] will rule no more. Be it so. In withdrawing from the ship of State, we may, at least, with pride look back upon the track she has traced upon the pathway of nations.... Sir, I neither deplore this loss of power, nor fear its consequences to the South. She will be more than ever watchful of her rights, more sternly resolved to maintain them.

Additionally, Stephen Mallory closed with new and revised material in his published remarks that was not used in his oral presentation:

> Sir, the union of these States must soon depend upon the constitutional and conservative action of this sectional party; and as successful aggression rarely pauses in its career, it becomes the duty of the South to learn, while time for calm reflection and counsel still remains, the position she is to occupy in this Union.

Conservative as I am, hopeful if not confident, that our darkening political heavens will grow brighter, and that we shall realize politically that the darkest hour is just before the dawn, I yet trust, nay I well know, she will never submit to that greatest of all degradation to a free people, a voluntary existence under a violated Constitution.

It is not for me to indicate the path she may, in her wisdom, pursue; but sir, wherever it may lead, be it gloomy or bright, my whole heart is with her, and she will find me treading it with undivided affections.

Senator Stephen Russell Mallory's impassioned oratory — one of his most important speeches and arguably his greatest speech — is notable in several respects. First, his opening words set an important mood, and although written in prose they suggest the artistry of the poet ("It came over my senses like cold northern blasts, telling of an icy origin...."). This elegant composition was spoken in the upper chamber, but was extensively revised for the published document. This recalls his study and reading of poetry as an adolescent.

Second, his sense of drama and sure hand in staging the event is unmistakable when he says, "A great national wrong has been done to the southern portion of this Confederacy" and "if we submit to our fate gracefully, our death may be without terrors; but submission or not, die we must!"

Third, Mallory breaks new ground when he acknowledges the unequal race between the North and South for expansion and concedes that slave states cannot win that race: "In my judgment, we must look inevitably to a preponderance of free States in this Confederacy." This idea could not have been popular among many southern radicals, but Mallory was acknowledging that efforts to equalize the number of free and slave states could not prevail. At the same time, he suggested that secession might be fast approaching: "With exultant tone we are told that she [the South] will rule no more. Be it so. In withdrawing from the ship of State, we may, at least, with pride look back upon the track she has traced upon the pathway of nations."

Fourth, his closure is especially well written and substantive, although it was not presented in its polished form in the upper chamber. Senator Mallory calls for the South to calmly reflect what role she is to occupy in the United States, and he expresses hope that somehow the conflict may be favorably resolved in a manner agreeable to both sides. However, as a realist, he warns that the South "will never submit to that greatest of all degradation to a free people, a voluntary existence under a violated Constitution."

Fifth, his closing published paragraph, which was not delivered in the Senate, is especially important: "It is not for me to indicate the path she may, in her wisdom, pursue; but sir, wherever it may lead, be it gloomy or bright, my whole heart is with her, and she will find me treading it with undivided affections."

Senator Mallory, even up to the last moment, would expect everyone to make substantial effort to find a peaceful solution. He always believed in the Union, and hoped that southern states could resolve their disputes with northern states by negotiating within the framework of the Union. But he made it clear that he would support secession if it became necessary and would remain with his state wherever she might go. He recognized that as a moderate occupying the middle ground, his options were rapidly diminishing as issues became increasingly radicalized. At the same time he had accepted that he did not know which path the nation may take, but whichever way Florida went he would follow. Here he had begun to sound like another politician named Abraham Lincoln who on April 4, 1864, would write, "I claim not to have controlled events, but confess plainly that events have controlled me."[30]

On March 23, 1858, the Senate approved admission of Kansas as a slave state, but on April 1 the House rejected the pro-slavery Lecompton constitution. A new constitutional convention controlled by the Republican Party met in 1859 and Kansas finally was admitted to the United States as a free state in January 1861.[31]

Throughout the first half of the 19th century, importation of African slaves, although illegal, was prevalent throughout North and South America. In 1807, the United States had abolished the African slave trade, but American-built ships occasionally illegally transported African Negroes into slavery in Cuba. In 1821 a U.S. fleet was stationed in Key West to deal with piracy and the illegal African slave trade. By 1850 the rising price of slaves significantly increased smuggling activity and brought pressure upon the U.S. government to repeal the ban prohibiting slave importation. Those who wanted to bring more slaves into the United States also wanted to expand slave territory by acquiring Cuba. By 1854 the Knights of the Golden Circle was promoting the establishment of a new slave empire in Cuba, Mexico and Central America.[32]

Slaves were used in the production of various commodities; primarily cotton in the United States, sugar in the West Indies, and coffee in South America. During these years, cotton production in the United States expanded throughout the South and westward until it peaked when Texas became a state in 1845. By then it had become clear that if cotton culture were to continue to flourish, new lands would be required in regions that were conducive to growing this fiber. Southern United States interests turned to the West Indies as a potential area for expansion of its slave empire. Because of its proximity to the United States, its strategic location at the intersection of the Gulf of Mexico, the Caribbean Sea and the Atlantic Ocean, and its ample supply of slave labor, Cuba became an object of acquisition by the United States.

Interest in Cuba was not a new phenomenon. Thomas Jefferson had written on this subject to President Monroe on June 23, 1823: "I candidly confess, that I have ever looked on Cuba as the most interesting addition which could ever be made to our system of States. The control which, with Florida Point, this island would give us over the Gulf of Mexico, and the countries an isthmus bordering on it, as well as all those whose waters flow into it, would fill up the measure of our political well-being."[33] By the 1840s this idea became connected with the concept of Manifest Destiny, a phrase that was used by leaders and politicians to explain continental expansion by the United States. Manifest Destiny became the rationale for acquiring Cuba, but the base reason was to amass more land and slaves to enable increased cotton production.

For some years, many southern citizens of the United States had expressed interest in purchasing Cuba. Some people saw the sale of Cuba as comparable to the sale of Florida by the Spanish. Spain had been unable to control the Seminole Indians in Florida and this had been a factor in their ceding Florida to the United States. Similarly, Spain was having difficulty controlling slaves in Cuba, and a number of slave revolts occurred in 1843 and 1844.[34]

On January 26, 1853, Senator Stephen Mallory addressed these issues in a speech in the Senate entitled, "Colonization in North America." These comments were the continuation of debate on a resolution dealing with commercial restrictions upon United States trade with Cuba, and also dealt with procuring that island. Mallory argued that restrictive laws hindered the United States in achieving favorable trade agreements with

Cuba. He added that these particular commercial restrictions were placed on U.S. trade by a bill enacted by Congress in 1834. He urged its repeal.

Next, Senator Mallory discussed the strategic location of Cuba in the Gulf of Mexico with respect to American trade emanating from southern states and westward. He said the Gulf had but one outlet, with Cuba in the middle of the body of water. The senator explained that the passage on the south side of Cuba was difficult to navigate because of opposing winds and currents during the season when the great agricultural wealth and cotton crop of the South were outbound toward the Atlantic Ocean. Consequently the preferred route taken was the narrow pass, 60 miles wide, between the north shore of Cuba and the Florida Keys. He insisted that if France or England should "ever acquire a naval position on the north shore of Cuba ... all the commerce and navigation of the Gulf, would be as effectually sealed as if a convulsion of nature had reared up a mountain barrier before it."[35] For these reasons, he suggested that Cuba must be acquired by the United States. This is so important, he said, that "no Power on earth, no party in the country, can preclude us from acquiring ourselves the Island of Cuba."[36]

Mallory had outlined the importance of Cuba as a potential site for a foreign naval station, which could interrupt United States trade routes, and, under the right circumstances, as a potential trade partner. Action on these matters was postponed, but they would be revisited in February 1859 when Senator Mallory made another speech urging the acquisition of Cuba.

The first session of the 33rd Congress convened on December 5, 1853. Some of the radical southerners suggested that the United States should go to war with Spain in order to acquire Cuba as slave territory. On April 3, 1854, pressure was increased on Spain when U.S. Secretary of State William Marcy instructed his minister in Madrid to attempt the purchase of Cuba from Spain for $120 million.

Slavery was the center of much Senate debate during the spring and summer of 1854 and Senator Mallory often was in the middle of it. On May 17, 1854, he presented a resolution requesting that it be referred to the Committee on Foreign Relations. The resolution was concerned with "africanization" of Cuba and reflected concern in the United States that Spain had a "settled design to throw Cuba ultimately into the hands of its negro population and to revive there ... the scenes of San Domingo's revolution...." This in turn would "excite the just apprehensions of the Government of the United States...." Mallory was suggesting that should Cuba come under control of slaves, it would be difficult for the United States to acquire that island. After agreeing to a minor amendment to the resolution, it was referred to the Committee on Foreign Relations.[37]

Reference to the San Domingo revolution pertained to the uprising in Haiti that occurred from 1791 to 1803, resulting in Haiti being proclaimed a republic. In 1844 Cuban black slaves had rebelled and this uprising was brutally suppressed. Another bloody affair had occurred in the United States in 1831 when a man named Nat Turner led a slave uprising culminating in the death of white American citizens. Largely unspoken was fear by some that if there were another slave uprising in Cuba, only 100 miles or so from American shores, slaves in southern states might follow suit.

Senator Mallory had a second opportunity to speak on africanization of Cuba when, on May 22, 1854, Senator Clayton (Delaware) presented a resolution concerning the West India slave trade and use of American vessels for this purpose. The resolution requested that the Committee on Foreign Affairs inquire into methods by which this illegal activity might be halted. Senator Clayton stated that it would be suicidal for

Spain to "Africanize Cuba by means of the emancipation of the slaves."[38] Senator Mallory agreed that such a course was not in the best interests of Spain and added, "For to Africanize Cuba, sir, is to arm the beastly and brutal African, fresh from the jungle, thirsting for blood, knowing no law, ignorant of all restraints, and to hurry him on to the slaughter of the white race and the desolation of the island!"[39] Mallory expressed the common prejudices of his day and then spoke of the Spanish culture to contrast it with that of the African Negro. His observations about the Spaniards undoubtedly were enriched through his first-hand experiences with his wife and father-in-law. Senator Mallory observed:

> The individual Spaniard of today has all the honor, pride, and character of his glorious ancestors, when Spanish captains and discoverers gave a new continent to Christendom; when her fleets covered the ocean, and when Castilian honor was a conspicuous, a brilliant example. In spite of the examples and the degradations of a court, the most corrupt in Europe — in spite of ages of misgovernment, the Spaniard retains his heroism and his virtue.[40]

On May 24, 1854, Senator Judah P. Benjamin, introduced similar resolutions that he asked be referred to the Senate Committee on Foreign Relations. The thrust of these resolutions was that Spain desired to emancipate her slaves in Cuba to prevent the United States from purchasing the island or taking it by force.[41]

In October 1854, three American diplomats, including the future president, James Buchanan, wrote a document that represented the views of many southerners. It came to be known as the Ostend Manifesto, and it required that Spain sell Cuba to the United States for the $120 million offered, or risk having the island taken by force. However, this blunt-force approach received much negative criticism and it was repudiated by the Pierce administration.[42]

The hope of purchasing or seizing Cuba had been a high southern priority for years and President James Buchanan expressed interest in obtaining Cuba in three of his annual messages.[43] On February 21 and 25, 1859, Senator Stephen Russell Mallory delivered a major foreign policy speech titled "Acquisition of Cuba" in the upper chamber. At that time the Senate was considering a bill to obtain Cuba by negotiation. Mallory initially attempted to minimize the accusation that attempts to secure Cuba were a sectional issue with the South trying to get another slave state into the Union. He said that attempting to balance the numbers of slave and free states was a delusion and that acquisition of Cuba was a national issue. Mallory contended there were as many northern men who wished to procure Cuba as there were southern men. He insisted that this matter dealt with the welfare of the entire nation, not just of a section of the country.

This first portion of his speech is transparent in its attempt to convince other senators that interests in the North wished to acquire Cuba and that it was a national issue. In fact it was a sectional issue; the South wished to obtain Cuba for the purpose of expanding United States slave territory. Mallory had adopted the traditional southern position and was attempting to justify his stance. There is no evidence that those in the North were as equally interested as those in the South in gaining Cuba. To suggest otherwise got Stephen Mallory in trouble.

In his speech, Senator Mallory asked, "Why is it that the State of Connecticut has adopted a resolution ... in favor of acquiring Cuba?" Senator Fessenden from Maine let Senator Mallory know this was factually incorrect. Instead, the resolution was made at a

Democratic state convention and not by the state of Connecticut.[44] Mallory had no response.

Mallory turned next to connecting procurement of Cuba with expansionism inherent in the Louisiana Purchase. He suggested that "acquisition of the Island of Cuba [is] the necessary consequence of the purchase of Louisiana."[45] This same line of reasoning had appeared six years earlier as a southern rationalization for procuring Cuba and Mallory used it in his January 26, 1853, speech, "Colonization in North America." In both the 1853 and 1859 speeches, Mallory linked the acquisition of Cuba with the Louisiana Purchase, but failed to adequately develop his argument for this coupling.

Stephen Mallory proceeded to explain the strategic importance of Cuba to America. Much of this part of his presentation was taken from his "Colonization in North America" speech. In fact that earlier speech may be viewed as a prelude to the present speech on gaining Cuba. In this immediate speech, Mallory asserted:

> Between Cuba on the south and Florida on the north, floats this vast commerce, upon which the hills of Cuba, like sentry-boxes, look down. Are we not justified, then, in asserting that the first contest — and this must be a naval contest — in which we shall ever become involved, will be here? It must necessarily be so; because no sea upon the habitable globe offers such a temptation to a maritime enemy against our commerce as the Gulf of Mexico.[46]

The senator expressed wishful thinking when he said, "This question of Cuba is an American question ... this Government looks forward to the time ... when the Gulf of Mexico shall be a closed sea, as much under our jurisdiction and control as is the Irish channel under those of England; and that no foreign flag shall then float upon its bosom but by the permission of the United States."[47] It should be noted that Mallory did not address the issue of foreign-flagged ships peacefully pursuing commerce in international waters in the Gulf of Mexico.

Mallory then reviewed the matter of importing slaves from Africa into Cuba and he stressed that treaties of 1817 and 1835 banned African slave trade. Nevertheless, the practice of importing African slaves into Cuba had continued unabated. He suggested that the United States should annex Cuba, abolish the African slave trade, and move the female slaves from the cities to the plantations (presumably they would procreate and obviate the need for importing slaves). Mallory said that Great Britain had attempted to interrupt that "middle passage" traffic and in the process had stopped and boarded American shipping, thereby creating a volatile situation. At the same time, he contended, England was interfering with efforts of the United States to secure coaling stations in the area and she consistently opposed America's efforts to procure Cuba. Mallory also asserted that Great Britain intended to develop "a free-negro soldiery" in Cuba, less than 100 miles from Florida. He suggested that slave uprisings could spread from there to the nearby shores of the United States. The senator inserted into the record excerpts of diplomatic dispatches that verified England's interest in gaining Cuba and freeing slaves.

Senator Mallory discussed his own views on freeing slaves:

> Emancipation, sir, has been a total, a wretched failure; and it has illustrated a singular feature of the negro race, namely: that, just as there are certain grains and fruits which the industry of man has redeemed, by careful culture, from their original and savage nature ... which, if withdrawn from his care, will relapse back

to their original type: just so does the African, in these colonies, when left to himself, relapse back, stage by stage to the original barbarism of his fathers.[48]

Here Mallory echoed traditional racial prejudice held by many southerners and some northerners.

The senator responded to a charge that "Cubans are Catholics, and therefore adverse to, and unfitted for, liberty; and that the Catholic Church is hostile to freedom." He refuted these allegations saying, "The enlightened Catholics of the world to-day would regard the transfer of Cuba to this country as a measure well calculated to advance the interests of the Church."[49] Mallory further refuted charges that Cubans were ignorant, were satisfied with Spanish domination, and desired no change. He could discuss these factors with authority because of his personal knowledge gained from having had extensive contacts with Cubans during his Key West days.

This session adjourned for the night, and Senator Mallory continued his speech on February 25, 1859. He opened by stating, "The Island of Cuba is essential to the general welfare of the United States, and to its military defenses; I endeavored to show its remarkable geographical position in a strategic military point of view."

Mallory then turned to a discussion of the United States' commercial relations with Cuba, saying that U.S. trade with Cuba was minimal because of restrictive tariffs. He presented some creative proposals that might encourage Spain to sell Cuba:

> We can purchase Cuba only by combining with a money consideration certain commercial concessions and advantages to Spain.... Connect the offer of money with a right of Spain to preserve her home trade with Cuba for a period—say forty years—and it would carry great weight. There would then be apparently no interruption to her commerce by the transfer, and the industrial interests of Spain would sustain no sudden sensation.... Spain needs money; she has long been on the verge of national bankruptcy.... [There is] the improbability of her retaining Cuba much longer....[50]

But what if Spain should reject these offers, Mallory asked rhetorically? "I would, in such case, act openly and fairly with her, and look directly at the contingency of taking Cuba and talking about it afterwards..."[51] Senator Mallory closed by saying, "Spain has established a Government there, [referring to Cuba] which is an ulcer upon the civilization of the nineteenth century; an ulcer doubly offensive because of its proximity to our shores...."[52]

With this speech, Senator Stephen Mallory displayed thoroughness of preparation and good organization of his thoughts. He strongly supported the southern cause and in doing so transparently dismissed arguments of opponents. While this address was not soaring oratory, it did contain some convincing arguments, the most creative of which was his bona fide proposal to induce Spain to sell Cuba by granting her certain commercial privileges. He was praised for his speech in the March 19, 1859, edition of the *Floridian and Journal*: "one of the very ablest speeches made in the Senate."[53]

Throughout the first half of the 19th century there was tension between the United States and Great Britain regarding the right of the British to board American-flagged vessels that were suspected of being involved in slave trade in the Atlantic Ocean. America was sensitive over the right of the British to search its vessels. England held that freedom of the seas applied to those using them for legal purposes; the United States contended its flag protected all its citizens from foreign interference, especially boarding by a British officer of an American-flagged vessel. When he was ambassador to England, John Quincy Adams had been asked if there was a worse evil than the slave trade. He replied that even worse would be his government giving permission to a British cruiser to stop and examine any vessel flying the American flag, for that would make slaves of all Unites States citizens.[54]

Slavery in the United States was legal, but the African slave trade was considered to be piracy, punishable by death. By an agreement of 1842, the British and United States navies jointly patrolled off West Africa to suppress the transatlantic slave trade. The American squadron, however, was not an effective policing force because the navy was too small and was stationed too far away from the African slaving coast.[55] Nevertheless, the slave trade had been reduced, primarily through British efforts.

By 1855 Cuba was the primary remaining bastion of slave traffic and many slave ships bound for Cuba sailed under the American flag.[56] Great Britain's navy was engaged in interrupting the illegal importation of slaves from Africa into Cuba "but successive presidential administrations, faithful to the obsolete issue of visit and search, refused permission to the British to search American vessels."[57] Consequently, to evade search, a slave ship need only raise the American flag and the Royal Navy, respecting American policy, would not detain and board her.

British-American relationships deteriorated when the British tired of this facade, and conducted what the United States considered to be illegal searches. English vessels began stopping and searching ships carrying the American flag when those ships were suspected of transporting slaves. Heavy African slave trafficking continued into Cuba. In 1858 England decided to increase its enforcement efforts, and began harassing American shipping. In April 1858, a British gunboat seized a United States vessel that had just left Havana Bay, and by the end of May English warships had boarded 116 vessels. Sixty-one of these were owned in the United States.[58]

Americans perceived this action by Great Britain as an insult to the flag. The United States Senate demanded a firm stand. Senator John Hays Hammond of South Carolina said, "If we intend war let us declare war.... We have just and ample cause of war. We have received the most flagrant insults...."[59] On May 31, 1858 Senator Mallory introduced this resolution in the Senate: "The recent proceedings of the British Naval Officers in the Gulf of Mexico, upon the high seas, in forcibly arresting and examining vessels of the United States, owned and navigated by American citizens engaged in lawful trade, are without justification and palliation, in derogation of the cherished rights of the American people...." The resolution asked that the president "be authorized to adopt immediate measures to arrest at once a continuance of such indignities."[60] Discussion ensued, and there was concern that a declaration of war was implied without giving the president proper authority to pursue war. On June 16, 1858, the Senate passed a resolution approving action of the president to send a naval force to the area to protect United States vessels on the high seas from search and detention by war vessels of any other nation. The British reacted by suspending their harassment of United States merchant ships and opened negotiations to determine how slave vessels might be deterred from fraudulent use of the American flag. War was avoided.[61]

The Seminole Indians were always problematic for Floridians; as the white population increased, the new settlers coveted lands on which Indians lived. Furthermore, black slaves who ran away from southern plantations often took refuge within Indian enclaves. The Federal government was pressured to convey Seminole Indians elsewhere. This led to the Wars of Indian Removal, the goal of which was to relocate the Seminoles from Florida to the Oklahoma Territory. The bloodiest of these conflicts was the Second Seminole War from 1835 to 1842. During Andrew Jackson's administration, the U.S. government spent $20 million and many lives to relocate the Indians to the west. However, the government could not convince all Seminoles to move voluntarily and military forces failed to capture and remove them to the Oklahoma Territory. By the early 1850s, Indians remaining in Florida were becoming troublesome again. White inhabitants in Florida were on guard against theft of their property and some feared for their lives. They urged removal of all Indians.

In response to pressure exerted by his constituents, Senator Mallory offered an amendment to the army appropriation bill on February 23, 1853, that read, "And be it further enacted, that for removing the Indians from Florida, the President of the United States be authorized to call into service as much of the volunteer force raised by the General Assembly of Florida, and under such conditions as he may deem necessary." Mallory explained that Indians still remained in Florida in violation of a treaty to move westward. He added that they would steal and otherwise harass white residents living at border settlements, and that probability of hostilities the next spring was high.

Senator Borland (Arkansas) opposed the amendment on the grounds that relocating Indians westward punished western states because native Americans would occupy lands that might be preferred by white settlers. He also said that putting Indians on his state's western frontier cut off Arkansas from expansion and development in that direction. Mallory replied:

> These Indians have made a treaty. They have agreed by a treaty, recognized by the Senate, to remove. Have we any right to set the treaty aside? Have we of Florida not a right to demand that the treaty shall be complied with? Have we not a right to ask that it shall not be violated? These men ... are a common band of cutthroats, outlawed by their own people, common renegades and murderers, who conceal themselves in the frontiers of Florida, and desolate them at pleasure.... The State of Florida considers their presence in her limits an intolerable evil not to be endured; and depend upon it these Indians must go out of the State, or they will be exterminated.

In plain language, Mallory was saying that Florida's Seminoles must go to the Oklahoma Territory or they must die. There was no negative response from any senators in response to this inhumane sentiment.

Senator Sam Houston (Texas) spoke of the cost of maintaining a Florida regiment in the field for one year and said that the expenses probably would be over $1 million. He proposed that for $15,000 necessary supplies could be given the Indians to prevent their starvation. He contended, "Starvation often drives the Indians to war and to encroachments.... I cannot vote for the amendment. I am satisfied that it would lead to a breaking out of hostilities...." Senator Mallory responded by pointing out failures of the Federal government in the past to deal with the problem and argued for passage of his amendment. Senator Houston expressed his fear that should forceful removal of the Indians be attempted at this time, another expensive war would follow. A vote was taken on Mr. Mallory's amendment and it failed by a vote of 19 to 24.[62]

The senator from Florida had made an impassioned plea to attempt to deal with the Seminole problem. He displayed his knowledge of the issues that was acquired through his first-hand experiences during the Second Seminole War. His amendment failed because the Senate was in no mood to get involved in another expensive war with the Seminoles, and western states did not desire that Seminoles live in their area. But through his efforts Mallory had aired a contentious issue that would not go away. He continued the struggle on an administrative level by contacting numerous appropriate government agencies and requesting their attention to the problem.

Senator Mallory also displayed his knowledge of army weapons when he spoke in the Senate on June 8, 1858, on the army appropriation bill. The Senate was debating whether money should be authorized to change the present musket into a breech-loading musket. Mallory enumerated many of the advantages of the breech-loading weapon and spoke of the evolution of the ball used in the musket. He declared his expertise as arising from the fact that "I have been using guns all my life; I buy every gun that is made. Whenever I hear of a gun invented, I send and get it. I try them all...."[63]

Later in the same hearing, Senator Mallory displayed his knowledge of primers that might be used in firing a gun when he questioned the extent to which "Maynard's primer" was used in actual service in the U.S. Army. The chairman of the Committee on Military Affairs, Jefferson Davis, replied that the original primers were defective but recently cement had been developed to waterproof them. Mallory commented, "I have no doubt that any fulminator, covered with gum shellac, as these primers are, made in Washington ... would prove very advantageous; but I think when you transfer these primers to a moist climate, a damp atmosphere, they are perfectly useless...." Davis replied, "I would, however, state what I am sure will be agreeable to the chairman of the Committee on Naval Affairs, that we think we have found a cement that is insoluble either in vapor or water." Mallory noted, "If that is the case, the primer is a very valuable discovery, if it can be protected from dampness, and be equally good under all states of temperature." In this instance Mallory has not only displayed his broad knowledge of many factors relative to warfare but there also appeared to be mutual respect between himself and Senator Davis, his future administrative chief.[64]

This session of Congress concluded on June 14, 1858, and a month later Stephen Mallory was with his family visiting at the home of his married daughter in Bridgeport, Connecticut. While there he received a letter from President James Buchanan dated July 7, 1858. The president offered him an important diplomatic post: assignment to Madrid as minister to Spain. Buchanan's letter to Mallory suggested he might be able to accomplish an objective that could not long be delayed. Undoubtedly the president was thinking of the acquisition of Cuba. Mallory was flattered to be considered for the position but declined the assignment due to "circumstances of a domestic nature." These circumstances probably were referring to the fact that after the death of his mother in 1855, he moved his family from Key West to Pensacola where Mrs. Mallory's relatives lived. By 1858 he had built their new home in that city and they were adapting to their new station in life.[65]

The distribution of government lands had been a contentious issue for the United States since the Revolutionary War because of controversy about land measurement and pricing. Initially, the sale of public land was a means to raise revenue for the Federal government, but western expansion of the nation, coupled with increased immigration, led to settling the land through homesteading. Public land sales originally were at fixed prices per acre; by 1854 the popularity of fixed prices gave way to a graduated scale that adjusted these prices to reflect actual value of the plot. Furthermore, preemption gave an individual the right to settle land first and pay later. Factory owners in the North opposed this policy fearing that it would draw cheap labor westward, away from the industrial base of the United States. On the other hand, southern states were fearful that generous homesteading legislation would attract farmers, who would oppose slavery, to the new states.

Amidst these conflicting currents, the Senate was deliberating a homestead bill. On July 19, 1854, Senator Stephen Russell Mallory rose to give a major address regarding this matter. He pointed out that the Federal government had given millions of acres of public lands to seven states for roads, railroads, canals, and rivers and had "not bestowed one acre upon Florida for such purpose."[66] He added that two of his bills for securing alternate sections of land for projected railroads passed in the Senate but failed in the House because land grants were administered, in his opinion, unwisely and unequally. Mallory continued with an explanation of why railroads and roads were so important to Florida and the nation. He followed with criticism of expenses associated with the operation of the General Land Office. Mallory added that many public lands in Florida were "maintained at prices which experience shows to be totally disproportioned to their value" and were still unsold after 20 to 30 years. "The leading object of the Government, in its disposition of the public lands," said Mallory, "should be their occupation, cultivation, and development, with a view to increase the resources, strength, and happiness of the country at large."[67]

Senator Mallory then responded to those who claimed that cheap, homesteaded land would attract a pauper class. He spoke emotionally: "Let your paupers go upon your lands, sow among the seeds of American liberty and law, and they will rise from the earth in the irresistible panoply of the American citizen to battle for freedom." Regarding the charge that homesteading attracted citizens from industrialized areas toward farming, Mallory used census data to refute this claim and added, "Sir, this steady march of emigration westward is irresistible."[68]

Mallory closed his speech by bringing to the forefront the interests of his state. "Florida," he proclaimed, "has reason to complain of the General Government; not only for maintaining within her borders this immense body of lands from twenty to thirty years exempt from taxation, at a price totally beyond their value; not only for shingling the State over with naval and military reservations, but for maintaining within her jurisdiction a band of worthless Indian cut-throats upon some of its most valuable soil."[69]

Stephen Mallory had made solid arguments for passing the homestead bill, stressing that it would benefit both Florida and the United States. It was a sound speech that was well organized and flowed logically. The principal points were well developed and coherent. Although it was not enacted into law, the debate most likely helped to pave the way for the Homestead Act of 1862.

Senator Mallory was provided the opportunity to take a moral stance regarding religious persecution and Catholicism. In May 1856 Senator Badger (North Carolina) had quoted a Catholic paper in St. Louis, *The Shepherd of the Valley*, as stating, "that as soon as the Catholics should obtain the supremacy in this country, there would be an end of toleration here." Mallory pointed out that the paper was not an official organ of the Catholic church and in fact the bishop of St. Louis had denounced it. He remarked, "It is the first time, Mr. President, in this body, that I have ever heard directly or indirectly the creed of any portion of our citizens presented as a matter of discussion." Although Senator Mallory seldom said anything in his public life about his religious views, he continued on this occasion to speak of religious toleration by the Catholic church, especially in colonial Maryland. Additionally, he pointed to contributions made by Catholics in the army and navy while noting that there were no Catholic chaplains for Catholic soldiers and sailors.[70]

As a young man in the 1830s and 1840s, Stephen Mallory had extensive experience as an inspector and collector at the Key West customhouse. He was able to draw upon this experience in the Senate on July 25, 1854. Under debate was a measure that provided for not funding customhouses where the amount of customs collected failed to equal the expenses of collecting them. Mallory opposed the amendment because it was based on the assumption that customhouses only collected revenue when in fact they also stored customs records. This was important when the Treasury Department in Washington burned, destroying all customs records since 1794. Fortunately, duplicate copies of these records existed in the customhouses.[71]

During this session of Congress, in contrast with previous legislative assemblies, Senator Mallory had dealt more extensively with national issues, and to a lesser degree, with Florida matters. However, he did not forget his obligation to embrace the interests of his constituents. He supported an appropriation for a survey of the harbor at Apalachicola, requested a $12,000 appropriation for investigation and surveys for constructing a canal across Florida, presented a resolution requesting that the secretary of war report to the Senate on the expediency of completing fortifications at Dry Tortugas and Key West, and participated in debate about a contract for mail service between Bainbridge, Georgia, and Apalachicola, Florida.[72]

On March 13, 1856, Stephen Mallory spoke in the upper chamber in support of a bill to appropriate $3 million for the "manufacturing and repair of small arms, equipping fortifications, and providing ammunition." This appropriation bill pertained to defense of the United States. Within this framework, U.S. relations with England were discussed. In the minds of some, Great Britain was becoming hostile toward the United States because of her possibly establishing a navy base and a coaling station in Cuba. Further, the *London Times* was taking an anti-American tone and some legislators feared another war with England.[73]

Senator Mallory opened his remarks by calming the fears of some: "I feel bound to say that I not only do not believe there will be war between Great Britain and the United States, but I believe that there should be none." He said the British should not be misled by the divisiveness in the United States over sectional issues. "If we should become involved in a war with Great Britain ... there will be within her limits no recreant to the cause or the country; nor will there be found upon her soil a man breathing any other than a determined spirit to see it out, honorably and successfully...." Mallory added that "local questions may disturb or divide political parties here ... many questions of a domestic character will always more or less divide us, but a public enemy will ever unite us.... [While] not believing there is any danger of an immediate rupture with Great Britain, I vote in favor of this bill ... on the further principle that preparation for war is, perhaps, the wisest means of avoiding it." Then Mallory discussed the defense of the United States, saying that England had armed many of her warships with heavy nine-inch guns and United States fortifications were defended with only 32- or 48-pounders (artillery) that would be quickly overcome by the larger guns. He contended that this appropriation bill must be supported so U.S. forts could be defended by nine- and 11-inch guns, the equal of those mounted on British warships. "Irrespective of our relations with foreign nations,"

Mallory proclaimed, "I think justice to ourselves requires that those fortifications should be armed at once, and armed effectually."[74]

A good politician never forgets his constituency and Mallory was always on guard to adequately represent local interests, especially when naval matters were involved. On August 18, 1856, there was Senate debate about establishing a navy depot at Brunswick, Georgia, and appropriating $200,000 for that purpose. Senator Mallory indicated his opposition to this bill. He argued that the United States already had eight navy yards; this was more yards than England had, and an additional yard was not needed. He appealed for further funding and upgrading of facilities at the Pensacola Navy Yard. However, the other senator from Florida, Yulee, not only did not support his fellow senator, but he made known his interest in establishing a naval depot at Beaufort, South Carolina. The bill was postponed until the next session of Congress.[75]

On other occasions, however, Mallory and Yulee worked in harmony. On February 27, 1856, Senator Mallory was looking at interests in his home state when a fortifications bill was being considered. It would provide an appropriation of $150,000 for construction, preservation, and repairs at Fort Jefferson on the Florida island of Dry Tortugas. Workers had to be transported to the work site because Fort Jefferson is about 68 miles west of Key West. Funding was needed immediately so that there would be no interruption of work during which workers might disperse. In this instance, Mallory and Yulee provided a unified front, but the appropriation was not approved.[76]

When the second session of the 34th Congress adjourned on August 30, 1856, Stephen Mallory returned to Florida to campaign for his reelection and for the national Democratic ticket. He spoke strongly on behalf of presidential nominee James Buchanan and defended himself from assertions that he was too moderate in his stance on slavery and states' rights. In his campaign speeches he talked about dangers facing the South and the nation and he proclaimed that the new Republican Party was responsible for the sad state of affairs in the United States. He supported the expansion of slavery and the Democratic Party.[77]

The Democratic ticket won in Florida. On December 24, 1856 the two houses of the Florida General Assembly met jointly and on the first ballot reelected Stephen R. Mallory to the U.S. Senate for six years commencing March 4, 1857. Mallory received 38 Democratic votes, four more than was necessary for his selection.[78]

A substantive matter with which Stephen Mallory was involved during this period was financial deficiencies in the post office. The postmaster general had recommended terminating the current contract to carry mail between Havana, Cuba, and the U.S. ports of Key West, Savannah, and Charleston by the steamer *Isabel*. Senator Mallory favored restoring service by *Isabel* because the contractor had provided good service over a 12-year period. He said that no one had expected that postage would pay for the route. On June 1, 1860, Mallory added, "I will give a faithful public servant a renewal of the contract for four years, during which time I hope we shall bring the Island of Cuba into the Union of the United States." The Senate rejected Senator Mallory's recommendations.[79]

In the dark of night on October 16, 1859, a band of 21 men captured the U.S. Armory at Harpers Ferry, Virginia. They were led by a fanatic abolitionist, John Brown, who had planned to seize weapons stored in the armory and distribute them to slaves who would join him in an uprising. He believed the oppressed could achieve freedom by striking back at their masters. However, Brown's attempt to free slaves was foiled when a company of U.S. Marines, commanded by Col. Robert E. Lee, took possession of the armory and captured him. The State of Virginia summarily "indicted, tried, and convicted Brown of treason, murder, and fomenting insurrection." He was hanged at Charlestown, Virginia, on December 2, 1859.[80] In the South there was fear of slave uprisings amid rumors of other armed abolitionists roaming the countryside inciting the slaves. In the North John Brown was lionized and honored as a martyr. On the day of his execution, northern church bells tolled for him and ministers preached commemorative sermons. Brown's hanging served to further tear asunder frail binds holding the nation together and propelled the Union toward disunion.

Senator Stephen Mallory spoke on the Harpers Ferry affair in the upper chamber on December 7, 1859. The Senate was considering a resolution offered by Senator Mason (Virginia) to inquire into facts surrounding the attempted seizure of the armory at Harpers Ferry. Senator Mallory opened his remarks by noting that southern men assembled in the chamber "represent a constituency moved ... with a consciousness in every homestead that their safety in this Union is in peril; that they are no longer wanted in the Union; that their fellowship is not sought, but repudiated. I think we are on the brink of a crisis such as this country has never seen before," Mallory added, "and I therefore feel deeply. In this case the cause of Virginia is the cause of the South. Our fortunes are united to hers. We feel proud of her attitude, proud of her high tone, proud of the legal and constitutional manner in which her executive and people have met this outbreak; and we expect to stand by her in any issue that she may make." He continued, "A sovereign State of this Confederacy has been invaded by northern men, with a large amount of northern capital, with arms manufactured in northern States, professing to have numerous friends and constituents behind them, and with arms calculated to arm some two thousand persons."[81]

This Harper's Ferry speech was one of Mallory's shortest speeches and one of his best. Its brevity coupled with its compressed and lucid state provided an impact not usually found in his other speeches. He had made clear he was a southern man, that Florida was firmly united in Virginia's cause, and that he would go the way of the South, no matter what.

Stephen Russell Mallory had dealt with a diversity of matters—some mundane and others of national importance—during his nearly 10 years as senator. However, his most memorable and important achievement would be strengthening and making more effective the United States Navy.

4

Strengthening the Navy

Stephen Russell Mallory's early Senate activities were necessarily constrained by his concentration on defending his right to be seated in the upper chamber. Nevertheless, he was able to redirect his attention to important naval matters.

On September 28, 1850, the naval appropriation bill abolished flogging as a form of punishment in the U.S. Navy on humanitarian grounds. President Millard Fillmore enacted the legislation in 1851.[1] However, a movement developed to restore this harsh means of maintaining order and efficiency aboard ships of war. Early in 1852 the Senate was called upon to consider a petition submitted by "certain citizens of Philadelphia in favor of the restoration of corporal punishment." Senator Stockton of New Jersey (formerly Commodore Stockton of the U.S. Navy) opposed renewal of what he and others considered to be a barbarous practice. Senator Mallory, who debated the matter on January 14 and 15, 1852, favored restoring corporal punishment because he believed flogging to be a necessary tool in maintaining naval discipline.[2]

This was Mallory's first major speech — he had been sworn into office only six weeks earlier — and he respectfully opened his remarks with praise for Senator Stockton and his extensive naval service, while acknowledging that Stockton had eloquently presented his case. But Mallory pointed out that the senator had presented personal opinions, not facts. The senator from Florida then established his own credentials:

> For twenty years I have been more or less familiar with shipping and seamen, and the views which I advance here have been derived from observation and conversation with seamen of every grade both in and out of the service. They are not hasty views; they have not been hastily adopted; they certainly will not be hastily abandoned.[3]

Senator Mallory unfolded a careful argument supporting the use of corporal punishment as essential to a properly functioning navy. He insisted that the nation's naval glory had prevailed because of use of corporal punishment. "Our Navy has attained the highest grade of preeminence," he said, and "It has attained it with the existence of this usage ... and we are now told that the continuance of this usage a moment longer, is to [result in] the destruction and ruin of the entire naval organization. Before the abolition of this punishment our Navy occupied the very first rank in efficiency and organization among the navies of the world. That rank it no longer holds."[4]

Stephen Mallory stated the U.S. Navy was no longer a superior organization due to abolition of corporal punishment. He spoke of how corporal punishment had been used by warships and the merchant marines of all nations in the world as far back as the thirteenth century.

Mallory then turned to the period when Stockton commanded the U.S.S. *Congress* from 1845 to 1847. He asserted that the commodore inflicted the lash 1,800 times during that period, exceeding the number imposed in a similar period by his successor. He stated that instant obedience was required to safely navigate a vessel and suggested that such obedience cannot be attained without at least the fear, if not the fact, of flogging. He spoke to the argument that flogging was degrading by indicating that it is the misbehavior that disgraces or degrades the individual, not the punishment. Mallory entered into the record a report from Commodore Stewart in which the naval officer spoke of the abolition of flogging and its negative effects upon the navy. The Senate then adjourned and the subject was continued the next day.

On January 15 Senator Mallory opened by distributing public documents to those present that would provide a factual basis for supporting corporal punishment. These were interrogatories completed by five commodores, six captains, 11 commanders, and one lieutenant. They were of the same theme: insubordination was becoming more common and navy vessels had become less efficient since abolishment of flogging. Mallory supported his arguments by summarizing a survey of mutinies in the British navy and he read from an 1851 report of the secretary of the U.S. Navy that lamented the absence of discipline. He related that court-martials had increased since prohibition of flogging. Senator Mallory also expressed his concern that the U.S. Navy was lagging behind the navies of Britain and France because of breakdown of discipline. He closed by suggesting that the entire matter should be referred to the Committee on Naval Affairs for investigation and production of a detailed report.[5] Mallory's arguments did not prevail. Legal flogging remained abolished in the U.S. Navy.

During a Senate exchange on May 6, 1852, Senator Mallory discussed specific timber used in constructing ships. Senator Hunter, who had questions about the type of wood used for planking on ships built for the Collins Steamship Line, had a humorous interchange with Mallory:

> Mr. Hunter (Virginia). The Senator from Florida (Mr. Mallory) who is acquainted with these subjects, tells me they are planked with pine, and not with white oak, as is usual with vessels of war.
>
> Mr. Mallory. I will say that every ship that I have happened to know anything about, built under naval directions, has been planked with oak planks.... The timbers and frames of naval vessels are live oak, and the timbers and frames of the Collins steamers are a mixture of live oak, locust, and pine.
>
> Mr. Badger (North Carolina). Well, be it so. I would ask the Senator from Florida one question. He says these steamers are planked with pine. Are they not planked with southern pine?
>
> Mr. Mallory. Certainly, sir.
>
> Mr. Badger. Enough said. If they are planked with southern pine, it is a great deal better than northern oak. [Laughter.][6]

It is noted that a serious subject had been treated with humor, perhaps to break the tension of the day. Also, Mallory had only been in the Senate for about five months, but was being referred to as the authority in ship construction as well as other naval matters.

Early in his Senate career, Stephen Russell Mallory showed interest in vessels clad in armor. On June 15, 1852, he testified on behalf of a resolution to build a floating battery for harbor defense. The battery would become the prototype of ironclads used in the Civil War. Mallory made reference to the experiments conducted by Robert L. Stevens in 1842 in New York Harbor using floating batteries that were clad in iron (the so-called "Stevens Battery"). The battery had received initial funding in February 1843 but remained incomplete. Mallory stated that military men had discussed such a concept for the past 200 years. "It is proposed to construct a floating battery of iron boiler plates," Mallory said, "capable of resisting a sixty-four pound shot, at a range of thirty yards. It is to be scarcely elevated above the water-line, and will have so much steadiness as to give the guns scarcely any motion."[7] The resolution subsequently passed but the battery was never funded or completed. As a strategist, Mallory was ahead of his time and his interest in ironclads would peak during the Civil War.

Some of the most important work Stephen Russell Mallory did in the 33rd Congress was related to improving the U.S. Navy. Since boyhood he had been interested in nautical matters and his knowledge on the subject, as well as his innate skills, led him to membership on the Senate Naval Affairs Committee. He became its chairman in 1853. When he first began his service on the committee, the U.S. Navy had languished. Acknowledging the poor condition of the navy, Mallory displayed his expertise in shipbuilding and promoted construction of ironclads. Fellow senators did not always agree with him, but they respected his judgment and integrity in naval matters. Mallory worked hard, particularly in 1854, to make the U.S. Navy a more formidable and efficient battle force.

On June 19, 1854, a bill "to improve the naval service" was reported from the Committee on Naval Affairs to the Senate. Committee chairman Mallory sponsored and introduced the bill by saying it "Prescribed the number and pay of the officers in each grade, provided for a retired and furloughed naval list, for an increase of the Marine Corps, for the establishment of a Bureau of Equipment, Orders, and Detail, and for the appointment of a judge-advocate for the naval service. It also made provision for the details necessary to carry out these objectives."[8] He discussed a series of amendments that had been worked out by the committee in consultation with navy Secretary James C. Dobbin. These amendments did not violate the principles enunciated by Mallory, but did revise implementing procedures. Due to time constraints, the Senate then discussed other matters, placing the navy bill on the agenda for the next day.

This proposed legislation came before the Senate on June 20 and Mallory discussed the bill while responding to questions. Senator Hunter (Virginia) posted challenges to a host of amendments and Mallory answered by giving some history of the bill's development. He said that the Senate and House naval affairs committees had held a joint conference with the secretary of the navy and they had reached agreement on important principles. It was agreed that the House committee would write a companion bill, but it was delayed due to technical and procedural problems. Mallory added that the present Senate bill and its details were "prepared under the eye and with the aid of the Secretary of the Navy, whose general concurrence in them I feel at liberty to state.... Among other features which the committees of both Houses regarded as essential, was that of establishment of the relative rank of the several grades of the service.... It seems ... just that the rights and privileges, no less than the duties, of every officer should be clearly defined." He added, "Naval strength, (or weakness,) from the character and design of the service, is altogether relative, and must ever be measured by that of its possible adversaries; and in determining what the condition and strength of our service should be, we have first to ascertain those of the only naval Powers whose ability to contend with us upon the sea is questioned." Mallory then compared the strength of the U.S. Navy in 1846 to that of the British navy in the same year to demonstrate the comparative weakness of the American navy. He asserted that U.S. ships must be of the equal of British ships; he advocated the use of the screw propeller rather than paddlewheel or sail, as well as more potent ordnance.[9]

Mallory then appealed to the patriotism of the members of the Senate when he said, "But, sir, in rising upon this occasion to speak for the Navy ... I came here to speak of its soul, its spirit, by which the service moves and has its being; and for these—for the men who sustain your flag, and represent your spirit upon the sea, who hold their lives in their hands whenever her interests or the honor of their country demand their sacrifice ... let me briefly remind you that, though inseparably connected, as it is, with national character, national rights, and even national greatness, disclosing, as it does, so many heroic deeds and memorable examples of devotion to country, it has received less attention from the fostering legislation of Congress than any other branch of the public service."[10]

The senator from Florida then explained each section of the bill. One portion requires closer attention because of controversy that would surround it later. That contentious section of the proposed legislation stated:

> The Secretary of the Navy shall [identify all officers] who are qualified to perform efficiently all their duties ashore and afloat; and ... with the approval of the President, shall retire, or permanently furlough, or drop from service, all officers who, in his judgment, are not so qualified. All officers on the retired list shall receive three fifths, and those on the permanent furlough list shall receive two fifths of the sea service pay to which they were entitled when retired or furloughed.[11]

Mallory discussed at length this provision requiring all officers to be examined to determine who are qualified to efficiently perform their duties aboard a ship at sea as well as on land, and to retire or permanently furlough those not so qualified. He pointed out that "many of the older officers are shown to be unemployed on shore, receiving large pay, while their juniors are performing their appropriate duties afloat upon less pay." He added that this situation must be corrected. Senator Mallory explained that pay scales, and extra pay, serve as a reward for exemplary service. Mallory also stated, "I regard seniority of rank as the only and the rightful element in naval promotion ... but, I say at the same time, that the Navy should be rigidly and frequently scrutinized, and that retirement and the Executive's power to furlough and dismiss must be promptly used, *to the end that every commissioned officer shall be fully competent for all and every duty which the country may devolve upon him* [italics in original]." To emphasize the need for a retirement list Mallory added, "Under the present system, lieutenants when promoted to commanders will be fifty-three, and commanders, when promoted to captains, *seventy-four years of age* [italics in original]." Senator Hunter replied that he felt the bill required additional amendments. Further consideration of the bill was postponed until the next day.[12]

The bill for improvement of the navy was discussed once more on June 21, 1854. Mallory offered further amendments that had been agreed upon by Senator Hunter after conferring with the navy secretary. Senator Mallory answered questions about some of the amendments, apparently to the satisfaction of all. The bill passed with the unanimous consent of the Senate.[13] On February 28, 1855, President Franklin Pierce enacted the legislation as the Naval Reform Act.[14]

Senator Stephen Russell Mallory and the Naval Affairs Committee had done a remarkable job in developing and shaping this bill. Mallory had displayed effective leadership and political talents, the most important of which was the ability to compromise without sacrificing principle. The committee had reviewed similar proposed legislation that had been written by the House Committee on Naval Affairs, and built on that base. Mallory and the committee members had thoroughly deliberated various aspects of the bill and constantly sought input from the secretary of the navy. This dedicated work with all interested parties enabled passage of the bill in both houses. Senate unification in this matter was remarkable in light of a developing schism on other issues and speaks well for the leadership and intellect of the chairman of the Senate Naval Affairs Committee.

The Naval Reform Act seemed popular when it became law in 1855 but the part of it creating the Naval Retiring Board garnered adverse criticism when it was implemented by the Navy Department. During a nine-month period between the closing of the 33rd Congress and convening the 34th Congress, Navy Secretary Dobbin had organized the Naval Retiring Board. The law required that the board judge the capacity of each individual to efficiently perform all of his duties both on sea and land. It met in June 1855 to select those U.S. Navy officers who should be retired and those who should be furloughed. Men retired were placed on the reserve list and removed from active duty. They were entitled to wear their uniforms and received three-fifths of their sea-service pay. Men furloughed were discharged from the U.S. Navy and received two-fifths of their sea-service pay.

The board identified those officers who should be retired and furloughed and notified the navy secretary of its findings. Secretary Dobbin reviewed the list and, with the approval of the president, Dobbin notified each officer of the decision. A number of those officers selected for retirement or furlough objected to being removed from active service. They contacted their senators who filed memorials in their behalf requesting reinstatement to active duty.

The most famous of these individuals was Matthew Fontaine Maury who was well known around the world as an oceanographer as well as an expert in the science of hydrography. Earlier in his career he had performed well at sea but had been injured and crippled in 1839. This led him into a different direction of study and writing that justly earned him praise throughout the world. Secretary Dobbin notified him on September 17, 1855, that he was being placed on the reserve list. Maury was indignant; he protested vigorously and believed he had been disgraced.[15] However, after legislative changes were made, Maury was restored to active duty in 1858.[16]

The 34th Congress assembled in December 1855 and began considering these memorials regarding retired or furloughed officers who desired reinstatement to active duty. About 68 naval officers filed appeals of this nature and for the next seven months the Senate discussed in detail various aspects of the Naval Reform Act. Those most preoccupied with the legislation were the members and chairman of the Committee on Naval

Affairs. Senator Mallory, as well as other senators, spoke extensively on these matters and their remarks are covered in about 200 pages of the Congressional Globe.

Reactions to the Naval Reform Act and work of the Naval Retiring Board by those affected covered a broad range of emotions and reasoning. Many officers who had been removed from active duty were angry because they felt that they had been discharged without due process. They believed they were entitled to a court-martial so they could clear their names. Others were incensed because they could not learn the reason why they were separated from the service after giving the nation years of honorable service. They requested they be allowed to review the records of the board so they might examine the rationale for their discharge. Others believed that the entire procedure and perhaps the act itself were unconstitutional. Most retired officers who had complained felt ashamed and disgraced because of the board's action.

Most of these negative criticisms were discussed in Senate chambers. Mallory said Navy Secretary Dobbin could not release a detailed report citing why each individual was retired or furloughed because none was kept — the law did not require one. Instead Secretary Dobbin merely had a listing of names of those affected. The senator said he understood, however, that individual board members had kept personal notes or logs regarding their part in the proceedings. Senator Mallory explained that the main problem facing Congress and the navy was an excess of officers available for legitimate employment at sea, resulting in men being assigned land duties that were inappropriate for naval officers who were perfectly fit for sea duty. While asserting that board decisions did not result from any specific action that questioned an officer's fitness for service, he suggested that removal from active service did not denote disgrace. The officer, he explained, had not broken military law and could not be subject to court-martial. Senator Mallory stressed his belief in the system of navy officers judging their peers to determine individual capacity and efficiency for public service. He conceded, however, that board members are not infallible and that errors in classification could have been made.

By February 1856 the Senate Committee on Naval Affairs under the direction of Chairman Mallory concluded that there was nothing wrong with the act itself, but the manner in which it was implemented was faulty. The committee believed implementation procedures could be improved by amending the law. Consequently, two changes were proposed: one was to establish a board of review to whom the complainant could state his case; the second was to give the president authority to restore the officer to active duty if it were recommended by the board of review.

In the following months a host of amendments were debated and a bill to "Promote the Efficiency of the Navy" was the product of these efforts. It contained details of implementation without restructuring the original act. On July 15, 1856, "S. 113" was passed by a vote of 26 to 11.[17] By January 16, 1857, the Senate and House had agreed on amendments to the bill providing that navy officers who had been dropped, furloughed, or retired could receive, upon their written request, a hearing by a court of inquiry to determine if the previous action should be reversed. The finding of the court was to be submitted to the president, and in the case of a retired officer, "the finding of the court, when approved by the President, shall be conclusive; and such officer shall be restored to the active list, to occupy that position and rank in the navy which he would have occupied had he not been retired under the action of the late naval board.... Provided, That the officers so restored or placed on the reserved list, shall be appointed to their places, respectively, by the President, by and with the advice and consent of the Senate."[18]

This amendment worked to the benefit of all and required compromise in order to avoid repeal of the law. Mallory and his supporters retained the principle of navy officers judging their peers to determine the suitability of individual officers to remain on active duty. Opponents were satisfied that the person aggrieved was getting a fair hearing through an appeal procedure. The role of the president was clarified and strengthened; Senate responsibility for providing advice and consent was retained.

Chairman Mallory and his committee had worked hard to amend the original act. This was probably the most extended and difficult debate on a single issue that Mallory faced during his Senate career. The resulting procedures produced a stronger framework for dealing with individual officers who could no longer fully perform their duties on land and sea and created increased efficiency within the navy. Mallory had exhibited a sense of calm and acceptance of criticism without reacting defensively. He carefully considered the views of his colleagues and faultfinders, while demonstrating skill in compromise and safeguarding important principles. These reforms became the foundation for further improvements in navy legislation in the next decade.[19]

Senator Mallory attended sessions in the upper chamber during which appropriation bills for the navy were being considered. One such debate took place on August 3, 1854, regarding the Naval Appropriation Bill for the year ending June 30, 1855. Part of the debate concerned funding the Pensacola Navy Yard for ongoing construction of a permanent wharf, a deep basin, and raising the walls of the basin. Senator Broadhead (Pennsylvania) proposed an amendment to strike out "continuation of deep basin, raising walls of dock basin." He wished these deleted because the dock construction contractors allegedly had not complied with their contract provisions and the dock was of no use.[20] Mallory spoke in favor of the provision contending that the dock was useful and practicable only if the deep basin and raising its walls were completed. He explained that within this basin a large scow is sunk beneath a ship and then floated to allow repair on the vessel. He pointed out that $993,000 spent for the dock would be wasted if the basin and wall were struck from the appropriation.[21]

The other Florida senator, Jackson Morton, who was Mallory's long-time political opponent, spoke in favor of the motion by Senator Broadhead to limit the appropriation. Morton proclaimed, "I look upon the establishment of this deep basin as perfectly unnecessary and worthless to the Government." Morton continued with rationale for his position. After he had finished, Mallory was responding when Morton interrupted saying, "Will my colleague suffer me to interrupt him for a moment?" Mallory consented to the request whereupon Senator Morton made a rather lengthy speech from the floor to further explain his position. Mallory then continued his explanation and Morton further interjected his opposition to Mallory's position. After extensive discussion, the Senate voted in favor of Senator Broadhead's motion.[22]

In reading the debate, it is clear that other senators were cautious about this portion of the appropriation bill due to the divisiveness and acrimony between the two Florida senators. Much of this antagonism was caused by the political affiliation of the two men — Mallory was a Democrat and Morton a Whig — but personal ill will also may have been involved. It was not the first or last time that these two would clash.

On June 7, 1858, Senator Mallory addressed the Senate in support of the Naval Appropriation Bill for the year ending June 30, 1859. The first matter addressed was the Naval Affairs Committee's amendment to construct a stone dry dock at the Pensacola Navy Yard for a sum of $100,000. Senator Hunter (Virginia) opposed the amendment because of the cost of the dry dock. Mallory reminded the Virginian that he had voted in favor of this project two years earlier. He illustrated the necessity for a dry dock by describing problems of a naval vessel needing repairs while operating in the Gulf of Mexico. That vessel would have to go to a northern navy yard because there were no such facilities available south of Virginia. Mallory explained that the present wooden dock was not practical in the southern climate and the Gulf of Mexico fleet must have a nearby dry dock available for repair so as to minimize time off station.

Hunter countered that a wooden dry dock had worked fine in California and he saw no reason why a more expensive stone dry dock was needed in Florida. Mallory explained that the sea-worm found in Pensacola waters eats through six inches of wood in 12 months. Consequently, the wooden dock had to be coppered every five years and, in addition, it was subject to dry rot. Senator Hunter and other senators were concerned with accuracy of the estimated money amount needed for the work and the current financial restraints in the treasury. Ultimately the amendment was rejected.[23]

Next, Senator Mallory submitted a motion to amend the Naval Appropriation Bill to provide for the construction of five steam screw sloops-of-war of 12-foot draft, four sloops of 14-foot draft, and one side-wheel steamer with 8-foot draft for a sum of $1,290,000. However, a member of the Naval Affairs Committee moved to delete the four steamers of 14-foot draft because of ship construction taking place elsewhere. He also was opposed because he believed the U.S. Treasury could not currently bear this large expense. Mallory defended his motion by comparing the American navy with that of Great Britain and France. He said, "England and France have a built navy; we have a navy to build."[24] Mallory proceeded to specify the numerical deficiencies in U.S. Navy ships in terms of their availability for defending the coastline and maritime commerce.

The ensuing extensive debate was expanded to include capability of the American navy to deal with Great Britain should the United States become involved in another war similar to the War of 1812. Some senators were concerned that British warships on slavery suppression patrol in the West Indies and Gulf of Mexico had insulted the American flag by boarding American-flagged vessels to determine if slaves were aboard. These senators were riled over these alleged insults and this led to debate on U.S. foreign policy. Senator Mallory objected to his amendment being connected to war measures since he had been attempting to focus on America's defensive posture rather than war preparation. The debate ultimately bogged down into a series of amendments. Late in the evening, the Senate voted on Mallory's original motion, defeating it by a vote of 24 to 20. Once again he planned to come back with this motion, mentioning on the floor that he would ask for five sloops on the next occasion.

Although he had lost this motion, he continued on through the night with others. One motion of interest pertained to improving the coal depot at Key West, Florida, for an amount of $20,000. This was approved. After lengthy and often acrimonious debate of many amendments pertaining to the appropriation, the Senate passed the Naval Appropriation Bill and adjourned late in the evening.[25]

The Senate reassembled the next morning, June 8, and approved without debate, by a vote of 19 to 17, an appropriation for five steam screw sloops-of-war. However, on June 12 the matter of the sloops came up again in regard to a joint conference report from the House of Representatives. The two houses of Congress could not agree as to the number of vessels that should be constructed. With this and other appropriation matters,

Senator Mallory always kept his eye on the ultimate goal: adequate funding for the United States Navy.[26]

Mallory had supported legislation for improvements of the Pensacola Navy Yard that he felt were not only important for the navy but also were of interest to the voters in his state. He probably was not discouraged by his motions that were defeated, for he was tenacious. He never gave up on something he believed in. For example, nine months later, on March 1, 1859, Senator Mallory mentioned that Pensacola had one of the finest harbors on the face of the earth but that it was necessary to "build a granite pier or wharf which protects a man-of-war in high northers. They would go ashore but for this pier.... To make a navy-yard, you are obliged to build that pier; it is indispensable...."[27]

Throughout this session of Congress as well as previous sessions, Mallory had worked for improving and expanding the Pensacola Navy Yard (that was actually located at Warrington, Florida, a suburb of Pensacola) so that the Gulf of Mexico fleet, rather than having to go to distant northern yards for repairs, would have a nearby facility available for repairs. Additionally, he campaigned for construction of warships in Pensacola, arguing that cutting Florida timber and sending it to northern yards was less efficient and more costly than transporting it to Pensacola. While these measures were intended to strengthen the navy, they also would improve Pensacola's economy. Such political plums were expected by a senator's constituency and were necessary for his reelection. In fact, Pensacola interests were critical of Senator Mallory for not doing enough for the city. Mallory countered this criticism by saying he had moved his home to Pensacola and would continue to work in Congress to strengthen the Warrington facility and increase the number of ships built there.

Through Senator Mallory's efforts, two steam sloops were built at the Pensacola Navy Yard: the *Seminole* and the *Pensacola*. The United States steam sloop *Seminole* was launched on June 25, 1859, and the *Pensacola* was launched on August 13, 1859. The *Pensacola* is of special interest because Stephen's daughter, Margaret, was her sponsor. It must have been a satisfying and heartwarming experience for both father and daughter.[28]

As early as 1852, Senator Mallory had expressed his objection to letting contracts for ocean vessels that were designed for two purposes: to carry mail and to be capable of conversion to warships. He saw the goals as being incompatible. On March 31, 1852, he stated his objections to a bill for contracting for transportation of the mails three times a month between New Orleans, Vera Cruz, and Tampico, Mexico, in steam vessels that could be converted to war vessels. Senator Mallory explained that such a vessel cannot be constructed to fulfill both purposes and that it would cost at least $150,000 to suitably strengthen the vessel so one battery could be put onboard. Another senator inquired if the British had contracted with the Cunard Line to design sufficient flexibility so that these mail carriers could be converted to warships. Mallory replied that the Cunard steamers were not adapted to war purposes and that the British navy consisted of an entirely different class of vessels. He asserted that Cunard steamers could act as troop transports, but they were not suitable for engaging in actual warfare.[29]

Three years later the same argument came up again. On February 27, 1855, Stephen Mallory spoke in the Senate regarding a bill providing for the transportation of United States mail in ocean steamers. The Collins Steamer Line offered to build five ships for this purpose and it was stipulated that they were to be "of great speed and sufficiently strong for war purposes." Mallory contended that the phrase "war purposes" was vague, but if it meant fighting a battle at sea the construction specifications for the ships were inadequate.

Senator Mallory then provided a lesson to the Senators on how a war vessel should be constructed. He said warships are timbered with the best of seasoned live oak, and planked with white oak. He added:

> The frames of the Collins ships are composed of white oak, locust, chestnut and cedar, and they are planked with pine. These different woods are all of unequal durability.... Their pine bottoms are an insuperable objection. Not that pine is less durable than white oak in our naval ships, but because it does not hold the bolts ... so well. The action of the powerful engines of these ships produces a constant tremulous action upon the hull, which ... tends to shake or disturb the bolts which hold the planking to the timbers; and the fibre of the oak resists the tendency far better than pine.[30]

Mallory stated that the Collins specifications sacrificed strength for speed; the frames were too far apart, leaving spaces covered only by pine planking that was susceptible to damage by shot or ramming. He explained:

> A ship of war must not only possess the power to destroy an adversary, but she must herself be able to withstand his [sic] shock. Consequently her boiler and all other vital parts of her machinery must be placed below the water-line.... The boilers of the Collins ships ... project far above the lower deck and ... the shaft of their paddle-wheels is three feet at least above the main deck.... Thus it will be seen that, to obtain speed, the boiler and the shaft are, in these ships, necessarily placed so high that for a length of near one hundred feet amid-ships ... there are but three beams in each of their two decks; and it is on one of these decks that it is proposed to mount the guns—guns which weigh, with their carriages, each ten tons.... I have said enough to show gentlemen their light, buoyant, and elegant structure, so admirably adapted to speed, but so unsuited for war purposes.[31]

After this speech, Stephen Mallory devoted much of his energy working as chairman of the Senate Naval Affairs Committee in various hearings and doing committee chores. The results of those activities appeared in the Senate in March 1860 when lengthy discussions took place regarding a bill for navy pay increases. Most of the committee recommendations were accepted without debate, but some required discussion and clarification. In one matter a fellow Senator challenged Mallory on pay increases for lieutenants. Mallory made clear where he stood: "Ever since I have been in Congress I have been endeavoring to get their pay increased. I have not ceased in that effort."[32] Ultimately the Senate completed its work on this bill, it was reconciled with the House version, and it passed the Senate on May 23, 1860, by a vote of 42 to 6.[33]

This same general pattern prevailed in considering the naval appropriation bill that originated in the House and had been referred to the Senate Committee on Naval Affairs. The first debates on the Senate floor commenced on June 16, 1860, and on June 21 the Senate concurred with the report of the conference committee.[34] Through his conscientious work with the Committee on Naval Affairs and on the floor of the Senate, Mallory had succeeded in financing and improving the United States Navy that only a few years later would give him so much grief.

Senator-elect Stephen R. Mallory had arrived at the United States Senate on the verge of the most cataclysmic event that can occur in any nation: a country becoming divided. He came on the scene in 1851, virtually unknown and knowing little of how the national legislative process functioned. Mallory had honed his political skills on the small stage of Key West, Florida, where he was well known and respected. He was familiar with politics on the local level and he had held important county positions, but he never had held a statewide post or a national position. With his characteristic perseverance and spirit of optimism, Mallory engaged in another productive period of self-study during which time he absorbed journals, logs, articles, and government documents so that he might become a worthy senator. Stephen Mallory earned respect in the Senate for his hard work, thorough preparation on issues of importance to him, and his ability to articulate his positions.

Stephen Russell Mallory grew into his Senate role through his intellect, energy, self-discipline, and his motivation to succeed. He was an excellent student who incorporated his early life experiences into his congressional work, which enhanced his performance as a polished politician and senator. Senator Mallory earned a reputation as an able man in specific areas of expertise and ability. This resulted in his appointment to the Senate Committee on Naval Affairs. He became committee chairman and played a significant role in strengthening the United Sates Navy.

One becomes impressed with the breadth and depth of Stephen Mallory's knowledge by reading his Senate speeches and remarks that cover a wide range of subjects. Although he was not known as an outstanding speaker, his Senate contributions were often eloquent in the style of the day; frequently they were comprehensively constructed with persuasive logic. Historian J. Thomas Scharf writes, "He was not a showy orator, but occasionally delivered speeches showing careful preparation and a clear knowledge of the subject treated."[35]

Even in this emotionally wrenching decade, when events were running counter to his wishes or his motions were defeated, he maintained an inner calm and appropriate decorum. However, he could debate a wily opponent with verbal skill and when necessary would not allow himself to be bullied. Stephen Russell Mallory was a man of principle; at the same time he was a pragmatist and an adroit politician who would not hesitate to negotiate and compromise on an issue when necessary. All in all he was quite skillful and successful as a United States senator. Clearly, Stephen Mallory had found his niche in the greater scheme of things and he looked forward to whatever opportunities might await him.

5

Secession and Fort Pickens

The first session of the 36th Congress adjourned on June 25, 1860, with the second session scheduled to convene on December 3, 1860. During the interim, the nation was holding its collective breath to see if an Illinois politician, Abraham Lincoln, would be elected president in November 1860.

Stephen Russell Mallory returned to his Pensacola home and found Florida in turmoil over possible secession. Florida radicals had watched the emergence of the Republican Party with concern ever since its inception. To appreciate the atmosphere to which Mallory returned, it is useful to trace the increasing importance of Florida radicals.

On November 14, 1854, Florida governor Broome had addressed the Florida House of Representatives and recounted the grievances of the South specifying that "fanatical organizations" in northern nonslave-holding states had pursued strong antislavery action, including attempting to repeal the Fugitive Slave Act, and proposing no further admission of slave states into the Union. Governor Broome said, "The South is calm and unmoved. She is prepared to abide by the Union, made by the Constitution, with equal rights under it. Beyond this, she will be forced to act upon the sentiment, 'A union of the South for the protection of the South.'" In a message on November 24, 1856, he told the House that the South "should let fanaticism know that she has made her last submission to unconstitutional exactions." Furthermore, "Her watchword should be read of all men, 'Equality in the Union, or independence out of it.'"[1]

This theme became prevalent. By November 22, 1858, Florida governor Perry recognized the increasing threat from the abolitionists and recommended reorganizing the state militia. Nomination of Abraham Lincoln for president by the Republicans in May 1859, coupled with the John Brown episode in October 1859 at Harpers Ferry, propelled Governor Perry to recommend to the Florida Senate that should Lincoln be elected president in November 1860, Florida should withdraw from the Union. The Florida Legislature concurred and passed resolutions authorizing the governor to cooperate with other slaveholding states should there be a Republican president. Opposition to these resolutions was negligible.[2] Some churches in Florida promoted secession when preachers called for disunion from the pulpit. For example, on January 4, 1861, in Tallahassee, the rector of St. John's church preached a strong sermon in favor of disunion and immediate secession. The Episcopal bishop of Florida, Francis H. Rutledge, "promised to pay into the Florida treasury, five hundred dollars when the state seceded." Late in the previous month, the Florida Baptist state convention had adopted a resolution expressing "their cordial sympathy with, and hearty approbation of those who are determined to maintain the integrity of the Southern States, even by a disruption of all existing political ties."[3]

Stephen Mallory returned to his home state to find an active secessionist movement. In several Florida counties "Minute Men" companies had been formed for the purpose of keeping track of abolitionists and to discourage those (sometimes through physical force) who were not in support of the radical southern position supporting immediate secession.[4] In Pensacola a company of "Minute Men" claimed that Senator Mallory was one of its members and that he was active in furthering secession.[5] However, this was never confirmed and it is not known if the group was using his name with his permission. Citizens of Pensacola were reported to be "agitated and excited" especially because secessionists and Union supporters off Federal ships in Pensacola Harbor were juxtaposed on the streets. Secession was the topic of the day and violent advocates of states' rights drew sailors into brawls. A man who professed to be in favor of the Union either quickly recanted or found himself in a fistfight. A naval officer stationed in Pensacola reported, "Men, women and children seem to have gone mad."[6]

The Democrats had split into three segments and they would field separate candidates for president. Mallory felt himself being moved by events rather than being in control of those events. When Florida had become a state, he was a strong Unionist, but later he modified his position by acknowledging the sovereignty of his state and its right to maintain slavery. For a long time he occupied a middle ground. While accepting the theoretical propriety of a state that was being treated unequally to withdraw from the Union, he still believed the aggrieved state should stay in the Union and attempt to work out its differences from within. As the secession movement progressed, Senator Mallory followed but still held faint hope that a seceding state would be allowed to depart in peace and come back into the Union after its grievances had been satisfactorily addressed. He abhorred civil war and would work diligently to avoid that eventuality until the very last moment.

On November 6, 1860, Abraham Lincoln was elected president. Throughout Florida there were calls for a convention to take Florida out of the Union immediately. In some Florida localities, the president-elect was burned in effigy.[7] Lincoln was not on the ballot in Florida, but the Constitutional Union party candidate for president, John Bell of Tennessee, received an unexpectedly large vote, suggesting that many Floridians favored maintaining the Union. When the Florida Legislature convened in the last week of November, Governor Perry's message to that body urged immediate secession from the Union. A bill calling for a constitutional convention regarding secession to convene on January 3, 1861, in Tallahassee was adopted on November 30 with minimal opposition. During the campaign to select delegates to the constitutional convention, the prime issue was whether Florida should secede immediately or delay that action until other southern states had acted.

A visitor to Pensacola on December 7, 1860, found the people in a state of excitement about separation, with speeches being made to bolster citizens in support of immediate secession. In that county's December election of delegates to the upcoming constitutional convention, the two unionist candidates defeated secessionist candidates in spite of Mallory's efforts to mute pro–Union sentiment and encourage votes

for the secessionists.⁸ But this was not the case statewide and delegates to the secession convention largely were slaveholders operating large plantations who were intent on protecting slavery. Since Florida had become a state, this planter class had controlled the legislature and the governor's office. Slaveholders would control the secession convention as well.⁹

On December 20, 1860, South Carolina seceded and that step added momentum to Florida's secession movement. This state of arousal in reaction to South Carolina's secession, along with a quick response by the radical element, placed Florida's December 22 election of delegates to the constitutional convention beyond the control of moderates.¹⁰

Immediately after South Carolina had seceded, leaders of the secession movement in that state met to speedily organize a confederation of southern states. On December 26 a committee recommended to the South Carolina convention that commissioners be sent to other southern state conventions to promote the cause of secession. The convention delegates approved these recommendations and by January 2, 1861, commissioners were named to "sow the seeds of revolutions across the Deep South."¹¹

The commissioner sent to Florida was Leonidas W. Spratt, who was one of the most strident of the radicals. He was a South Carolinian but previously had lived in Florida's Apalachicola area where he had practiced law and served as a probate judge. The main purpose of Spratt's journey to Florida was to ensure that South Carolina would not remain isolated in defending the rights of slave states.¹²

On January 7, 1861, Spratt addressed the Florida constitutional convention, focusing on the rise of the Republicans to power. In his speech he said:

> Within this government two societies have become developed. The one is the society of one race, the other of two races. The one is based on free labor, the other slave labor.... The one embodies the social principle that equality is the right of man; the other, the social principle that equality is not the right of man, but the right of equals only.

Spratt emphasized that two different civilizations had emerged and he claimed, "There is and must be an irrepressible conflict between them, and it were best to realize the truth." He continued by defending South Carolina against charges that she had acted precipitously and said that an overt act by Republicans was not a necessary precondition for secession. He explained, "the contest was inevitable."¹³ Furthermore, the commissioner promoted the idea of speedy action to form a provisional government consisting of seceded states and emphasized the necessity of uniting the region for protection against anticipated northern aggression.¹⁴

The Florida convention quickly reacted and a secession ordinance, along with a report in favor of immediate secession, was introduced. Former Whigs Jackson Morton and George T. Ward led the opposition to the ordinance. They tried to amend it to defer action until Alabama and Georgia had seceded, and they proposed to require ratification of the measure by Florida's citizens before it was enacted. These amendments were defeated by close votes. On January 10, 1861, Florida passed its ordinance of secession

Opposite: Mallory portrait, c. 1860. This Mathew B. Brady photograph probably was taken in Washington in December 1860 or January 1861 while Stephen R. Mallory was a senator from Florida. He retired from his Senate seat on January 21, 1861, and was confirmed as secretary of the Confederate States of America Navy Department on March 18, 1861. COURTESY OF LIBRARY OF CONGRESS, PRINTS AND PHOTOGRAPHS DIVISION, LC-B8172–1743.

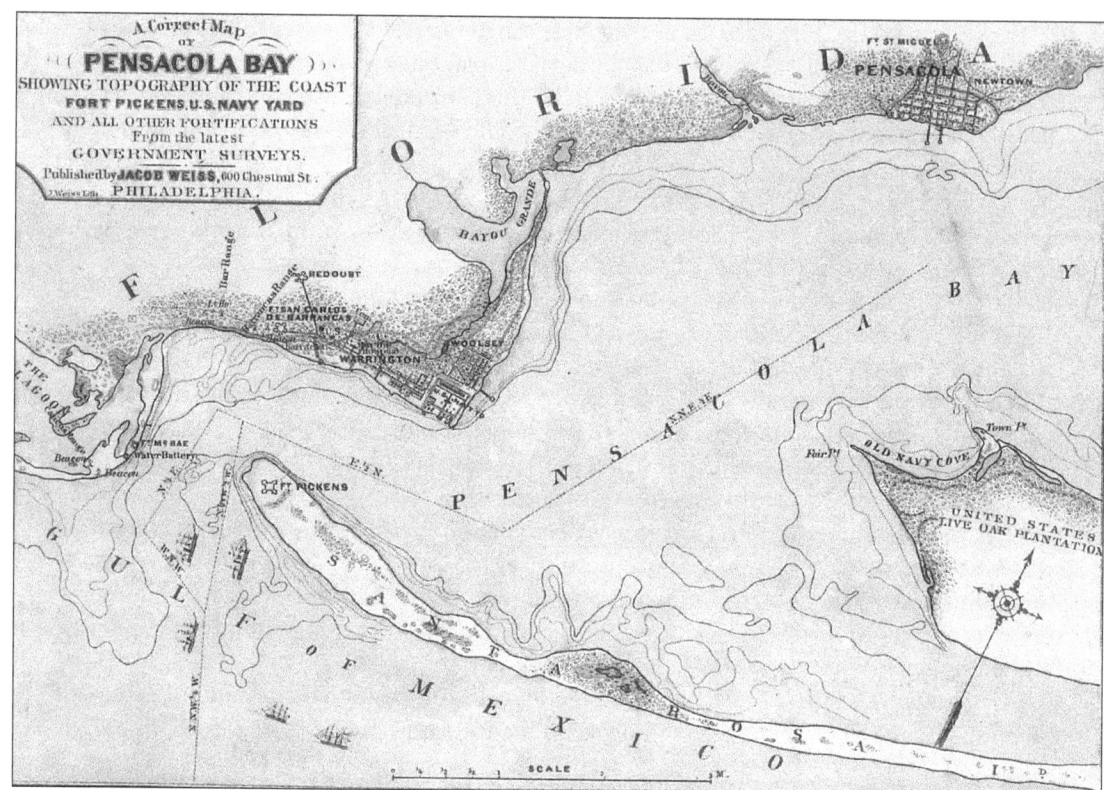

Pensacola Bay. This map of Pensacola Bay accurately depicts fortifications and coastal topography as it existed in February 1861. Guarding the bay entrance is Union-held Fort Pickens at the tip of Santa Rosa Island. To the west on the mainland is Fort McRae with his Water Battery and to the northeast is Fort Barrancas with its redoubt adjacent to the U.S. Navy Yard at Warrington, Florida. Forts McRae and Barrancas were occupied by Confederates. The well-designed locations of the forts exposed a hostile vessel entering the narrow bay entrance to triangulated fire. By 1862 Federal forces occupied all three forts. COURTESY OF LIBRARY OF CONGRESS, GEOGRAPHY AND MAP DIVISION, G3932.P45 186-.W4CW119.

by a vote of 62 to 7. However, in order to display unanimity, all 69 delegates signed it.[15] Mississippi seceded one day earlier, Alabama one day later.

In Washington, the second session of the 36th Congress convened on December 3, 1860. Senator S.R. Mallory[16] did not participate in Senate debate, but on December 27, in the Senate chambers, he wrote a letter to his friend James H. Hammond of South Carolina expressing his views about the current perilous situation. He was despondent and felt certain Lincoln would instantly seek to enforce the revenue laws. He foresaw the action that was to take place in Charleston Harbor and suggested that the new president would blockade all southern ports or the entire coastline.[17]

On December 21, 1860, Florida senator Yulee, anticipating the possibility of war, requested of Secretary of War John B. Floyd that he provide a list of U.S. Army officers who were appointed from Florida. Although it is not revealed why he desired this information the day after South Carolina seceded, it is likely he was interested in determining who might be recruited into the Confederate cause. Secretary Floyd, who reputedly was sympathetic to the southern creed and who would be appointed a Confederate brigadier general in May 1861, provided this information to Yulee on December 28, 1860. By early January 1861, Yulee and Mallory began working in concert, hoping that secession could be accomplished peacefully, but preparing for immediate action should war be inevitable. They both signed a letter to Secretary Floyd on January 2, 1861, requesting detailed information as to the amount of arms and ammunition at the various forts and arsenals in Florida. Undoubtedly this request was made to ascertain the strength of Federal strong points in Florida. A response was received the next day and the amount of detail was thorough and extensive. Among other things, it stated that at Fort Pickens there were 201 cannon of various identified types, and "4,974 projectiles of all kinds; 3,195 grape-shot, loose; 500 24-pounder stands canister shot; 12,712 pounds of powder, and 1,728 cartridge bags." Such information would be of value to an enemy. Apparently Florida's two senators requested additional information that same day. When they received no reply, they inquired when they might receive the requested data. On January 9 interim Secretary of War Joseph Holt replied saying, "the interests of the service forbid that the information which you ask should at this moment be made public." Apparently Holt, who would serve in both the Lincoln and Johnson administrations and who was described as "an all-out Unionist," had become aware that Florida would pass a secession ordinance the next day. The War Department now viewed the Florida senators as prospective enemies.[18]

Around this time, the general in chief of the army, Winfield Scott, concerned about the seizure of southern forts by "safety committees" of seceding states, wrote a letter dated December 28, 1860, to President-elect Abraham Lincoln with a copy to Secretary of War Floyd. While mentioning Fort Pickens, he was more concerned about Fort Taylor in Key West and Fort Jefferson at Dry Tortugas Island west of Key West. He asserted that these two forts were of greater value to the nation because of their strategic location that guards the drainages of the "upper waters of the Missouri, Mississippi, & Ohio rivers...." General Scott wrote about his concern: "There is only a feeble company at Key West for the defence of Fort Taylor, and not a soldier in Fort Jefferson to resist a handful of filibusters or a row-boat of Pirates...."[19]

On January 5 Yulee and Mallory participated in a caucus of southern senators that appointed a steering committee consisting of Mallory, Jefferson Davis of Mississippi and John Slidell of Louisiana. This committee passed a resolution urging southern states that had not yet seceded to do so as soon as possible. Later that day, Senator Yulee sent an important communication to Joseph Finegan, a Florida railroad operator from Yulee's home county, who had participated in the secession convention. It said, "The *immediately* [emphasis in original] important thing to be done is the occupation of the forts and arsenal in Florida. The naval station and forts at Pensacola are *first* [emphasis in original] in consequence. For this a force is necessary." He explained that the governor of Georgia was prepared to supplement Florida troops with Georgia state militia to accomplish this objective. He added, "Lose no time, for, my opinion is, troops will be very soon dispatched to re-enforce and strengthen the forts in Florida.... The North is rapidly consolidating against us...." Yulee added a postscript: "Lose no time about the navy-yard and forts at Pensacola."[20]

Two days later, on January 7, Senator Yulee sent Finegan a letter enclosing a copy of resolutions adopted after a meeting of senators whose states would be seceding. The resolutions encouraged each southern state to secede as soon as possible; made provisions for a convention to meet on February 15 at Montgomery, Alabama, to organize the

Fort Pickens. Currier and Ives published this lithograph of Fort Pickens at Pensacola Harbor. In this idealized image, the turbulent water around the fort represents the crisis in 1861, a larger-than-life United States flag symbolizes the resolve of the Union to resist southern demands for its surrender, and Fort Pickens gives the appearance of being impregnable. COURTESY OF LIBRARY OF CONGRESS, PRINTS AND PHOTOGRAPHS DIVISION, LC-USZC2, 2353.

Confederacy; asked for instructions as to whether delegates were to remain in Congress until March 4 to defeat hostile legislation; and appointed a committee "consisting of Messrs. Davis, Slidell, and Mallory, to carry out the objects of this meeting."[21] Also, the group thought that they should remain in their Senate seats as long as possible because "we can keep the hands of Mr. Buchanan tied and disable the Republicans from effecting any legislation which will strengthen the hands of the incoming administration." Clearly, preemptive actions were being taken and the South was going on a war footing.

On January 7, Georgia governor Joseph E. Brown sent a telegram to Florida governor Madison Starke Perry saying that Georgia would secede and asking, "Has Florida occupied the Forts?"[22] Two days later a telegram was sent by Senators Mallory and Yulee and Representative George S. Hawkins to Governor Perry stating, "Federal troops are said to be moving, or to move, on the Pensacola forts. Every hour is important. Georgia and Alabama if called will aid in the work, we think. The two seaboard forts are vacant. Chase, at Pensacola, built and knows the works." The next day Governor Perry transmitted this dispatch to the president of the Confederate convention, John C. McGehee. On January 10 "SRM" (S.R. Mallory) sent a telegram to Col. William H. Chase, a military engineer who commanded the land forces of the State of Florida at Pensacola, indicating that they were counting on him to get Pensacola's forts in Confederate hands: "All here look to you for Pickens and McRee."[23]

When with the Federal army in the 1850s, Chase had constructed fortifications at

5. *Secession and Fort Pickens* 69

Warrington Guns. This February 1861 photograph is of Columbiad guns of the Confederate Water Battery located below Fort Barrancas at Warrington, Florida. A tunnel connects the Water Battery and the fort. Both are across the bay from Fort Pickens that was occupied by Federal troops throughout the Civil War. Courtesy of U.S. National Archives and Records Administration, Photograph No. 77-HL-99-1.

and near the Pensacola Navy Yard. Two forts on the west side of Pensacola Bay protected the navy yard at Warrington, south of Pensacola. They were Fort McRee and Fort Barrancas. A smaller outpost, Fort Advanced Redoubt, protected Fort Barrancas from attack at the rear. A third military works, Fort Pickens, was located at the end of a barrier island to the east (Santa Rosa Island). It commanded the entrance to Pensacola Bay.[24]

Suddenly on January 12, there were indications that a peaceful settlement might not be totally out of the question. President Buchanan had become interested in a peace conference to be held in Washington on February 4 "for settlement of national difficulties."[25] By January 15 Florida's senators were aware that their state had passed an ordinance of secession. On that date they jointly signed correspondence to Governor Perry saying, "We have ceased participation in the proceedings of Senate, and only await receipt of authenticated ordinance [of secession] to retire formally."[26]

On January 18 through January 20 a series of messages dramatized the changing and confusing situation. On January 18 a telegram went to Governor Perry signed by Senator Mallory and eight other senators saying, "We think no assault should be made. The possession of the fort [Pickens] is not worth one drop of blood to us. Measures pending unite us in this opinion. Bloodshed now may be fatal to our cause." To Governor A. B. Moore in Alabama a telegram dated January 19 read, "Telegraph not to attack Fort Pickens. Florida Senators and friends think it unwise." Alabama senators Benjamin Fitzpatrick and Clement C. Clay, Jr., signed this message. On January 20 senators Yulee and Mallory wired Governor Perry: "The Southern Senators all agree that no assault on Fort Pickens should be made; that the fort is not worth one drop of blood at this time, and desire us to invoke you to prevent bloodshed. First get the Southern Government in operation. The same advice has been given as to Charleston, and will no doubt be adopted here."[27] This "one drop of blood" stance was developed after Mallory had consulted with Colonel Chase who wired him that he could not take Fort Pickens without a frontal assault using ladders and that would result in "an immense sacrifice of life and total annihilation of the garrison."[28]

Secessionists believed it was premature to engage in war until an operating government and an armed force had been established. Also, the South needed more time to entreat border states to join the cause. President-elect Davis expressed his opinion that the first blow by the South must be successful. Delays occasioned by peace initiatives may have worked to the advantage of the South because in the interim Confederate forces at Pensacola were strengthened.[29]

It is likely that some southern senators were grasping at a last chance for amity by responding positively to President Buchanan's offer of a peace conference. They were certain they would get a more equitable settlement through President Buchanan, who tended to be sympathetic to the southern cause, than they would from President-elect Lincoln, whom they viewed as antagonistic to their beliefs.

During this period, a special House Committee of Thirty-Three was pursuing a peace initiative in Washington. On December 29, 1860, the committee approved a proposal to admit New Mexico as a slave state, but it was defeated in Congress two months later. In February 1861 southern delegates gathered in Montgomery, Alabama, to organize a new government while at the same time the peace convention assembled in Washington. The peace conference accomplished little during the three weeks it met, but it sent a conciliatory recommendation to Congress where it was soundly defeated. However, one effect of these efforts to appease was to cool the southern ardor to attack Fort Pickens in January and February 1861.[30]

Finally, most southern senators felt they could delay no longer and Monday, January 21, was the day privately agreed upon by them to make a public declaration of their withdrawal from the Senate. Mrs. Virginia Clay, wife of Alabama senator Clement C. Clay, Jr., described the scene in the Senate on that day:

> The galleries of the Senate, which hold, it is estimated, one thousand people, were packed densely, principally with women, who, trembling with excitement, awaited the denouement of the day. As, one by one, Senators David Yulee, Stephen R. Mallory, Clement C. Clay, Benjamin Fitzpatrick, and Jefferson Davis rose, the emotion of their brother Senators and of us in the galleries increased.... As each Senator ... concluded his solemn renunciation of allegiance to the United States, women grew hysterical and waved their handkerchiefs, encouraging them with cries of sympathy and admiration. Men wept and embraced each other mournfully. At times the murmurs among the onlookers grew so deep that the Sergeant-at-Arms was ordered to clear the galleries; and, as each speaker took up his portfolio and gravely left the Senate Chamber, sympathetic shouts rang from

the assemblage above. Scarcely a member of that Senatorial body but was pale with the terrible significance of the hour. There was everywhere a feeling of suspense, as if, visibly, the pillars of the temple were being withdrawn and the great Government structure was tottering....[31]

Senator Stephen Russell Mallory commenced his last speech in the Senate with sadness, regret, and emotion. It was reported that he "wept as he spoke and drew tears from the eyes of many Senators and spectators in the crowded gallery."[32] He began with an indication of sorrow:

> I cannot feel ... but profound regret that existing causes imperatively impel us to this separation. When reason and justice shall have asserted ascendancy over party and passion, they will be justly appreciated; and this southern movement, demanded by consideration dear to freemen in every age, will stand proudly vindicated. Throughout her long and patient endurance of insult and wrong, the South has clung to the Union with unfaltering fidelity.

Mallory then summarized the consequences of the "insult and wrong" of which he spoke. "From the Union, governed by the Constitution as our fathers made it, there breathes not a secessionist upon her soil; but a deep sense of injustice, inequality, and insecurity [prevails] and to secure and maintain those rights which the Constitution no longer accords them, they have placed the State of Florida out of the Confederacy. In turning from the Union to the veiled and unknown future," he continued, "we are neither ignorant nor reckless of the lions in our path. We know that the prompt and peaceful organization of a practical republican government, securing liberty, equality, and justice to every citizen, is one of the most difficult ... duties devolving upon men."

Expressing his wish that the South and Florida could secede peacefully, Mallory said, "In thus severing our connections with sister States, we desire to go in peace, to maintain towards them an attitude not only of peace, but, if possible, of kindness...." But he warned that should the states remaining in the Union not permit this, the result may well be "one of the greatest calamities that can befall a nation ... a civil war embracing equally North and South." Then he cautioned that, "be our difficulties what they may, we stand forth a united people to grapple with and to conquer them. Our willingness to shed our blood in this cause is the highest proof we can offer of the sincerity of our connections."

The senator from Florida closed his remarks in a conciliatory manner saying, "we desire to part from you in peace.... We seek not to war upon or to conquer you; and we know that you cannot conquer us." Mallory acknowledged the kindness and courtesy he had experienced with many of his friends in the Senate and concluded by articulating, "We leave, with profound regret, those whom we will cherish in our hearts, and whose names will be hallowed by our children."[33]

Stephen Russell Mallory's swan song was full of melancholy, sadness, regret and depression. He said he did not like how things were turning out, but he felt that the South and Florida had been backed into a corner and had no choice other than secession. He expressed hope that the seceding states would be left alone to pursue their chosen course, but he admitted this was a slim hope. He dreaded a civil war, but made clear that the South would willingly shed blood and go the course. His speech was charitable and courteous. The next day Mallory, now a private citizen, left Washington to return to his home in Pensacola to determine how he might further support the aims of the Confederacy.

On January 10, 1861, the day the Florida ordinance of secession was passed, U.S.

Army Lt. Adam J. Slemmer, commanding Company G, 1st U.S. Artillery, having noted the approach of rebel troops in the area, spiked the guns at Fort Barrancas and blew up ammunition. In the meantime, Lieutenant Erben from the store-ship *Supply* assaulted Fort McRee and destroyed ammunition and spiked the guns bearing on Fort Pickens.[34] Lieutenant Slemmer collected Federal troops, munitions, and supplies and then occupied the most strategic and defensible installation in the area, Fort Pickens on the tip of Santa Rosa Island. Eighty-one men under his command now awaited a rebel attack upon their position. The fort was ideally located for a defensive position, but it was dilapidated and required much labor to make it stronger. Slemmer got his troops to work immediately. On January 12 a motley assortment of Florida and Alabama state militia intimidated aged Commodore James Armstrong and caused him, without a fight, to surrender the Pensacola Navy Yard, which was located across the bay at Warrington. The militia occupied Forts Barrancas and McRee as well. This group cautiously approached Fort Pickens, but did not attack the fort because of its strong position. The assemblage waited for further orders.[35]

After Mallory's arrival in Pensacola, officials from Alabama — Governor A.B. Moore and Senator Benjamin Fitzpatrick — met with him regarding the decision not to attack Fort Pickens, which had been communicated on January 18 by the nine southern senators. Mallory and Fitzpatrick said they and Senator Slidell had spoken with President Buchanan and the secretary of the navy. They had all agreed that no attack would be made upon Fort Pickens by either side during the remaining weeks of the Buchanan administration. Mallory also stated "that a special messenger had been sent by the Secretary of the Navy to the officer in command at Fort Pickens, directing that officer to prevent the ships which had been ordered to Pensacola from entering the bay. The officer sent was Captain Barron, of Virginia, in company with Mr. Mallory."[36]

On January 28, Mallory wrote to John Slidell in Washington indicating that the *Brooklyn* was sailing for Fort Pickens with troops but that no attack on that fort was contemplated at the present. Mallory told him that Buchanan should be advised that any attempt to land additional troops at the fort might result in war. He added, "We desire to keep the peace.... I am determined to stave off war if possible."[37]

The next day Secretary of War Joseph Holt wrote Lieutenant Slemmer at Fort Pickens to inform him that the *Brooklyn* was on the way with additional troops. However, Slemmer was instructed that he was to maintain a defensive posture and avoid a hostile collision with the southern state militia facing him. He was told he should fight only if attacked and make the best defense possible. On January 29 Holt and Secretary of the Navy Isaac Toucey sent another message to Slemmer and others saying that troops on the *Brooklyn* were not to be put ashore unless Fort Pickens was attacked. However, Federal ships were to remain on station offshore and would be permitted to unload provisions. Holt and Toucey informed all parties that "The President yesterday sent a special message to Congress commending the Virginia resolutions of compromise. The commissioners of the different States are to meet here [Washington] on Monday, the 4th February, and it is important that during the session a collision of arms should be avoided...."[38] Thus the "Truce of Pickens" was constructed, providing that southern forces would not attack Fort Pickens and the fort would not be strengthened with more troops.[39]

Since Lincoln's election, President Buchanan had pursued a course of doing everything possible to maintain the status quo, allowing the incoming president to deal with the problems of secession. Throughout this period, he displayed his capacity to avoid a showdown and to postpone a decision. The Fort Pickens reprieve was supported by Buchanan's peace conference in Washington that began on February 4. The conference continued for three weeks and produced a compromise that pleased no one. While the Pickens accord was being negotiated, Senator William H. Seward was "in Washington acting as untitled head of the Republican Party and self-designated savior of the Union.... He was looked upon as spokesman for the incoming administration.... He had chosen the path of conciliator."[40] Seward became the chief contact with southern statesmen who were trying to find a peaceful resolution of the conflict before Lincoln's inauguration. As a conciliator, he supported the Pickens agreement and urged the Senate to keep open the seats of southern senators who had vacated them. Seward hoped they might reoccupy them at some time in the future.[41]

The "Truce of Pickens" held until after Lincoln was inaugurated on March 4. The new president and his cabinet soon determined that Fort Pickens must be reinforced. On March 12 General Winfield Scott ordered troops aboard *Brooklyn* to disembark. His order reached the vessel on March 31 but the navy ship's captain refused to accept an order from an army officer. Authorization from a navy officer to land troops did not arrive until April 12. By then Fort Sumter had been fired upon and war had begun.

Both Fort Sumter and Fort Pickens were symbols of national pride for the North and sources of irritation for the South. There was every expectation that either might become a flash point. Were it not for the Pickens respite, it is quite likely that war would have commenced after guns were fired at Fort Pickens. Instead both sides honored the truce and chose to start a war at Fort Sumter in Charleston Bay.[42]

Stephen Mallory paid a price for trying to avert war through the "Truce of Pickens." For the rest of his life, detractors heaped abuse upon him, charging him with having pro-Union sentiments that were tantamount to committing treason against the South. He was a moderate, not a radical, who tried to avoid war, as did many others. Yet anyone who examines his record as a United States senator cannot fail to appreciate that he was a Southron who defended slavery and the concept of states' rights—the very core of the South's social, political and philosophical values.

The best example of his substantial southern and national sentiment and of his devotion to the Confederacy is evident in a letter he wrote to Florida governor John Milton in November 1861:

> Strange as it may sound to us, the Republicans and even the Democrats in the North are still dreaming of a 'reconstruction of the Union' and hug themselves with the belief that we would consent to a connection with them. I trust that those among us, and there are many here, who entertain such a dream will soon awake to its utter unreality. Upon no terms, and under no circumstances should we consent again to go into any Union with them.... We are a purer, nobler, braver and better people in all respects than they can ever become so long as the Puritan blood flows in their veins, and I know as well as I can know anything in the future that all mankind will so acknowledge us.[43]

In another letter to Governor Milton written two weeks earlier, Mallory discussed the Pickens episode and said he felt he had provided a most valuable service to Florida. He added, "I certainly am prepared to stand upon and sustain my cause; my only regret being that I may be compelled to speak well of myself & my action to defend myself against my enemies, than modesty would otherwise approve."[44]

Fort Pickens remained in Federal hands throughout the Civil War. When he reflected in later years on this chapter of his life, Stephen Mallory said it was a fatal error not to have taken Fort Pickens. With the fort remaining in Federal hands, access to Pensacola Bay was denied to the rebels who controlled the navy yard and no Confederate ship could reach the Gulf of Mexico. Eventually southern forces abandoned the Pensacola Navy Yard.[45]

From January 22 through mid-February Stephen Russell Mallory spent most of his time at home in Pensacola with his family while paying close attention to what was occurring in the area, especially at Fort Pickens. He could walk south on Palafox Street to the pier on Pensacola Bay where, on a clear day, he could gaze across the bay at the fort. Mallory was aware that the Confederate States of America was being organized in Montgomery, Alabama; he said he was unwilling to go to Montgomery and "give any ground for presuming that I wanted station or position."[46] But in mid-February he received a communication from his old colleague, Jefferson Davis, who asked him to meet with him in Montgomery. Mallory assumed he would be asked to serve in President Davis's cabinet and he resolved that he would decline the honor. But out of courtesy to his old friend, he felt he had to go to the interim Confederate capital to tell Davis he could not accept any public position. Stephen said goodbye to his family and departed by train for the short journey northward.

Part III

Confederate Navy Chief

6

Initial Moves

Delegates from seven slave states met in Montgomery, Alabama, on February 4, 1861, to begin forging a new nation. Those states, in order of their secession from the Union, were South Carolina, Mississippi, Florida, Alabama, Georgia, Louisiana, and Texas. By the end of June, four more states (Virginia, Arkansas, North Carolina, and Tennessee) would secede and join the confederation.

Representatives to the constitutional convention progressed rapidly and in only four days they unanimously approved a provisional Constitution of the Confederate States of America.[1] Most of it was copied verbatim from the United States Constitution, as was the later permanent constitution. The permanent constitution, however, had significant revisions pertaining to states' rights and slavery. It was debated from February 28 to March 11, 1861, and was unanimously approved.[2]

Delegates selected Jefferson Davis as provisional president on February 9. He was inaugurated on February 16 before a cheering crowd. As a band played "Dixie," he spoke these aggressive words: "The time for compromise has now passed and the South is determined to maintain her position, and make all who oppose her smell Southern powder and feel Southern steel if coercion is persisted in."[3]

The provisional constitution gave the pro-tempore Congress authority "To provide and maintain a Navy."[4] On February 12 the Congress named a Committee on Naval Affairs headed by Charles M. Conrad (who was a wealthy planter and lawyer from New Orleans) that was directed to prepare and report a bill to establish the Navy Department.[5]

President Jefferson Davis began selecting his cabinet. Stephen Mallory came to him with the notion of declining a cabinet post, but desiring to assist a navy secretary in any way possible. On February 21, 1861, the Confederate Congress passed an act establishing the Confederate Navy and Davis quickly nominated Mallory to lead the Navy Department. The Floridian determined he could not remove himself from consideration because two members of his state's delegation were assailing his honor by citing personal reasons for opposing him. "Of course I could not carry out my purpose," said Mallory, "and withdraw in the face of unknown opposition." The leader of the opposition turned out to be Mallory's old political foe, Jackson Morton. Disapproval of Mallory primarily was based

Jefferson Davis. This undated photograph of Confederate president Jefferson Davis probably was taken near the beginning of his presidency. Stephen Mallory was one of his confidants. COURTESY OF LIBRARY OF CONGRESS, PRINTS AND PHOTOGRAPHS DIVISION, LC-DIG-CWPBH-00879.

on his role in the Fort Pickens episode. His opponents believed the fort should have been assaulted and taken by state militia, but the "Pickens Truce" had prevented this. Because of his actions to avoid bloodshed at Fort Pickens, Mallory was unfairly branded as being unenthusiastic about secession.[6] Mallory had particularly bitter feelings about Morton. He believed that Morton held deep-seated ill will toward him and that he was a rather stupid, gauche person. He referred to him as a chucklehead.[7]

In the midst of opposition to his nomination, Mallory began lining up support from convention delegates and others he courted in Montgomery. He made alliances with two delegates from South Carolina, Thomas J. Withers and James Chesnut, Jr. Mr. Chesnut and his wife, the diarist Mary Boykin Chesnut, were Mallory's friends and were in contact with him throughout the war. It was Mary Chesnut who, on March 4, 1861, introduced him to Georgian Benjamin H. Hill, who also would be a close personal friend during and after the war.[8]

Appreciation of the Florida Legislature for Mallory's appointment was expressed in a joint resolution on December 17, 1861:

> Florida feels a just sentiment of pride in being represented in the Cabinet, and we deem it due to the occasion to declare our appreciation of the appointment by the President of the Hon. S. R. Mallory as Secretary of the Navy, in whose knowledge, experience, ability and patriotism the country may confide for the successful administration of the Department committed to his charge.[9]

The Confederate Senate confirmed Mallory as secretary of the navy on March 18, 1861, by a vote of 13 to six.[10] He was a popular choice for the post and most thought his selection was sound. Preceding him was a reputation for "clearness of reasoning and firmness of purpose ... [and] this made him acceptable to the majority of politicians and people."[11]

It was reported that the new secretary took the news of his confirmation in a rather detached manner. He was with Mr. and Mrs. Chesnut at a celebration and they were watching the raising of the Confederate flag. Stephen Mallory was talking with Mary Chesnut when Mr. Chesnut told Mallory he had been confirmed. "Mr. Mallory," wrote Mary Chesnut, "did not interrupt what he was saying to me but continued in the same placid voice. I did not find this very civil to Mr. Chesnut." She asked Mallory if he had heard this news before, and he replied that he had not. She queried him about why he had not acknowledged her husband's good news whereupon Mallory turned to Mr. Chesnut and thanked him with a "profound bow."[12]

Several factors influenced Jefferson Davis's selection of Stephen Russell Mallory as his navy secretary. First, he was from Florida. The state that a cabinet member came from was important; the new president believed it to be necessary to structure a governing body that equally represented interests of all new Confederate states in order to create a sense of unanimity and cohesion. Davis had been selected as president in order to reach a compromise between moderates and extremists. This required that he achieve balance in his cabinet. Mallory was viewed as a moderate and this impression interfered with his speedy confirmation.

Second, Davis knew and liked Mallory in addition to respecting his expertise in naval affairs. While Davis was secretary of war in the Franklin Pierce administration, he worked with Mallory and they also had served together as senators. President Davis was well aware of the dedication and leadership Senator Mallory had provided as chairman of the Senate Committee on Naval Affairs and he saw the result — a more efficient, improved, and stronger U.S. Navy. He believed there was no one else who had such broad knowledge and depth of understanding of naval matters as Mallory, irrespective of the fact that he had neither commanded nor served on a navy ship. He was aware that Mallory knew many naval officers and had a sound background in maritime law.

Third, Davis respected Mallory's personal characteristics of keen intellect, a strong drive to persist until the objective was achieved, and the ability to compromise without surrendering his principles.

Fourth, the president was a graduate of the United States Military Academy, had led ground troops in the Mexican War and generally viewed himself as an army expert. But in naval affairs he had no personal experience and had no problem delegating authority to Mallory. Davis believed he could trust the navy secretary to carry out his responsibilities with little oversight, in part because he assumed the navy role would be minor in comparison with the role of land forces.[13]

Jefferson Davis's vice president was Alexander H. Stephens of Georgia. Stephens, like Davis, initially had shied away from secession, but state loyalty had dictated his embracing disunion when Georgia seceded. He remained moderate in his views and was an early advocate of peace.[14]

Since Davis viewed himself as an expert in army matters, he had difficulty delegating to his six secretaries of war who became figureheads and "yes men."[15] His initial secretary of war was Leroy P. Walker, a prominent Alabama lawyer, politician, and ardent secessionist. What he lacked was administrative ability and early on "He was buried in the mass of details arising during the organization of the army and was not able to cope with them all."[16] President Davis had little confidence in Walker's ability to plan a general campaign. Consequently he dictated this activity himself and bypassed his war secretary. This pattern of the president running the war department persisted throughout the conflict and largely accounted for high personnel turnover in that department.

Robert A. Toombs was the president's selection for secretary of state. He was a wealthy Georgia planter who accepted this post with some hesitation because he had sought the presidency. He was not well used in his position because President Davis personally formulated all courses of action with other governments. In February 1861 Davis's foreign policy consisted of three goals: the South would seek peaceful separation from the Union, the Confederacy would negotiate with European nations for formal recognition, and the government would cultivate friendly commercial relations with all countries. To pressure Great Britain and France to grant formal recognition to the Confederacy, President Davis prohibited the export of cotton from summer 1861 to spring 1862. That action accomplished little other than constricting the flow of cash to the South. By late 1862 the Confederacy began exporting cotton again to finance the war effort.[17]

For secretary of treasury, Jefferson Davis selected Christopher G. Memminger, who had participated in the South Carolina secession convention and the provisional Confederate Congress. Memminger and Davis respected one another and the president gave him a free hand to run his department. Secretary Memminger's fiscal policy was to meet current expenses through sale of bonds and later treasury notes. Inflation and lack of public support for the purchase of bonds and notes made it increasingly difficult to raise money to finance the war.[18]

For attorney general, President Davis selected Judah Benjamin, who turned out to be one of his better appointments. Benjamin and Mallory had served together in the U.S. Senate where they both supported similar issues on occasion, including defense of the Naval Retirement Board. They respected one another and their mutual esteem flourished as a result of their work together in the upper chamber. Their friendship solidified during their service in the cabinet where Benjamin shifted from attorney general, to secretary of war, and then to secretary of state (a position he remained in from March 1862 until the end of the war). As attorney general, Benjamin gained Jefferson Davis's trust and soon became a favorite of the president. Judah Benjamin was "A human dynamo [and] a brilliant lawyer.... As Attorney General he had not been busy and was, therefore, able to cultivate, cajole, and advise Davis."[19] Benjamin was a confidant of the president throughout the war.[20]

Another solid appointment President Davis made was John H. Reagan for postmaster general. Reagan was a rough-hewn Texan who served in the same cabinet post throughout the war. He did a competent job in a relatively minor post as he kept mail moving during very difficult times. Reagan had a good relationship with Stephen Mallory and they became friends. Mallory seemed to enjoy the balance between the rough character of Reagan and the sophisticated demeanor of Benjamin.[21]

These were the men with whom the navy secretary would be working. Mallory would be closely allied with President Davis, who delegated responsibility to his navy secretary and permitted him to run his department without interference. Davis supported his navy secretary by attempting to secure resources needed to build and operate a navy and he deflected criticisms of Mallory's operation of the department.[22]

Judah Benjamin and John Reagan were also important to Stephen Mallory because they were his friends and both had the ear of the president. It was not uncommon for Mallory and Benjamin to spend considerable time with Davis. Frequently Mallory and

Confederate Cabinet Group Portrait. This illustration of the Confederate cabinet appeared in *Harper's Weekly* on June 1, 1861. It is a wood engraving from a photograph taken in Montgomery, Alabama. From left to right are Attorney General Judah P. Benjamin, Secretary of the Navy Stephen R. Mallory, Secretary of the Treasury C. S. Memminger (standing), Vice President Alexander Hamilton Stephens, Secretary of War Leroy Pope Walker (standing), President Jefferson Davis, Postmaster John H. Regan, and Secretary of State Robert Toombs. COURTESY OF LIBRARY OF CONGRESS, PRINTS AND PHOTOGRAPHS DIVISION, LC-USZ62-132563.

Benjamin would dine together and sometimes they took trips to visit the various battlefields near Richmond during McClellan's 1862 Peninsular Campaign.[23]

John Reagan described one battlefield experience he and Mallory shared in the summer of 1864. They heard firing northwest of Richmond that was unexpected because there were no Confederate troops in that sector. They rode horses to the firing, which was located close to a line of old, undefended trenches. There they found a Colonel Lyon, a prominent citizen who lived nearby, riding along the earthwork, waving as if giving directions. They inquired what he was doing. Lyon replied, "Commanding the forces; Reagan, you command the right; Mallory, you the left, and I will take the center." All three rode about shouting orders. The ruse caused Federal forces to fire upon them. The trio continued to shout orders to phantom troops, "with the shells cracking over us, until the firing ceased." Reagan said this "was one battle during the war which had not gone into history...."[24]

The most critical person in the cabinet as far as Stephen Mallory was concerned was the head of the treasury, Christopher G. Memminger. He was the moneyman and huge sums would be required to build and operate a navy. Finances would always be a problem for the Confederacy because the "peculiar institution" of slavery froze wealth. Money

Admiral Franklin Buchanan. This photograph was taken c. 1855–1861. Buchanan was the first commander of the Confederate ironclad *Virginia* but was seriously wounded in Hampton Roads during an attack on Federal warships on March 8, 1862. He was hospitalized and missed the battle between the *Virginia* and *Monitor* the following day. Later he oversaw the construction of the *Tennessee* and commanded it in the battle of Mobile Bay on August 5, 1864. COURTESY OF NAVAL HISTORICAL CENTER, NH 61161.

was consumed in buying and maintaining slaves and purchasing land for cotton production; only small sums of liquid funds were readily available for financing the war. Since there were few capitalists in the South and most wealthy men had little accessible currency, the amount of money that could be raised through taxation was limited and inflation would further aggravate the situation. In short, the South had a serious cash flow problem from the beginning.[25]

As a starting point, Secretary Memminger could only issue treasury notes and borrow, while acknowledging that this could only be a temporary measure. He recognized that cotton could not be converted to cash to finance the war effort until it was sold on the world market, and this could only be accomplished through maritime trade. At this juncture the treasury and navy secretaries recognized their mutual interests.[26] Cotton needed ships to go to market while a basic task of the navy was to protect the maritime trade. Obviously vessels were needed and the navy had precious few. Building ships in the South would take time, but existing vessels found throughout the Confederacy might be purchased immediately. Building ships in England and France, where all the facilities of great shipyards were available for speedy construction, was an option. Again money was needed to buy and build ships. Thus navy and treasury policy intersected.

The cumbersome mechanism for the navy secretary to obtain funding commenced with Mallory submitting an estimate of expenses and requesting an appropriation from Congress. After deliberating and approving a sum, Congress would send the navy's appropriation to the Treasury Department because the Confederate financial structure did not provide an independent budget for the Navy Department. Secretary Mallory would request necessary funds from the Treasury Department. Secretary Memminger would do his best to honor these requests, but sometimes he could not immediately comply due to the perilous condition of Confederate finances.

Mallory frequently discussed with Memminger the problem of getting department bills paid promptly. A particular issue for the navy secretary was that navy bills were paid with government bonds, which were unpopular with the public. Bond redemptions often were delayed from 24 hours to 40 days.[27] Incidents of this nature prompted Mallory to seek a solution from President Davis. On March 8, 1862, he wrote to the president saying failure of the Treasury Department to pay Navy Department bills in a timely manner "has been a constant source of embarrassment to the Department and of annoyance to its creditors and disbursing agents...."[28]

Not only was Secretary Mallory faced with the navy's financial problems, but he also had to deal with personnel problems. According to Durkin, "In March, 1861, the Confederate Navy Department possessed twelve small ships and approximately two hundred officers...."[29] These small ships were river boats requiring small crews resulting in more officers being available for placement than were needed.

To remedy the problem, Secretary Mallory did several things. Those who were experienced in firing cannon were ordered to direct army batteries at coastal defensive locations. Next, Mallory assured all officers that they would be assigned the same rank in Confederate service as they had held in the Federal navy. Then he borrowed from experiences he had while a United States senator when he drafted legislation establishing the Naval Retiring Board. The secretary persuaded the Confederate Congress to pass an act to "make promotion dependent solely on 'gallant or meritorious conduct during the war.'" This was a means to separate elderly officers, who were more suitable for deskwork, from those younger, more energetic and imaginative officers who were more competent for sea duty. This policy was codified by legislation in May 1863, which provided that older men unable to effectively perform sea duty remained in the regular navy where, with meritorious performance, they might advance in rank, but would not be assigned duty afloat unless transferred to the provisional navy. Younger, more energetic officers were placed in the provisional navy where they were assigned duties aboard ships and received promotions as merited by aggressive and effective performance of their responsibilities.[30]

Secretary Mallory sought out officers whose loyalty was assured and who could adequately perform assigned duties. Those who were aggressive and required minimal supervision often fared the best with the secretary and were amply and quickly rewarded. One example of a success story was James Bulloch, who became one of the South's most effective contracting agents in England and France and sacrificed his personal ambitions for command of a ship to serve the greater good. Another such example was Adm. Franklin Buchanan, who rapidly advanced from a desk job as chief of the Bureau of Details and Orders to command of the James River Squadron, and then to command of the new ironclad, the *Virginia*. After that assignment, he was hailed as a navy hero. In August 1864 he was given the most difficult task of defending Mobile Bay against Union attack. A third exemplification is Raphael Semmes, who gained worldwide fame as a most intelligent and aggressive commander of cruisers raiding enemy commerce. He worked well in isolation with minimal instructions and displayed outstanding initiative. All three men quickly were rewarded with advancement in rank. With the exception of Bulloch, they became famous and were considered heroes. Bulloch did so much of his work sub rosa, as was required by the nature of the job, that he received little renown.[31]

Confederate Navy Leaders. This painting was created for use in an official film on naval history in the early 1960s. It depicts an imaginary meeting of some of the leaders of the Confederate navy. Seated, left to right, are Capt. (later Adm.) Franklin Buchanan, Capt. Josiah Tattnall, and Cmdr. Matthew F. Maury. Standing, left to right, are Capt. George N. Hollins, Rear Adm. Raphael Semmes, and navy chief Stephen Mallory. COURTESY OF NAVAL HISTORICAL CENTER, NH 44520 KN.

Mallory generally was skilled at selecting the proper man for the job at hand, but he also made mistakes. One example of a poor choice was Mallory's assignment in 1861 of Lt. Beverly Kennon to direct the Ordnance Department at New Orleans. Kennon quickly bungled the management of that office by overspending his budget and squandering a total of $146,000 without approval. Before the secretary could get another man there to relieve him, Kennon made unauthorized expenditures reaching almost $500,000. Mallory removed him for insubordination and exceeding approved expenditures. Kennon transferred to Louisiana state service to command a gunboat where his daring and spirited initiative might be more fully appreciated. A year later he was back in Confederate service and performing well working with torpedoes and mining the Yazoo River.[32]

Another poor personnel selection that Mallory made was Capt. Victor Randolph. Randolph was given a position in the Navy Department where he immediately allied himself with politicians whom Mallory considered disloyal to the southern cause. To prevent him from dabbling in local politics, and because he believed Randolph could improve defenses at Mobile, he transferred him to that station. Randolph later implied to state and local officials in Alabama that the Navy Department in Richmond was ineffective. Mallory swiftly ordered Randolph back to Richmond for court-martial.[33]

A third illustration was Mallory's selection of Commodore Josiah Tattnall to command the *Virginia* in March 1862 after Admiral Buchanan had been wounded in action. Tattnall was forced to destroy the ironclad in the James River because of fear she would be captured by Union forces. Mallory was only a few miles away and Tattnall failed to notify the secretary of his intent. Mallory was furious when he learned the ironclad had been destroyed because he deemed the act to be premature. He thought Tattnall was incompetent and insubordinate; a court of inquiry followed. He was acquitted and Mallory then transferred Commodore Tattnall to Savannah to take charge of naval defenses between that port and Charleston. He did that job well and regained the confidence of the secretary.[34]

The above examples display Stephen R. Mallory's leadership style. In all six instances, he responded with alacrity both to reward good performance and to punish, or otherwise correct, poor performance. Even with his failure to place a man in a position at which he might excel — causing him to take corrective action — the secretary could give the person an opportunity to redeem himself. Tattnall did so in his new assignment at Savannah. Kennon acquitted himself though his excellent work with torpedoes.

Secretary Mallory displayed compassion for his men. Excellent medical care for the Confederate sailor was important to him. Under his direction, good navy hospitals and infirmaries were established and the wounded sailor who made it to a medical center could count on the best possible treatment where he stood an excellent chance of survival.[35]

Mallory saw to it that ordinary seamen were properly clad. He had his purchasing agents overseas ordering clothing, and he persuaded the Confederate Congress to authorize a clothing issue for the enlisted men. Shoes were hard to come by but one of Mallory's staff was able to find a local supply of leather for manufacturing sea boots. In Augusta, Georgia, a naval factory was erected to produce other footwear and uniforms.[36]

At the outset of his secretariat, Stephen Mallory was required to clearly define the role of the Confederate navy. President Davis realized that the South had no naval tradition and thought it would defend itself mainly through land battles. He saw the navy as an auxiliary force to the army supplying ships to augment the forts and shore batteries protecting the rivers and harbors along the southern coastline.[37]

This limited navy role was also reflected in the February 21 report of the Congressional Committee on Naval Affairs that was chaired by Charles M. Conrad. The preface to the report said committee members had "limited their enquiry to such naval means as might serve as auxiliaries to forts and arsenals and cooperate with land forces in the defense of rivers and harbors." First priority was given to protecting the New Orleans area and the Mississippi River from an enemy incursion. Conrad's report included a detailed defensive plan that was developed by Maj. (later Gen.) Pierre Beauregard, who had been involved in improving navigation of the lower Mississippi River after the Mexican War. Less detailed attention was given to defending the ports of Mobile, Savannah, and Charleston by strengthening those forts and providing additional batteries. The situation at Pensacola Bay, with Fort Pickens in control of Federal forces, was acknowledged.[38] While Mallory did not minimize the importance of these limited goals, he had no intention of constraining his strategic planning to such a narrow scope.

"An act to provide for the organization of the Navy" was approved on March 16, 1861, and Mallory acted quickly and boldly to build a fleet.[39] His first step was to create a Navy Department with people in key positions that he knew and trusted. For the most part he displayed a remarkable talent for selecting the best person for each job. He was careful to assess the qualifications of individual officers for sea duty as contrasted with desk duty, and he made appropriate assignments according to demonstrated skills, interests, and personal characteristics.

The organizational plan provided for the Office of the Secretary of the Navy, four operational bureaus, and a Marine Corps. The operational bureaus were the offices of Orders and Detail, Ordnance and Hydrography, Provisions and Clothing, and Medicine and Surgery.[40]

Secretary Mallory, two chief aides, four clerks, and one messenger staffed the secretary's office. At the outset, his two chief aides were his chief clerk, Edward M. Tidball, and Capt. French Forrest. Tidball had the same job in the U.S. Navy for 10 years and "would never be more than an energetic and competent bureaucrat."[41] But a bureaucracy needs bureaucrats and Tidball did his job well. Forrest served as the other chief aide for only a few weeks before Mallory transferred him to command the Gosport Navy Yard after it was seized by Virginia militia on April 21, 1861.[42]

Operational offices of the Navy Department were all located on the same floor in rooms connecting with Mallory's office.[43] Mallory selected the bureau chiefs. Most important of the operational units was the Bureau of Orders and Detail. It primarily was a personnel department that kept records of all human resources, made postings of sailors and officers as directed, and dealt with matters related to rank and promotion. This office also drafted and delivered orders as assigned by the secretary, and was involved with matters involving discipline and administration of military justice. Later this bureau was charged with other tasks seemingly inconsistent with its primary personnel function. These additional assignments dealt with supply and storage of coal, fitting out and replenishing ships (to a limited extent), and management of the Navy Rope Walk that manufactured cordage. The first chief of the bureau was Lawrence Rousseau, oldest of the captains who resigned from the United States Navy. Under his direction, the Bureau of Orders and Detail made a significant contribution in maintaining the efficiency and order of the navy. Later, Cmdr. J.K. Mitchell was in charge.[44]

The next most important office was the Bureau of Ordnance and Hydrography. It dealt with the manufacture, purchase, and distribution of ordnance and munitions and with all matters related to nautical instruments such as barometers, compasses, and charts. This office dealt with weapon standards and testing, and was in charge of nearly everything pertaining to navigation, such as lighthouses and buoys. It also coordinated the exchange of guns between the army and navy to meet the particular exigencies of the moment. Duncan M. Ingraham, and then George Minor, headed this bureau. The last chief was John M. Brooke, who took over in March 1863. Brooke, the inventor of the Brooke rifle and an outstanding officer of 18 years' service, was one of Secretary Mallory's most sound selections. The Bureau of Ordnance and Hydrography was efficiently managed and by late 1862 all navy ships were adequately armed.[45]

The third operational office was the Bureau of Provisions and Clothing. It provided food and clothing for all naval personnel and managed naval funds that provided pay for personnel. Heading this bureau was Paymaster John De Bree, who had served in the U.S. Navy for 44 years. He probably was of marginal effectiveness but he had a capable deputy, James A. Semple, who had similar experience but was younger and more energetic. The civilian agent appointed for food production and procurement, William F. Howell, was wise and resourceful and an excellent choice for that position. All these men worked well together and were said to have created a miracle. At war's end, although the army and many civilians were nearly starving, the navy never lacked food or clothing and sometimes supplied the needs of the army. On April 28, 1864, Paymaster De Bree, noting that the navy had a surplus of food, stated that it would be "an act of justice" should the navy reduce its ration so that more food would be available to the army.[46]

Dr. W. A. W. Spotswood directed the fourth operational office, the Bureau of Medicine and Surgery. He was a veteran of 25 years' service in the U.S. Navy in a similar though lesser capacity, where he had performed his duties efficiently. This office cared for the health of all navy personnel and provided medical care for the ill and wounded. It created four excellent hospitals (at Richmond, Charleston, Savannah, and Mobile) and infirmaries, provided ships with medical personnel including male nurses, imported medical supplies through blockade running, and operated a pharmaceutical laboratory in Richmond. The Bureau of Medicine and Surgery was another success story.[47]

Finally, there was a small Marine Corps that primarily dealt with security duties. The Marines functioned as guards aboard ships, at naval stations, and at shore batteries. Col. Lloyd Beall, a former Army paymaster with no Marine experience, was the commandant of this corps that at its height consisted of 753 officers and men. Mallory personally took the lead in establishing this unit, and saw to it that Beall was supplied with a capable cadre. Colonel Beall quickly trained these men to become a mobile striking force.[48]

In 1862, the secretary created small semiautonomous administrative units that were necessary because in the original organization certain tasks were divided between the Bureau of Ordnance and Hydrography and the Bureau of Orders and Details. This arrangement caused overlapping of responsibilities and confusion. One of these specialized units was the Department of Steam Engineering that was charged with planning, producing and distributing steam engines under the direction of the engineer in chief, William P. Williamson. A second specialized unit was the Office of Naval Constructor. John L. Porter was named chief and his office handled details of ship construction in various public and private yards.[49]

Other organizational problems were corrected later. For example, the task of supplying fuel and fitting out ships initially was assigned to the Bureau of Provisions and Clothing, but later was transferred to the Bureau of Orders and Details. These types of realignments were necessary when experience proved they didn't work well together. Additionally, in 1862 a fifth operational unit, the Torpedo Bureau, was added as use of torpedoes (mines) gained in importance.[50]

The organization of the Confederate navy was modeled after that of the Union Navy. However, it was missing one critical element. In *A History of the Confederate Navy*, author Raimondo Luraghi writes, "The most feeble point in the Confederate naval command was the absence of a chief of staff ... Mallory was all and everything: administrator and head of the navy, author and executor of naval strategy, and the man responsible for the conduct of maritime and coastal operations."[51] Not only was Mallory responsible for coordinating everything, but he also lacked a real sounding board and trusted subordinate to assist him in carrying out myriad chores. With a trusted chief of staff, Secretary Mallory could have delegated routine decisions and matters and freed his mind for full consideration of naval strategic and tactical concerns. In developing strategies, the Confederate navy chief tended at times to be naïve and unrealistically hopeful. A levelheaded subordinate might have encouraged Mallory to further consider and justify issues with which he was struggling so that sound conclusions could be reached. Possibly, the lack of a chief of staff simply reflected Mallory's management style, or conceivably it demonstrated his inexperience in directing a large organization.

Now that Secretary Stephen Russell Mallory had organized a Confederate Navy Department, there remained the unenviable task of building a navy from nearly nothing. Commenting on the path the navy secretary was to follow, historian Virgil Carrington Jones wrote: "Someone has described the Confederate Navy as a classical Greek tragedy, citing that its ships were born in adversity, nurtured on noble aspirations, and overwhelmed by irresistible odds."[52] That is an appropriate characterization.

Initially, the only nucleus of a southern navy was the steamer *Fulton* that had been captured in dry dock at Pensacola. She was a side-wheeler that was not seaworthy and would require an expenditure of at least $10,000 for repairs to get her into service by August 1. By late March, the Confederate navy consisted of the *Fulton* in dry dock, a second steamer and a tug, each armed with a single cannon; five revenue cutters carrying a total of nine guns; and two unarmed vessels.[53] Furthermore, the South lacked a merchant marine to engage in commercial trade and meet the Confederacy's need for manufactured goods.

This core of a southern navy was hardly a threat, even to a badly disorganized and relatively impotent Union navy. Author, historian, and former Confederate states navy officer J. Thomas Scharf has written, "The United States naval register of 1861 shows a total of 90 vessels, of which number 21 are designated as unserviceable, 27 available but not in commission, and 42 in commission; there were distributed to the home squadron 12 vessels...."[54] The remaining commissioned ships were stationed around the globe. However, the United States would react rapidly to strengthen its fleet.

Secretary Stephen Mallory's first job was to determine the type of sea power required for the task ahead. The naval committee of the provisional Congress had indicated that ships were needed only for cooperation with the army to protect rivers and harbors.[55] Building wooden vessels for even this limited scope was problematic because the South had little seasoned timber available. There were few skilled and able-bodied workmen available for cutting and trimming standing trees and fitting planks together. Other resources were lacking as well. Little hemp was available and few rope-works existed for manufacturing cordage. There were not enough iron and rolling mills available in the South to construct ironclad vessels. The only naval yard in the South was at Pensacola, but it was useless because Union forces controlled exit from and entry into Pensacola Bay through the occupation of Fort Pickens. Mallory recognized that he might be able to buy ships throughout the Confederacy, but the agrarian South had relatively few vessels available when compared to the North with its rich nautical heritage. Mallory thought that purchasing and building ships in England and France might be possible because he judged these nations would be sympathetic to the southern cause. The secretary concluded that the South could not successfully produce a counterpart to the North's naval force by attempting to match individual ships. He believed his best hope for defeating his opponent was to manufacture new and powerful types of vessels.[56]

While a United States senator, Stephen Mallory had strengthened the U.S. Navy, the same entity that he was now poised to try to destroy. In the U.S. Senate on April 2, 1852, he had referred to the "Stevens Battery" in New York Harbor and had proposed constructing a similar floating battery clad with iron boilerplates. In 1854 Senator Mallory had studied the progress of the British and French when they introduced ironclads into their fleets and he recommended that the U.S. Navy also use armor-clad warships. During this era, navies of leading world powers were in a state of transition. Motive power was changing from sail to steam engines driving screw propellers. The existence of wooden ships was threatened by the development of ships armored with iron.

On April 26, 1861, Mallory delivered his first Report of the Secretary of the Confederate Navy. He opened with a summary of progress made in procuring vessels for the navy. He added, "The expediency and policy of purchasing rather than building vessels at this time are obvious." He said it would take 12 to 18 months to build these vessels and that construction could commence after necessary preparations were made; while these preparations were underway, it would be desirable to purchase vessels.

The navy secretary proposed moving on to a bold new vista in the midst of a situation where initially his enemy would have complete mastery of the sea. Building on his past experience and knowledge of European efforts regarding ships clad in armor, he made this dramatic statement:

> I propose to adopt a class of vessels hitherto unknown to naval services. The perfection of a warship would doubtless be a combination of the greatest known ocean speed with the greatest known floating battery and power of resistance; and such a combination has been diligently but vainly sought, with but little regard to cost, by Great Britain and France. Vessels built exclusively for ocean speed, at a low cost, with a battery of one or two accurate guns of long range, with an ability to keep the sea upon a long cruise and to engage or to avoid an enemy at will, are not found in their navies, and only to a very limited extent in that of the United States, the speed and power of whose ships are definitely known. The latter power has built a navy; we have a navy to build; and if in the construction of the several classes of ships we shall keep constantly in view the qualities of those ships which they may be called to encounter we shall have wisely provided for our naval success.[57]

This section of Mallory's report hinted at three new concepts. First, "greatest known ocean speed" referred to a very strong steam plant perhaps driven by twin screws for maneuverability and speed. Second, "greatest known floating battery" referred to rifled (instead of smoothbore) cannon of larger calibers coupled with improved iron making. Third, "power of resistance" referred to the plating on the outside of the wooden frame.

Mallory had suggested in his report the intent to develop a new class of ironclad warships that floated low in the water due to their weight, and clad with thick iron protection that was angled to more effectively deflect ordnance fired at them. Finally, he included a caveat that was important because it predicted the ultimate failure of the Confederate navy. He suggested it would be necessary for the South to construct vessels that could counter the qualities of the enemy's ships. This was precisely what the South could not do. The North's resources and industrial might, along with its seagoing heritage, permitted the Union to build corresponding vessels—often in greater numbers—to respond to newly launched Confederate ships more quickly than the South could react. Time after time, the Confederacy either would have to put a vessel into battle before it was completely finished, or would have to destroy it before it was ready for battle because of the opponent's countermeasures.

Complicating the picture was the fact that early in the war the navy would be viewed as largely superfluous. The South anticipated an abbreviated conflict, and if the Confederacy did not win the war in 90 days, certainly Europe would intervene and come to the aid of the South. This expectation was reflected in funding for the war. Between February 1861 and August 1862, the Confederate Congress appropriated over $347 million, but less than $15 million of that sum was designated for the navy.[58] Even though Congress during later months frequently was responsive to Mallory's needs, this meager appropriation delayed purchasing or building ships.

Before the war had begun, the Confederate navy chief had explored the possibility of purchasing suitable vessels in the Confederacy, the North, and Canada. In mid–February 1861 Raphael Semmes, who had resigned his commission with the United States Navy, traveled to Montgomery to offer his services to the South. He visited President Davis who then sent him to northern states to purchase materials and hire mechanics to manufacture ordnance. While in the North he witnessed Lincoln's inauguration, and purchased percussion caps, light artillery, thousands of pounds of powder, and other munitions. In New York City, Semmes received a letter from Stephen Mallory dated March 13, 1861. Mallory asked that in addition to duties he was performing for the president, could he also purchase two or more appropriate steamers to be used for defense of the southern coast? Semmes searched but was unable to find suitable ships, primarily because such vessels had been obtained by the Union in anticipation of war.[59]

A few days later, on March 17, 1861, Secretary Mallory sent a team of navy officers to New Orleans to acquire any serviceable vessels that might be converted into auxiliary cruisers. Capt. Lawrence Rousseau headed this team but the results were disappointing. They were able to purchase only two small vessels, the *Habana* (that would become the *Sumter*) and the *Marquis de la Habana* (that would become the *McRae*). Ultimately the *Sumter* was placed under the command of Raphael Semmes and he selected Lt. John M. Kell as his second in command. They went on to fame in the *Sumter* and later in the fast ocean cruiser *Alabama*, which was built in England for the Confederacy.[60]

On April 17, 1861, Commander Semmes met with Secretary Mallory and offered his views on interrupting the Union's commerce. He suggested targeting their maritime trade because he believed the North's strength arose from its wealth; destroying its commercial shipping could enervate the enemy. Raphael Semmes wrote:

> Wealth is necessary to the conduct of all modern wars, and ... the enemy's chief source of wealth ... [was] a commercial marine that was second only to that of Great Britain.... It became an object of the first necessity ... to strike at his commerce. I enlarged upon this necessity, in the interview I was now holding with Mr. Mallory, and I was gratified to find that ... [he] agreed with me fully in opinion.

Mallory then began to search for a man who might acquire vessels in Great Britain that could be used to destroy United States commercial shipping.[61]

The navy secretary's life was about to become intertwined with that of James Dunwoody Bulloch, whom he would choose as his purchasing agent in England. Bulloch was born near Savannah, Georgia, on June 25, 1823, and joined the United States Navy at the age of 16. After a successful career, he resigned in 1853 to pursue work in private shipping. He was hired by the Cromwell Steamship Line and commanded the mail steamer *Bienville* that sailed between New York and New Orleans. The ship was berthed in New Orleans when the Civil War commenced. He decided to go with the South, but as a man of honor, Bulloch determined that he must return *Bienville* to her rightful owners in New York. On April 13, 1861, he wrote a letter to Confederate attorney general Judah P. Benjamin offering his services to the South and sailed back to New York in command of the *Bienville*.[62] Bulloch arrived there on April 22 and the next morning he found a letter to him from Benjamin. It read, "The Secretary of the Navy desires you to come to Montgomery without delay."[63] When Bulloch arrived at Mallory's office in Montgomery on May 8, 1861, the secretary said, "I want you to go to Europe. When can you start?" In his postwar memoirs, Bulloch says he was taken aback by this announcement of a foreign mission but he responded, "I have no impedimenta, and can start as soon as you explain what I am to do."[64] Bulloch summarized Mallory's review of the mission: "It was thought to be of prime importance to get cruisers at sea as soon as possible, to harass the enemy's commerce, and to compel him to send his own ships-of-war in pursuit, which might otherwise be employed in blockading the Southern ports."[65] Mallory detailed the type of vessels he was seeking and how they might be obtained. He then asked Captain Bulloch to go to his hotel, fully consider the matter, make such notes that would be necessary to help him memorize details, and return to his office the next day.

When Bulloch returned the next morning, Mallory examined the notes Bulloch had prepared and expanded his thinking on certain matters. Concerning getting ships out of Europe, Mallory related his expectation that the European powers would recognize the Confederate government and grant to Confederate cruisers that same shelter and privileges conceded to all belligerents by all nations. The secretary added that the Confederacy would need to respect laws of neutrality, including England's Foreign Enlistment Act and any neutrality proclamation that might be issued. Mallory impressed upon his agent the need to act with haste and granted him wide discretionary powers. He provided Bulloch with details of financing and persons whom he was to contact.[66]

James D. Bulloch destroyed his notes so his mission would not be compromised should he be arrested. He arrived safely in Liverpool, England, in early June. On the day Bulloch had departed from the secretary's office, Mallory wrote a letter to him confirming that he was to purchase or build six steam vessels driven by propellers. Speedy execution of the directive was expected. Mallory defined the purpose of these vessels:

> The class of vessels desired for immediate use is that which offers the greatest chances of success against the enemy's commerce ... our ships must be enabled to keep the sea, and to make extended cruises ... they shall be no larger than may be sufficient to combine the requisite speed and power, a battery of one or two heavy pivot guns and two or more broadside guns, being sufficient against commerce.[67]

In his letter, Secretary Mallory specified that Bulloch was to engage in financial arrangements with "some well known and established English commercial house ... and seek their cooperation...." The Secretary concluded his letter with a "shopping list" of war materiel that was to be sent back to the Confederacy on the swiftest available ship. On June 4, 1861, the agent called upon the commercial house Fraser, Trenholm and Company, and obtained from their local agent, Charles K. Prioleau, a line of credit he could use.[68] Within a month Bulloch had purchased a quantity of naval supplies and had arranged for the first keel of a foreign-built Confederate cruiser to be laid (ultimately she would named the *Florida*).[69]

On May 10, 1861, Secretary Mallory followed up on the section of his April Report to the president pertaining to the adoption of a new class of vessels when he wrote to Charles M. Conrad, chairman, Committee on Naval Affairs. In this message, the secretary explained the resistance of iron plates to heavy ordnance that was tested in 1845. He also described the success of the British during the Crimean War in reducing a fort in 1855 using vessels clad in iron that were undamaged by return fire from the fort. He noted that in 1857 France began constructing 10 ironclad ships, and he discussed the qualities of one of these ships, the *Gloire*. After citing the successes of England and France in developing ironclads, Mallory promoted the value of such vessels over that of wooden ships. He wrote, "I regard the possession of an iron-armored ship as a matter of the first necessity. Such a vessel at this time could traverse the entire coast of the United States, prevent all blockades, and encounter, with a fair prospect of success, their entire Navy." He contended that should the Confederacy try to match the Union navy wooden ship by wooden ship, they could not succeed, but that using iron to fight against wood could compensate for the inequality of numbers. Mallory added that an agent of the Navy Department would go to England soon to purchase vessels of the type recommended.[70]

One week later, Mallory wrote a letter to Lt. James H. North, directing him to proceed to England where he was to call upon Confederate officials and agents regarding obtaining vessels clad in iron. Specifically, Mallory called North's attention to the French frigate *Gloire* that "is regarded as the most formidable ship afloat." He suggested that other armored frigates of this class might be available for sale or might be constructed in France for the Confederacy. The secretary stated that the Confederacy needed two of these ironclads, each armed with six or eight guns. Mallory wrote, "We want a ship which can not be sunk or penetrated by the shell or shot of the U.S. Navy at a distance at which we could penetrate and sink the ships of the enemy, and which can not be readily carried by boarders." North was instructed to provide ordnance for the guns and to work in concert with Bulloch.[71]

Mallory obtained the necessary financing for both types of vessels. For the six steamships that Bulloch was to obtain, Mallory secured an appropriation of $1 million; for the two ironclads that North was to obtain he secured an appropriation of $2 million.[72] The secretary picked the right man for obtaining cruisers in England. James Bulloch was an exceptional and energetic man who served the Confederacy splendidly throughout the Civil War. But Mallory's judgment turned out to be poor in picking James North to obtain the ironclads. North lacked initiative. After making some cursory examinations of an ironclad frigate in England, he went to France where he failed to find a suitable vessel. Of this trip, historian Raimondo Luraghi caustically comments, "What North accomplished in France other than acting as a tourist is not clear."[73]

Meanwhile the politically important state of Virginia had come into the Confederacy. That state's secession was not official until a referendum had been ratified on May 23, 1861. However, this was a mere formality because Virginia had effectively joined the Confederate States of America on April 27. Ten days later Virginia invited the Confederate government to make Richmond its permanent capital. That offer was eagerly accepted because of Virginia's large population, crucial resources, her heritage, and a wish to solidify the Confederacy.

On May 31 President Davis signed an act relocating the capital to Richmond. On that date, Mallory arrived in Montgomery by train from Pensacola and stopped long enough to buy some dresses for Mrs. Mallory. He departed on the evening train and reached the new Confederate capital on June 3.[74] The next day he moved into his new office in the old Mechanic Institute at Franklin and Ninth streets. This structure came to be known as the War Department Building. The official government guide offered a quaint description directing a visitor to the secretary's office on the second floor: "right hand side. Enter through Chief Clerk's office, last door but one...."[75]

Mallory's wife and three children probably did not immediately join him in Richmond, but there is evidence they were there by 1862. His fourth child, Margaret ("Maggie"), had married Henry R. Bishop and was living in Bridgeport, Connecticut. In November 1861, Union officials became concerned that private correspondence between the Mallory family and Margaret constituted a security risk. She was living in Yankee territory and mail service had been cut off between the South and the North. Nevertheless, Mallory family mail was passing through the Baltimore, Maryland, Post Office. On November 29, 1861, the consummate showman, P.T. Barnum who was a concerned neighbor, wrote a letter to Secretary of War Simon Cameron from his home in west Bridgeport, Connecticut, saying, "Mrs. Bishop is in constant correspondence with her parents and their letters are mailed to her in Baltimore." In response, Assistant Secretary of State F.W. Seward wrote to Maj. Gen. John A. Dix in Baltimore forwarding Barnum's information. He requested, "Will you please adopt such measures for the suppression of this correspondence as in your judgment are necessary and proper?"[76]

Apparently, Mrs. Bishop was a loyal southerner while living in the North. Perhaps an open display of her loyalty occasioned Mr. Barnum's letter to Washington. Her mother reported:

> When the war broke out a friend sent her a pretty little confederate flag. She hung it over her étagère in her parlor, this pretty souvenir that had run the enemy's lines without being confiscated. Some Yankee soldiers heard that she had the flag displayed in her parlor and demanded its surrender. She bravely replied that her home was her castle and she could do what she pleased within it. That night her home in Bridgeport was burned to the ground.[77]

Stephen Mallory necessarily pushed aside any concerns he might have had about Maggie's safety and concentrated upon the demands of his job.

7

Ironclad Victories and Defeats

Immediately after his March 1861 confirmation as Confederate Navy secretary, Stephen Mallory defined the navy's role and enunciated his strategy for control of the seas and interior waterways of the South. He concluded that he could not counter the immense resources of the North by matching individual wooden ships, but instead knew that his best chance of defeating the Union fleet was to develop armor-clad warships. Building upon his knowledge of ancient Roman galleys and early European experiments with warships and floating batteries plated with iron, he conceived of a powerfully propelled ironclad ship that was capable of sinking her enemy by ramming or use of cannon fire.

Secretary Mallory began to implement this strategy when the South occupied the fine facilities of the Gosport Navy Yard at Norfolk, Virginia, that had been abandoned by Federal forces and then occupied by Southern troops on April 21, 1861. He arranged for employment of a large labor force at the yard for preparing ammunition for captured guns and distributing them to states. He also authorized the establishment of a naval laboratory and a machine shop. The secretary ordered the purchase of a Nasmith hammer to enable completion of naval steam engines that were in short supply.[1]

During early June 1861, Mallory held discussions with John Mercer Brooke, John Luke Porter, and William P. Williamson concerning the construction of a great ironclad, heavily armed, and capable of propelling herself rather than being towed. By June 23, John M. Brooke had completed preliminary drawings of such a vessel. Mallory approved Brooke's drawings, rather than a competing design that had been submitted by naval constructor John L. Porter; he directed Porter to draft detailed drawings. Brooke and Williamson went to Norfolk the next day to find machinery for the proposed ironclad. They could find nothing suitable, but Williamson examined the engines of the burned *Merrimack* and found them to be in good condition. The idea of converting the *Merrimack* to the desired ironclad was conceived at this point, and on July 11, 1861, Mallory ordered that the conversion commence immediately.[2]

In organizing leadership for the vessel's construction, Mallory made a major error by dividing the conversion responsibilities among the three men and placing no one person in charge of the project. John Porter was in charge of construction, William

Williamson overhauled the machinery, and John Brooke remained in Richmond to supervise the preparation of the armor and armament. This arrangement caused discord, especially between Porter and Brooke. Brooke was the designated liaison officer who made inspection visits and suggested alterations to Porter who was irked, perhaps because the Brooke design had been selected over his design or because Brooke, an equal, was in effect supervising his work. The animosity increased later when serious weaknesses were discovered in the vessel when it became operational. All of this could have been avoided had the secretary appointed a line officer to be totally responsible for the project with the naval constructor in charge of actual construction. Mallory did not make this error again.[3]

John M. Brooke was responsible for the iron plates and the acquisition of heavy guns.[4] Mallory was about to spring his technological surprise for the enemy: arming the vessel with heavy ordnance. The armament that was devised and prepared by Brooke consisted of "guns of a class never before made, and of extraordinary power and strength."[5] The ironclad would be named the *Virginia*. The new rifled gun developed by Brooke was first used in battle aboard the *Virginia* in its famous engagement with the *Monitor*.

Mallory signed the order for initial production of the Brooke Gun by Tredegar Iron Works on September 21, 1861, and followed it on October 31 with an order for 12 more guns. Later, Mallory wrote James Bulloch in England:

> Our ordnance experiments have been useful and interesting, and we have demonstrated beyond question the great superiority, of banded guns over those not banded.... In strength, accuracy, and range it is superior to all of our guns.[6]

By summer 1861, the Federal government was strengthening the blockade by interdicting shallow draft vessels being used to transfer war and civilian goods from major Confederate ports to nearby coastal and riverine locations. From this activity, Union strategy evolved of opening new land fronts upon southern coastlines and inland waters. Federal strategists now became determined to launch invasions by sea and establish second fronts. Because of its location near Hampton Roads and Fort Monroe where the Federal home fleet was located, the primary target area was the outer banks of North Carolina and waters behind those barrier islands. From there the Union planned to move southward and seize locations for establishing supply depots and coaling stations.[7]

In his first four months in office, Mallory had strengthened defenses of the South Carolina–Georgia coastline where he anticipated that Federal forces might attack. For the defense of that area, Mallory had purchased and equipped four steamers; contracts had been made with local builders to construct gunboats, each with three heavy guns, to support the steamers. He had also purchased five small armed steamers from the State of North Carolina to defend shallow coastal waters.

In anticipation of a Union attack, Secretary Mallory intended to use ironclads as the prime defensive measure. Matthew Fontaine Maury disagreed with the secretary. Maury still harbored ill feelings toward Mallory because of his role in the Naval Retiring Board before the war when he was threatened with retirement from the Federal navy. He rejected Mallory's defense and championed a scheme to use small, fast gunboats, armed with a large pivot-mounted gun, to overrun Union vessels and damage or destroy them. Maury believed they would be more effective than Mallory's slow ironclads, would be more maneuverable in shoal waters, and would not require a large expenditure of money and resources. Maury's boats would come to be known as the Mosquito Fleet.

With the support of his political backers in the Confederate Congress, Maury was able to get his plan approved. It was decided that the gunboats would be used to defend Hatteras Inlet. This was an important strategic location because from here there was access to the Dismal Swamp Canal that led to Norfolk and the Gosport Navy Yard.[8]

The U.S. Navy first struck at Hatteras Inlet on August 27, 1861, and gained control of Pamlico Sound. Six gunboats of the Mosquito Fleet under the command of Flag Officer Samuel Barron were brushed aside without difficulty; Barron was taken prisoner, and Fort Hatteras and neighboring Fort Clark surrendered. With the easy defeat of the Mosquito Fleet and its commander a prisoner of war for the next two years, Mallory's concept of using ironclad gunboats was strengthened.[9]

The Federal amphibious group gained control of nearby Ocracoke Inlet and then struck South Carolina. The initial amphibious expedition off that coast consisted of 51 ships and over 12,000 troops. Federal forces seized Port Royal and Beaufort in November 1861. A similar expedition seized Roanoke Island in North Carolina in February 1862 and defending Confederate vessels were destroyed at Elizabeth City. On March 14, 1862, Union forces seized New Bern on the Neuse River in North Carolina, threatening the interior of that state. A Federal military group then laid siege to Fort Pulaski protecting Savannah, Georgia. That fort surrendered on April 11. In March 1862 Federal operations commenced in north Florida when Fernandina, Jacksonville, and St. Augustine were occupied by Union troops.[10]

Clearly these United States amphibious operations overwhelmed meager defending forces in the coastal areas, opening a new front in the war and threatening invasion of the southern interior by sea and river. Suddenly there loomed the possibility of a Federal strike toward the Norfolk, Virginia, area, jeopardizing urgent Confederate naval construction at Gosport Naval Yard. The negative impact upon the morale of southern citizens was significant. Those living near the sea could never be sure when another invasion fleet might appear on the horizon. As a result there was a mixture of fear and panic resulting in Southrons fleeing toward the interior. The Confederate response was to place the coasts of East Florida, Georgia, and South Carolina into a military department under the command of Gen. Robert E. Lee, who strengthened fortifications around major port cities, obstructed waterways leading into the interior, and withdrew Confederate troops to an inner defensive line to position them out of range of Union Navy guns.[11]

The Confederate navy chief revised his strategic planning in light of the success of Federal forces. He came to realize that the most important role for the Confederate navy at this point was coastal defense; if the Federals were to follow up they could open additional fronts and threaten the very existence of Confederate armies. He reasoned that this operation was more important than breaking the blockade and thereafter he focused on coastal defense. It is likely that he and General Lee discussed Lee's reduction of his defensive perimeter. Subsequently, Mallory took similar action. As time went on and as more Confederate ironclads were commissioned, the coastal defense strategy produced an unanticipated benefit. That plan, which increased protection of major port cities, succeeded in sealing off remaining Confederate ports from seaward attack making them more defensible. In a sense, the rebels had developed a counter-blockade to maintain the status quo and prevent blockading vessels from making incursions into the South's open ports, and it was successful. The ports of Charleston, Savannah, and Wilmington were not entirely closed until they were threatened (or occupied) by Sherman's troops approaching from their overland route late in the war.[12]

Stephen Mallory was most concerned about United States amphibious operations in North Carolina for many reasons, the most important of which was the threat against Norfolk where the *Merrimack* was being converted to the *Virginia*. In the fall of 1861, when attacks were launched on the outer banks of North Carolina, the *Virginia* had been under construction for about three months. Building delays irked the Confederate navy chief and he put 1,500 men to work on the ironclad to preserve his head start on the Union. In daily messages he urged the men to speed up the task, and insisted that work be continued at night and on Sundays. He recognized that his most potent enemy was not money, but time. The secretary anticipated that the Union would, at some point, react swiftly to harness its industrial might for construction of countermeasures. Before time ran out, he needed to get his "ultimate weapon" in action.

There were a host of delays. The engines that were raised with *Merrimack* required extensive repair. Iron sheets could be rolled only in one-inch thickness and they had to be piled on top of one another to produce three inches of protection. Testing of that sheathing revealed that it could not withstand the impact of projectiles that might be fired at it. There was further delay as the Tredegar Iron Works revised its equipment to make two-inch plates. The southerners ran out of iron and began searching for scrap iron. The inadequate railroad system could not transport iron products to Norfolk in a timely manner because of a shortage of engines and cars. In addition, rails were beginning to wear due to heavy use. The innovative new muzzle-loading rifled gun required extensive testing and suitable ammunition had to be developed. Finally, there were problems recruiting sailors to man the *Virginia*.[13] These delays continued into February as boilers were installed and workers skilled in affixing iron plate were impressed. Ammunition was slow to arrive and engine lubricating oil was hard to find. Finally, *Virginia* was commissioned and launched on February 17, 1862. One week later she had her commanding officer, Capt. Franklin Buchanan, who also was given the rank of flag officer in command of the James River Squadron.[14]

The order from Mallory to Buchanan to take command of the *Virginia* revealed Mallory's strategic and tactical thinking. He wrote, "The *Virginia* is a novelty in naval construction, is untried, and her powers unknown, and the Department will not give specific orders as to her attack upon the enemy. Her powers as a ram are regarded as very formidable, and it is hoped that you may be able to test them.... [E]ven without guns the ship would be formidable as a ram." Then the secretary inserted a pipe dream: "Could you pass Old Point and make a dashing cruise on the Potomac as far as Washington, its effect upon the public mind would be important to the cause." Mallory stressed the importance and urgency of the coming action saying, "The condition of our country, and the painful reverses we have just suffered, demand our utmost exertions, and convinced as I am that the opportunity and the means of striking a decided blow for our Navy are now for the first time presented, I ... know that your judgment and gallantry will meet all just expectations. Action-prompt and successful action — now would be of serious importance to our cause...."[15]

Mallory viewed the ironclad vessel as the single weapon he might develop that would have a chance to even the odds against a resource-superior enemy. He saw the ironclad as an ultimate weapon that could win the war. But Mallory's idea of making "a dashing cruise on the Potomac" was an illusion that avoided reality. The *Virginia* could not cruise to Washington because the vessel's draft exceeded the depth of the Potomac River. Also, it was unreasonable to expect the ship to be unmolested throughout its journey. Furthermore, iron could conquer wood just as long as the enemy had only wood. If enemy forces countered with iron, the odds changed. Historian Jay W. Simson puts it succinctly: "any weapon is an ultimate weapon if only one side is so equipped."[16] In time the Federal government, because of its immense resources and industrial strength, quickly defended itself with similar ironclads.

The secretary was aware that the Federal ironclad *Monitor* was coming south and it became necessary for Mallory, the eternal optimist, to proffer the pipe dream because it supported his determination to avoid hopelessness. This private dream permeated his "ultimate weapon" philosophy by suggesting that an "ultimate blow" could be delivered by this powerful ship. The phrase, "Could you pass Old Point and make a dashing cruise" fits neatly into his philosophy that encompasses daydreams and hope. Stephen Mallory was a man who could nearly always see the silver lining around the darkest cloud; this premise had become a part of his being.

He continued similar thinking a few weeks later and this suggests how thoroughly unrealistic expectations of a rosy outcome were embedded in his psyche. On March 7, 1862, he wrote to Buchanan:

> I submit for your consideration the attack of New York by the *Virginia*. Can the *Virginia* steam to New York and attack and burn the city? ... Once in the bay, she could shell and burn the city and the shipping. Such an event would eclipse all the glories of the combats of the sea.... The Brooklyn ... navy yard and its magazines and all the lower part of the city would be destroyed, and such an event, by a single ship, would do more to achieve our immediate independence than would the results of many campaigns. Can the ship go there? Please give me your views.[17]

Buchanan replied that the *Virginia* would probably founder if she encountered a gale or a heavy swell because she was not seaworthy and was unable to operate on the high seas. He also felt that because of her draft *Virginia* would have difficulty crossing the bar off New York while under fire. He expressed concern that the ship might not withstand the fire of coastal batteries and following enemy vessels.[18]

Secretary Mallory did not follow through on either the Washington or New York raids, but that did not mean that his pipe dreams would be forgotten forever. Mallory implemented another idea based on fantasy on May 7, 1864, when he sent orders to Acting Master Thomas E. Hogg:

> You will proceed with the men under your command from Wilmington by the shortest and safest route to the port of Panama. At that port you will take passage on board either the *Guatemala* or *San Salvador*, the two Federal screw steamers trading between Panama and Realejo. After reaching the high seas you will ... capture the vessel in the name of the Confederate States.... Having secured the steamer, organized your crew, and hoisted the flag of the Confederate States, you will adopt prompt measures to arm your vessel and proceed to cruise against the enemy of the Pacific.... You will endeavor to strike a blow at the California trade and whalemen in the Pacific....[19]

This project barely began before it was discovered and terminated. By November 9, 1864, Thomas Hogg and his men had boarded the steamer *Salvador* in Panama Bay and the master of that vessel became suspicious. He notified H.K. Davenport, commanding the Federal warship U.S.S *Lancaster*, that men were aboard who intended to capture his ship after sailing into international waters. On November 11 Commander Davenport took Hogg and his six cohorts into custody for participating in this plot. They were imprisoned at Mare Island Navy Yard in California on January 1, 1865, and later were transferred in military custody to Fort Alcatraz, California, while awaiting trial by court-martial.[20] Stephen Mallory had exhibited a dramatic flair but this notion was impractical and failed.

Both sides knew the other was building some type of armor-clad warship. Although the Union navy headed by Gideon Welles was slow to respond, a contract for the construction of an ironclad was awarded on October 4, 1861. The industrialized North sprang into action and it was able to construct this innovative vessel expeditiously. Various shops and rolling mills produced the parts for the ship while the hull was being constructed in a shipyard. When the iron plate, turret, fittings, engines, bolts and nuts were available, they were brought to the finished hull in assembly-line order. The keel was laid on October 25, 1861, in Long Island, New York, three and one-half months after construction on the *Virginia* had commenced. On January 30, 1862, the Union vessel *Monitor* was launched on Long Island Sound. The fact that this vessel could be built in only 95 days strongly suggested there was no possible way the South could keep pace with the industrial resources of the North.[21] On February 20, 1862, Welles ordered the commander of the *Monitor*, Lt. John L. Worden, to proceed to Hampton Roads, Virginia.[22] Destiny was about to bring *Monitor* and *Virginia* together.

To meet the impending threat, Captain Buchanan had developed a combined army-navy plan designed to deny the James River waters to the Union. Three coordinated actions were planned. The *Virginia* would strike from Norfolk toward the mouth of the James River, a small Confederate squadron in the upper James River would sail down to join the ironclad, and Gen. John Magruder would move overland against the enemy positions at Newport News.[23] The plans did not work out because of lack of a unified command structure. General Magruder was never enthusiastic about the operation and simply refused to participate, citing bad road conditions. Because of a gale, the Confederate squadron remained anchored six miles upstream and arrived late. Buchanan was not deterred by the turn of events because he was aware from newspaper accounts that the *Monitor* was sailing south toward Hampton Roads. He needed to destroy the Union fleet before the *Monitor* could interfere.

Virginia descended the Elizabeth River toward the enemy in midmorning on March 8, 1862. The *Monitor* would not arrive in the vicinity for one more day, giving the *Virginia* a small window of opportunity to validate Mallory's thesis that an ironclad could shatter a wooden fleet. The *Virginia* was destined to become the most celebrated vessel in Confederate naval history. The Union sloop of war *Cumberland* was the first to literally feel the strength of the *Virginia*. She was rammed and quickly sank. Steaming up the James River, the *Virginia* sank two transports and seriously damaged the frigate *Congress*, which was beached. Finally, the ironclad heavily damaged the steamer *Minnesota*, but broke off the action as evening descended. The ironclad *Virginia* had engaged and decimated a Federal wooden fleet by gunfire and ramming while suffering only minor damage. She had made naval history by not being limited to acting as a floating battery.[24]

That first days' work demonstrated that Secretary Mallory was clearly on the right track when insisting upon purchasing or building a fleet clad in iron to counter overpowering numbers of Federal wooden ships. Confederates were elated by the havoc wrought by the ironclad. On the Union side, there was panic and dejection. A huge explosion shortly after midnight finalized the first engagement between an ironclad and a wooden fleet. The *Congress* had continued burning after the battle and shattered the night "with such a deafening, terrible crash that windows miles away trembled, sending a gigantic plume of flames to an incredible height, like the eruption of a volcano."[25]

The next morning the *Monitor* arrived to confront the *Virginia* in the first engagement between two ships clad in iron. The vessels battled and battered each other for four hours, but neither could sink the other. Armor had triumphed over the gun. The two giants called it a day and withdrew. These two days made wooden fleets obsolete and the two armored vessels became the prototypes for the great battleships of World War II.[26]

The *Virginia-Monitor* engagement had demonstrated the superiority of iron over wood and the need to develop better guns to pierce iron plates. The Union had proven that it could quickly manufacture an ironclad and neutralize the southern ironclad. According to naval historians Raimondo Luraghi, Jay W. Simson, and William N. Still, Jr., the Confederacy had won a strategic victory at Hampton Roads because the *Virginia* thereafter dominated the waters and the *Monitor* declined to contest the area again as long as *Virginia* remained. Control of the James River by the Confederates altered Union general McClellan's plans for conduct of the Peninsular Campaign against Richmond.

The James River's waters remained firmly in Confederate hands for the war's duration and this fact contributed significantly to defense of the southern capital. Capturing Richmond was a principal goal of the Union from the beginning of the war. The *Galena*, the *Monitor*, and the *Naugatuck* were all Union naval vessels that attempted to take Richmond by sailing up the James River, but they could not get past Confederate gun emplacements at Drewry's Bluff to engage the James River Squadron. Ultimately that squadron consisted of the *Richmond, Fredericksburg, Virginia II,* and *Texas*. To these Mallory added the *Patrick Henry* (formerly *Yorktown*) and *Thomas Jefferson* (formerly *Jamestown*) that he had purchased from the State of Virginia.[27] These ships closed the back door to Richmond, but ironically they never fought a major battle. Their presence alone, coupled with the Drewry's Bluff guns, was a sufficient deterrent to keep the Union navy at bay.[28]

Confederate navy secretary Stephen Russell Mallory was elated over the outcome of the epic battle between the *Virginia* and the *Monitor* because it proved to him and the world the importance of vessels clad in iron, which he had believed in since his days as a United States senator. But now he was looking to the west. Mallory had become aware of strengthening Federal forces on the Mississippi River. The Union was massing ironclad gunboats to the north in the Cairo area and improving its blockade to the south at the mouth of the river. Because of his concern about the Federal buildup in the upper Mississippi River, he ordered Capt. Lawrence Rousseau to strengthen the defenses in that area. He authorized Rousseau to construct five gunboats, and to purchase four other steamers and armed barges to serve in conjunction with them.

In an undated memorandum, Mallory revealed the ambitious plans that he wanted implemented before the enemy could launch countermeasures. On May 14, 1861, he secured an appropriation for the construction of a large ironclad gunboat in New Orleans under the supervision of his agents there, Asa and Nelson Tift (Asa had been his friend from his early Key West days). The Tift brothers also were given a contract to build two smaller ironclads and John Hughes and Company of New Orleans was awarded a contract to assemble one armor-clad vessel. Additionally, Secretary Mallory had four more ironclads under construction at Norfolk and others were to be built at Savannah, Charleston, and New Orleans.[29]

Monitor and Virginia. The famous battle between the two ironclads, *Monitor* and *Virginia*, took place on March 9, 1862, and forever changed the face of naval warfare. In this painting by Raymond Bayless, the Confederate *Virginia* is in the foreground and the Federal *Monitor* is at the right rear. At the left, the Union vessel *Minnesota* is firing at the *Virginia*. COURTESY OF NAVAL HISTORICAL CENTER, NH 84512 KN, AND U.S. NAVY ART COLLECTION, DONATION OF RAYMOND BAYLESS, 1975.

The brothers had the novel idea that ordinary carpenters (not skilled ship carpenters that were in short supply) could be utilized to build a ship if she were built on straight lines with the four corners connecting at the ends. Nelson Tift fashioned a model of the ship that would become known as the *Mississippi*. The idea gained the approval of experts in the field, and the Tifts offered their services, without compensation, to the Confederate Navy Department. On August 26, 1861, Asa and Nelson Tift formalized the matter by submitting a letter to Secretary Mallory offering "to give to the Government the use of the invention and to superintend and direct, as your agents, the construction and completion of one or more vessels, without pecuniary compensation from the Government for our service, or any other reward than that which every citizen must feel who can, in any way, contribute to the defense of our country."[30] Mallory accepted the offer "with the conviction that an efficient ship, to drive off a blockading fleet, can be constructed on your plan for less money and in a shorter time than upon any plan hitherto devised, and that in her construction your services, thus patriotically tendered, will be important to the speedy and economical completion of the work." The secretary said his hope was that the vessel could be completed by December 15, 1861.[31] The ship would be a monster. She was to be 260 feet long, displacing 4,000 tons, carrying 20 guns including four 7-inch Brooke rifles, and propelled by a huge steam power plant.[32]

Asa and Nelson Tift went to work in New Orleans on September 18, 1861. That same day Mallory signed another contract for an ironclad ship with a well-known builder, E.C. Murray. He built his vessel in a yard adjacent to the Tift yard, and on occasion the two parties worked together. Murray's vessel, named the *Louisiana*, was to be smaller than the *Mississippi*. She was designed to displace 1,400 tons and be 264 feet long. Her armament was to be 16 guns including two 7-inch Brooke rifles. The projected delivery date was January 25, 1862. The combined cost of the *Louisiana* and the *Mississippi* was estimated to be in excess of $600,000.[33]

While the two giant ironclads were being constructed, the Confederates became concerned about Federal gunboats that were concentrating at the junction of the Ohio and Mississippi rivers near Cairo, Illinois. In August 1861 an entrepreneur from Memphis, Tennessee, John T. Shirley, proposed building two ironclads in Memphis to parry forces to the north. He swiftly was awarded a contract to provide two vessels by December 24, 1861, at a cost of $76,920 each. They would be clad with railroad iron and would be 165 feet long. Their draft would be no more than eight feet and they would be fitted with rams weighing two tons.[34]

Navy secretary Mallory had begun to accumulate a formidable force that might be interposed between the enemy's vessels at Cairo and his blockading ships that had arrived at the mouth of the Mississippi River. He hoped he could keep waters in between free from Federal incursions, but he was a realist. He recognized that threatening U.S. Navy vessels were floating in water, while his ironclads were sitting on land. The imponderable question in Mallory's mind was that of time. Would there be time to get these southern warships in water?

Mallory was placing all his hopes on the four ironclads he was constructing on the Mississippi River, two at Memphis and two at New Orleans. In Memphis, contractor Shirley had to start by constructing a shipyard, putting together sawmills, felling and transporting timber, and acquiring railroad iron.[35] Shirley stated, "I sent to New Orleans, St. Louis, Mobile, and Nashville for ship carpenters, at considerable expense, with very little success. I applied to every commanding general for details of men, which were refused."[36] He asked Secretary Mallory to intercede in his behalf. The secretary wrote to the local commander, General Polk, on December 24, 1861: "The completion of the ironclad gunboat at Memphis by Mr. Shirley is regarded as highly important to the defenses of the Mississippi. May I ask, therefore, that you will extend to this Department the necessary aid? The men may be furloughed for this special service, and the highest current wages will be paid them."[37] General Polk's response was to send Shirley six men, when he needed hundreds. Although the go-ahead had been given to Shirley in August to build two ships named *Arkansas* and *Tennessee*, their construction did not commence until October 1861. Due to many problems, Shirley eventually gave up attempts to build two ships at once and concentrated on building the *Arkansas*. The *Tennessee* ultimately was destroyed at the work site.[38]

Meanwhile, on the lower Mississippi the Tift brothers and E.C. Murray were busy building their vessels in adjacent shipyards, which they too had to build from scratch, at Jefferson City on the Mississippi River near New Orleans. Murray was constructing the *Louisiana*; the Tifts, the *Mississippi*. Both contractors had problems similar to those encountered by Shirley in Memphis. There was an abundance of skilled workmen in the area's eight shipyards, but they were primarily employed in building small river gunboats.

Perhaps Mallory's lack of sensitivity to the local labor situation in New Orleans contributed to the delay in constructing the *Mississippi*. In November construction was halted due to a labor strike. The workers were striking for wages identical to those received by carpenters sent from Richmond by Mallory to work on the *Mississippi*. Although the Tifts agreed to the pay raise, the men continued to feel resentful because the government had not hired local workers to build the vessel. Furthermore, the strike had delayed construction for six days. Due to these disruptions, the secretary ordered Confederate station commanders at New Orleans to assume control of ship construction if the builders were not doing everything possible to expedite their completion. In late March 1862, Mallory directed Cmdr. Arthur Sinclair to assume command of the *Mississippi* when she was commissioned, and to aid the Tifts in completion of the ship. From that point on, station commanders supervised all naval construction.[39]

Murray's first tasks in building the *Louisiana* were to contract for 1.7 million cubic feet of lumber and to acquire engines, boilers, and shafts. There were problems from the beginning. The lumber contract originally was with a Florida firm but the Union blockade made it impossible to deliver the timber. The contract had to be revised in order to secure delivery from nearby sources. To obtain the hardware, Shirley had to buy a river steamer, *Ingomar*, and scavenge from her four engines and drive shafts. The drive shafts did not fit the new hull and others had to be built. Iron was difficult to get but he found 500 tons that had been seized by the Confederate government.[40]

By February 24, 1862, Mallory, who was concerned about slow progress in building *Louisiana*, wrote to Cmdr. John K. Mitchell, in command of the New Orleans Naval Station:

> The importance of having the ordnance and ordnance stores ready for the *Louisiana*, an ironclad vessel being built by Mr. Tift, in time, is apparent to you; and you will make all proper exertions to have guns and carriages ready. If they can not be finished in time otherwise, you will endeavor to stimulate the parties to work night gangs of men upon them.... You will keep the Department advised of everything connected with the subject which you may deem of interest, and every effort will be made here to facilitate your operations. You are relied upon for getting these batteries ready.[41]

The secretary wrote Mitchell again on March 15, 1862, urging him to see to the early completion of *Louisiana*. He added, "Not a day must be lost."[42]

In an adjacent yard, the Tift brothers began assembling necessary materials for constructing the *Mississippi* and had similar difficulty locating lumber. The required 2 million cubic feet slowly began to appear, and on October 14 the first section of the keel was laid. As was the case with Murray, the Tift brothers also encountered many delays, but the hull rapidly took shape because of the simplicity of its straight-line design and the fact that 600 men had been put to work. Multiple problems were encountered with mechanical and metal parts. It was difficult to find a firm that could manufacture engines in a timely manner and additional boilers had to be built to propel the huge boat. There were no local workmen who could shape the mold for casting propellers, and even simple items such as nuts and bolts had to be secured from sources throughout the South. There was no shop available to build the big central drive shaft. Ultimately a salvaged shaft was found and sent by ox-drawn wagons to Richmond where Tredegar Iron Works remodeled it. The army and navy competed with each other in securing from dwindling iron supplies the amounts needed for their important projects. These problems connected with building ironclad ships in the South produced waste, excessive expenditures, and delay. Naval historian Raimondo Luraghi correctly assesses the central reason for these numerous problems when he states, "Builders were hindered by the South's Achilles' heel, the veritable reason for its final defeat: the flimsiness and inferiority of its industrial plant."[43]

Secretary Mallory did his best to solve problems in constructing the *Mississippi*. He sent his chief engineer, James A. Warner, to New Orleans for an inspection. Warner determined that the propulsion power for the ironclad was inadequate and that more boilers were needed.[44] When Nelson and Asa Tift appealed to Mallory for help in casting the propellers, the secretary sent them the foreman of the Gosport Navy Yard, a blacksmith and two pattern makers to resolve the dilemma.[45] Mallory was involved with the Tift brothers on at least a weekly basis in 1862 through exchange of telegrams and letters as he assisted them in dealing with a host of problems.[46]

At the same time Mallory was coping with other issues. Federal forces were on the move in the north. Fort Donelson fell on February 17, 1862; Nashville, Tennessee, fell a few days later; the Confederate defenses at Columbus, Kentucky, had to be evacuated on February 28; and on April 7 the Federal capture of Island No. 10 opened the Mississippi River as far south as Memphis. Confederate intelligence agents who had gotten jobs in Federal shipyards at St. Louis sent reports to Mallory "of an imminent movement of the enemy in force down the Mississippi against New Orleans."[47] Many Confederate military and civil officials feared such a move from the north; a number of Union captain Farragut's own officers believed forts to the south of New Orleans could not be passed. Mallory correctly assessed that an attack was coming, but he thought it would come from the north. His judgment proved to be wrong, but he correctly perceived that there was an urgent need for the ironclads under construction at New Orleans to be finished.[48] To this end Secretary Mallory spared no effort. He wrote the Tift brothers on March 11, 1862, regarding the *Mississippi* saying, "You will please urge on the completion of the ship you are building with all dispatch. Can you not induce night and Sunday work?"[49]

In the east, Federal troops began moving toward the peninsula between the James and York rivers in Virginia for their first assault on Richmond. Mallory was feeling this pressure and was anticipating a need to abandon Norfolk when he wrote to Capt. S.S. Lee, commanding the navy yard there. On April 24, 1862, the secretary wrote Captain Lee urging him to accelerate his work on another ironclad (*Richmond*) because the safety of Norfolk depended on its early completion. Captain Lee expressed concern about working at night as Mallory had suggested earlier. The secretary wrote in response:

> You think that the yard would be endangered by fire were men to work at night upon the *Richmond,* and you say that candles or open lamps would have to be used.... With an overwhelming force at your doors, and the prospect of losing Norfolk within twenty days distinctly before us, it will not do to limit the work upon this vessel to one-half this available time.... I think you will be able to find lanterns and to organize a corps of men, boys, or girls even, to hold them and thus enable the mechanics to work at night. If practicable it must be done.[50]

In Mallory's missives to the Tift brothers and to Captain Lee, we see a man who is feeling pressed from both east and west. Nevertheless, he remains determined to do all possible to block the enemy, if not defeat him. He also recognizes that his most precious commodity — time — is rapidly diminishing.

Meanwhile the secretary was making progress in fulfilling his ironclad program on the Mississippi River. On February 6, 1862, the *Louisiana* was launched. She made an impressive figure resting in the water for the first time and excited a huge crowd. Unfortunately she was unprepared for combat; she had no armor, no engines, no weapons, and no shafts. On March 2 Mallory appointed Cmdr. Charles F. McIntosh to take charge of the vessel and see to her completion. One major problem involved its weaponry. It was planned that *Louisiana* would be armed with four rifled guns and 12 smoothbore cannons made in New Orleans. The rifled guns proved to be unreliable, causing delay. Finally, four Brooke 7-inch rifled guns that were cast in Norfolk were made available to accompany 12 broadside smoothbore cannons.[51]

Problems with the central drive shaft resulted in agonizingly slow progress on the *Mississippi*. On March 15, 1862, Secretary Mallory shared the bad news with Asa and Nelson Tift when he wrote, "The Tredegar Works have disappointed us terribly. The shaft is not ready, and, although promised from day to day, may not be ready for a week.... Work night and day to get your ship done, without regard to expense."[52] The shaft was completed on March 22, but now it was learned there was no railroad car in the South that could transport the manufactured product. A special car had to be built. On March 24 the Tift brothers were advised that the shaft was being shipped on that date. Mallory sent them a telegram: "It is a beautiful piece of work. Strain every nerve to finish ship. Expend money to encourage mechanics if essential to speedy completion. Work day and night."[53]

The great central shaft finally arrived and its installation commenced on April 17. Cmdr. Arthur Sinclair was now in command of the ship and the secretary wrote him saying, "Every possible exertion must be made to complete her at the earliest moment."[54] The *Mississippi* was launched on April 19 but her upper works were unarmored, the central shaft was not connected to the engines, the engines were not fully installed, and several guns had not been placed in position. The Tift brothers thought she would be ready by May 10, 1862. However, on April 18 a Federal mortar boat fleet opened fire on the forts to the south of New Orleans.[55]

Mallory still believed the Union ironclads in the Cairo area were a more serious threat than those near New Orleans. Both he and President Davis expected the main attack to come from the north. They were convinced that Union navy secretary Welles would follow the Anaconda Plan developed by General Scott and descend the river toward New Orleans. Secretary Mallory believed forts defending New Orleans could deal with wooden ships coming upriver from the south, while Federal ironclad ships coming downriver from the north would need to be countered by the rebel ironclads *Louisiana* and *Mississippi*. However, Cmdr. George Hollins, who was in charge of the upriver flotilla, did not agree with Mallory and wished to bring his ships down to fight the Union fleet south of New Orleans.

As the Tifts and Murray were constructing their two giant ironclads, a smaller ironclad named the *Manassas* (formerly the *Enoch Train*) was being completed. Confederates had obtained this New Orleans tugboat and converted her to an iron-plated ram in fall 1861. She had been a New Orleans tugboat that was converted to an iron-plated ram. *Manassas* displaced 387 tons and was 134 feet long. She was armed with one 32-pounder carronade mounted on the bow.[56]

By the fall of 1861, Union blockading ships had gathered in large numbers at the mouth of the Mississippi River and the Confederates were determined to initiate a skirmish with them. On October 11, 1861, Lt. Alexander F. Warley seized the *Manassas*, which was under private ownership as a privateer, on behalf of the Confederate navy. Warley's ship was absorbed into Hollins's so-called "Mosquito Fleet," consisting of six lightly armed riverboats. In the early morning of October 12 the naval group struck the Union intruders. As was the case with most Confederate ironclads, the *Manassas* was underpowered and limited in maneuverability. Consequently she was mainly utilized as a ram and her first combat action was colliding with a Union warship. The ensuing fracas resulted in Union ships fleeing to the safety of the Gulf of Mexico, providing the Confederacy with its first naval victory. Five months before the *Virginia*'s success, the *Manassas* became the first Confederate ironclad to ram a Union warship and introduce the concept of "ram fever" into Northern lexicon.

After disagreement with military and civilian officials, Mallory relented and allowed the *Louisiana* to proceed to a worsening situation south of New Orleans. She was underway on April 20, but because of unfinished work on her propulsion system she could not be steered and was towed southward. During the night of April 23–24, Capt. David G. Farragut unleashed his attack on Fort St. Philip and Fort Jackson below New Orleans. The *Louisiana*, still unable to navigate and moored in the river near the forts, waited for the enemy to approach. Because she was stationary, the *Louisiana* was able to fire only six of her 16 guns at the passing Federal fleet, while the enemy's return fire bounced off her armor. The Union ships bypassed the *Louisiana* and proceeded to receive the surrender of New Orleans on April 25. In the meantime, work continued on the *Louisiana*. Her engines were connected to the screw propellers and she was ready to go into action. On April 28, however, troops in the two forts deserted and the vessel was deprived of supporting fire from the guns in these forts. The *Louisiana* was trapped with nowhere to go. It was doubtful that she could have penetrated the blockading fleet and escape to sea, and it was feared she would be captured by the enemy. That prospect was unacceptable; the *Louisiana* was scuttled.

Manassas also was engaged in the Battle of New Orleans. On April 24, 1861, she helped to defend forts below New Orleans. Lieutenant Warley successfully rammed the Union vessels *Mississippi* and *Brooklyn*, but a short time later, due to battle damage, *Manassas* caught fire, exploded and sank. She was one of the few ironclads destroyed in combat rather than being scuttled or destroyed by Confederates.[57]

Upriver, the Confederate *Mississippi* was still unfinished and had no propulsion system. It was decided to tow that vessel northward while workmen aboard labored on her. On April 24 two smaller ships attempted towing the *Mississippi* upriver but failed because of their insufficient power. Instead all three vessels slipped downstream, and the decision was made to let the current carry the ironclad toward New Orleans where she might engage in battle. Upon her arrival in the area, the *Mississippi* found confusion, defeat, panic, and the entire Union fleet waiting for her. To allow the vessel to fall into enemy hands was unthinkable; the executive officer, Lt. James I. Waddell, set the ship afire.

Stephen Mallory had lost most of his ironclad fleet in the Mississippi River; the *Mississippi* had been fired, the *Manassas* had exploded in combat, the *Louisiana* had been scuttled, and the *Tennessee* would be intentionally destroyed in June. Only the *Arkansas* remained to face the Federal flotilla. Mallory had run out of time and Farragut wrote, "We were too quick for them."[58]

It was not so much that Farragut was "too quick for them," but that the Confederates were too disorganized to establish an effective defense. The fragmented command structure is obvious when looking at assignments. Gen. Mansfield Lovell, who commanded land forces in New Orleans, wished to coordinate land and naval forces but he was informed by President Davis and the secretary of war that he had no authority over the navy. Furthermore, his authority over land forces did not extend beyond the New Orleans city limits. In addition he had asked the War Department for more troops and guns but Davis pulled these resources out of New Orleans for the Battle of Shiloh. Outer land defenses were the responsibility of Maj. Gen. Johnson Kelly Duncan. He and Lovell disagreed on how best to defend New Orleans. In January 1862, Lovell was instructed to seize 14 riverboats that would become the River Defense Fleet under army, not navy, control. To complicate matters, the Louisiana governor fitted out two small state-owned gunboats.

The Confederate navy structure was even more muddled. Between August 1861 and March 1862, there had been a revolving door of people commanding in New Orleans. Secretary Mallory first sent Lawrence Rousseau to buy ships on the Mississippi River. He met limited success and Commodore George N. Hollins replaced him. Mallory clashed with Hollins and Cmdr. John K. Mitchell took over on February 1, 1862. On March 29, 1862, Mallory ordered Cmdr. William C. Whittle to New Orleans as naval commandant. Roles and responsibilities were unclear. Whittle believed he was to be in command of the naval station exclusive of the vessels under Mitchell's command. It is not clear whether Mallory intended to divide the command or did not communicate clearly. With this turnover of key command personnel, it is no wonder that harmony was difficult to achieve.[59]

Close coordination was absolutely necessary when Confederate army and navy forces were defending river highways in the west. At New Orleans the two forces did not act in concert with each other. A vagueness in the Confederate command structure existed at the cabinet level where President Davis did not demand a close alliance between army and navy planners. This lack of collaboration permeated the local command. There were instances of lack of understanding as to mutual objectives. Awkwardness existed where naval officers were outranked by army officers; as a consequence, generals attempted to exercise control over naval units without having the requisite knowledge and understanding of naval operations.

A unified command would have improved the command structure, but there was no precedent for such an approach in Mallory's experience. He would have done well to imitate his enemy's organization. Union navy secretary Gideon Welles had commissioned Capt. Andrew Hull Foote on September 6, 1861, as flag officer of the Mississippi River Squadron, and he specified that naval operations were to be under command of the War Department. Flag Officer Foote, in close cooperation with Gen. Ulysses S. Grant, hammered Forts Henry and Donelson into submission in February 1862. That success produced a permanent unified command structure and close army-navy cooperation that Secretary Welles insisted upon. Secretary Mallory and President Davis never fully adopted this concept although later there were instances of close cooperation of the Confederate Navy Department with General Beauregard in Charleston and General Lee in Carolina coastal waters.[60]

No one person can be blamed for the loss of New Orleans because there was an abundance of condemnation to be collectively shared, but Secretary Mallory cannot be absolved from his miscues. It was Mallory who overruled his local naval commander, George N. Hollins, who had always argued that the Union attack would come upriver from the south. It was the secretary who decided the threat was from the north, not from the south, and the president concurred. As late as February 27, 1862, the New Orleans army commander, Gen. Mansfield Lovell, also subscribed to the view that the most urgent threat to the port city was from Union forces gathered in the north rather than those forming in Mississippi's delta.[61] It was Mallory who sent the Tift brothers to New Orleans rather than using local shipbuilders, and it was he, among others, who did not press strongly for close army-navy collaboration. And it was Mallory who did not place responsibility with a single individual for department teamwork with contractors, the City of New Orleans, and others.[62]

In fairness to Mallory, it needs to be stressed that he had multiple responsibilities, and much of his attention during this period was diverted toward the *Virginia* in the James River and Hampton Roads. Perhaps if he had organized the Navy Department with a chief of staff and had assigned that individual to go to New Orleans and unify command structure, improvements could have been made that would have led to a more effective fighting force. However, it is doubtful that this alone would have saved New Orleans because it would not have appreciably quickened completion of the ironclads. Without these fully functioning southern vessels, it is unlikely that Farragut's naval force could have been turned back.[63]

On the same day that New Orleans surrendered, there were still two Confederate ironclads upriver at Memphis. The work on the *Arkansas* was nearly complete, and Lt. Henry Kennedy Stevens had been appointed as her executive officer. Most of the armor had been attached, and her engines were on board, ready for installation. The other ironclad, *Tennessee*, was not as advanced in her construction. Planking was not complete, equipment was not aboard and, most importantly, iron with which she was to be clad was on the other side of the river. Only the *Arkansas* was immediately ready to defend Memphis.[64] Cmdr. Charles H. McBlair was concerned about the safety of the *Arkansas* and decided to immediately take his ship to the Yazoo River north of Vicksburg. He loaded necessary equipment on barges, and these along with the vessel were all towed to the Yazoo. The *Tennessee* was left to her fate at Memphis.[65]

In May, on the upper reaches of the Mississippi River, the Southern River Defense Fleet, consisting of eight gunboat-rams, had succeeded in ramming two Union ironclad gunboats, the *Cincinnati* and *Mound City*. These ships did not sink because of shallow water, but the South enjoyed a rare victory. Southern fortifications to the north had fallen to the Union, but the Confederacy decided to make a stand at Memphis. At sunrise on June 6, 1862, the Southern River Defense Fleet attacked five Union ironclads and four rams while Memphis residents watched the show. The Federal rams worked effectively, crippling Confederate vessels that were then further damaged by gunfire. Only one Confederate vessel escaped downriver. The Mississippi River was now open to the Union from Cairo, Illinois, to Vicksburg, Mississippi. In response to this fluid situation, the southern ironclad *Tennessee*, still on her slipway in Memphis, was burned and destroyed on June 5, 1862.[66]

On the Yazoo River, Commander McBlair did not make sufficient progress in finalizing construction of *Arkansas*, and on May 24, 1862, Secretary Mallory replaced him with Lt. Isaac N. Brown. Stephen Mallory told Brown to finish the ship, sparing no expense, and he did so utilizing civilian help at Yazoo City. By July she had become a formidable warship measuring 165 feet long, clad with iron more than four inches thick, and carrying 10 guns including two 8-inch Columbiads, two rifled 6-inch guns, and two 100-pounder Dahlgrens. On July 4 *Arkansas* passed her engine trials.[67]

In New Orleans, Captain Farragut had been ordered to advance upriver toward the strategic town of Vicksburg. On May 2 he sent a portion of his squadron to the north. His ships reached Vicksburg on May 18, but Farragut found the town too heavily defended to take with his existing force. He retired to the south but returned a month later with a stronger force consisting of 4,500 troops, 10 fieldpieces and Cmdr. David D. Porter's 17 mortar boats. By July 1 more reinforcements arrived and Union squadrons continued pounding the Vicksburg fortress with a barrage that had commenced June 27.[68]

The situation was looking grim for the Confederacy but there was a gleam of hope that an "ultimate weapon" might turn the tide. Perhaps the *Arkansas* could fill this role much as *Virginia* had done in the east? Gen. Earl Van Dorn had been placed in command of the army district encompassing south-central Mississippi and eastern Tennessee. On June 24 he requested of President Davis that the ironclad be removed from navy control and placed under his command. The president, anxious to prevent the fall of Vicksburg, consented even though Van Dorn knew little about naval strategies and tactics and overrated what the *Arkansas* could accomplish. Van Dorn sent a telegram dated June 27 in which he suggested that the *Arkansas* could run through the Union fleet and sink the transports. He closed by saying, "It is better to die game and do some execution than to lie by and be burned up in the Yazoo."[69]

The commander of the *Arkansas*, Lt. Isaac N. Brown, incensed by the tone of the telegram, said he would engage in battle when the ship was ready. On July 15 the vessel's preparations were completed and she passed into the Mississippi River with a mammoth assignment. The *Arkansas* was to break through Union squadrons then make for sea and her ultimate destination, the Confederate port of Mobile. Odds were heavily stacked against *Arkansas* but with a stroke of luck she surprised two Union squadrons at anchor 12 miles north of Vicksburg that were unready for combat. While steaming through this group she engaged them in an artillery duel and in 30 minutes reached the protection of Vicksburg's batteries. The *Arkansas* later was engaged in a night duel with eight Union vessels and on July 22 a Federal force made a final attack upon her. Yet Captain Farragut's force got the worst of it; they gave up trying to sink her and retired to New Orleans. Thus, in a remarkable effort, the *Arkansas* had caused the first major Union campaign against Vicksburg to fail and had opened 250 miles of the Mississippi River from Vicksburg to Port Hudson.

The Confederates were so exhilarated with their success that Van Dorn gave the *Arkansas* another important task. She was to sail at once to Baton Rouge, Louisiana, to support a southern land attack. On August 6, while the *Arkansas* was engaged in battle with the Union ship *Essex*, her heavily strained engines failed and she drifted aimlessly. The engines could not be repaired and the executive officer in command (Brown was on sick leave) could not permit the ship to fall into enemy hands. She was scuttled, set ablaze, and blew up. *Arkansas* was gone.[70] This marked the end of the five ironclads, Mallory's "ultimate weapons," in the Mississippi River.

Like the *Virginia* in the east, the *Arkansas* in the west had also achieved a strategic victory of sorts. With her run through the Federal fleet, she had delayed the fall of Vicksburg for a full year and enabled the Confederates to control a large segment of the Mississippi River. This in turn allowed the Trans-Mississippi Department to remain in contact with the rest of the Confederacy. In retrospect, it may have been ill advised to squander this precious resource. Naval historian Jay W. Simson speculates that if the *Arkansas* had remained at Vicksburg in a defensive role, she might have been able to prevent the crossing of Grant's army from the west to the east shore of the Mississippi in 1863.[71]

By May 11, 1862, Gosport Navy Yard was taken by the Union. It was a tragic loss to the Confederacy, which had no other shipyard comparable to this magnificent facility. Worst of all, the mighty *Virginia*, the ship that had contributed so much to the South and had changed naval warfare forever, was gone. Fearful that Union forces would capture her, Flag Officer Tattnall destroyed *Virginia* by fire on May 11, 1862, without any orders from Secretary Mallory. A court of inquiry later found that "The destruction of the *Virginia* was, in the opinion of the court, unnecessary at the time and place it was effected."[72]

The Navy secretary was devastated because the Confederacy had counted on these vessels to counter the overpowering strength of the Union. Mallory's gambit had been a stroke of courage and persistence, an effort to check the strength of the Union Navy with a technological advance while facing naysaying by his critics. Although he had made mistakes, he exhibited outstanding leadership in advancing the five ironclads and failed primarily because he ran out of time and resources.[73]

Secretary Mallory was severely depressed over the loss of his navy in the Mississippi River. On April 30, 1862, the secretary wrote to James Bulloch, his agent in Liverpool, about the current situation:

> New Orleans has fallen, the enemy has the Mississippi, and our struggle has commenced in earnest. This is a heavy blow, but it serves but to nerve our people to greater resistance. Surrender or concession are not thought of, but on the contrary we are, if possible, more than ever resolved to conquer and maintain our independence.[74]

This demonstrated persistence in the face of adversity was typical of the man. After the initial shock of loss of the *Virginia* and *Arkansas* diminished, Stephen Mallory, although despondent, analyzed the achievements of these ironclads. Both of them had displayed their potential for causing fear and destruction among Union fleets, and neither of them had been destroyed by the enemy, but by their own crews. The secretary was convinced that he should continue to make every effort to build a powerful ironclad navy.[75]

Mallory wrote in his diary, "The destruction of the Navy at New Orleans was a sad, sad, blow, and has affected me bitterly, bitterly, bitterly! The Destruction of the *Virginia* was premature. May God protect us and cure us of weakness and folly."[76] To his wife he wrote on May 11, 1862:

> I do not know how you discovered that the naval losses on the Mississippi affected me; but the fact is ... that they almost killed me, and I am ashamed to say that I have lain awake night after night with my heart depressed and sore, and my eyes filled with tears, in thinking over them. Our men fought splendidly, and merited by their gallantry the victory they had not the force to achieve. This has made me very weak, and neutralized the effect of all the medicine I have taken; but I am getting over it.[77]

His mood could not have been improved by negative comments coming from some of his enemies in the press. The *Charleston Mercury* mocked Mallory by reporting that he "no doubt did all that a man in a permanent trance can do." The *Wilmington* (North Carolina) *Journal* cast an aspersion at him writing, "It is said that at first, the Montgomery government resolved to ignore a navy. Thinking they need have no navy, they naturally thought nobody was needed as Naval Secretary, and so, to be consistent they chose Mr. Mallory."[78]

On June 24, 1862, Mallory wrote this in his diary: "I am as sick as I am disgusted with the carpings and complaints of ignorance and presumption, that I have not built a Navy!—I feel confident of having done my whole duty, of having done all that any man could have done with the means at hand. I have my own approbation at least."[79]

In the Mississippi River, the loss of five ironclads in Mallory's attempt to defeat the North was a lethal blow to him personally and to the South's war efforts. In the face of such an event it is human for men to look for someone to scapegoat and Stephen Mallory was to become the target of censure. Two weeks after the destruction of the *Arkansas*, Charles M. Conrad, chairman of the Committee on Naval Affairs and a long-time critic of Mallory, introduced a resolution in the Senate, and Henry S. Foote of Tennessee introduced a similar document in the House. The gist of the resolutions was to express a lack of confidence in Mallory's leadership and to abolish the office of secretary of the navy, transferring its powers and duties to the secretary of war.[80]

Charles Conrad may have been angry about the loss of New Orleans. He had been a lawyer there and owned property in the area. Also, he may have been chagrined that he had not been selected as navy chief. Henry Foote was antagonistic toward Mallory and a persistent critic of President Davis. He initially opposed the secession of Tennessee and was against continuing the war. Of Mr. Foote, Mallory wrote to his wife, "[He] is a fool and is crazy besides, and hates the Administration and the President with an intense hatred." He added, "I have much to be proud of and nothing whatever to regret in my administration.... Knowing that the enemy could build one hundred ships to our one, my policy has been to make such ships, so strong and so invulnerable, as would compensate for the inequality of numbers."[81]

Mallory was not a man to be trifled with and he sought vindication. He believed the country ought to know of his deeds and efforts, for he felt he had done all possible to build a navy and direct affairs of the department. He believed he bore minimal responsibility for loss of New Orleans and the ironclads. To the contrary, he felt he had introduced technological advances to conducting warfare that had been little known to anyone a year earlier. Furthermore, the secretary believed he had done all possible to bring the Mississippi River ironclads into the fray fully armed and equipped, but had simply run out of time. Consequently, he desired a full hearing that would validate his efforts. He encouraged his supporter in Congress, Ethelbert Barksdale, to oppose the Conrad-Foote moves by introducing a resolution asking for the appointment of a joint House-Senate committee to investigate the conduct of the Navy Department. This proposition was approved on August 27, 1862. It blocked the Conrad-Foote resolutions that could not be pursued until the joint committee reached its own conclusions. If the joint committee reached a finding that was favorable to Mallory, the initial resolutions would be doomed.

The joint special committee consisted of five members each from the Senate and House. From the House, the members selected were Foote and Barksdale, plus William W. Boyce, James Lyons, and Lucius Dupré. From the Senate, the members were Clement C. Clay, Jr., Thomas J. Semmes, Augustus E. Maxwell, James Phelan and Robert M. T. Hunter. Hunter resigned later and was replaced by Robert L.Y. Peyton. Mallory welcomed having Foote on the committee, although he was unfriendly to the secretary, because his presence would blunt charges of a fixed group. Barksdale was Mallory's ally, and Senator Clay was a close personal friend. Clay was named chairman of the committee and would be able to influence the direction and focus of the group. The rest of the committee members were reasonably objective and Mallory expected to get a fair hearing.[82]

The joint committee first met on September 4, 1862, when procedural rules were developed. Specific areas of inquiry were identified and Secretary Mallory was invited to be present whenever a witness was being questioned. At the outset he was asked to submit certain documents and respond to certain queries, which he began to do on September 5. These responses were available to the committee for its second meeting on September 8.[83]

Most of the areas for questioning dealt directly with the events leading to the loss of New Orleans. A number of witnesses were asked how the Navy Department had conducted its affairs during and before that battle. The theme of responses was that things had progressed as well as might be expected when taking into consideration difficulties in procuring laborers and materials. Another area of questioning pertained to the unusual contract with the Tift brothers for construction of the *Mississippi* and the subsequent destruction of the ironclad. The testimony revealed nothing nefarious in the contract. Actually it disclosed that the unusual arrangements with these civilians were positive factors furthering Confederate interests. Regarding the destruction of the vessel, the consensus was that there was no really safe place to take the ship to complete construction when considering the threats from both upriver and downriver. As might be expected, at the outset of the hearings the most unfavorable (to Mallory) questioning of witnesses came from Senator Foote, but frequently chairman Clay ruled against him for leading witnesses. When Foote objected, Clay called for a vote of the committee to determine if it would support the chair's ruling, and it did so. From that point on, the pro-Mallory faction generally controlled the proceedings.[84]

Charles Conrad was a witness for the prosecution and he charged that Mallory lacked intelligence and energy in leading the Navy Department, that he did not appreciate the importance of ironclad ships, that he was slow in getting the work done on these vessels, and that this led to poor performance of ironclads on the Mississippi River. Conrad proceeded with a host of charges on specific issues that Mallory partially rebutted through submission of documents.[85]

The joint committee completed its examination of witnesses on March 24, 1863, having consumed over six months of effort.[86] It ended its work without affirming any serious evidence of malfeasance in office by the navy secretary or neglect in carrying out his duties. It became apparent to all that Stephen Mallory had been faced with many serious problems and that for the most part he had dealt with them in an intelligent and energetic manner. The probe did disclose that he had made some mistakes and errors in judgment.

The final committee report cleared him of all charges. The portion of the narrative summarizing committee findings reads:

> Taking into consideration the poverty of our means and the formidable power and boundless resources of our enemy at the beginning of this war, our people have no sufficient cause for shame or discouragement in the operations of our Navy. What has been and is being done to resist the enemy on the waters of our rivers and on the sea, should inspire confidence, and excite strong hope that our Navy will yet

prove an efficient and worthy ally of our noble armies in achieving our independence. It has already won the admiration and applause of neutral nations for its gallant and glorious achievements. And if we should succeed in getting into service the war vessels completed and in progress of construction, the committee believe that our naval triumphs will yet rival the heroic and brilliant achievements of our land forces.[87]

Mallory was vindicated but at the price of having to devote much valuable time and effort that should have been directed toward dealing with relentless war pressures.[88] The committee cleared Stephen Mallory of malfeasance primarily because his supporters on the joint House-Senate group adroitly dealt with his detractors. Especially important was the naming of Mallory's close friend, Clement C. Clay, Jr., as chairman. He was able to control the direction of the inquiry.

Some historians have not been nearly so kind to Mallory in examining his role in the fall of New Orleans. Chester Hearn has been especially critical of Stephen Mallory in his well-researched book, *The Capture of New Orleans, 1862*. He claims that had Confederate forces been able to attack vulnerable enemy forces as they were assembling in the Mississippi River from the Gulf of Mexico around April 18, 1862, they would have been able to wreak havoc upon the fleet. The trouble was that Mallory had run out of time in preparing his ironclads for battle. Hearn asserts this delay was crucial and was the consequence of a poorly coordinated army-navy command structure and squandered resources. He argues that Mallory "spread his meager financial resources all over the South and Europe on a grandiose building plan that could never be implemented. He failed to concentrate his limited funds on the resources available to him.... [A]nd this failure had no effect on changing his administrative habits." Hearn caustically adds that Mallory was "like a semiskilled engineer trying to operate a complicated apparatus equipped with 10 puzzling drive gears but no manual of operation. He kept shifting gears, hoping to find the right one."[89]

While Hearn makes a cogent argument and heaps criticism upon the secretary, he pays little attention to Mallory's consistent and intensive efforts to build a navy where none had existed before. Although Hearn is unduly harsh with Mallory, the joint special committee was very kind to him. The truth of the matter probably lies somewhere between these two extremes. Although it is conjectural, it is possible that had Mallory concentrated on building just one ironclad, he might have gotten it into battle in time to disperse the attacking naval force. After all, the *Virginia* had accomplished such a feat the previous month. But one must ask: was it best for Mallory to have tried and failed, or not to have tried at all?

8

Commerce Raiders

Secretary Mallory had framed the use of sea-roving commerce raiders as a strategic objective in 1861. The purpose was to use these ships either to destroy United States–flagged ships carrying war materiel, or capture and release ships not carrying such cargo after they signed a ransom bond agreeing to pay a certain sum to the Confederate States of America at war's end. This objective derived from Mallory's notion of not being able to match his enemy ship for ship. Rather than choosing to attack the enemy's strongest point, he decided the South's best opportunity would be to strike at the Union's weakest point — its unprotected merchant marine. His vessels would utilize hit-and-run tactics, always avoiding conflict with enemy warships and targeting defenseless merchantmen. He believed that the successful prosecution of this goal would produce economic hardship within the United States and perhaps draw some ships from the Union blockade so that southern ports would become more accessible to overseas vessels importing manufactured goods.

Stephen Mallory's initial step to fulfill this commerce-raiding strategy was to purchase two steamers that were named *Sumter* and *McRae*. He appointed Raphael Semmes as commander of the *Sumter* on April 18, 1861, and Lt. John M. Kell was named as his second in command.[1]

On April 22, 1861, Commander Semmes arrived in New Orleans, inspected the *Sumter*, and proceeded to convert the ship according to his specifications. He had been arranging with a local foundry to have four howitzers cast for the *Sumter*. Cost factors and lack of brass for their manufacture led Semmes to write Mallory requesting that cannon and ammunition from the recently captured Gosport Navy Yard at Norfolk be shipped to him immediately by rail.[2] However, the shipment was delayed because the guns had been taken off the train to make room for other war goods. During this delay, Semmes installed a new mainmast and full set of sails. There were other problems: necessary water tanks had to be built, carriages for the guns had to be manufactured, primers had to be made by a local chemist, small arms and ammunition for the crew had to be located, and 2,700 pounds of powder were needed for the guns. The armament consisted of an 8-inch rifled gun and four 32-pounders, but Semmes had trouble getting the powder to fire the weapons. Finally, through Mallory's intervention, he was able to secure the

Sumter—Confederate Raider. The *Sumter* was the first commerce raider to go to sea (June 30, 1861) and performed well under the command of Raphael Semmes. In January 1862 she anchored at the British colony of Gibraltar to undergo extensive repairs and was blockaded by Union ships. *Sumter* was sold and converted to the blockade runner *Gibraltar*. In July 1863 she delivered rifled cannons to the South for use in defense of Charleston. Captain Semmes went on to fame with the sea raider *Alabama.* COURTESY OF NAVAL HISTORICAL CENTER, NH 98.

necessary powder from the Baton Rouge Army Ordnance Department, only to have it seized during the delivery process by the State of Louisiana.[3]

But by mid-June, the *Sumter* finally was crewed, loaded, commissioned and ready to go to sea. The secretary's instructions to the commander were to "do the enemy's commerce the greatest injury in the shortest time."[4] But Semmes encountered additional problems. He found that two Union ships, the *Brooklyn* and *Powhatan*, blocked Mississippi River passes. Only in the dark of night would he be able to evade Union vessels and dart into the Gulf of Mexico. However, to navigate in the dark he needed a pilot and no such civilian would come forth due to apprehensiveness about anticipated dangers. Semmes sent a letter to the chief pilot demanding a helmsman for his use in running the blockade. He threatened to send an armed force to arrest a pilot, if necessary, and bring him on board.[5] The matter was resolved on June 30, 1861, when Commander Semmes noted that the *Brooklyn* had left her anchorage to pursue a sail seen on the horizon. *Sumter* was able to dash through the blockade past *Powhatan* and gain the open sea.[6]

Three days later the *Sumter* captured her first prize near Cuba, the Union merchant ship *Golden Rocket*. The captured crew was taken aboard the *Sumter* and the Union vessel was set afire. This signaled the beginning of hostilities against the United States merchant marine.[7]

Semmes's usual practice upon capturing and destroying a merchant ship was to place the crew upon the *Sumter* and either transfer them to a cooperating freighter passing nearby or release them in a neutral port. He treated them humanely, never putting them in irons and giving them the same food as his crew.[8] Upon stopping a boat, designated crew would board the vessel and inspect the manifest of the captured ship. If the cargo was found to be contraband of war, both the ship and cargo would be destroyed, frequently by setting her afire, but sometimes by cannon fire to give the crew training and target practice. If, on the other hand, the cargo was found to be bona fide neutral goods, the ship would be permitted to depart after execution of a ransom bond.[9]

The paymaster on board the capturing vessel usually executed the ransom bond. This document stated that the master of the released ship obligated the owners to pay a specific sum to the Confederate government within 30 days of the close of war. For example, such a bond was issued when the *Sumter* seized the *Montmorenci* of Bath, Maine, on November 25, 1861; it was released upon execution of a ransom bond for $25,000. On January 18, 1862, the master of the bark *Investigator* signed a similar ransom bond when captured and released by the *Sumter* in the Strait of Gibraltar.

The *Investigator* would be the last vessel falling captive to the *Sumter*. During her cruise she had seized a total of 18 vessels, eight of which had been destroyed. Mallory's vision had been validated by her success. The value of property destroyed exceeded the cost of *Sumter* and she had terrorized enemy shipping that caused a diversion of enemy ships to hunt her down.[10]

On January 18, 1862, Semmes had his ship anchored at Gibraltar when he wrote the Confederate States commissioner in London requesting funds for necessary repairs and purchase of fuel. He received these funds, but the U.S. consul applied pressure upon the British making it impossible for him to purchase any coal. Semmes then found that his craft was not seaworthy and that the boilers needed to be replaced. However, he could not get vital work done at Gibraltar. Furthermore, three Union warships were on blockade station and observing his movements.

Semmes received permission from James M. Mason, Confederate commissioner in London, England, to lay up his vessel. On April 3, 1862, he wrote to Secretary Mallory informing him of the *Sumter*'s disabled condition and explaining his reasons for decommissioning the vessel and leaving a few crew members to look after her. He told Mallory he had discharged the remaining crew and had instructed his officers to report to the Navy Department for further assignment. Semmes then went to London to confer with Mason and in June shipped to Nassau where he found a dispatch from Mallory dated May 2 assigning him to take command of a new vessel, the *Alabama*.[11]

McRae, the sister ship of the *Sumter*, had also been purchased in April 1861. She was a wooden steamer of 830 tons with a sloop rig and initially was armed with a 9-inch pivot gun and six 32-pounders.[12] Mallory originally had identified her as a cruiser, but later she was reclassified as a riverboat and became engaged in various actions on the Mississippi River, the most important of which was the Battle of New Orleans.[13]

Nearly forgotten in history was a third vessel that was seized at the beginning of the war in the port of Charleston, South Carolina. Formerly a side-wheel merchant steamer that ran between Charleston and New York City, she was fitted out as a cruiser and named the *Nashville*.[14] She was of 1,221 gross tons, had powerful engines, and was armed with two small guns. The *Nashville* departed Charleston to carry mail to England, and on November 19, 1861, she seized and burned a northern freighter, the *Harvey Birch*. The *Nashville* arrived in Southampton, England, on November 21, 1861, creating a sensation since she was the first Confederate warship to enter a port in the Old World. Also in port was the Union cruiser *Tuscarora*. This forced British foreign secretary Lord Russell to interpret Great Britain's neutrality rules. He determined that the *Nashville* was a warship of a belligerent power with a regular crew and was entitled to the same privileges as any belligerent ship. She could not improve her fighting power, but could make any repairs necessary to return to sea. Additionally, the British ruled that the *Tuscarora* could not leave until 48 hours after departure of the *Nashville* on February 3, 1862. The import of this ruling was that the request by the United States that Great Britain outlaw Confederate warships from English waters was denied once and for all.

Nashville returned to Savannah with a cargo of Enfield rifle-muskets, and during the journey destroyed a second Union merchant ship. The *Nashville* was sold to private parties later that year and became the blockade runner *Thomas L. Wragg*. Subsequently, she became the privateer *Rattlesnake* and was destroyed by the Union in 1863. This single round-trip by the *Nashville*, coupled with the activities of *Sumter*, closed the first phase of Mallory's commerce-raiding strategy. The second phase would open with the employment of more powerful cruising raiders.[15]

In England, Confederate agent James Bulloch, was involved in constructing two ships that were to be used for raiding United States merchant marine vessels. He had reached Great Britain in early June 1861 and found there were no suitable ships available for purchase. Later that month, he signed a contract for construction of a vessel with William C. Miller and Sons shipbuilders, whose yard was located on the Mersey River in Liverpool. The ship, which was modeled after a Royal Navy screw sloop, was to be a fast steamer, 185 feet long. After completion, she was to be armed at sea with rifled guns. To mislead Union agents, this vessel came to be known as the *Otero*, but later she would gain fame as the *Florida*.

Bulloch signed a contract for a second steamer with Birkenhead Ironworks, a shipyard located on an estuary of the Mersey River opposite Liverpool. This contract was for a larger and more advanced vessel. It was to be over 211 feet long, and would be powered with 1,000-horsepower steam engines that could propel her at 12 knots. After leaving the yard, she was to be equipped with two 7-inch rifled pivot guns and four 4.5-inch guns in broadsides. This ship was the 290th hull laid by the Birkenhead firm and initially she was identified only as "290." Later she would be named the *Alabama*.[16]

The Confederate agent proceeded with caution in England because he had been identified as a man with southern ties. United States consular agents watched him carefully for any violations of Great Britain's neutrality. On May 13, 1861, Queen Victoria issued a Proclamation of Neutrality that acknowledged the Confederacy to be a belligerent power. On June 1, 1861, she issued an order that closed British and colonial ports to prize ships from both sides. The Foreign Enlistment Act of 1819 guided ship construction in England. Under its provisions, British subjects could legally equip a ship outside British dominions even if the intent was to cruise against a friendly state. British subjects could equip a ship within British dominions if it was not done with the intent to cruise against a friendly state. Under this act, the mere building of a ship within British dominions by any person was not an offense, whatever the intent of the parties, because the offense was not the building, but the equipping.[17]

James Bulloch hired a leading Liverpool solicitor, F.S. Hull, to guide him in order to avoid violating British domestic law. Bulloch was scrupulous in this respect; he made certain he never took any weapon on board a ship under construction — not even a penknife — until she left British waters. To disguise the identity of the first hull, he not only gave her an Italian cover name of *Otero*, but also persuaded the local agent of an Italian firm, John Henry Thomas, to pretend to be the supervisor of her construction and have *Otero* registered in his name as owner. All this subterfuge worked perfectly; even

Charles Francis Adams, the United States minister in London, did not suspect anything until *Otero* had been under construction for four months. Similar secrecy would cover hull "290."[18]

Stephen Mallory had ordered his agent to secure arms and bring them to the Confederacy. Bulloch had collected most of the armament in June 1861 and then purchased a fast, iron-hulled steamer named the *Fingal*. Her ample stowage was loaded with four rifled naval guns and carriages, 800 projectiles, 1,000 Enfield rifles with bayonets, 500 revolvers with ammunition, sailors uniforms, and 400 barrels of gunpowder. On an account for the Confederate army as well as the states of Georgia and Louisiana, the ship carried an additional 14,000 Enfield rifles and 1 million cartridges. With the cargo secured, Second Mate John Low took command of the *Fingal* and secretly departed. In order to not arouse suspicion, Bulloch boarded the *Fingal* at sea on October 15, 1861. To the delight of the South and the chagrin of the North, *Fingal* successfully ran the blockade, arriving in Savannah, Georgia, on November 12, 1861.[19]

From Savannah, James Bulloch went to Richmond to meet with Secretary Mallory. A British mail packet, the *Trent*, had been stopped by a U.S. warship, the *San Jacinto*, near Cuba on November 8, 1861, and two Confederate commissioners sailing to posts in England and France were taken prisoner. Great Britain was incensed about these men being seized from a British vessel and viewed it as a gross violation of international law. England demanded an apology and the release of the envoys. The Trent crisis nearly brought the United States and England to war and strengthened the hopes of southerners that Great Britain would grant diplomatic recognition to the Confederacy. Mallory was apprised of this situation before Bulloch arrived at his office. The optimistic outlook for diplomatic acknowledgement encouraged Mallory to consider having armor-clads built in Great Britain.

During his meeting with Bulloch, Mallory discussed his ideas about building ironclads for offensive purposes in England and France. He formulated his thinking and provided written instructions to Bulloch on November 30, 1861. The agent was directed to arm and equip a war vessel to be named the *Manassas* and he was to do so "without infringing the laws of Great Britain.... [Y]ou will leave England in command and will proceed against the enemy ... the department ... desires to impress upon you the importance of rendering your vessel as formidable and your cruise as destructive to the enemy as practicable.... A speedy recognition of our Government by the great European powers is anticipated...."[20] In January 1862, Mallory, writing to Bulloch, confirmed his intent: "I am very anxious to commence the construction in England by contract of an ironclad sloop of war of four to six guns...."[21]

The Confederate agent returned to his ship in Savannah and found it to be effectively blockaded. He was able, however, to return to England on a blockade runner from Charleston. Arriving in Liverpool on March 10, 1862, Bulloch's immediate responsibility, before turning to building armor-clads, was to arrange for the escape to sea of two commerce raiders that were now nearing completion.[22]

The first of these vessels, *Florida*, having passed her sea trials, set sail on March 22, 1862, for her secret destination of Nassau in the British Bahamas. The *Florida* arrived there on April 28 and on May 8, her new commander, Lt. John Newland Maffitt, came aboard. To avoid violating British neutrality, *Florida* had departed Liverpool without any weapons on board, but the U.S. consul in Nassau, Samuel Whiting, contended that *Florida* had violated British neutrality laws by apparently loading munitions of war on the vessel. She was seized by the local admiralty court and was not released until August, after the court determined there was insufficient evidence to hold her.[23] The *Florida* then sailed to a prearranged destination on the high seas where she was met by another ship sent by Bulloch. That vessel carried armaments that were transferred to the commerce raider. Misfortune struck the *Florida* when a few days later half the crew, including Maffitt, came down with yellow fever. The scourge was out of control and Maffitt had no choice other than finding a Confederate port where all on board could receive medical care.

On September 4, 1862, the *Florida*, following a running battle with Federal ships, successfully penetrated the blockade at Mobile Bay. The vessel was quarantined in the bay with a steamer that functioned as a hospital ship anchored alongside. After one month, the quarantine was lifted. The *Florida* needed to repair her battle damage and it was not until the night of February 16, 1863, that she was able to run the blockade and escape to open sea.[24]

Before the *Florida* departed Mobile, Secretary Mallory provided general guidelines to Lieutenant Maffitt, but avoided giving detailed instructions, relying instead upon the lieutenant's good judgment and discretion. The secretary instructed Maffitt that his goal was "to do the enemy's commerce the greatest injury in the shortest time." Mallory added, "The strictest regard for the rights of neutrals can not be too sedulously observed, nor should an opportunity be lost of cultivating friendly relations with their naval and merchant services and of placing the true character of the contest in which we are engaged in its proper light." In light of the episode at Nassau, and fearful that Federal forces were intercepting messages, the navy chief closed with an explanation of techniques for communication using ciphered messages.[25]

In less than three months after departing Mobile in mid–February, the *Florida* had captured and destroyed 11 merchantmen. On May 6, 1863, she captured her 12th vessel, the brig *Clarence*. Lt. Charles W. Read, one of Maffitt's daring young officers who previously had served with distinction aboard the *McRae* and the *Arkansas*, proposed a plan. He would take *Clarence* (as an auxiliary of the *Florida*) on a separate raid into Hampton Roads; by stealth he would bypass Fortress Monroe and capture or destroy an enemy warship or merchant vessels. He asked for a crew of 12 men and a small howitzer. Maffitt approved the venture and provided framework for it by specifying, "The *Sumpter* (a Cromwell steamer) is now a kind of flagship anchored off Hampton Bar, and at midnight might be carried by boarding. If you find that impracticable, the large quantity of shipping at the fort, or in Norfolk, could be fired, and you and crew escape to Burwell's Bay, thence making your way in safety to the Confederate lines."[26]

Lieutenant Read departed and made his first capture on June 6, 1863, about 150 miles from Bermuda. The victim was the bark *Whistling Wing*, laden with coal for the Federal fleet. She was burned. The next day, Read intercepted the Yankee schooner *Alfred H. Partridge* out of New York bound for Matamoras, Mexico, with a cargo of "arms and clothing for our citizens in Texas." This seemed to Read to be a "strange but gratifying mission for a ship flying the stars and stripes," and he released her after the captain signed a ransom bond. It is likely that Lieutenant Read had misinterpreted for whom the arms and clothing were destined. There was a significant body of German Texans devoted to the Union and these supplies probably were meant for members of the Union Loyal League. Through 1862, league members had been fleeing the Lone Star state to join the First Texas Cavalry (Union) in New Orleans. At the time the *Alfred H. Partridge* was stopped, the Union was planning an invasion of Texas that would commence in the fall of 1863. The

Florida and Jacob Bell. This engraving depicts the destruction by the Confederate commerce raider *Florida* on February 13, 1863, in West Indian waters, of the clipper ship *Jacob Bell* bound from Foo-Chow, China, to New York. COURTESY OF NAVAL HISTORICAL CENTER, NH 59293.

First Texas Cavalry (Union) participated in the Rio Grande Expedition under the command of Gen. Nathaniel Banks and departed New Orleans on October 26, 1863. The United States hoped loyal Germans would escape Texas to join the Union army, or would participate in a civil uprising in conjunction with this invasion. This may clarify Read's misinterpretation of the mission of the *Alfred H. Partridge*.[27]

The *Clarence* then proceeded toward Hampton Roads, and Lieutenant Read reported, "On the 10th of June, when off Cape Hatteras, I received such information as convinced me that it was impossible to carry out the instructions of Commander Maffitt." He departed that area for a raiding cruise along the northeast coast of the United States. The *Clarence* proved to be a poor sailing vessel. After Read seized the bark *Tacony* on June 12 and found it to have better sailing qualities, he transferred everything to the *Tacony* and burned the *Clarence*. From June 12 to June 24 he burned and bonded a total of 19 sailing vessels.[28]

On the morning of June 25, Read transferred everything from *Tacony* to another captured ship, the *Archer*, scuttling the *Tacony*. At sunset on June 25, he anchored in the harbor at Portland, Maine, with other ships at anchorage believing him to be an excursion boat. At 1:30 A.M. the following morning, he captured the U.S. Revenue cutter *Caleb Cushing*.[29] However, he was trapped in a light wind and could not set fire to shipping in the harbor. By the time he was able to get out of the harbor, the capture of *Caleb Cushing* had been discovered, and he was pursued at sea by three steamers carrying armed citizen volunteers. About 15 miles offshore the three pursuers and *Caleb Cushing* exchanged fire. Read ran out of ammunition, set the cutter on fire, and surrendered.[30] He and his crew were imprisoned.

During their adventures, Lt. Charles W. Read and his crew had ample opportunity to engage in maritime gossip with their prisoners and read Yankee newspapers. In his diary, Read related, "The latest news from Yankeedom tells that there are over 20 gunboats in search of us."[31] That was no exaggeration. Read's raids had spread panic along the northeastern coast and pressure mounted on Union navy secretary Welles to respond. He was unwilling to weaken the blockade, but he sent a dozen nonblockading vessels in chase.

Panic spread as the predator cruised the coastline. On June 13 Welles sent this telegram to Rear-Admiral Lee at Newport News: "Yesterday morning the privateer *Clarence*, a captured sailing vessel, fitted out by the *Oreto*, captured three vessels within 8 miles of Cape Henry. The bark *Tacony* they are fitting as a cruiser. Send out anything you have available."[32] Lee responded by sending out seven warships. Welles sent similar telegrams to Commodore Stribling at the Philadelphia Navy Yard ("Can the *Shenandoah* go in pursuit?"), and to Rear-Admiral Paulding at the New York Navy Yard ("Send what vessels you can in pursuit."). Paulding responded that he would send out six vessels. On June 14, Welles sent orders to the navy yards at Boston, New York, and Philadelphia to "Charter or seize half a dozen moderate-sized, fast vessels; put on board an officer, a dozen men, plenty of small arms, and one or two howitzers; send them out in various directions. Take any vessel that can be sent to sea within the next forty-eight hours." From New York Navy Yard on June 14 at 7:00 P.M. Commander Paulding wired, "The yacht *America* is here with twelve midshipmen on board. May I give her a suitable crew and send her in pursuit of the *Tacony*? Also the *Marion* is here and might cruise for a week. May I send her? The *Sabine*, with some addition to her crew, might go for a week on this service. The *Virginia* is just leaving." Welles approved these actions. On June 14, President Abraham Lincoln wrote to Secretary of the Treasury Salmon P. Chase: "You will cooperate, by the revenue cutters under your direction, with the Navy in arresting rebel depredations on American commerce and transportation and in capturing rebels engaged therein."[33]

Hysteria spread so rapidly on the United States eastern shores because no one had thought any southern raiders would have the arrogance to patrol so closely to the coast. Southern daring brought the war home to northern citizens who were largely insulated from the pain of the conflict. In the coastal raid, Lieutenant Read's mission was to destroy as much maritime property as possible in the shortest time. One might speculate that the Confederate raid probably did not decrease the northern will to fight and it might have had the opposite effect. On the other hand, it certainly buoyed Confederate spirits and morale. Mallory must have delighted in recounting the tale of Lieutenant Read's small sailing vessel being hunted down by all the available steamships of the Federal navy. It was one of the few times he could enjoy the achievements of the underdog who could not be crushed in spite of all the might of the Federal navy.

After much success as a raider, *Florida*'s career ended on October 7, 1864, when she was rammed and surrendered to the Union cruiser *Wachusett* while anchored at the neutral Brazilian port of Bahia.[34]

When James Bulloch, returned to England from America in March 1862, he found that good progress had been made in construction of the second cruiser that later would be named the *Alabama*. After the *Florida* secretly left for the open sea, he turned his attention to the *Alabama* and found that the quick departure of *Florida* from her berth had stimulated interest in the *Alabama* by English authorities; the United States minister to Great Britain, Charles Francis Adams; and American agents.

At this time Bulloch also was considering the ironclads that Mallory had ordered him to have built, but he expressed his anxiety about getting these vessels past British inspection and out to sea. To Secretary Mallory he wrote, "The British Government seems to be more determined than ever to preserve its neutrality, and the chances of getting a vessel to sea in anything like fighting condition are next to impossible.... If the present rigid watchfulness of the custom-house officials continues, and it is found impossible to get No. 2 [*Alabama*] out as a proper fighting ship, I will do the next best thing, fill her up with arms from a ship chartered to supply her at an out port, and make a dash for some harbor on our Gulf or Atlantic coast."[35]

Bulloch had every reason to feel apprehensive because it appeared that spies indeed were at work. Also, United States minister Adams was increasing the pressure upon the British government to interpret British neutrality laws in a manner that would preclude the Confederates from getting their ships to sea. Looking ahead at building ironclads, Bulloch reasoned that it would be even more difficult to pass off as a merchant ship a vessel that ultimately was to become a warship. This was so because the design of ships had changed. Bulloch's future ships would be built of iron, not wood, and the use of the screw propeller and steam engine, plus the vessels' designs for use of armament, made it appear that they could only be used as ships of war. Great Britain had the obligation under international law to enforce its neutrality in the face of any inefficacy of its domestic law.[36]

But for now, Bulloch's primary concern was to get the commerce raider, "290," to sea. As time passed, reports from spies became more accurate. On June 13, 1862, an observer reported that 200 powder cases were ordered for the vessel, 60 of them had been placed on board, and the balance was to be delivered at week's end. One week later another spy warned that the ship was planning to depart on June 27. Rumors were that she was sailing on behalf of the Spanish government, but the gateman reported she was under control of the Confederacy. Furthermore, the agent reported, "She may go out any tide and sail in two or three hours' notice. The crew is engaged to go to a certain place, then they will be told where they are to go to; if they don't sign articles to go there, they will be told to go home. Everything as regards time of sailing, where she is bound for, name &c. is kept a profound secret." Another report: "On Friday, July 18th, two dozens of swords were taken on board the '290.'"[37]

In spite of these pressures, Bulloch's mind was clear and focused. While arranging for construction of ironclads, he took extraordinary steps to ensure that the *Alabama* safely reached the sea by disguising her identity and destinations. The ship had been named *Enrica* to encourage the rumor that she was a Spanish ship and then was placed her under command of Matthew J. Butcher, an English national, to enhance the deception that the Confederacy was not involved with the vessel. But U.S. minister Adams pressured the British to seize the *Enrica*. Bulloch's mole in the British Foreign Office alerted him of a July 26 submission of a document by the United States requesting the vessel be seized. At the same time, Bulloch received further intelligence from another agent in Southampton indicating that the Union vessel *Tuscarora* had arrived in the area with orders to prevent *Enrica* from gaining access to the sea. Bulloch acted swiftly and obtained permission

Officers of Confederate Raider Alabama. Pictured are two officers aboard the *Alabama.* In the foreground is the commanding officer, Capt. Raphael Semmes, who is standing by his ship's 110-pounder Blakely pivot gun. In the background, standing by the ship's wheel, is Lt. John M. Kell, his executive officer. This photograph was taken in August 1863 during Alabama's visit to Cape Town, South Africa, where Semmes supervised badly needed repairs. The officers were entertained in Cape Town and in return held a shipboard "open house" that, according to Captain Semmes, produced a gathering of the "better classes." COURTESY OF NAVAL HISTORICAL CENTER, NH 57256.

to take his ship on an engine trial. He did so at dawn on July 29, 1862, with guests aboard to witness the "trial." Shortly thereafter, British agents arrived at the shipyard to seize *Enrica* and discovered she had left. She had anchored in Moelfra Bay on the Welsh coast and the guests were returned to Liverpool by another boat. The next morning *Enrica* sailed to Terceira in the Azores where she was equipped with armament delivered by another vessel. Raphael Semmes arrived as her new commander and the *Alabama* was fully prepared to fulfill her mission and her destiny.[38]

On August 24, 1862, the Confederate flag flew above the cruiser *Alabama* for the first time. Lt. John M. Kell, second in command, described the scene:

> By order of Captain Semmes all hands were summoned aft to the quarter deck. Mounting a gun carriage the captain read aloud his commission as captain in the Confederate Navy, followed by his orders from the Secretary of the Navy, Hon. Stephen R. Mallory, to take command of the ship we were now to christen the *Alabama.* All officers stood with heads uncovered, as in the presence of Sovereign Authority, and while this ceremony was going on slowly ascending to the peak and royal mainmast head were the ensign and pennant of the new man-of-war. At the

Alabama. Harper's Weekly published this line engraving in 1862. It depicts the *Alabama* taking aboard sailors before departing from a merchant ship that she has captured and set on fire. COURTESY OF NAVAL HISTORICAL CENTER, NH 58738.

conclusion of the captain's words and a wave of his hand a gun was fired, officers and men gave a deafening cheer and the band played "Dixie," the anthem of the new-born Confederacy.[39]

Alabama had begun her journey into history to become, along with *Virginia*, one of the most revered ships in the annals of the Confederate States navy.

In the fall of 1862. Secretary Mallory had sent the famed oceanographer Matthew Fontaine Maury to England on a secret mission. As an expert in torpedo warfare, he was directed to obtain electric cable, insulation material, and other equipment required to improve the reliability of electrical ignition for exploding torpedoes. He was also instructed to try to obtain additional cruisers for commerce raiding.[40]

Maury saw a vessel in Dumbarton, Scotland, in March 1863 that he thought might be suitable as a commerce raider. She was named the *Japan*, and was a 600-ton iron-hulled, screw-driven steamer with a brigantine rig that had been built in 1862. Maury purchased her for the Confederacy as directed by Secretary Mallory. On April 1, 1863, the *Japan* sailed from Grenock, Scotland, and was renamed the *Georgia*. She was fitted out at sea with guns and ammunition consisting of two 24-pounders and two 22-pounders and was commanded by Maury's cousin, William Lowndes Maury. During her tour of duty, she captured nine Union merchant marine vessels. However, she was found to be unsuitable for commerce raiding because of inadequate sail power and consequent inordinate use of coal. She was sold to a merchant in Liverpool, England, on June 1, 1864.[41]

Shenandoah. This photograph shows the *Shenandoah* hauled out for repairs in February 1865 at the Williamstown Dockyard, Melbourne, Australia. Note the fresh caulking beween her planks. This Confederate raider cruised the Pacific Ocean where she decimated the U.S. whaling fleet. After the war concluded, she was surrendered to British authorities in Liverpool, England, making the *Shenandoah* the only Confederate navy ship to circumnavigate the globe. Courtesy of Naval Historical Center, NH 85964.

Historian Frank Lawrence Owsley, Jr., has calculated that all Confederate commerce cruisers and the captured ships they outfitted as raiders destroyed about 200 Union vessels. The value of these losses was estimated to be between $15 million and $25 million. The *Alabama* accounted for nearly $5 million of this loss while *Florida* and her satellites accounted for $4 million worth of destroyed commerce. Another raider, the *Shenandoah*, destroyed about $2 million of the enemy's commerce.[42]

The *Shenandoah* is a particularly interesting vessel because of her productivity and unique assignment. On July 18, 1864, Mallory wrote Bulloch about purchasing another commerce raiding cruiser to replace the *Alabama* that had been sunk by *Kearsarge* a month earlier. As early as August 19, 1864, the imaginative and creative secretary of the Confederate navy had suggested operations against the Yankee whale trade after discussing it with his staff. He contacted Bulloch and specifically mentioned that the *Sea King* might be a suitable vessel for such a mission.[43] The secretary suggested general specifications he desired in such a vessel, but made it clear to Bulloch that his ideas were but evidence of his anxiety to get another sea raider on the water. Mallory wrote to Bulloch, "Do not wait for instructions, but do the best you can under the circumstances."[44]

As was his nature, James Bulloch proceeded with alacrity. For some time he also had been looking at the *Sea King* in Glasgow, Scotland, and he judged her to be a prime candidate to become a commerce raider. She was 222 feet long, displaced 1,160 tons, and carried an 850-horsepower engine. Through a British agent, he bought the *Sea King* in fall 1864. The ship put to sea on October 7, 1864, and sailed to Madeira, Portugal, where she was christened the *Shenandoah*. In that port she was outfitted, armed, and crewed. She departed under the command of Lt. James I. Waddell on October 19, 1864, and sailed for the Cape of Good Hope toward her ultimate destination, the northern Pacific Ocean.[45]

On that same day, James Bulloch had provided Lieutenant Waddell with detailed instructions for the voyage and enclosed a memorandum from Secretary Mallory. His mission was to destroy or disperse the American whaling fleet in the Pacific Ocean. Mallory directed Waddell to proceed to Sydney, Australia, and then northward to the Okhotsk Sea where he could expect to intercept the whaling fleet.[46]

Lieutenant Waddell planned to capture whaling charts that would detail loci of sighted whales and would suggest where whaling ships might be found. He took charts from four whalers in early April before destroying the vessels in the Caroline Islands. Around April 15, 1865 (having no way to know, of course, that General Lee had surrendered his army), the *Shenandoah* sailed for the Okhotsk Sea. In that area, Waddell found few available prizes and in May he pointed the bow toward the Aleutian Islands and the Bering Sea. He arrived there the next month and from June 22 to June 28 *Shenandoah* captured 24 whaling vessels. With the whaling fleet cleared out, Waddell headed south. On August 2, off the tip of Baja California, the skipper hailed a British bark, the *Barracouta*. The entry in *Shenandoah's* logbook reads, "Having received by the bark *Barracouta* the sad intelligence of the overthrow of the Confederate government, all attempts to destroy the shipping or property of the United States will cease...." Captain Waddell had Shenandoah's guns stowed below and decided he would surrender his ship in England rather than going to a United States port where he might be jailed. He returned by way of Cape Horn, thus circumnavigating the globe. On November 6, 1865, at Liverpool, England, he lowered the Confederate flag for the last time. *Shenandoah* had captured 38 vessels during her eight-month cruise.[47]

Although he may not have been aware of it, Stephen Russell Mallory, by dint of his creative mind and ceaseless energy, had launched one of his most successful single commerce raids of the war. Whale oil from the northern Pacific did not light lanterns in New England that winter.

9

Southern-Built Defensive Ironclads

Secretary Mallory developed another strategic objective related to building ironclads in the South with the goal of defending the coastal waters, harbors and rivers of the Confederacy. Ports had to remain open for the Confederacy to import necessary manufactured goods, war materiel, civilian goods, and commodities. Waterways required guarding to prevent Union armies from threatening the rear of rebel armies.

Experiences at New Orleans and elsewhere had demonstrated that land forts were not impregnable, or could be bypassed, and could not be relied upon to defend an important area. The action of the southern ironclad *Arkansas* at Vicksburg had suggested that such a vessel could operate as a floating fortress and hold off a Union fleet by working in concert with guns on land. The success of the *Virginia* clearly demonstrated the powerful destructive potential of a single ironclad. Consequently, Mallory's strategic undertaking involved building ironclads in the South and stationing them in appropriate rivers and harbors. Their purpose was to blunt Union attacks on southern coastal or riverine military strongholds, or deflect combined Union navy and army amphibious operations that were attempting flanking attacks upon strong Confederate positions.

One necessary corollary of this strategy was to locate the manufacturing capacity of the South farther inland, away from the coastal zone, so it was less vulnerable to attack and more easily defended. This requirement was clearly demonstrated by the loss of Gosport Navy Yard. However, much of the equipment located there had been sent inland prior to its abandonment.

This defensive strategy also required that ironclads be armed with guns more powerful than those used by the enemy. To ensure penetration of Federal armor, the South would need to use rifled guns with larger calibers and higher muzzle velocities than those of Federal vessels.

In spite of the loss of Confederate ironclads in the Mississippi River and destruction of the *Virginia* in the spring of 1862, Navy Secretary Mallory began building his home defense fleet by laying the keel of a new iron-plated gunboat at Norfolk shortly after the *Virginia* had fought the battle at Hampton Roads.[1] By April 22, 1862, the secretary became concerned about the safety his newest ironclad, now called the *Richmond*. Union forces were gathering in strength outside Hampton Roads and he feared that Norfolk would soon fall. Mallory wired Capt. S.S. Lee commanding the navy yard in Norfolk saying, "Organize night gangs of carpenters on the *Richmond*. Put all the men in the yard upon her that can advance her completion. Stimulate the men by offers of reward for early completion."[2] By early May, the *Richmond* had been towed up the James River to the Rocketts Navy Yard near Richmond, Virginia, where she was fitted out and by October 1, 1862, she was ready for commissioning. The *Richmond* was the initial vessel in the Confederate home defense fleet and spent the remainder of the war in the James River on guard duty preventing U.S. forces from reaching the Confederate capital.[3]

As this vessel was being fitted out, another port was feeling vulnerable to attack from the sea. Charleston, South Carolina, was the busiest port in the Confederacy and was a prime Union target. Because of accomplishments of the *Virginia* in Hampton Roads early in 1862 and the ability of the *Arkansas* to run the gauntlet of Farragut's Union fleet on the Mississippi River in the summer of 1862, Stephen Mallory, along with the rest of the world, realized the potential of a vessel clad in armor and accepted the fact that the wooden warship had become outmoded. From this point on, the secretary gave priority to development of armored ships.

At the beginning of 1862, the Confederate navy had five ironclads under construction. The Battle of Hampton Roads on March 8 and 9, 1862, justified Mallory's faith in such vessels and on May 1 the Confederate Congress authorized further construction of these ships. The secretary immediately sanctioned, or was responsible for constructing, 14 new ironclads.

Secretary Mallory had thought that the *Virginia* might be used for missions outside protected waters, but Buchanan's report of her poor seagoing qualities and her lack of adequate power made him reconsider. In the fall of 1862, Mallory consulted his staff on this matter and changed his ironclad policy. He decided to build in the South only smaller ironclad defense vessels to protect the Confederacy's riverine and harbor waters. Mallory had relinquished the idea of breaking the blockade with these ships. Instead he favored building or buying larger seagoing ironclads in England or France to be used as offensive weapons to break the Union blockade. However, the southern public still expected that ironclads constructed in the South during and after the last half of 1862 would be capable of breaking the blockade.

As the pressure of the blockade increased, this unfulfilled expectation induced the public to subject Mallory to criticism. Gen. Pierre Gustave Toutant Beauregard was an outspoken critic of Mallory. He found fault with the design of the ironclad harbor defense vessels by saying they were "unseaworthy by their shape and construction...."[4] Mallory replied, "Certainly they are unseaworthy, as vessels usually are that are built as these were, for harbor defense chiefly. They are not expected to go to sea.... To have made them seaworthy would have decreased their defensive power."[5] He explained that would have meant sacrificing mobility, speed, and shallow draft. This elucidation apparently did little to diminish criticism.

Two armor-clad ships were constructed in Charleston and were launched by October 1862. They were the *Chicora* and the *Palmetto State*. They were of the same class as the *Richmond* and were designed by John L. Porter, the naval constructor who had been chiefly responsible for building the *Virginia*.

General Beauregard announced on September 24, 1862, that he was assuming command of the Department of South Carolina and Georgia at the direction of the War Department. The general believed in a unified command to include naval forces operating in his department. He exercised operational control over the Confederate navy forces in Charleston; the commanding officer of the naval squadron, Duncan N. Ingraham, worked in close coordination with the general. But Stephen Mallory, who disliked Beauregard and mistrusted him, maintained direction of naval construction.

On the day he assumed command, General Beauregard made clear he was in charge of operations of the *Chicora* and *Palmetto State*. He announced he would be attacking the Federal blockading fleet in the near future. All was ready by the evening of January 30, 1863, and the surprise attack was launched as the *Chicora* and *Palmetto State* slipped out to sea. Just before dawn the two ironclads spotted the Union blockader *Mercedita*. The *Palmetto State* rammed and heavily damaged the *Mercedita*, while the *Chicora* fired upon and disabled another blockade vessel, the *Keystone State*. The *Chicora* then partially disabled the Union ship *Quaker City*. The Federal force dispersed and was not followed by the less seaworthy and slower Confederate ships. The Confederate armored vessels won a victory of sorts because they had scattered a Federal squadron and demonstrated the difficulties the Union might have in any anticipated offensive naval action against Charleston. However, it was a hollow achievement because the rebels did not capture or sink the Union ships and the blockade was not cleared.[6]

At Savannah, Georgia, the Confederate steamer *Fingal*, having run the blockade in November 1861, was still trapped. Mallory decided to use the hull in a manner similar to the *Merrimack* and transform her into an ironclad. He again turned to Asa and Nelson Tift to alter the ensnared ship.[7] This was a big ship that displaced more than 1,000 tons and was 204 feet long, but her draft of 17 feet limited her use in shallow waters. Her battery consisted of two 6.4-inch rifle broadsides and two pivot 7-inch rifles. In August 1862 she underwent an engine trial and was christened the *Atlanta*.[8] After a series of delays, the new ironclad headed toward the Union blockading fleet on March 19 and March 30. On the first occasion the Corps of Engineers did not clear obstructions in time; on the second occasion she grounded. The moves served to alarm Rear Adm. Samuel DuPont, commanding the Federal South Atlantic Blockading Squadron, who moved two ironclads to the Savannah blockade.[9]

The *Atlanta* was under the command of Lt. William H. Webb. He advised Secretary Mallory that he intended to move down the Savannah River where he would "break up and raise the blockade between here and Charleston, and on returning to look into Hilton Head, damaging the enemy there as much as possible, and then to enter the Savannah River, where I can remain to cut off supplies for Fort Pulaski. After returning from this cruise, I may proceed to the southward as far as Fernandina.... I assure you the whole abolition fleet has no terror for me...."[10]

Mallory often selected officers for command who possessed initiative and boldness. However, in this instance, the secretary feared that Webb's plan was reckless. Mallory suggested that he wait for completion of another ironclad, the *Savannah*. Webb, who apparently was eager to experience glory of a great victory, rejected Mallory's suggestion. The secretary made a mistake by permitting Webb to reject his suggestion.[11]

Atlanta moved into Warsaw (Wassaw) Sound around 5:00 A.M. on June 16, 1863, and promptly grounded. This event caused the vessel to lean at such an angle that she could not effectively fire her guns. The Union ironclads *Weehawken* and *Nahant* spotted the *Atlanta*, closed to 300 yards, and pounded the inert Confederate vessel into submission.

The battle, which became target practice for the Federal vessels, lasted 15 minutes before the *Atlanta* surrendered. She was the first southern ironclad to fall into enemy hands.[12]

Following her capture, the *Atlanta* was crewed by Federal sailors and taken under her own power to Port Royal, South Carolina. On June 21, a telegram was sent by Acting Rear-Adm. Samuel P. Lee to U.S. Navy secretary Gideon Welles reporting that *Atlanta* "steers well and made 6 knots against a head sea going to Port Royal. She was completely provided with instruments and stores for a regular cruise. She had a ram, a saw, and a torpedo on her bow.... She will soon be ready for service under the flag of the Union."[13]

Upon the loss of the *Atlanta*, rebel defenders of Savannah turned to another armorclad named the *Georgia* (not to be confused with the commerce raider *Georgia*) that had been launched in October 1862. Her engines were so weak that the vessel could not be propelled against the current. Consequently, she was reclassified as a floating battery and was anchored below Savannah near Fort Jackson. The floating battery protected Savannah until the city fell to the Union in December 1864, at which time she was destroyed.[14]

After the loss of New Orleans in April 1862, Mallory became concerned about the security of the important port of Mobile, Alabama. The State of Alabama also was worried about Mobile's defense and purchased an old lighter named the *Baltic* that formerly had transported cotton from Mobile to ships in the lower bay. On May 2, 1862, she was converted to an ironclad and was transferred to the Confederate government. The *Baltic* was placed at the Mobile Naval Station under the command of Lt. James D. Johnston. She was adequately armed, but her propulsion system was obsolete, making her slow and difficult to steer.[15] Lt. Charles C. Simms, one of her officers, described the *Baltic* as "rotten as punk, and is about as fit to go into action as a mud scow."[16] Nevertheless, she was engaged in the important task of laying 180 stationary torpedoes (naval mines) at the entrance to Mobile Bay. She gained fame as the first minelayer in American naval history.[17] By late spring of 1864, she was decrepit and worm-eaten. Her iron plate was removed to be used on the *Nashville*, and the *Baltic* was decommissioned.[18]

Late in 1862 Secretary Mallory ordered construction of ironclads on the Yazoo River at Yazoo City, Mississippi, and the Red River at Shreveport, Louisiana. Because he was concerned about protecting these work sites from Union incursions, on September 24, 1862, Mallory wrote Secretary of War George W. Randolph requesting military protection for this construction activity.[19]

At Yazoo City, workmen began converting the gunboat *Mobile* into an ironclad and a contract had been signed for construction of an unnamed paddle-wheel ironclad. At Shreveport, a contract had been let for delivery of another ironclad in six months. Mallory also considered constructing a pair of ironclads on the Tennessee and Cumberland rivers, but the project was abandoned because the sites were too exposed to enemy raids.[20]

Meanwhile, Federal forces were placing increasing pressure on the Vicksburg, Mississippi, area. At the nearby Yazoo River, conversion of the *Mobile* was not going well because the Confederates lacked nearly everything needed to complete the work. As Union forces closed in on Vicksburg, the unfinished ironclad had to be destroyed to avoid its falling into the hands of the Yankees. When Vicksburg surrendered on July 4, 1863, Confederate shipbuilding in that region ended.[21]

An ironclad was launched at Shreveport on April 14, 1863, and no effort was spared in fitting out the ship that was christened the *Missouri*. Substantial delays were encountered in completing the vessel. The contractor had difficulty getting iron, had to build his own blast furnace, tried to seize an ironworks in Texas, and finally used railroad rails.

He encountered difficulty finding skilled carpenters for her construction. Guns intended for the *Missouri* were seized by the army to be used at Grand Gulf forts during General Banks's Red River campaign. Finally, the *Missouri* was commissioned on September 12, 1863, but she remained stranded in Shreveport due to a low water level.[22] The Red River campaign opened the following spring. Union forces advanced toward Shreveport but were defeated on April 8 and 9, 1864, at the battles of Mansfield and Pleasant Hill. The *Missouri* never engaged in combat. On June 3, 1865, Lt. Jonathan Carter, her commander, surrendered her to a Union naval officer. The *Missouri* was the last Confederate ironclad to surrender in home waters.[23]

In Texas, there was a small naval force that was uniquely organized. The Texas Marine Department, Confederate States Army, was established in 1861 and was charged with the defense of coastal waters and rivers, specifically in the Galveston area. In August 1861, the secretary of war ordered a navy officer, Cmdr. William W. Hunter, to command this department that was part of the army, apparently with Secretary Mallory's assent. The awkward nature of this arrangement became apparent on November 8, 1861, when one of the vessels in the Texas Marine Department, the *Royal Yacht*, was captured and burned by crew from the *Santee*, a Union blockader. This was of sufficient import that a description of the action was published in the *Houston Telegraph* and Commander Hunter provided accounts of the engagement to both his army commander, Gen. P.O. Hebert, and his navy commander, Secretary Mallory.[24]

In September, 1862 Mallory wrote Hunter asking that he submit monthly reports to the Navy Department. Hunter explained that he had been submitting reports to the commanding general of the District of Texas. He gave Mallory a summary of his activities with the Texas Marine Department and obeyed the secretary's directive to maintain a crew for the schooner *Dodge*. On December 8, 1862, Gen. J.B. Magruder, commanding the District of Texas, New Mexico, and Arizona, countermanded this directive and ordered that the *Dodge* be dismantled and sunk as an obstruction in the Trinity River. Thereafter General Magruder reassigned Commander Hunter to obstruct and defend the Trinity River by building scows and supervising laborers. On April 11, 1863, the naval commander without a ship was detached from service under the War Department and returned to Richmond.[25] This clumsy command structure did not work well, but that became immaterial after the fall of Vicksburg and Port Hudson in the summer of 1863. When the Union gained control of the Mississippi River, Texas was detached from the Confederacy and Mallory had no further dealings with that small navy.

From the beginning Secretary Mallory encountered persistent problems in his attempt to construct ironclads. The difficulties primarily were due to the South's agrarian economy and an underdeveloped industrial base. The main problem was procuring iron. The Confederate navy chief needed iron — lots of it — to manufacture armor for his ships. The Confederacy never had enough iron, and both the navy and the army competed for what was available. Iron ore and coal deposits were not large enough to meet war needs and they diminished as Union forces encroached upon southern soil.

Mallory assessed the multitude of problems he was facing in creating a navy where none had existed before and moved with his customary speed and energy to resolve them. On May 20, 1861, he sent Capt. Duncan N. Ingraham to assess the capability of certain rolling mills to produce "wrought-iron plates of from 2 to 3 inches in thickness." Ingraham was directed to visit the Tennessee Iron Works on the Cumberland River in

Tredegar Iron Works. This view of Tredegar Iron Works at Richmond, Virginia, was taken in April 1865. This was probably the most important industrial facility in the Confederacy, manufacturing iron products for the armed forces. COURTESY OF LIBRARY OF CONGRESS, PRINTS AND PHOTOGRAPHS DIVISION, LC-DIG-CWPB-02886.

Stewart County, Tennessee, and the Daniel Hillman & Co. rolling mill in Kentucky. Last he was told to check out a rolling mill at or near Atlanta, Georgia.[26] On May 23 Captain Ingraham reported that the Tennessee Iron Works "are not prepared under any circumstances to do such heavy work." He added that Daniel Hillman's Kentucky rolling mill was only 40 miles from the Ohio line and the owner was preparing to close that operation so as not to endanger the property. Ingraham reported on May 28 that he had visited the Atlanta ironworks and rolling mill. That firm was named Schofield & Markham and the owner told him that only railroad iron was being made there and that it would be difficult to adapt the mill to production of the required iron plates.[27]

Though this was grim news for Mallory, he was not easily discouraged. He acted to improve the situation by having the navy assume control of the Schofield & Markham firm. Renamed the Atlanta Rolling Mill, it was adapted to roll plate of the required size and by August 7, 1862, Cmdr. George Minor stated that the mill had produced 10,000 tons of plate.[28] By late 1861 contracts had been made with other firms by the Navy Department. In a joint contract with the War Department, the Tredegar Iron Works in Richmond, Virginia, agreed to make iron plate along with boiler iron, cannon, ammunition and other iron products. In a separate contract Tredegar agreed to produce "3,000 tons of Catawba cold-blast charcoal iron." Similar contracts were let with eight other firms for iron plates as well as charcoal pig iron, gun iron, steel, and sheet copper. An ominous indicator of future difficulties is found at the end of a report: "The department has dispatched agents to buy up all the scrap iron to be found."[29]

The urgent search for scrap iron extended to railroads. The navy turned to iron railroad tracks that could be used for shaping iron plates. At first they used worn out tracks. As the need for iron plating increased, the navy sought portions of track that were seldom used and cannibalized them for manufacturing iron plate. This was self-defeating because the South's railroad system was barely adequate for war at its outset and through the years deteriorated track and equipment could not be replaced. This led to virtual collapse of the southern railroad system.

At war's beginning, the South had one of the best iron works in the nation, the Tredegar Iron Works in Richmond, Virginia, that was led by Joseph R. Anderson. Unfortunately Anderson did not immediately gear up his factory for a war that countless people believed would last no longer than 90 days. The fact that he failed to stockpile supplies cost him and his business dearly. Less than a month after the war started, Anderson turned down a large lot of tin that was available in New Orleans because he thought the price was too high. By the end of May, and for the next six months, he could not cast bronze field pieces because neither tin nor copper was available. He needed pig iron produced in Tennessee and Georgia, but could not get it shipped in an expeditious manner to his factory. Due to an archaic transportation system, an abundance of iron ore could not be shipped and accumulated at mines, delaying production. Even worse, railroads could not deliver Tredegar's finished products, such as iron plate and cannons, because flatcars were unavailable. Additionally, Tredegar Iron Works was deluged by the requested amount of iron plate needed to construct the *Virginia*. From October 1861 to February 1862, Tredegar rolled 732 tons of plate for the *Virginia* and nearly the entire capacity of the factory was expended for five months. Production of other necessary iron products for the army was given lesser priority. All these factors probably compromised army field operations.[30]

In October 1862 while engaged in defending North Carolina waters, Secretary Mallory contacted Secretary of War Randolph and raised the question of removing iron rails from two railroads in order to produce ironclad boats. Randolph replied that enemy pressure had prevented this from being accomplished.[31] But Mallory was persistent and on November 4, 1862, he wrote to the governor of North Carolina, Zebulon B. Vance, informing him that an agent (Capt. William F. Lynch) had been sent to North Carolina to secure railroad iron for plating gunboats. Lynch, who did not have a good personal relationship with Vance, returned empty-handed and reported to Secretary Mallory that the governor controlled the railroad iron. Mallory assured Governor Vance that he would be properly compensated if permission were granted for removal of the iron.[32] Vance replied that he was a mere stockholder in the railroad company and did not control the iron. The navy secretary refused to be disheartened and persisted in the search for iron. On November 21, 1862, Mallory's perseverance was rewarded when Governor Vance informed him that consultation with the railroad directors resulted in the release of iron taken from torn-up track that was located nearest the enemy. Vance added that Mallory could also have bolt iron from destroyed bridges across the Neuse River.[33]

On February 13, 1863, the secretary once more wrote Governor Vance, calling his attention to about 707 tons of railroad iron that was located at Lawrenceburg, North Carolina. The secretary requested it be released to him "with the understanding that it will be used exclusively for plating gunboats and batteries now nearly ready for it in your State."[34] Vance replied that he could have the iron only if it could "be exchanged for the old iron on the different roads of the State. They are rapidly running down," Vance explained, "and are applying for the same iron. I suppose their worn-out rails would answer the same purpose for rolling."[35] One week later Mallory wrote to Maj. Gen. D. H. Hill at Goldsborough, North Carolina, asking his assistance in obtaining 10 or 12 miles of railroad iron to be rolled into iron plate with which to clad ships traversing North Carolina waters.[36]

Mallory was desperate and would use any kind of iron that could plate his ironclads. These interchanges between Vance and Mallory illustrate the difficulties associated with a strong states' rights stance conflicting with weak centralization of power within the Confederate government. North Carolina governor Vance, a strong states' rights man, had a series of clashes with President Davis and other Richmond officials over rights of North Carolina as opposed to rights of the Confederate government. Mallory intervened personally on many occasions with Governor Vance and their correspondence was not always amicable. As late as November 1863, Mallory was still having difficulty securing railroad iron through the governor's office.[37]

Initially there was no rolling mill in the South that could produce the two-and-one-half-inch plate that was required for ironclads. In time, the Tredegar Iron Works in Richmond, Virginia; the Atlanta Rolling Mill in Georgia; and later the Shelby Iron Company of Columbiana, Alabama, all manufactured limited amounts of armor plate.[38] However, there never was enough iron plate available to meet the Confederate navy's needs and this factor frequently caused unconscionable delays in commissioning Confederate vessels subsequent to their launch. In fact, there were instances of these vessels still having iron plating attached to their hulls as they sailed toward an enemy engagement.

The South also had limited capability for manufacturing other iron products such as heavy guns, shell and shot for artillery, small arms, ship engines, anchors, chains, and nuts and bolts. At the beginning of war the Confederacy had only two cannon foundries, the Tredegar Works in Richmond and the Bellona Foundry located on the James River approximately 15 miles from Richmond. Both foundries worked at a frenzied pace to meet the needs of the Confederate armed forces for heavy guns; the navy and army frequently were in competition for this artillery.[39]

A shortage of marine engines also existed. Remedies for a limited supply of engines were exacerbated by the fact that in the past such engines for southern steamers had been manufactured by northern industries. Mallory initially met this need by scavenging obsolete engines from other vessels, and then contracting with southern firms that produced small steam engines. One such firm was the Columbus Iron Works in Georgia. Rented by the Navy Department, it came to be known as the Columbus Naval Iron Works. By October 1862 it was producing naval engines and boilers of high quality; two years later, 60 percent of the power plants for armored ships under construction in the South came from this plant. In addition, some engines were obtained from Europe.[40]

Secretary Mallory's procurement troubles continued in his search for other essential metals. As Union forces seized rebel territory, the Confederacy's limited supply of copper dramatically decreased. The navy also needed tin and zinc, metals that were unavailable in the South. Blockade runners imported these three metals into the Confederacy. The navy's requirement for lead was partially met by a large supply in southwestern Virginia. It too was supplemented by blockade running.[41]

The Confederate Navy required coal for operating its steamships. Nearly all the coal available in the South (located primarily in Virginia and Alabama) was "soft" bituminous coal rather than the higher-grade anthracite. The paucity of manpower presented problems in mining ample supplies of this material. Once coal was mined, southern railroads could not meet diverse requirements and workloads imposed upon them. Since different railroad gauges were used from state to state, the system always had been inefficient and the war effort only magnified the predicament. Railroads required heavy maintenance that could not be supplied because of the lack of workers, resulting in rolling stock wearing out prematurely.

The ability to turn ore into iron was likewise minimal, as was the manufacturing capacity to shape plates and manufacture other iron products. The South had a limited supply of iron ore and an insufficient number of smelters. Before the war, the South produced around one-sixth of the iron ore extracted in the nation, but most of it was located in Kentucky, western Virginia, and Tennessee. These mines soon fell into Union hands. Production of iron depended upon furnaces where iron bars were manufactured and then rolled into sheets in a rolling mill. There were less than 39 furnaces in the Confederacy and the few available rolling mills were of insignificant size.

Getting iron for rolling mills was not the only complication Secretary Mallory encountered in equipping his armored vessels. The shortage of manpower was especially serious with respect to mechanics and other skilled workers. On March 14, 1862, Mallory wrote to Secretary of War Benjamin that construction of iron-plated sloops at Memphis, Tennessee, was being delayed due to scarcity of craftsmen. He requested that Benjamin order the army to detail as many skilled men as possible to complete the work. President Davis indorsed Mallory's request and urged immediate action.[42]

In 1864 a number of naval facilities reported that shop tools were often idle due to lack of mechanics to work them. The Naval Station at Charlotte, North Carolina, reported a steam hammer was often idle. The work force was so small that crank axles could not be forged to replace those broken on six locomotives, and necessary munitions of war could not be manufactured as desired. The Naval Ordnance Works in Atlanta reported it was understaffed in important manufacturing positions and could not keep up with orders for munitions. The Selma Cannon Foundry reported it had insufficient blacksmiths for completing guns in a timely manner. Secretary Mallory brought these matters to the attention of the president on July 1, 1864, and requested, "that details to meet these demands be made from conscript camps or the Army."[43]

Insufficient manpower was always a major problem because so many workers and skilled laborers also were needed to fill the rank and file of southern armies. There never were enough men to mine the coal, to maintain the railroads, to operate factory machinery, to produce the ingots, and to roll the plates in the foundries.[44] In short, there simply were not enough men in the South to meet the varied needs of the Confederacy.[45]

A major obstacle in building the Confederate navy's ships was finding locations for boat yards. The Pensacola Navy Yard at Warrington, Florida, a minor shipyard, was available but it was of little value since the harbor was effectively closed by Union occupation of Fort Pickens and by the Federal blockade. On April 20–21, 1861, the Virginia State Militia was able to seize the Gosport Navy Yard at Norfolk, Virginia, but was forced to abandon it one year later.

Due to loss of shipbuilding and subsidiary facilities occasioned by the abandonment of the Gosport Navy Yard and the fall of New Orleans in 1862, it was necessary for Secretary Mallory to have shipyards built from the ground up throughout the South. For protection, these had to be dispersed, creating the disadvantage of decentralization. Many of the new yards had to be built in a field or sandy bank of a river. The water had to be deep enough for launching, with timber and other necessary materials readily available. Mallory believed these primitive accommodations would be suitable for the small ironclads he had in mind.

The secretary began thinking about such shipyards as early as October 1861. On

October 20, 1861, Mallory broached the subject of building a steamer at St. Marks, Florida, located on the Gulf Coast below Tallahassee, when he sent a note to Florida governor John Milton. On November 2 he wrote another letter to Governor Milton: "I want to build a ... gunboat at St. Marks. Can it be done?" On November 19 Mallory wrote to Milton again saying, "I have under contract four gunboats in our State, & greatly wish to build one of eight [foot] draught at St. Marks, for that port."[46]

In North Carolina important shipyards were located at Wilmington, Tarboro, and Charlotte. In South Carolina, the center for ship construction was at Charleston and nearby Mount Pleasant while at Florence a similar facility was built in 1863 on the Great Pee Dee River. Primary shipyards were located at Savannah and Columbus in Georgia. In Alabama industrial activity was centered in Selma where the Confederate Naval Foundry and Iron Works was located as was the Selma Navy Yard and Ordnance Works. The major shipyard in Mississippi was located at Yazoo City, but that site could no longer operate following the siege of Vicksburg in 1863. After the Battle of New Orleans in April 1862, the only remaining shipyard in Louisiana was found in Shreveport. This summary is not exhaustive, but it serves to illustrate the extent to which Secretary Mallory and his staff went to develop shipyards. Without this all-out effort, there could not have been a home defense fleet.

Although the supply of iron was always wanting, that was not the case with raw materials needed for shipbuilding. At or near these shipyards, there was an abundant supply of proper wood with which to build vessels. Two excellent trees used for ship construction were found in the South: the live oak and the pitch pine. The oak was a hard, durable wood that was used for the ship's frame while the pine, which was used for planking, was firm and abundant.

After Gosport was relinquished, the largest shipyard in the South was the Confederate Navy Yard at Rocketts Landing on the James River outside Richmond, Virginia. It became the base, construction site, and headquarters of the James River squadron. To safeguard this important base, the Confederate Navy mined and barricaded the James River, defending it with wooden and armored vessels. Nearby was the Graves Shipyard. The important Tredegar foundry, that supplied most of the metal products required by the army and navy during the war, was located in downtown Richmond on the James River.[47] This critical location was protected from Union incursion by various Confederate vessels, batteries on riverbanks, and by mines and obstacles in the water.

In addition to shipyards, the remainder of the infrastructure—foundries, ordnance stores and laboratories, and marine machinery works—were moved inland. Most of these were in operation by 1863. This was a mammoth accomplishment that was superbly coordinated by the Navy Department staff.[48]

Many auxiliary manufacturing operations also had to be created. Some of them had been developed just after the outbreak of war but it was necessary for those near the coast to be moved inland to avoid Federal encroachments. To illustrate how this impacted one community, it is useful to examine the Charlotte, North Carolina, area. Charlotte was well inland, had a major railroad junction, a substantial labor supply, and requisite commercial facilities. This location soon became a major manufacturing and distribution center.

When Secretary Mallory anticipated the loss of the Gosport Naval Yard in the spring of 1862, he turned to Charlotte as the location to which he would transfer machinery and skilled workmen. He succeeded in doing this before Gosport fell into Union hands. By the summer of 1862, laborers occupied the Mecklenburg Iron Works and expanded it along the tracks of the North Carolina Railroad. The new Charlotte Naval Yard was established and employed about 300 machinists and foundry workers. Factories in Charlotte manufactured mines, anchors, gun carriages, marine engines, propellers, and shafts. Other industrial facilities were built to manufacture additional items of war. The Confederate State Acid Works produced chemicals necessary for making fulminate of mercury, a component of percussion caps. Sulfuric acid was needed for wet cell batteries that ignited electric torpedoes and provided power for the South's telegraph system. The Mecklenburg Gun Factory produced ordnance and small arms. Other factories manufactured wooden canteens, belt buckles, and wire. The North Carolina Powder Manufacturing Company produced gunpowder in its mill until August 1864 when an accidental explosion destroyed it. In January 1865 another disaster struck when there was an accidental fire in the Confederate storage warehouses resulting in destruction of large quantities of foodstuffs, blankets, clothing, and other items.

Industrial production at Charlotte was an essential element in building and maintaining the Confederate navy. Secretary Mallory could not have attained the success he experienced had not industrial centers such as this been developed.[49] The Confederacy and the navy secretary persevered, producing many sound warships and accoutrements.[50] Starting without a fleet and facing enormous odds, the Confederate Navy Department was able to construct at least 150 warships during the war, only about half of which were completed and commissioned into service. Nevertheless, this was a significant achievement and credit goes to the navy secretary and his naval constructor, John Luke Porter.[51]

Problems accompanied Secretary Mallory's success in building a navy. By January 1862 he experienced severe difficulties procuring seamen for his growing navy. On January 10, 1862, he wrote to the chairman of the Committee on Naval Affairs in the Confederate Congress suggesting that a bounty be allowed to encourage men to enlist as seamen, with the amount of the bounty per seaman graduated according to length of the enlistment period.[52] In September 1862 Mallory wrote to the secretary of war requesting that seamen who were in the army, and wished to enlist in the navy, be permitted to do so.[53] In May 1863 the Confederate Congress passed an act providing that all persons in the army who wished to be moved to the navy, and whose transfer the secretary of the navy had applied for, were to be assigned to navy service. In accord with this law, Mallory requested that about 600 identified men fitting these criteria be transferred. The secretary of the army replied to Mallory that army commanders did not particularly appreciate the need for sailors and resented the loss of their experienced soldiers. Mallory replied with sympathy that he was anxious that these transfers be made in a "manner least detrimental to the Army...."[54]

In preliminary steps to challenge Federal strong points in coastal and riverine waters of North Carolina and to protect the flank of General Lee's army in Virginia, Secretary Mallory began laying keels for ironclads and commenced construction of five armored vessels in North Carolina in 1863. The *Raleigh* and *North Carolina* were being built in Wilmington to protect that important port and the other three were under construction on North Carolina interior rivers because the shipyard locations were relatively isolated and safe from Union attacks. Secretary Mallory and Gen. Robert E. Lee were concerned about Federal incursions into the heartland that might threaten to flank General Lee's army. Earlier there had been Union invasions up the Neuse, Tar, and Roanoke rivers, and Mallory had agreed to work cooperatively with the army for the prevention of further intrusions. At Whitehall on the Neuse River, the Confederate navy was building the armored ship *Neuse*; at Tarboro on the Tar River, a contract had been signed for delivery of an unnamed armor-clad vessel by March 1, 1863; a third ironclad was being built at Edward's Ferry on the Roanoke River, with a planned launch date of April 12, 1863.[55]

Union troops interrupted construction of the *Neuse* on December 15–16, 1862, by shelling the hull, but she was repaired.[56] On July 20, 1863, Federal troops entered Tarboro on the Tar River where they found and burned the unnamed ironclad ship under construction. General Lee wrote to President Davis expressing his concern about Federal forces at his rear, and encouraged completion of the armored vessels under construction. Lee wrote, "I regret very much that the boats on the Neuse and Roanoke are not completed. With their aid I think success would be certain. Without them ... the fruits of the expedition will be lessened and our maintenance of the command of the waters in North Carolina uncertain. I think every effort should be made now to get them into service as soon as possible."[57]

The third boat, located at Edward's Ferry on the Roanoke River, came to be known as the *Albemarle*. An indefatigable effort was required to build her. There was no shipyard there, so work took place in a cornfield, largely with the help of local people. Iron again was a problem. After long negotiations with North Carolina's governor Vance, railroad iron was obtained for making plates. *Albemarle* was dragged into the river on October 3, 1863. By the end of November, both *Albemarle* and *Neuse* had been launched and were being fitted out.[58]

Progress was being made in constructing similar vessels elsewhere. In Charleston the keel for a large armed boat, measuring 180 feet long and covered with 600 tons of iron plates, was laid down in November 1862. She was completed toward the end of 1863 and was named the *Charleston*. In Savannah, another ironclad named the *Savannah* was being built in August 1862. The *Savannah* was commissioned on June 30, 1863, and was one of the finest ironclads that had been built for the Confederate Navy. She was said to be a "well-constructed and a very fine ship...." With a battery of four 6.4-inch Brooke rifles she was formidable.[59]

A contract for construction of a second vessel in Savannah was signed in December 1862. She also was large, measuring 175 feet in length, and was named the *Milledgeville*. Because of deficiencies in the South's industrial machine, this vessel was not launched until December 21, 1864, and then was scuttled to avoid capture by the Union when Savannah fell shortly thereafter.[60]

Secretary Mallory was also alert to problems in the western theatre. At a shipyard in Columbus, Georgia, a large 189-foot ironclad was under construction. She was named the *Muscogee* and then changed to the *Jackson*. Once again, the lack of iron and skilled labor slowed her construction, and she would not be completed until the end of 1863.[61]

Mallory was most concerned about defense of the port at Mobile, Alabama. About 200 miles to the north of Mobile, the town of Selma, Alabama, was converted into a large industrial complex. A navy yard was built in Selma and two ironclads, the *Huntsville* and the *Tuscaloosa*, were built there in 1862. However, their engines were so weak that they could be used only as floating batteries. Mallory needed additional armored ships for harbor defense at Mobile. To meet this requirement he had a large paddle-wheel ironclad, the *Nashville*, built at Montgomery, Alabama, and a second powerful armor-clad, the *Tennessee*, constructed at Selma. The usual delays—lack of iron and skilled labor—were encountered. Nevertheless the two ironclads were launched on February 8, 1863, and the

Tennessee was about to get her guns as the year ended. However, *Nashville* was not progressing well because there was not enough iron for her plating.[62]

Another essential requirement for Mallory's armored defensive fleet was naval cannons that were superior to those used by the U.S. Navy. In Mallory's report to President Davis dated April 26, 1861, he stated, "Rifled cannon are unknown to naval warfare; but these guns having attained a range and accuracy beyond any other form of ordnance, both with shot and shell, I propose to introduce them into the Navy...."[63] The rifled naval cannon in which Mallory put his faith was the Brooke Rifle, invented by Lt. John Mercer Brooke. Mallory selected him as the head of the Office of Ordnance and Hydrography in March 1863 after he had served a year as chief of ordnance. Secretary Mallory had a knack for selecting good men for important positions and Brooke was a most fortunate choice for this responsibility. He was a fellow Floridian who had demonstrated intelligence and a bit of genius in previous scientific work.[64]

By 1863 the Brooke Rifle was being produced in the Selma Naval Foundry, and in June of that year Brooke named his valued collaborator, Capt. Catesby ap R. Jones, as the foundry commander. Against great odds, this foundry produced at least 100 heavy naval cannons during the war.[65] The principal problems for Jones were shortages of iron and inadequate skilled labor. For example, he explained his difficulties about lack of manpower when he wrote to Brooke on May 14, 1864:

> We now cannot turn out more than one gun a week, but with a proper number of mechanics could turn out three a week, and in a few months one a day.... In addition to our present force we could employ with great advantage to the Government twenty-five molders, twenty-five machinists, and twenty blacksmiths....[66]

Meticulous care was given to the manufacture of these guns and powder, and constant improvements were being made as dictated by experience with the ordnance in the field. By the end of the war, it was generally acknowledged that the Brooke Rifle was one of the most effective cannon in the Confederate navy. Mallory wrote to the President on July 1, 1864, praising the Brooke Rifle:

> The reports of the enemy's naval officers commanding iron-clad ships concur with the results of our own experiments in showing that the heavy navy rifles are the most effective ordnance yet used against those vessels. Their range and accuracy are very satisfactory; and, while some of them have been fired without visible strain from 500 to 1,500 times in conflict, none of them have burst when properly handled.[67]

The Brooke rifled and banded gun frequently was an important component of the ordnance on southern-built ironclads. This strong offensive power harmonized with the defensive iron sheets fastened to ship hulls.

As 1863 ended, Secretary Stephen Russell Mallory had made great progress toward his goal of creating a home defense fleet for protection of important southern harbors and waterways. This was accomplished through great individual effort. To compensate for the inadequacies of the industrial complex in an agrarian society, Mallory created manufacturing capabilities where none had previously existed and moved facilities inland to minimize the Union threat to them. Although he faced many difficulties Secretary Mallory, through his Herculean efforts, made significant progress in developing a formidable southern-built ironclad defensive fleet.

10

Foreign-Built Offensive Ironclads

Another strategy that Stephen R. Mallory framed was the development of an offensive weapon to counter the Union blockade of the South. His intention was to build ships with good seagoing qualities in England or France, plate them with armor, and equip them with rifled guns. Their mission would be to cross the Atlantic Ocean, attack enemy blockading ships and clear at least part of the barrier.

The effectiveness of ironclads had been demonstrated by the use of floating batteries during the 1854–1856 Crimean War. A naval revolution followed as ironclad vessels began supplanting wooden vessels. France laid down the ironclad steam screw frigate *Gloire* in 1858 and she went into service in 1860. In 1862 Great Britain put *Warrior*, her first iron ship, into service. By 1861, France and England had a total of 28 ironclads built or under construction. Undoubtedly Mallory carefully followed this activity, which may have stimulated his interest in building offensive ironclads overseas.[1]

On January 14, 1862, Mallory wrote to James Bulloch with firm directions as to what he hoped to achieve. Mallory said he wanted steel or ironclad vessels constructed in England or France and he specified that he desired "to have an armored steam sloop of moderate size, say of about 2,000 tons, and to carry 8 or 10 heavy guns" that might be based on drawings by Naval Constructor Porter and Chief Engineer Williamson. Stephen Mallory then related his vision:

> The model which I have shows very clean, sharp, and beautiful lines of a 2,300-ton ship; but the principal novelty is in the manner of mounting the guns, which are placed amidships in an iron casemate, the two after and forward guns in which are so pivoted as to fire in broadside or fore and aft. Besides these, two heavy guns are pivoted near the ends. The decks are clear and all accommodations are below them. The hull is ironed and is low in the water, and by the device of the single casemate much iron is dispensed with.

Mallory closed with a sense of urgency saying, "I submit this plan for your information only, but so anxious am I to have an ironclad ship built that, should you and

Lieutenant North, with whom I associate you in this matter, be able to contract or to make the preparatory arrangements to contract for an armored or steel or ironclad ship, you will proceed with all dispatch to prescribe the character of the vessel, and I will place the funds in England at once."[2]

A distinguishing feature of the ironclad ship was the presence below the waterline of a ram on the bow that was an iron piercer projecting forward six or seven feet. Thus, the ironclad ship also became a potential battering ram. The use of this supplemental weapon revived an old technique of sea war that had become viable once more as a result of steam engine development. Functionally, a vessel of shallow draft with powerful engines would be able to nimbly navigate southern rivers and quickly strike with her guns or, with her ram, penetrate an enemy ship's hull below her waterline and protective armor.[3]

About eight months later the navy chief returned to the subject once more when he revealed his hopes for the ironclads that were under construction. In a letter to Bulloch dated September 20, 1862, Mallory wrote, "Not a day, not an hour, must be lost in getting these ships over, and money is of no consequence in comparison to the speedy accomplishment of this work. If we can succeed in getting them to sea, armed, manned, and equipped, we would go to New Orleans at once and regain the Mississippi."[4]

James Bulloch, who had returned to Great Britain in March 1862, was proceeding briskly in carrying out Mallory's orders for building armored vessels. He turned again to the Laird Brothers, owners of the Birkenhead Ironworks, the same firm that had constructed the *Alabama*. Mallory's agent had not yet received the $1 million appropriation for two ships, but the Laird Brothers accepted his order on faith. On July 4, 1862, Bulloch wrote to Mallory: "[I] have contracted for three [*sic*: two] armored ships, the first to be ready in March, the second two months later." He added cautiously, "If money does not fail, there will be no delay in the execution of the contracts."[5]

The Lairds again used numbers indicating the sequence in which ships were built to identify these boats (they were numbered "294" and "295"). The vessels were to be identical and innovative. Each of them had a length of 230 feet and a beam of 42 feet. Their 350-horsepower engines would be capable of making 10 knots. They had watertight compartments that could be flooded or emptied, thus altering their draft within a range of from six to 15 feet above the water line. The maximum thickness of the iron plating was 5.5 inches. The ships had a pair of revolving turrets, each of which would house two 9-inch rifled guns. The most ominous feature of the vessels was a long underwater ram, made of solid iron, extending seven feet from the prow of the ship. Because of this feature, they were referred to as "Laird rams."[6]

The Union recognized the threat these ships posed and Gustavus Vasa Fox, the assistant secretary of the Union navy, feared they had nothing that could counter them. Bulloch worried about how long he could sustain the charade that these ironclads, with their twin turrets and underwater ram, were being constructed for commercial trade.[7] Secretary Mallory apparently had the same concerns because he wrote Bulloch on August 8, 1862, saying that it was of great importance to hasten the building of the ironclads and encouraging him to pay a bonus to ensure early completion.[8]

A month later, the Confederate navy chief expressed his angst to Bulloch about financial matters. Due to Confederate cash-flow problems, Mallory feared the Confederate treasury might fail to meet Bulloch's financial requirements, and he discussed alternative means of satisfying these obligations.[9] Ten days earlier Bulloch had written Mallory (their letters crossed in the mail): "The work is going on to my entire satisfaction, and if funds do not fail you shall have two formidable ships ready in the early spring."[10]

Bulloch's next report to Mallory, dated November 7, 1862, revealed that bad weather had delayed some aspects of the construction of the ships, but work continued in heated sheds to counter the effect of short, foggy days. Bulloch also discussed factors for consideration in getting the first vessel out of the country without violating British neutrality laws. He suggested that the first ship might be ready to leave around April 1, 1863, and the second in June 1863.[11]

Before the end of 1862, Mallory was feeling more assured about financing his ironclads in England when he learned from Confederate commissioner James Mason that cotton bonds could be used to obligate the Confederate government to deliver that fiber (at the rate of eight cents per pound of cotton) to the holder of the certificate, with the delivery being made "at any port in possession of the Confederate States when demanded by the holder of the bond, after reasonable (say 30 or more days) notice or within three months or more after a peace."[12] At the sale price, the bond purchasers could anticipate handsome profits at the end of the war. At this time, the Confederacy had enough cotton on hand that at eight cents per pound it was worth $16 million. Early in 1863, the treasury secretary received a request from the navy secretary for $3 million in cotton certificates (of the $16 million available) with which to finance the building of the ironclads overseas.[13]

On January 23, 1863, James Bulloch wrote again to Secretary Mallory sharing his views of the political climate in Great Britain. Bulloch had become convinced that the British government was moving toward compliance with the United States' request for seizure of the ships he was building. He asserted that "the hope of getting the ships out seems more than doubtful, indeed hopeless, unless there should be a change in the political character of the ministry.... If we get money and I contract for other ships," Bulloch added, "I should go to French builders."[14]

Bulloch had already explored that possibility but could not proceed because he was without funds. The financial firm of Erlanger and Company stepped into the breach and floated a large loan based on cotton bonds in major European financial markets. Preliminary negotiations for the Erlanger Cotton Loan began in October 1862 in Richmond, although Confederate officials viewed it as a device for increasing Erlanger's wealth. Subscribers would be able to buy cotton for the bargain price of $30 a bale and profits by the takers of the loan would be enormous. It was a poor deal for the Confederacy, but the money was desperately needed. Subscription books were opened on March 19, 1863, and were heavily oversubscribed, but the net receipts for the Confederacy of the £3 million loan were estimated to be a little over £1,250,000. As bad as the deal seemed, it kept the stream of supplies coming into the Confederacy. The proceeds were to be paid by Erlanger to the Confederacy in eight installments. Treasury Secretary Memminger received the first payment on March 24, 1863.[15]

Secretary Mallory prepared estimates for building ironclads in France, the Confederate Congress secretly appropriated over $5 million for these vessels, and Mallory soon forwarded over $630,000 to Bulloch. Mallory's agent had already inspected shipbuilding yards in Bordeaux, France, and had inquired about French neutrality laws and their interpretation. By July 16, 1863, Bulloch and French shipbuilder Lucien Arman had signed a contract for constructing two ironclads that were to be completed in 10 months. They were to be approximately 171 feet in length, displace 1,000 tons, and were to be armed with one large 10-inch 300-pounder Armstrong in the bow, and two 6-inch guns in a turret at the stern. Powerful engines would produce a speed of 12 knots at full load.[16]

Meanwhile, Bulloch's hopes had improved for the ironclads in England. Writing to Secretary Mallory on July 9, 1863, Bulloch ebulliently proposed that when the armor-clad ships were ready to go to sea they should proceed directly to Wilmington, North Carolina. One vessel would make for New Inlet, and the other for the main channel at the mouth of the Cape Fear River. "By steaming quietly in at early daylight, they might entirely destroy the blockading vessels; not one should be left to steal away and to make known the fact of the ironclads being on the coast." After completing the work at Wilmington, the two ironclads "might sail southward, sweep the blockading fleet from the sea front of every harbor from the Capes of Virginia to Sabine Pass, and cruising up and down the coast could prevent anything like permanent, systematic interruption of our foreign trade for the future." Bulloch continued with additional fatuous ideas. The ironclads could go up the Potomac River and strike Washington, creating a diversion for General Lee. They could raid Portsmouth, New Hampshire, demolish the navy yard there, and afterward threaten to destroy the town unless $50 million were paid. Then they could attack Philadelphia, Pennsylvania where "once in front of the city they could dictate their own terms."[17]

In addition to the two ironclads in France, the two Laird rams under construction at Liverpool were progressing well. One ("294") had been launched on July 4 and it was expected that both would be ready for sea by October 1863. On August 30, 1863, Secretary Mallory detailed Capt. Samuel Barron to take command of the emerging force as flag officer, aboard either of these ironclads. Mallory reiterated to Barron that the mission of these ships was to raise "the blockade of our coast."[18]

Bulloch still was concerned about possible interference by British authorities with the departure of the ironclads. U.S. minister Charles Francis Adams let the British know that the United States was most distressed about the destruction of her merchant fleet by the commerce raiders *Florida* and *Alabama*. In turn, Great Britain began reconsidering its neutrality policy. Bulloch tried to safeguard the ironclads by clandestinely arranging for a French shipbuilder, Bravay and Company, to buy the unfinished vessels and complete their construction in accord with his requirements. Bravay and Company agreed that when the ships were beyond British jurisdiction, they would sell them to Bulloch at the sale price plus a commission.

Adams was well aware of the severe threat posed to ships of the Union blockade by the Laird rams. On July 11, 1863, he wrote to Lord Earl Russell, the British foreign secretary, suggesting that if the vessels were delivered to the Confederates, a state of war could exist between the United States and Britain. The situation escalated after Adams received a letter from Russell declaring that his government could not find sufficient evidence to warrant seizing the two rams. Adams sent a letter dated September 5, 1863, to Russell containing a phrase that electrified the atmosphere: "One of the ironclads is about to leave.... It would be superfluous in me to point out to your Lordship that this means war."[19] It was a life-and-death matter for the United States, which did not know if it could cope with these two powerful vessels.

Lord Russell responded by sending an order to the customs officer at Liverpool to halt the delivery of the two ships until their legal status could be determined. He also moved to prevent a repetition of the *Alabama* debacle where the ship had slipped off hours before a similar order was to be served. He sent a British gunboat to seal the exit from the Mersey River while a detachment of royal marines boarded the vessels. The Confederacy lost these two powerful ships; eventually the British purchased them for Her Majesty's Navy for £220,000. After debts were paid, a portion of this money was turned over to the Confederates. These funds, plus those gained from sale of other seized vessels in France, enabled Bulloch to purchase blockade runners.[20]

The Confederacy's hopes for constructing a powerful ironclad fleet in France were dashed as well. A month after the events at Liverpool, an informant visited the U.S. minister in Paris and offered him documentation that the two ironclads being built at the Arman shipyards in Bordeaux were being built for the Confederate navy. To disguise the affair, Bulloch had asserted that the ships were being built for Egypt and he had given them fictitious names, *Cheops* and *Sphinx*. Ultimately, Emperor Napoleon III forbade departure of the vessels. Arman managed to sell them to two other countries with the *Sphinx* going to Denmark. However, in 1864 the Danes decided they did not want the vessel and Arman offered to sell the *Sphinx* to Bulloch, who assented. By January 1865, Mallory had the first and only foreign-built ironclad in the Confederate Navy.[21]

The *Sphinx* was placed under command of a Virginian, Capt. Thomas Jefferson Page, and left Copenhagen with a provisional Danish captain and crew, with Page aboard. She sailed toward the English Channel, encountered a gale and nearly foundered. Captain Page managed to get into a safe harbor and later the *Sphinx* was met at sea by the Confederate blockade runner *City of Richmond* that provided crew and supplies. In late January 1865, the ship was commissioned into the Confederate navy and renamed the *Stonewall*. Although she was not seaworthy, she struggled toward America enduring heavy seas and near mutiny. Captain Page expressed his anxiety about his new vessel when he cautioned Flag Officer Barron: "You must not expect too much of me; I fear that the power and effect of this vessel have been too much exaggerated. We will do our best."[22] Upon reaching Nassau in the Bahamas on May 6, 1865, Captain Page learned that southern forces were surrendering. He then headed for Cuban waters where *Stonewall* was cornered by U.S. Navy ships at Havana. Ten days later, he was able to convey his vessel to neutral Spain in return for $16,000 to pay off his crew. The only foreign built ironclad that Mallory was able to put to sea became a ship without a nation and met an inglorious end.[23]

These events in Great Britain and France in late 1863 were a calamity of the highest order for the Confederate Navy Department. A potential attacking force had been struck down in just two months, not through battle, but through effective Union diplomacy and political maneuvering. In his unique way, Stephen Mallory described how the two countries rejected Confederate efforts to get ironclads built on their soils:

> While John Bull put his foot squarely down and said to the "so-called Confederate Government," "Don't come here to get any more ships and kick up a row; damn me, I'll not stand for it," France, ... exhibited about as much good faith and sincerity as might be expected from any professional Jeremy Didler.[24]

What Mallory and Bulloch failed to appreciate was the fact that both nations had acted out of self-interest.

At this point it may be useful to look at the character of James Bulloch to whom Secretary Mallory had entrusted great responsibilities. Bulloch had been given the freedom to operate independently and carefully maneuver within the diplomatic and political structures of England and France, accomplishing all that could be reasonably expected of him. After the war, Raphael Semmes left us a valuable character sketch of James Bulloch:

> I had spent some days with him, at his quiet retreat, in the little village of Waterloo, near Liverpool.... He was living in a very plain, simple style, though large sums of public money were passing through his hands, and he has had the honor to come out of the war poor. He paid out moneys in good faith, to the last, even when it was quite evident that the cause had gone under ... he had greatly assisted me, by his counsel and advice, given with that modesty and reserve which always mark true ability.[25]

Historian Philip Van Doren Stern also heaps praise upon Bulloch by stating that the man was "the ingenious planner, the good technician, the astute businessman, the honest administrator of huge funds, the man who was responsible for the most effective moves his government made beyond its borders...."[26]

After all the efforts they had made to build an ironclad fleet in England and France, Stephen R. Mallory and James D. Bulloch must have been bitterly disappointed. Mallory had experienced similar feelings a year earlier when New Orleans and the Gosport Navy Yard fell into the hands of the enemy but he had come out of his sad state clearly focused on the future.

Bulloch and Mallory had both been pleased with the success of the *Fingal* as a blockade runner and began considering further operations of this nature. After the *Florida* and *Alabama* got to sea, Bulloch gave his attention to acquiring another ship to run the blockade. In February 1863, Mallory wrote Bulloch of the immediate need for a blockade runner to bring six months' naval supplies, mostly clothing, for 3,000 men. The navy secretary authorized Bulloch to "purchase a steamer for this purpose and to place a naval officer in charge of her.... A light-draft, fast steamer is desirable, and I perceive that a new class of such vessel, with two propellers, has been successfully devised."[27] In October 1863, Bulloch purchased for this purpose a 700 gross ton ship, the *Coquette*, placing her under command of a Confederate navy officer, Lt. Robert R. Carter. This fast, 200-horsepower, twin screw, iron steamer arrived in Wilmington from Bermuda on May 12, 1864, with a load of marine engines and ordnance stores. She was capable of carrying up to 1,259 cotton bales on her return cruise.[28]

The Confederate army had been meeting some of its needs with its blockade running operation consisting of five ships transporting war materiel. North Carolina's governor Vance had purchased a ship, the *Ad-Vance*, for the same purpose.[29] On February 6, 1864, the Confederate Congress passed legislation regulating blockade running activity. The legislation centralized dealings of cotton within the War Department and this activity was placed under the aegis of Col. Thomas L. Bayne. He controlled the amount of cotton to be shipped overseas in payment for goods supplied; this had the effect of nationalizing all foreign trade of the Confederacy. "King Cotton" became the financing medium for obtaining needed supplies in the Confederacy.[30]

Colonel Bayne had under his supervision agents who were placed at specific southern ports. In Florida the agent was Maj. A. B. Noyes who was located at St. Marks. On March 29, 1864, a conference was held between Major Noyes and the secretaries of war, treasury, and navy where it was decided that two steamers would be procured to conduct trade between Gulf ports in Florida and Havana or Nassau. It was agreed that the Navy Department would take charge of the first vessel and place an officer in command.[31]

The shipping giant in England, Fraser, Trenholm and Company, agreed to furnish the Confederacy with eight steamers. That firm would operate the steamers until they were purchased by the Confederacy through transfer of one-half the outbound cotton to the company. When the value of the cotton covered the value of the ship plus a 20-percent commission, it would be relinquished to the Confederate government. At that point, the rebels either could keep the civilian crew or replace them with naval personnel.

James Bulloch, Mallory's agent, handled the arrangements in England. He purchased four ships from Jones, Quiggen and Company located in Liverpool (*Bat, Stag, Owl,* and *Deer*) and four more vessels (*Lark, Wren, Albatross,* and *Penguin*) from Laird and Sons, also in Liverpool. Bulloch supervised all work.[32]

The Navy Department continued running the blockade with the *Coquette*, Lieutenant Carter commanding. This ship had to be taken out of service in March 1864 due to various mechanical problems. Following repairs, the *Coquette* made five trips through the blockade carrying thousands of bales of cotton between May 9 and July 11, 1864. Unfortunately, her career ended that summer. Her boiler tubes were fouled with silt and Mallory ordered her sold.[33]

By August 24, 1864, the Confederate Navy was operating the *Owl* between Bermuda and Wilmington. She was under the command of John N. Maffitt of *Florida* fame. In early 1865, Commander Maffitt took the *Owl* to Havana where he joined with *Lark* and *Wren*. These latter two light-draft vessels had not been turned over to the Navy Department but had been built for the service of the Confederacy. As senior officer, Maffitt was ordered to see that they ran the blockade to ports in Florida, as well as Galveston, bringing in supplies of clothing and shoes for the navy and small arms for the army.[34] *Owl* joined *Lark* and *Wren* for numerous round trips between Havana and Galveston in spring 1865. On May 25, 1865, the *Lark* was the last steam blockade runner to enter and leave a Confederate port.[35]

On February 18, 1864, James Bulloch had written to Secretary Mallory expressing that "Although sorely disappointed in reference to ironclads, from which we were justified in expecting so much, there are means at hand by which the enemy can be greatly annoyed and harassed." He then suggested that the Confederate navy should take over the blockade running business to supply the needs of the South. Bulloch revealed a creative slant as he wrote, "If registered in the name of private individuals and sailed purely as commercial ships they could trade without interruption or violation of neutrality between our coasts and the Bermudas, Bahamas, and West Indies." Suddenly, he asserted, the blockade runner could be converted to gunboats and destroy Union blockaders. Bulloch explained how this might be done:

> When three or more of the vessels happened to be in harbor at the same time a few hours would suffice to mount a couple of heavy guns on each, and at early dawn a successful raid might be made upon the unsuspecting blockaders.... After a raid or cruise the vessels could be divested of every appliance of war, and resuming their private ownership and commercial names, could bring out cargoes of cotton to pay the cost of the cruise....

Like Mallory, Bulloch was a man who could tolerate a setback and immediately plunge into planning for the next depredations upon the enemy, no matter how fanciful the plan.[36]

On March 21, 1864, Mallory enlarged upon Bulloch's ideas when he wrote that commerce raiders could destroy commercial New England fishing fleets around the globe. "From distant points such vessels could be suddenly assembled at a blockaded port," Mallory wrote, "open it for sixty days and again separate." He thought this might "turn the trading mind of New England to thoughts of peace."[37] On April 6, 1864, Mallory further expanded on this concept when he wrote to Flag Officer Samuel Barron and said that vessels "might strike a blow at the enemy off Wilmington, during the summer, and then separate to meet for a blow at another point. I commend the light infantry system to your judgment."[38] This operating mode seemed to fascinate the secretary. The next day he wrote in the same vein to Bulloch: "Such ships as ours ... could make a united dash at New England fisheries and ports, then separate for reunion at Wilmington or Charleston, where at times they might strike a telling blow.... Such a system of alternate united and separate action — naval light infantry tactics — has never been adopted upon the sea...."[39]

Mallory emerged from despair over the loss of foreign-built ironclads to combine tactics associated with commerce raiding, blockading running, and hit-and-run attacks upon blockading vessels. These tactics evolved from experimentation beginning in 1863 with "David" class torpedo boats being employed to attack Federal warships and fast gunboats manned with commandos being used to assault and capture Union warships and merchant marine vessels.

11

Technically Advanced Weapons

Secretary Stephen Russell Mallory developed strategies associated with using technically advanced weapons of destruction. He consistently expressed interest in applying technology that might give the rebels an advantage over their stronger opponents. The secretary put key men in responsible positions and encouraged them to think and plan creatively. He nurtured this productive climate by avoiding micromanagement and accepting responsibility for inevitable errors that resulted from experimentation. This was not a minor matter for people would die or be wounded in the course of these events.

The Confederate army and navy were well aware of previous efforts to make water a hostile environment for enemy boats. One method was to use inert obstructions such as sunken ships and piles of rocks to block interior waterways and harbors. Such obstructions were utilized throughout the war by both sides. Technically advanced weapons arose from the application of scientific knowledge, particularly in the fields of metallurgy, engineering, and chemistry. These principles led to manufacture of the torpedo or mine. During the Civil War, the torpedo was an explosive device in the water that blew up either at or below the surface. If it was moveable and delivered to an objective by floating it in the current or attaching it to the end of a shaft attached to the bow of a boat, it usually was referred to as a torpedo. But if it was anchored to river or harbor bottoms in a fixed position, it often was referred to as a mine.

The torpedo or mine was developed after the invention of explosive gunpowder in the 16th century, but these early devices could be exploded only while on the water's surface. A true underwater mine was invented by an American, David Bushnell, around 1771. This device was used to sink a schooner during the War for Independence in 1777. This underwater mine, carried by a small submersible boat, was detonated by a time device. After 1777 the use of mines progressed rather quickly while submarine development lagged behind as designers struggled with navigational problems.[1] The advancement of mines progressed relatively quickly because inventions enabled them to be exploded either by percussive contact or use of electricity. Although the Confederates did not invent mines or torpedoes, they were the first to use them in a disciplined manner and as important strategic components in warfare.

The person behind the development and use of torpedoes was almost certainly

Stephen Mallory, or Matthew Fontaine Maury, or both. Both Mallory and Maury had ample opportunity to promote torpedo warfare, since in the summer of 1861 Mallory named Maury as head of the Bureau for the Defense of Coastal Waters and Rivers, a part of the Office of Ordnance and Hydrography. Maury was appointed after he demonstrated the potential of this weapon by exploding a percussion torpedo on the James River near Rocketts Navy Yard. Thereafter, this bureau laid a number of torpedoes (mines) in both the Mississippi and James rivers.[2]

In its simplest form, the torpedo was a metal canister, barrel, or similar container filled with explosives. In the water, the torpedo (or mine) usually was placed in a fixed position and anchored to the river or sea bottom with a weight. The device was tethered to a chain or rope and allowed to float upward to an appropriate distance below the water's surface. Torpedoes could be detonated by contact or electricity. The contact torpedoes exploded as "horns" on the device were broken when striking a ship's bottom. This set up a chemical reaction igniting the charge. The main disadvantage with the contact torpedoes was that they would explode equally well when struck by friendly or enemy hulls. The electric torpedo was fired by use of wires connected to it that ran to batteries on shore. These proved to be less reliable; faulty detonating equipment resulted from difficulty in obtaining necessary wire or rubber for underwater insulation. Also, torpedoes or mines could be strung together and floated into a target.

The Confederate navy developed an imaginative and effective delivery technique when the "spar" torpedo was created. In this application, 50 to 100 pounds of powder were packed into a thin metal container at the end of a 30-foot wooden or metal rod. The watertight canister at the end of the spar was delivered by a small vessel and lowered into the sea so as to strike an enemy vessel below the waterline. Later, torpedoes were delivered in similar fashion by submarines. These explosive devices posed both physical and psychological threats to the enemy and compelled the Union to divert resources and energy to deal with them.[3]

The first Confederate torpedo (mine) attacks took place on July 7, 1861, in Hampton Roads. However, these devices failed to explode and Union sailors recovered them the same day. Other such attacks took place that summer but failed, probably due to water leaking in the floating cask that usually contained about 25 pounds of powder.[4] Through months of experimentation along with design modifications and innovations, Confederate torpedoes became more dependable. By late 1862, they had become an important component of southern naval strategy.

This developing stratagem demanded new organizational units. In October 1862 the Confederate Congress created three new organizations: the Torpedo Bureau, the Submarine Battery Service, and the Secret Service Corps. The Torpedo Bureau was placed in the War Department under the direction of Gen. G.J. Raines. Its function was to protect against inland attacks on Confederate forts and prevent landings along the southern coasts by planting land torpedoes (or mines). The Submarine Battery Service was a similar structure placed in the Navy Department under command of Lt. Hunter Davidson, Matthew F. Maury's successor. Two months earlier, Maury had been sent to Europe to obtain electrical cable and related equipment that was indispensable to torpedo warfare. The function of this group was to defend the waters approaching Richmond, particularly the James River, and other similar waters. In practice the War Department's Torpedo Bureau and the Navy Department's Submarine Battery Service worked closely with one another to defend against enemy depredations.

The Secret Service Corps, part of the Navy Department, was commanded by Capt. Thomas E. Courtenay, and was assigned to attack the enemy with explosive devices in acts of sabotage.[5] One of the most effective tools utilized was a torpedo disguised as a piece of coal that would have the desired result when it went into a furnace. One victim of this wile was the troop transport *Greyhound* that sank in the James River on November 24, 1864.[6]

The Submarine Battery Service manufactured torpedoes, some of which were planted in the Yazoo River in Mississippi. The most dramatic demonstration of the power of these torpedoes occurred on the Yazoo on December 12, 1862. The 500-ton ironclad Union gunboat *Cairo* was going up the river clearing numerous planted torpedoes. Suddenly, two of them exploded in succession, one under her port quarter and the other under her port bow. *Cairo* sank in 12 minutes. Afterwards Rear-Adm. David D. Porter wrote in his report, "His [Lieutenant-Commander Selfridges's] vessel is a great loss to us. She was in splendid order and had just been made shot-proof with railroad iron, where she was before vulnerable."[7]

The Confederacy continued to plant torpedoes throughout southern harbors and waterways, at Charleston, Mobile, the Cape Fear River near Wilmington, and on the Savannah River at Augusta, Georgia. Torpedoes claimed many victims. On February 28, 1863, the ironclad *Montauk* struck a torpedo and sustained serious damage on the Ogeechee River near Fort McAllister, Georgia.[8] On July 13, 1863, on the Yazoo River, the large ironclad gunboat *Baron De Kalb* hit a torpedo and while she was sinking another torpedo exploded at her stern. She went under in 15 minutes.[9] Additional Union vessels ran afoul of torpedoes in the James River in 1863 and 1864. In August 1863 the gunboat *Commodore Barney* was seriously damaged and in May 1864 the 542-ton gunboat *Commodore Jones* was sunk with a third of the crew going down with her.[10]

Federal forces dreaded torpedoes and Secretary Mallory believed the devices were just as effective as an army corps. Naval historian Spencer C. Tucker writes, "Torpedoes sank more Union warships during the war than any other means used by the South." Another naval historian, Raimondo Luraghi, suggests that during the war the Confederate torpedoes may have "destroyed or disabled some fifty Union warships, a fleet equal (at the time) to about thirty thousand tons of shipping. Never during the conflict did any other Confederate naval weapon cause such havoc in the Union Navy."[11]

Anxiety about Confederate torpedoes caused the Federal army and navy to divert resources to be watchful. For example, in 1864 thousands of United States soldiers were transferred from combat posts to scrutinize the riverbanks of the James River to guard against placement of torpedoes and mines.[12] Additionally, in the spring of 1864 a large Federal amphibious force was assigned to the James River for minesweeping duties. This force consisted of "the *Tritonio*, the *Stepping Stones*, the *Delaware*, eleven armed cutters ... and 175 sailors, marines and soldiers" to clear the left bank of the James River of Confederate troops and protect the vessels.[13]

Another advanced weaponry used was the submarine. This term applies to a vessel that could be operated both above the water and fully submerged. The submarine is not to be confused with a vessel that is capable of only being partially submerged. Some attack boats were constructed with tanks that could be filled to make a larger portion of the hull lie beneath the water line. The Confederates used both types of vessels in several important naval engagements.

The submarine had been invented before the Civil War but the Confederate navy

Cairo—Union Ironclad Gunboat. This vessel was photographed on the Mississippi River in 1862. On December 12, 1862, the *Cairo* was clearing mines on the Yazoo River when two of them exploded on her port side. She sank in 12 minutes. COURTESY OF NAVAL HISTORICAL CENTER, NH 61568.

developed such boats that were truly combat-ready and were put to practical use, while the U.S. Navy merely toyed with the idea. The next step for Secretary Mallory was to deliver torpedoes directly to targets of choice. Submarines or torpedo boats could carry these explosive devices and accomplish this mission. Once submarine development progressed to the point where the vessel could be safely submerged and returned to the surface, thought was given to the best method for sinking enemy ships. As the ability to navigate a submersible improved, the Confederates experimented with the use of a torpedo placed at the end of a long spar that was attached to the submarine's bow.[14]

Early southern experiments with submarines began in New Orleans, but were transferred to Mobile when the Crescent City fell to the Union. Financial aid came from a wealthy sugar dealer, Horace L. Hunley. The fourth submarine constructed, which was to become the most famous, was christened the *Hunley* in his honor. Because the presence of the Union blockade at Charleston Harbor made an inviting target, the submarine was transported by railroad to that city in August 1863.[15]

On the evening of February 17, 1864, the *Hunley* steered toward the enemy in Charleston Harbor. The submarine, with her contact spar torpedo extended, slammed into the screw sloop-of-war *Housatonic*. The resulting explosion heavily damaged *Housatonic*'s stern on the starboard side, and she sank within a few minutes. *Hunley*

Hunley. The Confederate Navy vessel *Hunley*, the first submarine in history to sink an enemy warship, did so on February 17, 1864, when she sent the Federal warship *Housatonic* to the bottom using her extended spar torpedo. *Hunley* never surfaced until she was raised through salvage efforts on August 8, 2000. This sepia drawing by R.G. Skerrett was done in 1902 after a painting then held in the Confederate Memorial Literary Society Museum, Richmond, Virginia. It is believed to be an accurate image of the submarine. COURTESY OF NAVAL HISTORICAL CENTER, NH 999, AND NAVY ART COLLECTION.

apparently was severely damaged by the same explosion, and also sank. This was the first recorded incident in history where a submarine had sunk a warship.[16]

As might be expected, the Union was most perturbed. Union Rear-Admiral Dahlgren wrote, "I have attached more importance to the use of torpedoes than others have done, and believe them to constitute the most formidable of the difficulties in the way to Charleston. Their effect on the *Ironsides*, in October, and now on the *Housatonic*, sustains me in this idea." He recommended that a reward of $30,000 be offered for the capture or destruction of each Confederate submarine.[17]

Meanwhile, another weapon was being developed under Secretary Mallory's creative leadership. This was the first torpedo boat or assault boat in history. Capt. Francis D. Lee suggested the idea for such a vessel to General Beauregard who supported the project and referred him to Mallory. Captain Lee called upon the secretary on October 18, 1862. He reported that Mallory studied the design and "expressed his deep interest in the undertaking and his entire willingness to furnish everything in his power to make its accomplishment as early as possible."[18] After early experiments that were failures, the rebels designed a cigar-shaped boat that was 54 feet long and five feet six inches wide. The vessel was protected by metal plating and was powered by a steam engine in the center. The boat was fitted with tanks that could be filled and emptied of water to affect her buoyancy. This enabled her to lie low in the water partially submerged. A moveable spar that could be controlled from the inside was attached to the bow. The spar was 14 feet long and at the end was fastened an explosive device containing 100 pounds of gunpow-

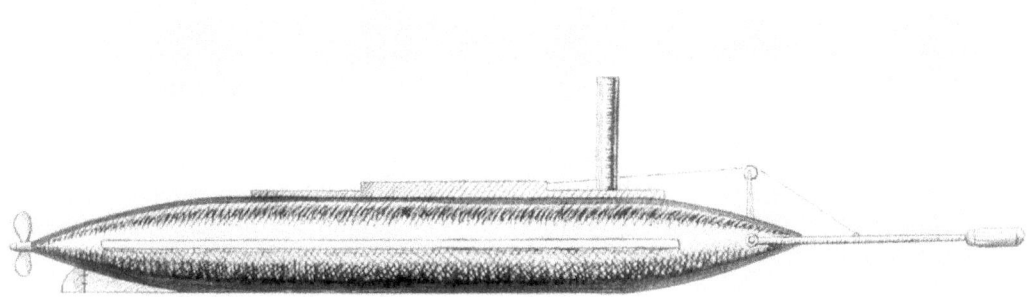

***David*—Torpedo Boat.** This pen-and-ink drawing shows the profile of the *David* with her spar torpedo deployed. On October 5, 1863, the vessel exploded her weapon against the hull of the Union warship *New Ironsides*. The Federal vessel was heavily damaged and out of action for over a year. COURTESY OF NAVAL HISTORICAL CENTER, NH 95242.

der. This model was built on the Cooper River near Charleston and was launched in Charleston Harbor. She was christened the *David*. After training, her crew steered her toward an enemy vessel, the ironclad *New Ironsides*, on the evening of October 5, 1863. At around 9:00 P.M. the *David* raced toward her target and with the spar lowered she caused a huge explosion against the hull of the *New Ironsides*. The ironclad remained afloat but was heavily damaged and was out of action for more than a year while being repaired in Philadelphia. *David*, though shaken, returned intact to Charleston.[19]

The Union navy was impressed with the performance of the *David*. Rear-Admiral Dahlgren wrote, "Among the many inventions with which I have been familiar, I have seen none which have acted so perfectly at first trial. The secrecy, rapidity of movement, control of direction, and precise explosion indicate, I think, the introduction of the torpedo element as a means of certain warfare. It can be ignored no longer.... By all means let us have a quantity of these torpedoes, and thus turn them against the enemy. We can make them faster than they can."[20]

Both General Beauregard, in charge of Charleston's defenses, and the Confederate Navy Department followed up the initial success of *David* with further attacks by this torpedo boat and another recently constructed similar boat, the *Squib*. Construction of new torpedo boats followed in short order, not only in Charleston, but also in Wilmington, North Carolina, and Mobile, Alabama.[21]

The greatest difficulty in constructing these assault boats was getting the engines with which to propel them. Secretary Mallory became involved personally in trying to acquire good engines and other weapons system support items. On April 16, 1864, he wrote to Bulloch in England and provided him with a description of small marine engines and boilers to be used in torpedo boats. He asked Bulloch to, "Please have twelve made as early as practicable and sent over to us.... We want also 25 miles of good insulated wire, suitable for marine batteries, to which electrical currents are to be sent. We also want one thousand of the best gun cotton, to be used for torpedoes."[22]

Some Union officers were impressed with the "David" class of vessels and urged they be replicated for the Federal Navy. U.S. Navy rear admiral Dahlgren suggested to Secretary Gideon Welles that a vessel similar to *David* be constructed. He wrote to Secretary Welles saying, "I ... request that a number of torpedo boats be made and sent here with dispatch...."[23]

All of these new weapons—submarine, torpedoes (mines), and torpedo boats or assault boats—struck fear into the enemy and served as prototypes for modern weaponry. Torpedo boats became the forerunners of the famed patrol torpedo (PT) boats of World War II vintage, and submarines were antecedents for those constructed for destroying shipping in World Wars I and II. These weapons were developed because Secretary Stephen R. Mallory, driven by the desire to gain the upper hand through employment of technical surprise, exercised his imagination and creativity and had the courage to risk failure because of the potential rewards that might be gained.

12

The Beginning of the End

Through 1864 and 1865 Secretary Stephen R. Mallory saw his navy achieve some remarkable victories as well as suffer some agonizing defeats. The secretary was well aware that the South was losing the war but he would not be deterred from doing the best possible job with the meager resources still available. The feared sea-raiders *Florida* and *Alabama* were operating and the *Hunley* had sunk the *Housatonic*. Although he would fail in his attempt to develop an offensive ironclad fleet in England and France, Mallory had succeeded in putting afloat a considerable defensive ironclad fleet to protect southern coastal and riverine waters. This homeland defensive force was growing with the most recent additions, the *Fredericksburg* and *Virginia II*, joining the *Richmond* on the James River. Furthermore, the keel was laid for a fourth powerful ironclad, the *Texas*.[1]

All was quiet at important southern ports on the east coast. Charleston Harbor seemed to be under effective control by Confederate navy and army forces, especially since the intimidating armored ship *Charleston* had been added to the local squadron.[2] At Wilmington the ironclad *Raleigh* had joined her sister ship, the *North Carolina*, to strengthen the defenses there.[3]

However, Mallory was concerned about two locations: Mobile Bay and the North Carolina sounds. North Carolina coastal waters invited Union penetration inland, threatening Lee's army in Virginia with a flanking movement. Mobile was a prime Union target because an important railroad terminus was located there and linked the rebel supply line running into the interior with blockade-running activity in Mobile Bay.

The secretary was concerned about weak Confederate defenses at Mobile that were attributed primarily to the usual problems of lack of iron and unavailability of labor. In early 1864 two newly constructed ironclads were being prepared for battle. The *Tennessee* had received her guns but still lacked crew and officers. The *Nashville*, which had been launched the previous June and then towed to Mobile, was being fitted out. However, iron was not available for the *Nashville* and priority was given to the completion of the *Tennessee*.[4] The navy and army had not always worked cooperatively with one another in the past, but in this instance it was in their mutual interests to do so. Since Mallory was unable to secure sufficient numbers of sailors to man the *Tennessee*, he asked that

Tennessee—Confederate Ironclad Ram. The *Tennessee* was built in Selma, Alabama, and was commanded by Admiral Buchanan in the August 5, 1864, Battle of Mobile Bay. The ironclad was battered into submission and surrendered. Buchanan was wounded and taken prisoner. COURTESY OF NAVAL HISTORICAL CENTER AND U.S. NAVY ART COLLECTION, NH 83805 K.

soldiers be transferred to the navy. Ultimately 110 men were transferred to the ironclad, but they needed training to make sailors of them. Admiral Buchanan was in command and he quickly saw to it that they were drilled to fire the guns.[5]

The *Tennessee* took her station on Mobile Bay on May 18, 1864, and anchored 10 miles from Fort Morgan along with two gunboats, the *Selma* and *Morgan* (and later the *Gaines*). The *Tennessee* was powerful. "She displaced 1,273 tons, was 209 feet long with a 48-foot beam ... her outer decks were armored with 2-inch sheet iron. She carried a formidable battery of six rifled Brookes: two of 7.5 inches ... and four, of 6 inches...."[6] The main problem for Mallory and Buchanan was the fact she was the only available ironclad. Time and iron had run out and other ironclads would not be completed in time for the Battle of Mobile Bay. However, there were supplemental defenses including obstacles in the water and a triple line of anchored contact mines that narrowed the channel so that an invader would have to enter Mobile Bay under the guns of Fort Morgan. Confederates waited for the inevitable attack.

Federal armed forces were gathering for this great confrontation and had planned a coordinated land-water assault. Adm. David G. Farragut gathered a suitable naval group including four ironclads. Additionally, he asked for at least 3,000 soldiers for the operation; by August 2, 1864, 2,400 troops were in place on Dauphin Island to the west, poised to attack Fort Gaines.

At 6:30 A.M. on August 5, Farragut attacked with his fleet. The ironclad *Tecumseh* opened fire and gunners at Fort Morgan returned fire with its rifled guns. The *Tecumseh* was hit, went off course into the torpedo field, struck a mine causing an explosion, and sank. Farragut continued forward. In spite of heavy fire from Fort Morgan resulting in alarming losses, his ships entered Mobile Bay. During a long battle, the three remaining Union ironclads took on *Tennessee*. For an hour the Confederate vessel underwent a ferocious pounding from Union 11-inch cannons. Her armor began to fail from the assault; she lost her steering, and began taking on water. *Tennessee* was effectively disabled and surrendered at 10:00 A.M. The Union had won the battle but at a disheartening cost in lives and in destruction and damage of naval vessels. The Federal ground forces, strengthened by 2,000 more troops, would carry out a land campaign against the forts but Fort Morgan would not surrender until August 23.[7]

The town of Mobile remained in southern control and continued as a manufacturing center with road and railroad connections to the interior. It was well defended by two forts, torpedo fields, a naval squadron, and about 10,000 soldiers. The Yankees were forced to delay an attack on the town due to losses incurred during the ill-fated 1864 spring invasion of the Red River valley in Louisiana. That northern defeat caused significant depletions of troops, ships, horses, wagons, and guns. The Union paused to replenish and reinforce its western army during the fall and winter. In January and February 1865, Union general Canby began receiving reinforcements, and by March he was able to muster an army of over 45,000 men. These troops moved toward Mobile on March 26, 1865, supported by a naval squadron consisting of five ironclads and other vessels. Confederates exacted a heavy toll on this force. Torpedoes (mines) sank a total of two big Union ironclads and six other vessels. Nevertheless, the Confederates were forced to evacuate Mobile on April 12, 1865.[8]

The Confederate loss of Mobile Bay and the town of Mobile were largely due to the fearsome strength of Yankee navy and army forces. Rebel planning was generally sound, given their meager resources, but there was no unified control. Buchanan directed naval forces and Maj. Gen. Dabney H. Maury presided over the forts. Their command responsibilities were not clearly defined and there was not the level of army-navy coordination that had existed earlier at Charleston Harbor between General Beauregard and Commander Ingraham.[9] But the southerners had inflicted heavy losses on the Northern navy, primarily because of technical superiority in the design and use of torpedoes.

Stephen Mallory's other concern was with the North Carolina sounds and low country. Gen. Robert E. Lee was interested because they could be used by a Yankee armed force bent on threatening his flank. Furthermore, Lee's army was starving and if the South could control this territory an ample spring harvest could feed his troops. General Lee wrote President Davis about this situation on January 2, 1864:

> The time is at hand when, if an attempt can be made to capture the enemy's forces at New Berne, it should be done. I can now spare troops for the purpose, which will not be the case as spring approaches.... The garrison has been so long unmolested, and experiences such a feeling of security, that it is represented as careless. The gun-boats are small and indifferent, and do not keep up a head of steam. A bold party could descend the Neuse in boats at night, capture the gunboats, and drive the enemy by their aid from the works on that side of the river, while a force should attack them in front.[10]

General Lee's letter stimulated a combined army-navy operation that would result in the last great victory for the Confederate States of America. Navy secretary Mallory began putting the plan into motion on January 15, 1864 when he ordered Cmdr. James W. Cooke and Assistant Naval Constructor William A. Graves to oversee fitting out the ironclad *Albemarle* to hasten its completion. Cooke was to become the ship's commander upon her commissioning and Mallory stressed the urgency of the task by writing him saying, "You will make a weekly report of your progress, and you will not hesitate to adopt any measure necessary to the prompt completion of the work."[11]

On April 12, 1864, Confederate brigadier general Robert F. Hoke was ordered to command this combined operation and the chosen target was Plymouth, North Carolina. The *Albemarle* was being completed on the Roanoke River that empties into Albemarle Sound where Plymouth is located. General Hoke planned to advance toward Plymouth with about 7,000 troops and 30 field guns in coordination with the *Albemarle* that would attempt to neutralize the Union naval squadron protecting Plymouth. The town was defended with about 3,000 troops. Its strongest protective point was Fort Williams that was located in a position that enabled gunners to fire upon roads approaching the town.[12]

General Hoke inspected the *Albemarle* and was impressed with the imposing ironclad. She was 152 feet long, was propelled by two screws, carried a draft of only nine feet, and was armored with two Brooke 8-inch rifles that could fire in any direction. The General explained the situation to Commander Cooke and discussed the role the navy was to play. Cooke agreed to get underway for the battle on April 17. On that day, General Hoke commenced a probing attack; the next day he attacked across the entire front. His army was pinned down and battered, not only by the defensive troops but also by 21 guns of the Union navy squadron. On the night of April 17, Cooke weighed anchor to navigate toward Plymouth, towing behind him a raft fitted with a blacksmith shop to finish bolting iron plates on the vessel. Cooke had trouble with the propeller and rudderpost; at 10:00 P.M. on April 18 the *Albemarle* dropped anchor three nautical miles above Plymouth. About four hours later, the *Albemarle* got underway for Plymouth and after sunrise engaged the enemy fleet. Cooke rammed the Federal gunboat *Southfield*, quickly sinking her. The *Albemarle* next engaged the *Miami* and caused extensive damage with her rifled guns. The *Miami* fled downriver with two other gunboats, but Cooke did not pursue. Instead, he turned the *Albemarle*'s guns on Union fortifications, pounding them through the day and into the night. At dawn on April 20 the Confederate infantry attacked, and *Albemarle* played a supporting role by bombarding Union troops. That morning the Federal garrison surrendered.[13] The Confederates captured about 3,000 prisoners along with 28 cannons, 5,000 rifles, 700 barrels of flour, and various other supplies and ammunition. The navy was delighted to seize 300 tons of coal.[14]

This Confederate success at Plymouth, North Carolina, demonstrated outstanding planning and execution in a combined navy-army operation. The power of one ironclad vessel was a decisive factor and served to validate Secretary Mallory's faith in that type of ship. Confederates were elated. On May 17, 1864, the southern Congress issued a joint resolution of appreciation saying that "the thanks of Congress and the country are due and are tendered to Major-General Robert F. Hoke and Commander James W. Cooke and the officers and men under their command for the brilliant victory over the enemy at Plymouth, N. C."[15] In an extract from the report of the Secretary of the Navy of the Confederate States, dated April 30, 1864, Mallory wrote, "The signal success of this brilliant naval engagement is due to the admirable skill and courage displayed by Commander Cooke, his officers and men, in handling and fighting his ship against a greatly superior force of men and guns."[16]

The whole affair was a tremendous morale boost for Southrons and was timely because much misery would soon follow for the rebels. About a week after Mallory's April 30 statement, the Federal army under the direction of General U.S. Grant commenced a major offensive campaign to annihilate General Lee's army. The campaign would open in the Battle of the Wilderness and end at Appomattox Court House less than a year later.

Not only was the general populace buoyed by the South's victory, but so was General Hoke who turned toward the other North Carolina coastal stronghold — New Bern. It was intended that the *Neuse* would participate in this battle, but in her bid to move toward New Bern she ran fast aground a Neuse River sandbank from which she could not extricate herself despite major efforts.

General Beauregard had now assumed command of all forces in the area and he decided to use the rebel ironclad *Albemarle* in a risky venture. He ordered Commander Cooke to take the armored ship out of the Roanoke River into Albemarle and Pamlico sounds, which were infested with Union ships (but no ironclads), and sail up the Neuse estuary to New Bern. Southerners were aware that there was a powerful Yankee squadron consisting of seven ships mounting 56 cannons that would be opposing the *Albemarle*, which had only two rifled cannons. However, rebels were confidant that these wooden ships could not withstand shelling from the two Confederate guns and that the *Albemarle* could prevail against return fire because of her iron plates.[17]

On May 5, 1864, the *Albemarle*, accompanied by two tenders, steered toward her next battle. It began in late afternoon; the two forces exchanged fire, and the Union gunboat *Saccacus* rammed *Albemarle*. The collision caused *Albemarle* to heel, but she was not seriously damaged. The *Saccacus* was crippled by the collision and received heavy fire from the ironclad just after being bashed. The *Saccacus* lost her steering and she drifted aimlessly away. Later another Federal ship withdrew because she was almost sinking. Fighting stopped near sunset. The Union ships had all suffered serious damage, and two were disabled. The *Albemarle* was unable to continue her cruise because her smokestack was badly damaged. This caused steam pressure to drop so low that the ship could not make way. Furthermore, the muzzle of one of her two guns had been destroyed. Commander Cooke anchored to make repairs; he was determined to get to New Bern as soon as possible to support General Hoke's land attack upon that Federal stronghold.[18] However, the rebel army had withdrawn from in front of the town after being ordered to do so by General Beauregard. The Confederate offensive had been cancelled to reposition rebel soldiers in defensive positions against Union general Grant's advance. The *Albemarle* returned to Plymouth where she remained to protect Lee's flank against any enemy attack from that quadrant.[19]

The day after *Albemarle* weighed anchor to steam to New Bern, the ironclad *Raleigh* sailed from Wilmington, North Carolina, accompanied by two gunboats. Her mission was to attack the Federal blockading fleet. At around 8:00 P.M. on May 6, 1864, she engaged two Union vessels that withdrew when they saw their projectiles were not damaging the *Raleigh*. The southern ironclad followed them out to sea, some sporadic firing occurred, and at sunrise on May 7 a battle ensued between *Raleigh* and four U.S. Navy ships. Projectiles from the northern ships were ineffective and the Federal force fled. *Raleigh* returned to Wilmington but ran aground on a falling tide. As the ebb tide continued, the ironclad, grounded on a sandbar, broke her back (probably due to the weakness of the hull) and was lost.[20] However, the *Raleigh* had demonstrated her usefulness in keeping the enemy fleet at bay—as had *Albemarle*—and validated Mallory's theory about the efficacy of such vessels employed as a home defense fleet. Secretary Mallory's ironclad defense of the southern coastline now consisted of 12 vessels and constituted "an almost insuperable obstacle for the enemy."[21] Further, "the Confederate ironclads, overcoming great obstacles, had succeeded in implementing the defense strategy that Mallory had assigned them."[22]

Stephen Mallory was not satisfied with defensive action and was eager to go on the offensive should there be reasonable opportunity to do so. An alternative had arisen earlier in the war when an imaginative officer, Lt. John Taylor Wood, came to him with a proposal for partisan warfare. Wood suggested development of an organization for conducting riverine sorties against the U.S. Navy, by using small, fast attack boats in hit-and-run assaults. The strike force would be a small group of perhaps 15 to 20 men to a boat that by stealth would make quick, destructive raids in enemy-held territories. Mallory enthusiastically endorsed this concept and put it into play in late 1862.

On the night of October 7, 1862, Lieutenant Wood commanded a raid by two boats that were transported by wagons to the Potomac River. Fifteen sailors, who were chosen by Wood from James River Squadron personnel, manned the craft. The raiders found the U.S. schooner *Francis Elmore* loaded with hay anchored in mid-channel near Bluff Point. They captured her, set her afire, and took the crew as prisoners.[23] The commander led another raid on the evening of October 28, 1862, when he and 25 armed men in four boats captured the merchantman *Alleghanian* that was anchored in Chesapeake Bay about 20 miles off the mouth of the Rappahannock River. The vessel was bound from Baltimore for London with a load of guano. The officers and pilot were taken prisoner and the remaining 10 seamen were ordered into their lifeboat. Then the vessel was set afire.[24]

A more elaborate and ambitious commando raid, again led by Commander Wood, took place in August 1863. He led a raiding party of 82 officers and men in an amphibious operation that involved four boats carried on wagons. His second in command was 2nd Lt. Francis L. Hoge. The objective was to capture an enemy warship, and Wood established a base along the Piankatank River that empties into the Rappahannock River. There he met Col. Thomas L. Rosser, commanding the Fifth Virginia Cavalry Regiment, who was to play a supporting role. Rosser placed his cavalry in the village of Urbanna, Virginia, on the Rappahannock River. On the evening of August 23, 1863, Commander Wood and his men launched their boats. Early in the morning they sighted two enemy gunboats, the *Satellite* and the *Reliance*, on the Rappahannock River. About 70 crewmen were aboard the two enemy ships. Lieutenants Wood and Hoge, each in command of two boats loaded with a total of 60 men and officers, steered toward their separate targets for a simultaneous attack. Wood attacked the *Satellite* and after a short but intense firefight the gunboat crew surrendered. At the *Reliance*, Hoge's group had a more difficult time subduing that crew, perhaps because Hoge was seriously wounded when the attack commenced. The *Reliance* ultimately surrendered and Wood took charge of both captured vessels. At daylight he returned the prisoners to the care of Colonel Rosser at Urbanna. Rosser supplied him with 30 sharpshooters to complete the crews for further operations.

Wood had decided to use the captured gunboats to attack enemy shipping but he found that the engines of the *Reliance* were not working properly. Therefore he took the *Satellite* in search of merchantmen. On the second night out he captured three enemy schooners: the *Golden Rod*, *Coquette*, and *Two Brothers*. Ultimately, all three schooners and the two captured gunboats were stripped of everything of value and burned, after which the raiders returned to Richmond.[25] On February 14, 1864, the Confederate Congress passed a joint resolution "of thanks to Commander John Taylor Wood, and the officers and men under his command, for daring and brilliant conduct."[26]

Another organizer of commando warfare was John Yates Beall, whom Mallory appointed as acting master in the Confederate navy. Beall gathered 20 volunteers to man two boats, the *Swan* and *Crow*, and on the night of September 18, 1863, the commandos captured the sailing merchantman *Mary Anne* and the schooner *Alliance* in Chesapeake Bay. The next night they captured three other schooners: the *Horseman*, *Pearsall*, and *Alexander*. Beall transferred his raiders to the *Alliance* and tried to take her into southern waters while chased by three enemy gunboats. In the process he ran aground and the vessel was scuttled, after which part of her valuable cargo was saved and taken to Richmond.[27]

On November 10, 1863, Beall and his crew of 14 men launched their boats, but were captured at daylight. Union brigadier general Henry H. Lockwood joyously telegraphed that his men had captured "the notorious Captain Beall himself."[28] General Lockwood further stated that the prisoners were not entitled to be treated as prisoners of war, since he considered them to be partisans.[29] Lieutenant Colonel and Assistant Adjutant General Chesebrough replied:

> As to the prisoners themselves, they will be held for the present, not as prisoners of war, but as pirates or marauding robbers, until the further pleasure of the Secretary of War, to whom the matter will be submitted, shall be known. Not being protected by commissions or any orders produced from the pretended rebel Government, they will probably be tried as pirates or as robbers, either in the United States court or the local court, unless ordered to trial by military commission.[30]

Affairs were turning ugly and President Davis reacted. The Confederacy had in irons a number of Union prisoners upon whom he threatened reprisal should the Confederate prisoners be treated contrary to the laws of war. In the end, reason prevailed and a prisoner trade was worked out. Beall and most of his men were exchanged on May 5, 1864.[31]

Now it was time for the commandos to go to a more comprehensive and difficult assignment. New Bern, North Carolina, still in Federal hands, constituted a strategic vexation for General Lee's army similar to that experienced at Plymouth. In January 1863, Lee had sent troops to try to clear New Bern of Federal forces without seeking help from the Confederate navy. That attempt failed largely because of the bombardment of Confederate troops by two Union gunboats. Lee turned to Mallory with a plan to use Commander Woods' men to capture one of the gunboats. He believed his troops could succeed if fewer Union cannon opposed them. Secretary Mallory agreed to a joint army-navy operation. He and Wood decided that three parties of raiders should be organized and trained by Lt. Francis L. Hoge. This was accomplished in January 1864. The three groups, plus a Marine unit, consisted of 253 officers and men. The commandos united at Kinston, North Carolina, with 12 boats and two large launches. Each of the launches could carry a maximum of 45 men and a 45-pounder field howitzer.

Lieutenant Wood divided the flotilla into two groups. He selected Lt. Benjamin P. Loyall as his second in command. The two groups, with the exception of the launches that were still being unloaded, began moving toward New Bern on the evening of January 31, 1864. At dawn the next day, Gen. George E. Pickett launched the coordinated Confederate land attack; the Union commander sent his most powerful gunboat, *Underwriter*, up the Neuse River to support the Federal troops. On the evening of February 2, Wood and Loyal reconnoitered with two boats. In the dark of night, Wood spotted the *Underwriter* and determined it would be the principal target for the commandos.

The *Underwriter* was a powerful gunboat. She was 186 feet long, had 800-horse-power engines, and was armed with five heavy guns. Lieutenant Wood planned to place the two Confederate boats on either side of the *Underwriter* and subject her to converging fire. The rebels attacked in the early morning of February 3. They got close to the Federal gunboat before the Union sailors could depress the cannons and open fire. Both sides loosed a hail of small arms gunfire, but the southerners gained the deck and a hand-to-hand engagement followed. The commandos captured the ship, but were unable to start the engines due to lack of steam pressure. The nearby Federal fort began shelling the ship and, because it could not be moved, the *Underwriter* was set on fire and abandoned. The vessel blew up around 5:00 A.M. but General Pickett decided to forgo the assault upon New Bern.[32]

Although the *Underwriter* had to be destroyed and Confederates did not recapture New Bern, Mallory's vision of the efficacy of a rapid strike force was confirmed. Such activities evoked much enthusiasm by both sides. They became popular in the Confederate navy and many squadron commanders emulated the concept. The assistant secretary of the Union navy, Gustavus V. Fox, expressed his determination to have a similar unit in his organization.[33] The Confederate Navy commandos had proved their mettle and took on additional projects throughout the remainder of the war. Some of those engagements are summarized below.

In 1863 Secretary Mallory developed a plan to strengthen the Confederate capability for destroying northern commerce. He determined he would have his commerce raiders concentrate on merchant fleets in the northeast, particularly in the vicinity of New England. This area was chosen because targets of opportunity were plentiful and were relatively undefended by the United States Navy. Since these raids were to be in coastal waters, rather than the open ocean, raiders would no longer be protected by the space of open ocean; speed was to be used as the prime defense for the new raiders. These ships were to cruise to one place, sink ships, and then dash to another area before Union ships could locate them.

To unleash these attacks, Mallory needed a new kind of vessel. The secretary outlined his needs to James Bulloch in a letter dated August 19, 1864. He wrote that he intended to possess two armed vessels and "use them for dashes at the enemy's commerce and for blockade running at pleasure." Here was a new wrinkle. As Bulloch had suggested earlier to him, Mallory would combine, in the same vessel, the capacity for both commerce raiding and blockade running. The secretary outlined the features needed in such a ship. "The first and greatest requisite is speed at sea ... [and] draft of water should not exceed, deep loaded, ten (10) feet." He specified that "Power [is] to be applied to one screw, if speed can be had; if not, then to two...." Further, there was to be "A clear sweep for the forward and after pivot gun to be secured." Mallory added that he had recently purchased a vessel that met these criteria. She was a blockade runner that had been built on the Thames River in England and had passed through the blockade at Wilmington several times. This twin-screw ferry, the *Atalanta*, had been fitted out with three guns, and was renamed the *Tallahassee*.[34] John Taylor Wood commanded her and the crew consisted of 120 officers and men. The executive officer was Lt. William H. Ward and Capt. Edward Crenshaw was in charge of marines.[35]

On the night of August 7, 1864, the *Tallahassee* sailed out of Wilmington, eluded her pursuers, and on August 11 captured her first prize, the *Sarah A. Boyce*. Twenty miles outside New York Harbor the raider captured a number of ships and then moved toward the New England coast, capturing more vessels. She entered the neutral port of Halifax, Nova Scotia, Canada, loaded 80 tons of coal, and returned undetected to Wilmington. In the course of a 20-day raid she had alarmed the enemy who sent out ships to try to find her, frightened coastal residents, and caused much physical and psychological damage. "She had eluded and mocked the powerful Union squadrons and captured thirty-three merchantmen, of which twenty-six were destroyed, two released, and five bonded."[36]

The *Tallahassee*, renamed the *Olustee* to deceive the enemy, left port for her second raid on October 26, 1864, with Lieutenant Ward in command. She captured and destroyed six merchantmen off the capes of Delaware before returning to Wilmington. Following this raid, her battery was removed and she operated as a blockade runner under another name (*Chameleon*). On December 24, 1864, she proceeded to Bermuda to obtain provisions for the Confederate army, could not find an open Confederate port on the East Coast, and decided to sail to Liverpool, England, where she arrived on April 9, 1865.[37]

The former blockade runner *Edith*, renamed the *Chickamauga*, launched a third raid in Atlantic Ocean coastal waters on October 28, 1864. She was at sea until November 19, 1864, and destroyed six merchantmen.[38]

The summer of 1864 was crucial for both sides. In the east, General Grant was beginning his push through The Wilderness and Spotsylvania on the way to grinding down Confederate general Lee's army that was defending Richmond and Petersburg. In the west, Union general William T. Sherman was well on his way toward capturing Atlanta and commencing his march eastward across Georgia and the Carolinas. The Union navy defeated the southern navy at the Battle of Mobile Bay. Doom was prevalent in the South. Diarist Mary Boykin Chesnut wrote, "Since Atlanta I have felt as if all were dead within me, forever. We are going to be wiped off the earth."[39]

It was plain to everyone that things were going badly for the Confederacy and that her days were numbered. But Stephen Mallory, always the optimist who could see the silver lining in every cloud, was upbeat in his message to the president on April 30, 1864. He wrote in a way that suggested the Confederacy would live forever when he spoke of the necessity of providing education and training for navy officers. Mallory acknowledged that many southern midshipmen had received good education and training aboard the school-ship *Patrick Henry*. But he observed that their scholastic work could not be suitably accomplished aboard ship. He recommended the erection of additional permanent housing at Drewry's Bluff to fulfill the educational needs of midshipmen. The secretary also said that additional quarters were needed to house a proposed increase in the number of students from 106 to 150 young men, and he closed by proposing that six additional teachers be employed.[40] This was a remarkably optimistic outlook for the future in contrast to the factually based pessimism of the day.

The Confederate navy sustained a heavy blow when two of its famous cruisers that had done so much to boost the rebels' morale were captured or destroyed. The first loss occurred on June 19, 1864, when the cruiser *Alabama* was sunk in a battle with the U.S. cruiser *Kearsarge* just off Cherbourg, France.[41] On October 7, 1864, the cruiser *Florida* was anchored at the Brazilian port of Bahia for supplies and repairs when, at around 3:00 A.M., the U.S. cruiser *Wachusett* rammed and captured her. The *Wachusett* towed the *Florida* out of the neutral port to sea.[42]

Twenty days after the *Florida* was captured, another tragedy befell the navy. In April and May 1864, the ironclad *Albemarle* had proved her worth by defeating Federal naval forces in battle, and was standing guard at Plymouth, North Carolina, on the Roanoke River. By her mere presence, she denied the Union fleet access to the interior, protecting General Lee's flank in Virginia. The *Albemarle* was attacked on the evening of October 27, 1864, when U.S. commander William B. Cushing moved a 45-foot steam barge, fitted with a spar tipped with an explosive device, toward the Confederate ironclad. In spite of heavy southern small-arms fire, the barge reached the *Albemarle*. Cushing exploded the torpedo that opened a hole in her hull, and she sank in eight feet of water. Federal army and navy forces immediately retook Plymouth, leaving Lee's flank unprotected.[43]

The *Albemarle* was the only Confederate ironclad destroyed by a single enemy weapon. Author-historian William N. Still, Jr., states, "Of the twenty-two armored vessels completed and more than thirty laid down but not finished, four were captured and the rest (other than the *Albemarle*) were destroyed by the Confederates to avoid capture." The destruction of their own ships by Confederate sailors affected their morale. Still cites a sailor from the *Savannah* who predicted, "if we are attacked we will follow the course of the other ironclads and either blow up or get captured."[44]

This same glumness prevailed among civilians. Secretary Mallory was proud of his accomplishments in constructing ironclads, but was chagrined when one of these ships had to be destroyed so the enemy could not capture it. One day at the Rocketts Yard he had a group of ladies for inspection and lunch aboard a new ironclad. As they departed the genial Mallory said, "Well, ladies, I have shown you everything about them." One lady replied, "Everything but one, the place where you blow them up?"[45]

United States general William T. Sherman captured Atlanta, Georgia, in September 1864, and began his famous march to the sea on November 15, 1864, heading for Savannah, Georgia. On November 27, 1864, Confederate general William J. Hardee, who was defending the Savannah area, sent a message to Flag-Officer William W. Hunter, requesting help from the Confederate navy in defending Savannah from Sherman's march. Hunter responded by ordering Lt. J.S. Kennard to take the gunboat *Macon* up the Savannah River to defend the bridge of the Charleston & Savannah railroad.[46] However, the army and navy defense failed and Sherman's troops continued their advance. Hardee's army retreated and escaped entrapment with the help of the guns of the ironclad *Savannah*. It guarded a vital bridge preventing the Union troops from cutting off the rebel flight. The *Savannah* remained on station to protect the rear guard of the retreating army and presently Federal troops approached and opened fire upon her. *Savannah* defended the position and then retreated, but found she could not escape through a southern minefield. She was trapped. At 11:00 P.M. on December 21, 1864, her crew set her ablaze and she exploded. On Secretary Mallory's order, other vessels in the Savannah area were destroyed, as was the shipyard. Savannah was evacuated.[47]

A few days later, Federal forces mounted an attack on Wilmington, North Carolina. On Christmas evening, the Union launched an amphibious operation against Fort Fisher that guarded an entrance to the Cape Fear River. In spite of a frightful bombardment, the fort held. On January 13, 1865, the Federal army and navy launched another attack on Fort Fisher. Eight thousand troops were landed near the fort and advanced under covering naval fire. It was a hard-fought battle, but Fort Fisher fell to the Union on January 15, 1865.

Secretary Mallory noted the numerous enemy naval resources that were engaged in this attack and, with his characteristic verve, decided this presented an opportunity to go on the offensive. He decided he would move the James River Squadron down to General Grant's main supply base at City Point, Virginia, before the Union ironclads at Fort Fisher could return to the James River. His objective was to cause Grant to give up the siege of Petersburg.

On January 16, 1865, Secretary Mallory ordered Flag-Officer John K. Mitchell to move promptly toward City Point because "In a short time many of his [the enemy] vessels will have returned to the river from Wilmington.... If we can block the river at or below City Point, Grant might be compelled to evacuate his position.... I regard an attack upon the enemy and the obstructions of the river at City Point, to cut off Grant's supplies, as a movement of the first importance to the country and one which should be accomplished if possible."[48]

But Mitchell got a case of "the slows" and did not respond. Mallory wrote him again on January 21:

> You have an opportunity, I am convinced, rarely presented to a naval officer, and one which may lead to the most glorious results to your country. I deplore that you did not start immediately after the freshet, and have deplored the loss of every day since. You will, I trust, start tomorrow, and may Heaven make you and your squadron an instrument for the invigoration of our great cause.[49]

At 9:00 P.M. the same day Mallory sent a telegram to Mitchell urging him on. The secretary said, "Your movement is being delayed fatally, I fear. Unless you act at once action will be useless."[50]

Mitchell's squadron moved at dawn the next day, but it retired when exposed to heavy fire by Union batteries on the riverbanks and by the big guns of the ironclad *Onondaga*. In disgust, Mallory replaced Mitchell with Rear Adm. Raphael Semmes, former captain of the *Alabama*. Semmes could do little because the Federal ironclads had returned from the Fort Fisher expedition and the small Confederate squadron was outnumbered. The Confederate navy secretary had to give up this offensive move. It was to be his last.[51]

Meanwhile, General Sherman was advancing across South Carolina. After crossing the Savannah River, he threatened to surround Charleston. At this point, one of the main goals of the Confederacy was to husband its dwindling army manpower. On February 14, 1865, General Beauregard evacuated Charleston. That left the Confederate warships in the harbor stranded with no avenue of escape. During the night of February 17–18, the fleet was scuttled. Three successive explosions marked the demise of the *Palmetto State*, the *Chicora*, and the *Charleston*. On February 22, the city of Wilmington was the next to fall to the Union army. On March 13 the ironclad *Neuse* had to be scuttled to prevent her capture.[52]

The Confederacy would, however, go out with a fight. Torpedoes were still in the water causing mayhem for the Union. On January 15, 1865, the powerful Union ironclad *Patapsco* was testing Confederate defenses at Charleston near Fort Sumter, when it struck a torpedo and sank in less than a minute, causing the loss of 62 men.[53] On March 1 Rear Adm. J.A. Dahlgren, commanding the South Atlantic Blockading Squadron, was on board his flagship, the *Harvest Moon*, steaming near Georgetown, South Carolina. Dahlgren was waiting for his breakfast in his quarters when, at 7:45 A.M., there was a loud explosion. The *Harvest Moon* had struck a torpedo that blew up between the main hatch and wardroom bulkhead. The ship sank in five minutes. Dahlgren wrote dryly, "It had been reported to me that the channel had been swept, but so much has been said in ridicule of torpedoes that very little precautions are deemed necessary, and if resorted to are probably taken with less care than if due weight was attached to the existence of these mischievous things."[54]

With the fall of Wilmington on February 22, 1865, all Confederate seaports had been closed to commerce save Galveston in Texas. On May 24, 1865, the blockade runner *Lark* successfully ran the blockade out of Galveston. It was the last ship to do so during the war.[55]

Things had gone no better for Robert E. Lee's Army of Northern Virginia in the trenches fronting Richmond and Petersburg. Lee was facing relentless pressure from the Federal army of Gen. Ulysses S. Grant while, at the same time, looking over his shoulder at Gen. William T. Sherman's bluecoats advancing across the Carolinas who were attempting to consolidate with Grant's troops. Throughout the summer of 1864, Grant's army had continuously sidestepped southward forcing Lee to extend his right flank to Petersburg. During the winter, the Army of the Potomac began to turn Lee's flank with westward movements that threatened the rear of the Army of Northern Virginia. By March 1865 General Lee had to consider abandoning Petersburg and Richmond in order to save his army from encirclement. Lee made one last major attack upon Grant on March 24–25, smashing through Federal lines, but Grant counterattacked, regaining lost ground. The Union's headlong assaults continued with Lee's army ever retreating. The Federal army could no longer be held at bay. A one-sided Union victory was gained at the road junction of Five Forks on April 1 and Grant ordered an all-out attack for the next morning. Lee could not contain the avalanche and conceded that to save his army he must flee westward. General Lee sent a message to President Davis advising him that he could no longer stem the tide.

13

Southern Strategies and Outcomes

Noted historian and author James M. McPherson has identified two fundamental strategies of war. One is a national plan that is formed from political goals; the second involves military tactics by which armed forces implement these goals.[1] It is noted that strategies are never static since they are constantly being reshaped in response to the exigencies of war.

At the outbreak of Civil War, Confederate president Jefferson Davis succinctly enunciated the South's philosophy in his first message to the Confederate Congress: "We seek no conquest, no aggrandizement, no concession of any kind from the State with which we were lately confederated; all we ask is to be let alone."[2] This thoroughly defensive plan was reflected in Charles M. Conrad's February 21, 1861, report of the Congressional Committee on Naval Affairs that recommended a limited supporting role for the Confederate navy.

By May 1861, Confederate navy secretary Mallory had developed two initial naval military plans that, while defensive in nature, were more expansive then that envisioned by the Conrad committee. The first goal was to create a small fleet of fast wooden cruisers whose purpose would be to harass the United States merchant marine worldwide and create economic havoc within the Union. This defensive approach was the logical extension of President Davis's issuance of letters of marque and reprisal that were intended to destroy Union shipping. Regarding this plan, Mallory's Confederate agent, James D. Bulloch wrote, "Primarily the purpose was to destroy the enemy's commerce, and thus to increase the burden of war upon a large and influential class at the North, and the collateral purposes were to compel the United States Navy Department to send many of their best ships abroad for the pursuit of the Confederate cruisers, and to increase their naval expenditure, which it was thought would tend to weaken the blockade, retard the preparation for attack upon exposed portions of the Southern coast, and also to add largely to the aggregate cost of carrying on the war."[3]

Secretary Mallory's second strategic undertaking was more advanced technologically and was of greater vision. For years he had been thinking about using ships clad in iron—

the next logical progression in naval warfare. On May 8, 1861, Mallory sent a message to the Confederate Congress outlining his views on the importance of ironclads and said, "I regard the possession of an iron-armored ship, as a matter of the first necessity. Such a vessel at this time could traverse the entire coast of the United States, prevent all blockades, and encounter, with a fair prospect of success, their entire Navy."[4] This planning also was essentially defensive in nature, but it contained an element of offensive tactics when it suggested that this ironclad, the "ultimate weapon," might destroy the entire Federal fleet. Regardless of whether defensive or offensive tactics were used, the intent of the goal was to eliminate the threat of a Union blockade designed to suppress the South's ability to wage war.

Conceptually the secretary had a more advanced intellectual grasp of naval warfare techniques than most and he had the courage, tenacity, and energy to attempt expeditious implementation of his ideas. It is also accurate to say that Mallory was naïve in his optimistic assumption that his ultimate weapon could defeat the Union navy because the secretary assumed his opponent would not react in a timely manner with appropriate countermeasures. However, the fact that the strategy did not ultimately fulfill the vision may not reflect faulty planning. Instead one must acknowledge that the South's deficiencies in manufacturing and industrial capability played a central role in Mallory's failure to produce sufficient numbers of high quality naval vessels. Of ships built in the South, Bulloch wrote:

> The very best vessels which it was possible to complete were mere make-shifts. They were plated either with layers of thin iron, insufficiently bolted, or with ordinary railway metals; and the difficulty of bending the plates and rails and fashioning the timber backing compelled a resort to the weakest forms of structure, ... But the inefficiency of the vessels in respect to strength and suitability of design was still further increased by the want of sufficient motive-power to admit of their being properly manoeuvred.[5]

Stephen Mallory's foresight is remarkable when compared to the Union Navy Department personnel. About two months after Mallory's energetic moves toward purchasing and building ships covered with iron plate, U.S. secretary of the navy Gideon Welles, with little sense of urgency, recommended that a board be created to study the wisdom of building ironclads. That board was appointed a month later. Mallory took advantage of a three-month head start by approving plans on July 11, 1861, for construction of the *Virginia*. The Federal board made its recommendations on September 18, 1861, and the Union's *Monitor* was built even though the chief constructor of the Federal Navy Department at first condemned this vessel.[6] Mallory believed that if he could only act boldly and quickly and put ironclads to sea while the other side was still in the planning stage, he might have the great opportunity to contest iron against wood and destroy the blockading fleet. He was correct in his assessment. It was, as noted by Leslie S. Bright, "a question of iron and time."[7]

The die was cast in 1861 when Stephen Mallory began to implement his twin strategies of destroying the American merchant fleet with his fast wooden cruisers and defeating the wooden Union blockaders with his southern built-ironclads. He hoped that Federal forces would cooperate by diverting ships from blockade duty to pursue and attempt destruction of Confederate cruisers. This would allow southern ironclads to pick apart remaining blockaders while cruisers evaded their pursuers in the vastness of the ocean.

But it did not work out as Mallory had hoped. Union secretary Gideon Welles did not take the bait. He kept his blockading vessels on station.

By late 1862, President Davis had moved from a strictly defensive national strategy to a more proactive stance, determining to strike offensively with concentrated forces at points of perceived Federal weaknesses. Thus, a purely defensive stance had evolved into elective offensive operations that were compatible with defensive strategy. This "offensive-defensive" approach gave recognition to the idea that the best defense may be a strong offense that is utilized in specific tactical situations. For example, the president supported the offensive use of Confederate army forces at Shiloh in 1862 and Gettysburg in 1863.

Correspondingly, Confederate navy secretary Mallory also moved increasingly toward offensive-defensive planning in employment of his naval resources. Throughout 1862, he began developing and implementing revised designs to cope with difficulties experienced early in the war: a tightening Union blockade, the losses of New Orleans and Gosport Navy Yard, and Federal amphibious operations resulting in forays into the southeastern seaboard that threatened Lee's armies and southern manufacturing plants. Secretary Mallory knew that the Union threat from the sea and rivers had to be adroitly managed if the South were to have any chance of winning the war, or drawing it out long enough that the North might sue for peace. He acknowledged Union superiority in terms of quantity of manpower, industrial capacity, natural resources, and ships. The secretary comprehended that the South's best chance against numerical dominance was to utilize revolutionary technology that was emerging in England and France. Having read widely, Mallory understood how these advances might be applied in the American Civil War; he recognized that technological surprise would benefit him most in this unequal affair. This became the underpinning for his evolving strategies. As the pieces began to fall together, Stephen Mallory enunciated a four-part blueprint that would channel Confederate naval activities.[8]

1. First in this four-part design was the goal of constructing and deploying sea-roving commerce raiders to destroy United States merchant vessels. This represented an expansion of his initial 1861 goal of purchasing or building commerce raiders in the South. The original effort had produced a successful raider, the *Sumter*. This amplified plan would result in the raiders *Florida* and *Alabama* being constructed in Great Britain and cruising the high seas in 1862. Other raiders would follow.

2. The second strategic undertaking was building ironclads in the South for defensive purposes. This protective plan was a revision of the original 1861 goal. These armor-clad vessels would be built to a smaller scale than those behemoths that had been constructed on the Mississippi River in 1861. These new boats of shallow draft with powerful guns were intended for riverine warfare and for action on protected bays, particularly on the coast of North Carolina. As tactics evolved, these ships occasionally would be used offensively in combined army-navy operations against Federal fortifications.

3. The third part of the design was to construct armored ships of seagoing quality in England and France. Their mission was to cross the Atlantic Ocean and destroy Union vessels blockading the southern coastline.

4. The fourth approach was to develop and introduce into warfare technically advanced weapons of destruction. The secretary was convinced that use of such weapons was the prime hope for offsetting the North's naval advantages.

These four strategic goals composed the doctrine for all Confederate navy operations from mid-1862 until the close of the war. Here we examine how successful the Confederate navy was in achieving these goals.

1. *Commerce Raiders*

The first goal was to build and deploy commerce raiders upon the high seas to destroy United States merchant vessels. This objective was a success if one considers only numbers of ships demolished. Various sea raiders reduced the size of the United States merchant marine by destroying "249 Union-owned vessels with a total value of $8,639,999.82."[9] The North, however, had extensive shipbuilding capacity to draw upon for replacement of destroyed vessels. Insurance rates increased dramatically but the North had sufficient wealth to deal with this expense. Furthermore, American international trade continued by transferring cargos to ships registered in neutral countries, which Confederate vessels dared not touch. Additionally, Federal navy secretary Gideon Welles was unwilling to divert any Union warships to permanent patrol duty in the Atlantic Ocean, choosing instead to use all those vessels to strengthen the blockade. In hindsight this appears to have been a wise decision by Welles.

Additionally, commerce raiders did not achieve economic strangulation of the North as desired by Mallory. In fact, as historian Jay Simson correctly asserts, the commerce-destroying effort largely was irrelevant. He points out that southern cruisers did not hurt the Union economically because the North was in the midst of a major economic boom consisting of industrial economic expansion in the northeast and increased prosperity in the farm states resulting from gains in exports of agricultural products, particularly wheat. These national achievements largely cancelled losses experienced by shipping interests.[10]

Another way of looking at the effectiveness of commerce-destroying sea raiders is to examine claims for reparations made by the United States upon Great Britain for her role in allowing sea raiders, primarily the *Alabama* and the *Florida*, to escape to sea and fulfill their objective of destroying U.S. merchant vessels. The Geneva Tribunal was created to arbitrate claims sought by the United States. On September 14, 1872, the tribunal adjudged that the British government was to pay the United States a sum of $15,500,000 for damages done by *Alabama*, *Florida*, and several lesser vessels. The claim was promptly paid.[11]

George W. Dalzell, in his book *The Flight from the Flag*, contends that $15 million worth of damage to ships and goods was of no great matter even in those days. In contrast, he estimates that the United States destroyed or captured blockade runners valued at approximately $31 million. He asserts that if one assesses the economic impact on the merchant marine caused by sea raiders, the outcome is of minor importance. However, he acknowledges that these Confederate vessels wielded a more important weapon than guns, namely fear of their activities. This in itself fueled the flight from the flag — the transfer of cargoes to ships flying neutral flags. Thus, American flagged maritime commerce was driven from the sea not to return, partially due to the depredations of Mallory's sea raiders.[12]

Sea-raider successes in destroying vessels of the American merchant fleet produced unintended negative consequences for the Confederacy. Mallory believed that under British laws and regulations a ship, regardless of its ultimate intended purpose, could be built in England, without interference by Great Britain, as long as it was not armed in that nation. Even though Bulloch warned him, Mallory did not acknowledge that Great Britain's attitude began shifting on this matter when that nation became aware of the unfavorable response by the United States to achievements by the *Alabama* and *Florida*. When American diplomats alerted their British counterparts that Confederate ships constructed in neutral English waters were destroying a significant portion of the American merchant fleet, the British became concerned especially when the United States suggested that war might be in the offing. The British, who remembered their difficulties in America during previous military engagements, did not wish to risk involvement in a similar conflict with the United States. Great Britain began revising its interpretation of neutrality obligations and eventually decided that a ship that could reasonably be used as a warship could not be built in British waters, even if she were later armed on the high seas. The French reacted in similar fashion. The ramifications of these expedient shifts in interpreting neutrality commitments are discussed below in assessing goal number three pertaining to foreign-built offensive ironclads. Mallory failed to anticipate this policy deviation and was angry about English and French alteration in political attitudes that arose largely because of Confederate commerce raider accomplishments.

On balance, this strategic goal must be considered a failure. Although Confederate sea raiders did interrupt United States maritime commerce and undoubtedly buoyed lagging Confederate morale, economic strangulation of the North did not follow. Southern commerce raider activities had negligible impact upon the capacity of the United States government to effectively wage war.

2. *Southern-Built Defensive Ironclads*

Mallory's second goal of constructing ironclads in the South for defensive purposes was a qualified success. Through a superhuman effort, Secretary Mallory and his staff, often in cooperation with the army, were able to construct many fine ironclads and place them judiciously in defensive positions. One sterling achievement was production of the ironclad *Virginia*, whose battle with the *Monitor* forever changed the face of naval war. Mallory can hardly be praised enough for fully supporting and encouraging construction and operation of this important warship. Later in the war, Secretary Mallory's development and placement of ironclads in the coastal waters of North Carolina produced southern naval victories that served to protect General Lee's flank and delayed the surrender of his army.

However, this success in the east was countered by Mallory's unsuccessful defense of the Mississippi River that opened the way for the penetration of the South by Union navy and army forces. His ironclads on the Mississippi River were not completed in time to become a factor in that conflict. The industrial might and superior resources of the North overwhelmed the South. Lack of iron and time was a race that Mallory ran and lost but arguably there was no one else who could have done better.

3. *Foreign-Built Offensive Ironclads*

The objective of constructing armor-clad ships overseas for attacking the Union blockade was a well-conceived project that required much imagination, persistence and courage. Yet it was a colossal failure costing huge sums of money and having no impact on the blockade. No Confederate ship built through this initiative ever saw action in the war. Responsibility for this failure cannot be placed on Mallory and Bulloch alone, for too many factors were beyond their control. These included serious financing problems facing the Confederate government, difficulty with efficient communications hampered by vastness of the Atlantic Ocean, Confederate government failures in foreign relations, skills of United States diplomats in pressuring Great Britain, and other imponderables. Especially critical was the inability of Confederate foreign policy and diplomatic efforts to blunt aggressive diplomatic moves and impediments exerted by the United States on Great Britain thus causing her to reexamine her interpretation of neutrality statutes. These forces energized both England and France to seize or otherwise deny prospective Confederate warships the opportunity to fulfill their planned missions. Confederate foreign policy and diplomacy could not counter these factors.

But even if the ironclads had gotten to sea, what then? It is probable that the United States would have reacted by concentrating her numerically superior ironclad fleet to isolate rebel cruisers. In fact when the *Stonewall* arrived in Havana, Cuba, Federal warships concentrated nearby and effectively barricaded the Confederate ironclad. Author Frank Merli asserts, "Bottled-up rams could break no blockade."[13]

One must question the resources that were squandered on this project. The South, unlike the North, did not have the luxury of ample financial reserves that could be dissipated. The four ironclads that were contracted in Great Britain and France cost a total of about $2 million.[14] However, the return on the investment was nil. While the plan was imaginative, there was some evidence it might not work well. In 1862 the French ironclad *Normandie* made a transatlantic trip and the crew was debilitated by the constant heat and humidity that turned the ship's interior into a veritable steam room.[15] This suggests that a Confederate armored ship arriving at the American coast after a transatlantic voyage would not be in sufficient fighting trim to engage in combat with blockading vessels. One cannot be certain that Mallory and his staff had fully evaluated operational problems that might come into play in a situation such as this.

One of Mallory's most admirable personal characteristics was his persistence. However in this instance that quality became a negative attribute since it caused him to hold an inflexible position that resulted in his failure to release resources sorely needed elsewhere. This probably was one of his more important mistakes, but at the same time it must be remembered that this was a most difficult war for the South to win. Mallory, a desperate man, was always trying the best to neutralize, if not defeat, his enemy. Desperate men take long chances and need not necessarily be berated when outcomes are unsuccessful.

4. *Technically Advanced Weapons*

The fourth strategy, introducing technically advanced weapons of war, was admirably accomplished even to the point of exceeding Mallory's own optimistic dreams. For the first time in history a submarine, the *Hunley*, sank a warship. Additionally, partially submerged torpedo boats, or assault boats, became intimidating weapons commanding respect especially after the *David* had seriously damaged a Union warship. Torpedoes or mines, whether delivered by a submarine, a partially submerged assault boat, or planted on land or in water, created angst among enemy personnel. Confederate planners placed high value on torpedoes as weapons of war because they were effective, relatively inexpensive, and could be transported easily. The critical goal of developing and using technically advanced weapons of war was an unqualified success.

Full evaluation of these four strategic goals requires consideration of how the dimension of time affected the end results. Time was an important factor contributing to the Confederate navy's inability to neutralize or defeat the Union navy. At the beginning of war the Confederacy had no navy but Union ships were dispersed and could not blockade principal southern ports as well as the entire southern coastline.

In 1861 the Confederacy had time, before the blockade became effective, to get iron plating and equipment imported from England and Europe and begin compensating for its own deficiencies. But it did not.

In 1861 the Union hesitated in producing ironclad ships. The Confederate navy gained a lead of several months when it produced the *Virginia* and with concerted effort might have maintained that lead. But it did not.

The Confederate States of America became an entity in mid-February 1861; war did not commence for nearly two months. Within that time frame the Confederacy could have begun building a stronger navy by purchasing ships in Europe, immediately contending that this was not an act of war but an effort to protect its ports and waters. But it did not.

Timing turned out to be the South's worse enemy. It had faced that issue once before and had accepted a reprieve. On January 9, 1861, the Union steamer *Star of the West* sailed into Charleston Harbor to supply Fort Sumter and was fired on by South Carolina artillery. War did not begin then because neither side was ready to engage in hostilities. Now the Confederacy had the opportunity to move quickly toward full mobilization for the impending conflict but instead allowed itself to be maneuvered into firing the first shot of the war at Fort Sumter on April 12, 1861. From that time forward, Confederate navy secretary Stephen Russell Mallory was always running out of "iron and time."

14

Confederate Collapse and Prison

Sunday, April 2, 1865, was a balmy day. As President Jefferson Davis worshipped that morning at St. Paul's Church in Richmond, he was approached by a messenger and given a telegram from General Lee who advised the president that Grant's army had breached his lines causing massive casualties. Lee said he could not regroup his defensive lines and was unable to defend Richmond any longer. He advised immediate evacuation of the capital. President Davis left church without a word but the news quickly spread throughout Richmond and the populace began fleeing.

The president of the Confederate States of America summoned his cabinet and at noon told them of Lee's predicament. He ordered that the government be withdrawn from Richmond, and that cabinet members report at 8:00 P.M. that evening to the Richmond & Danville railroad depot. President Davis planned that the government would go south to Danville, Virginia, join with the remaining army of Gen. Joseph E. Johnston in North Carolina, and move to a safe location. During the rest of the day, boxes of official records and papers were packed; what was left of the archives was burned, including valuable naval records. The Treasury Department's remaining gold along with deposits in Virginia banks were also gathered for the railroad journey. Everything of military and industrial value was put to the torch and by nightfall, as troops withdrew, looters took over.[1]

Secretary Mallory ordered Rear Admiral Semmes, commanding the James River Squadron, to destroy all his ships that evening and then have his sailors join with Lee's forces. They were to be given rations for the march and be equipped for duty in the field.[2] Mallory also sent an order to Capt. William H. Parker, superintendent of the Confederate States Naval Academy, to have his company of 60 midshipmen act as escort and guard for the Treasury Department money. They were available because Admiral Semmes would destroy their school ship, the *Patrick Henry*, along with the remainder of the fleet. The officers and midshipmen arrived at the railroad depot that evening and found the treasury train loaded with boxes and kegs of coinage, gold, and silver amounting to over $1 million and weighing around 10 tons. Passengers were loaded until late evening and the treasury train departed shortly after midnight.[3] Ultimately the train's treasure was unloaded to wagons and arrived in Abbeville, South Carolina, on April 30.

A second train was at the depot for President Davis and his cabinet. It left the station at around 11:00 P.M. before the treasury train departed and at midnight the James River Squadron vessels were set afire. According to eyewitnesses, "A series of frightful explosions rocked the city, now aflame, with shocks like those of earthquakes. The shells in each ship's magazine, thrown high in the dark sky, exploded in bunches at different times. It was a hellish pyrotechnical spectacle."[4] Except for the few Confederate ships that still existed at sea, that was the end of Mallory's navy.

During the flight of the cabinet toward Danville, Stephen Mallory wrote brief portraits of other cabinet members. He recorded that John Reagan, the postmaster general, was "silent and somber, his eyes as bright and glistening as beads, but evidently seeing nothing around them, now whittling a stick down to the little end of nothing without ever reaching a satisfactory point...." Of Secretary of the Treasury Trenholm, he wrote that Trenholm "was provided with abundance of supplies for the inner man, including some 'inexhaustible' hampers of 'Old Peach,' all of which he shared generously with his companions." Mallory's friend, Judah Benjamin, was, he said, noted for his "'Epicurean philosophy' and hope and good humor refused to desert him. He rallied his associates over their mournful faces as he munched a sandwich with great relish, 'and, with a never-give-up-the-ship sort of air, referred to other great national causes which had been redeemed from far gloomier reverses than ours.'"[5]

The presidential train rolled slowly through the night and arrived at around 5:00 P.M. the following afternoon, April 3, at the railroad depot across the Dan River from Danville, Virginia. The presidential party remained there for five days waiting for news from General Lee. On April 9, 1865, a courier arrived from the Army of Northern Virginia with a message advising the president that Lee had surrendered at Appomattox Court House. President Davis assembled some of his cabinet and staff to consider the communication. Mallory said they "carefully scanned the message as it passed from hand to hand, looked at each other gravely and mutely, and for some moments a silence, more eloquent of great disaster than words could have been, prevailed."[6]

That night the Confederate government moved on to Greensboro, North Carolina, where the party stayed for one week. They were not well received there due to significant Union sentiment and fear by citizens that Yankees would punish them for harboring the cabinet. Some cabinet members were "quartered in a leaky, dilapidated box car, which they dubbed the 'Cabinet Car.' But they made the best of the unpleasant situation. They drew bread and bacon from their Navy Store and foraged for eggs, flour, and coffee; Colonel Lubbock of Davis's staff helped divert the little group with some of his Texas stories; Mallory, with yarns of the Seminole Indian War, and Benjamin with his inexhaustible wit and humor."[7]

On April 15, President Davis conducted a conference with Generals Johnston and Beauregard asking their opinions as to next steps. They replied that terms should be asked of Sherman in order to end the fighting. The president gave them the authority to pursue that course and General Johnston sent a request for a meeting with General Sherman to discuss concluding hostilities. Sherman was receptive to the overture and the two generals met between their lines at noon on Monday, April 17. They worked out an agreement for ending the conflict subject to approval by their respective governments.[8]

The Confederate government left Greensboro on April 15 by wagon train and meandered southwesterly to Charlotte, North Carolina. On April 24, Davis received the propositions agreed to by Generals Johnston and Sherman and, after discussion with his cabinet, approved them. Secretary Mallory had provided to President Davis a lengthy and detailed analysis as to why he believed the Johnson-Sherman agreement was acceptable and fair and should be supported.[9] The Federal government, however, rejected the settlement, believing it to be too conciliatory in light of Lincoln's assassination on April 14, 1865, which some believed had been a Confederate government plot. Terms more favorable to the Union were agreed upon on April 26. That same day Davis and his party, along with escorting troops, continued their journey toward the South Carolina-Georgia border.

On the morning of May 2 President Davis's group arrived in Abbeville, South Carolina. The treasury train was there with Captain Parker in charge. Secretary of the Navy Stephen R. Mallory issued his last order when he directed Parker to deliver the treasure to Gen. Basil Duke, who was in charge of the guard accompanying the president, and then disband his command.[10]

While at Abbeville, Stephen Mallory decided there was little more he could offer the Confederacy. He had no navy to whom to give commands and few prospects of building a similar organization elsewhere. He knew his wife and children were in Georgia and were nearly destitute. Mallory told Davis on May 2 that he was considering resigning because he could not flee the country with him or go to the Trans-Mississippi Department. He added that if Davis went to Florida to escape capture, he would remain with him since he knew the state well. Davis revealed nothing about his plans.[11] That night Mallory wrote a resignation letter but did not offer it to the president.

The presidential entourage left Abbeville for Washington, Georgia, that evening. Apparently President Davis hoped to go cross-country with a small military escort to join forces in the Trans-Mississippi Department under Kirby Smith's command. At Washington, Georgia Mallory submitted his letter of resignation dated May 2, 1865, to the president. Mallory told Davis he would leave on May 4 for Atlanta on his way to La Grange, Georgia, where his wife and children were staying at the home of his old friend, Benjamin Hill. He had decided not to flee any longer, awaiting any fate that might befall him at La Grange. In his resignation letter Mallory wrote:

> The misfortunes of our country have deprived me of the honor and opportunity longer to serve her, and the hour has approached when I can no longer be useful to you personally. Cheerfully would I follow you and share whatever fate may befall you, could I hope thereby in any degree to contribute to your safety and happiness. The dependent condition of a helpless family prevents my departure from the country, and under these circumstances it is proper that I should request you to accept my resignation as Secretary of the Navy.
>
> In thus terminating our official relations, language fails to give expression to my sense of your patriotic devotion to our common country, or to the grateful promptings of my heart for the kindness, consideration, and courtesy which you have extended to my humble efforts to serve her. May God watch over and protect you; and may the smiles of Heaven be upon the pathway of yourself and your loved ones.[12]

Jefferson Davis, accepting Mallory's resignation, replied:

> It is with deep regret that I contemplate this separation. One of the members of my first cabinet, we have passed together through all the trials of the war and the not less embarrassing trials to which the Congress has of late subjected the Executive. Your minute knowledge of naval affairs and your counsel upon all important

Mallory Portrait c. 1865. This undated photograph is from a carte-de-visite and most likely was taken near the end of the war. Compare this mage with that found in Mallory's 1860 portrait on page 64. In the interval between the two photographs, the man has dramatically aged and his face reflects the wear and tear of his responsibilities. BY PERMISSION OF THE MUSEUM OF THE CONFEDERACY, RICHMOND, VIRGINIA.

measures have been to the Administration a most valuable support. For the zeal, ability, and integrity with which you have so long and so constantly labored, permit one who had the best opportunity to judge, to offer testimonial and in the name of our country and its sacred cause to return thanks. I will ever gratefully remember your uniform kindness and unwavering friendship to myself; and will fervently pray for your welfare and happiness in whatever position you may hereafter be placed.[13]

By chance an old political foe of Davis's, Brig. Gen. Louis T. Wigfall of Texas, was passing through Washington, Georgia, on his way to the Trans-Mississippi Department to join the fight with Gen. Kirby Smith. Mallory decided to join him on the train trip to Atlanta. From there he went to La Grange, Georgia, to the home of his friend Benjamin H. Hill, who had been a senator from Georgia in the Confederate States Congress.[14]

Benjamin Hill's home was a splendid old mansion in a community of fine antebellum homes. It has been described thus:

> In the double parlors are heavily carved black Italian mantles [mantels]. The thirty-foot Corinthian columns rest on a veranda, eleven feet wide that runs around the front and sides of the house. Apple and peach orchards, a scuppernong vineyard, oak and hickory groves and a juniper walk were features....[15]

There Stephen Mallory had a joyful but short reunion with his wife and children.

They came in the dark of the night. Stephen Russell Mallory and Benjamin Hill were arrested at Hill's home on May 20, 1865. Mallory was "charged with treason, and with organizing and setting on foot piratical expeditions against the United States commerce and marine on the high seas."[16] Mrs. Mallory described what took place:

> At half-past twelve o'clock, we were aroused from sleep by a heavy knock at the door, and a threat of breaking it open followed before any one had time to answer. When a light was Procured the servant opened the door, and some twenty armed men entered to arrest my husband.... Mr. Mallory was hurried off like a malefactor, without being given even enough time to put on proper clothing. They would not listen to the tears and entreaties of his wife and children to let him remain with them only until daylight.[17]

Benjamin H. Hill, Jr., recorded his view of the same event and corroborates Mrs. Mallory's account:

> We had retired, and about midnight were aroused by loud knocking at the front door. I at once, and without dressing, rushed down to my father's bedroom. I found him already awake. A search was made for a match but there was none in the house, and I went outside to the servant's house for the purpose of getting a light. What was my consternation on opening the rear door to find the house surrounded by soldiers, who, stood with muskets on guard. Securing the light, I returned at once, but in the meantime the officer at the front door had secured an entrance and with a dozen men was in the bedroom.... My father was placed in front of the soldiers and the order given to march ... at the front gate [we] found another detail with Mr. Mallory [in their charge].[18]

Acting upon instructions from Secretary of War Edwin M. Stanton, Capt. G.H. Kneeland of the Fourth Indiana Cavalry, with a guard of 12 men, was ordered to proceed with Mallory, Hill and former Maj. Gen. Howell Cobb to Fort Lafayette in New York Harbor.[19] Fort Lafayette "was built on a small rock island lying in the Narrows between the lower end of Staten Island and Long Island."[20] Mallory and Hill were marched to a special train and taken north to Atlanta. On the morning of May 25, 1865, Captain Kneeland left

Atlanta with his prisoners to proceed through Nashville, Tennessee, on the journey to New York.[21] On June 3, 1865, the prisoners arrived at Fort Lafayette.

Prison commandant Brig. Gen. Martin Burke had been instructed to treat the men as political prisoners, confining them in separate cells.[22] Evidently Mallory and Hill objected to being kept in separate cells; the adjutant general's office of the War Department stated on June 13 that the secretary of war had "no objection to their being in the same room, provided their safe custody is insured and that they have no communication with persons outside."[23]

This prohibition against contacting people outside the prison must have been rescinded since Mallory records numerous instances of writing letters to his family and receiving responses. His first letter from prison, dated June 7, 1865, was to his wife. Mallory's second letter to Angela Mallory was dated 10 days later. In it he expressed sorrow about separation from his family, but encouraged his wife. He wrote:

> Take courage then, my loving wife. Believe with me that properly presented, my case will have the favorable consideration of President Johnson. I am anxious to take the oath of allegiance and to do what I can to evoke order from chaos, & in good faith, to aid the administration to harmonize the country. As a slaveholder I regard the institution gone, and I am prepared to conform to our new status. I want no station, I care not to cast another vote, but want to see a strong government.

Mallory closed on a personal note:

> Oh if I could but see you for an hour!—Kiss our little ones for me. Tell my noble boy Buddy [Stephen, Jr.] that I long ardently to see him. And tell my servants that I count upon their good faith until we meet. God grant that I may be able to do something for them to start them fairly in their new life.[24]

By early May President Johnson's reconstruction efforts were progressing. Provisional governors were being established in former Confederate states and constitutional conventions were being called. People who had been slaves were free but were denied civil rights and voting rights. But at the same time, the administration began losing control of its moderate policy to the radical Republicans in Congress who desired a more punitive program against the South.[25]

The shift toward a more severe plan had an impact on Mallory and other political prisoners since there was the possibility they could receive a death sentence. In November, Secretary of War Stanton received a legal opinion from Judge Advocate General Joseph Holt regarding Mallory's criminality. Holt wrote that Mallory was an administrator of a department in the Confederate government "whose only business, in the absence of a navy, was simply the authorization and direction of a general system of piracy...." Holt stated that Mallory was one of the original conspirators of the rebellion and he suggested this in his legal opinion, "some atonement is yet to be made for the hundreds of thousands of lives sacrificed thereby.... The experience of the world has shown that great crimes never have been and never can be repressed without punishment.... If the leaders in an unprovoked attempt to assassinate such a nation as this have not forfeited their lives, then it is not believed to be within the compass of human depravity to incur such forfeiture." Holt recommended that Mallory be put on trial for treason as soon as possible.[26]

Another individual who was in sympathy with these vindictive aims was Gen. Alexander Sandor Asboth, who had been in command of Federal troops in West Florida. On December 10, 1865, he wrote to Secretary of War Stanton regarding an article in the *New York Herald* that advocated clemency for Mallory and other southern leaders. The article took this position because Mallory had tried to prevent the war by establishing the Fort Pickens truce. General Asboth wrote that this line of reasoning was false because Mallory was writing "treasonable dispatches" in January 1861 while still a United States senator. These documents have been referred to earlier, and all pertain to communications written before January 18, 1861, advocating secession and prompt seizure of Fort Pickens.[27] They were issued before the peace initiative that caused the Fort Pickens truce; the general failed to tell the full story, instead selecting only those documents that would be injurious to Mallory's cause.

Against this backdrop, Stephen Russell Mallory wrote one of the most important personal letters of his life. This missive, dated June 21 and addressed to President Andrew Johnson, was a petition for pardon and restoration of United States citizenship. Mallory, the prisoner, humbly stated he deemed it proper "to state frankly certain circumstances of my own case." He continued:

> I am now over fifty years of age, and from the casting of my first vote to the secession of my State my political life ... [I] was devoted to the maintenance of the Union. I was never a member of a convention or of the Legislature of my State, and never advised or counseled her secession. When first elected to the U.S. Senate ... I was known to be opposed to disunion in any form ... [and] no word or sentiment of disloyalty to the Union ever escaped me. Florida, by a convention of her people, formally seceded, and at the command of the convention, through her governor, I withdrew from the Senate ... and retired to private life. I never was and never can be regarded as a leader of secession. I always dreaded the perils of secession, and believed that ample remedies for all political evils or wrongs, present and prospective, could be more justly, wisely, and advantageously secured in the Union than out of it. Whatever might be the argument in favor of secession I could only regard it as another name for revolution, and to be justified only as a last resort from intolerable oppression.

He then changed his tack and turned to the planned attack on Fort Pickens:

> Knowing that such a step would precipitate the country into civil war ... and determined to omit nothing in my power to preserve peace and facilitate reconciliation, I addressed by telegraph the most urgent remonstrance against it to the officer in command, and had the good fortune thus to avert a dire calamity. For my interference in this matter ... I endured the bitter hostility of leading men in my own State.

He closed by saying he had not sought the office of secretary of the Confederate navy, and that although he opposed secession he had no choice but to follow where Florida led.[28]

The prisoner had submitted an apologia. He selected material that would further his cause, ignoring factors that would be harmful to him. Mallory interpreted information in a way that would support his defense. The self-serving nature of the document must be recognized, but it must be placed in context. Many people in the United States desired to punish rebels for their transgressions. Mallory may have thought he was fighting for his very life.

In mid-July Mallory was morose. His friend, Benjamin Hill, had been released and Mallory wrote, "He is gone, and I am here alone."[29] It had been a month since he had sent his letter requesting a pardon to President Johnson and he had not received a response. He was becoming more anxious and had no way of knowing whether he would be subjected to severe punishment. Believing the president was ignoring his plea he turned elsewhere for help.

On July 2, 1865, Mallory wrote a letter to Zachariah Chandler asking for assistance in securing a pardon. Chandler had served in the United States Congress as a senator from Michigan; he was a strong abolitionist and Radical Republican. Chandler and Mallory had served together in the Senate although they were on opposite sides of the aisle. In spite of their differences, Chandler, the abolitionist, and Mallory, the slave owner, became friends.[30] In his letter to Chandler, Stephen Mallory repeated most of the same arguments contained in his June 21 letter to President Johnson. In addition, he stressed the matter of freed slaves and the ballot box. Mallory wrote:

> There will be little difficulty in getting the State governments into healthy working order if common sense is allowed to prevail in the incipient measures. The negroes' present and future I do not regard as questions of much difficulty ... I know of many negroes whom I would trust with the ballot, and the number will steadily increase, and they must, at no distant day, become voters, under certain qualifications, as they have in the British West Indies, and in some of the Northern states where slavery once existed.

Mallory closed with a plea saying, "If you can consistently with your views aid me you will have my grateful recollections for your kindness."[31]

Chandler replied to Mallory on July 29, 1865, asking permission to forward Stephen's letter to the president. Chandler said, "Your letter accepts the logic of events, and I desire to lay it before the President. Shall I do it?"[32] Chandler apparently received a positive response; he forwarded Mallory's letter to President Johnson saying, "Inclosed [sic] I send you a letter from Hon. S.R. Mallory which speaks for itself.... As you know the case better than I can, it is not necessary for me to express an opinion."[33]

Stephen Mallory also used his powers of persuasion with Brig. Gen. Martin Burke, the prison commandant. In August he had the opportunity to increase his chance of release from prison by providing Burke with information about the raiding cruiser *Shenandoah*. It was still operating in the Pacific Ocean since its commander did not know the war had ended. Mallory wrote down the cruising route of the vessel so that Federal authorities could locate it and urge her commander to surrender. In response, General Burke wrote to Secretary of State Seward recommending that Mallory be paroled.[34]

William Waters Boyce wrote to Secretary of State Seward in Mallory's behalf on July 29, 1865. Boyce had served in the U.S. Congress as a representative from South Carolina from March 1853 until December 1860. He was one of the signers of the Confederate Constitution and had been a member of the Provisional Congress as well as the first and second Confederate congresses. In 1862 Boyce had served on the joint special committee of the Confederate House and Senate to investigate the conduct of the Navy Department. Boyce scribed:

Mallory was forced into the secession vortex.... At Montgomery he was one of the very few who avowed a willingness to go back into the Union on the basis of a satisfactory compromise. He lost his popularity in Florida at the beginning of secession because he aided to prevent an attack on Fort Pickens. Since the break down of the Richmond Government he was very anxious to go home and be a good and loyal citizen. I am perfectly satisfied he is anxious to go home and act as you would desire — in the interest of peace, harmony, and fraternity. Permit me, therefore, to invoke your kind offices in his behalf.[35]

In September 1865, Secretary of War Edwin Stanton made an inspection tour of Fort Lafayette and visited Mallory in his cell. The prisoner recorded that Stanton listened carefully to him as he explained his views on politics, the Confederate revolution, his desire to take the oath of allegiance to the Union, and his wish to obtain a pardon and assume all the duties of a citizen of the United States. Mallory feared the interview had not gone well. Perhaps Stanton might have been prejudiced against him, he thought, because of Stanton's having been counsel to David Yulee in opposition to Mallory's right to the contested Senate seat in June 1852.[36]

Another visitor came to see Mallory in October 1865. That visitor had just been released from prison at Fort Warren in Boston Harbor and paused in New York City while waiting for permission from Washington to visit his old friend. He was the able former postmaster general of the Confederacy, John Reagan. Reagan wrote, "I had a very pleasant meeting with my old associate."[37]

Around this time, Angela Mallory and Stephen had discussed the possibility of her traveling to Washington to make a personal appeal to the president in Stephen's behalf. Later, Mrs. Mallory talked with the president but felt she had failed because the chief executive, although he listened politely, was unresponsive.[38]

Mallory's reaction to what Angela perceived as a failed mission was to write another note to President Johnson:

Permit me to throw myself upon your generous kindness. Hearing nothing of my petition to you ... I feared that I failed in the statement of my case.... I have been four months as a prisoner; I am impoverished and ruined; my wife and children, helpless and dependent, are to me a constant source of mental anguish. Her anxiety led her to your presence in my behalf recently, but she had not the power to say to you what filled her heart. I recognize fully your policy for the restoration of harmony to a united people, and I will pledge my good faith to aid it to the extent of my power.[39]

William Marvin had been Stephen's friend in Key West since boyhood, had schooled him in law, and Stephen had practiced law in his Key West prize court. Judge Marvin had become provisional governor of Florida and in October 1865 he wrote to President Johnson in behalf of his old friend. He said he would not comment on Mallory's political history because the president "knows it as well or better than I do." But Marvin stressed that Mallory could be permitted to return to Florida "without any injury to its interests. Mr. Mallory has the gout badly, which the dampness of the prison exasperates. His family is in Connecticut and he would like to visit them. I think if were set at liberty on parole I can be surety for his keeping it."[40]

On November 14, 1865, Angela Mallory wrote another letter to President Johnson from her daughter's home in Bridgeport, Connecticut:

> I come again before you Mr. President as a suppliant for Mercy & Clemency to my husband. From information derived from undoubted authority, I fear sir, that my husband's feelings toward the Government have been misunderstood, and that is the cause of his detention in prison, when others have been released. Let me beg of you to read his application for pardon and you may be assured that his sentiments expressed in that document are the true and sincere expressions of his conscientious convictions. Gov. Marvin knows my husband well, and were he not satisfied of his honesty, he never would have recommended him to your clemency.

Adding a personal note, Mrs. Mallory wrote, "My husband's health is failing him, and unless released from imprisonment, I fear that his days will not be long. Return to my children their father and to me my husband."[41]

As Christmas approached, Mallory was suffering from poor health and low spirits. On December 5, 1865, he noted in his diary, "Am I to be released or not? Patience, fortitude, resignation, manhood befriend me! Suffered much pain for days back. But I must not complain."[42] Mallory feared he was making no headway in obtaining a pardon, in spite of all his efforts and those of his wife. His mood did not improve when he heard that Secretary Stanton was urging that he be tried for treason.

But Angela was not to be beaten down. She informed her husband that, regardless of the bad news about Stanton, she was going to Washington to plead her cause again with the president. Stephen worried about his wife; he had heard nothing from her. Finally, he got a note from her on January 24. She reported that although President Johnson received her kindly, he stated he was unable to grant a pardon. He told her that God "is our only hope and therefore we must trust Him and carry our crosses with patience, hope, and confidence." She found these words to be comforting.[43]

Angela Mallory was permitted to visit Stephen at Fort Lafayette about this same time; she found him to be suffering from gout and heart palpitations. She wrote to her friend Mrs. Clement C. Clay about the health of her husband:

> It makes my soul sink within me when I see my husband languishing in a prison and I can not help him out. He suffers all the excruciating torments that no other disease but the one he has can inflict, without a word of complaint.... I who for seventeen years witnessed the great sufferings which he undergoes know that he can not bear it much longer. I would not be surprised if some morning when Gen. Burke goes into Mr. M's room to see that he has not escaped, if he finds nothing but his body there, for his soul can not be detained by earthly prisons.[44]

These were some of the darkest days for Stephen and Angela, and there was little to dispel the gloom. In the past, Stephen had frequently been the optimist who proclaimed that even the darkest cloud had a silver lining. That was not the case this time.

But forces of change were at work. Mallory had originally been charged with treason for several reasons, the most important of which was the belief that the Confederate government had been involved in the plot to assassinate Lincoln. But no direct link was established between the assassin, John Wilkes Booth, and Confederate officials.[45] When Andrew Johnson assumed office, people recalled his 1864 statement that "Treason must be made odious, and traitors must be punished and impoverished...."[46] Despite this kind of rhetoric, Johnson's pardon policy became quite lenient. Historian Eric Foner points out that by 1866 President Johnson had granted over 7,000 pardons.[47] Furthermore, there had never been any bill of particulars that enumerated specific acts of treason by

Mallory. Moreover, most Americans felt that punishing former Confederate leaders would be counterproductive in the emerging atmosphere of reconciliation.[48]

Governor Marvin was continuing to work in Mallory's behalf, and had made a strong presentation for his parole. Finally, both Seward and Stanton recommended Mallory's release. President Johnson, who had never desired to punish Mallory, may have been persuaded, more than she thought, by Angela's two visits to him.

On March 10, 1866, former Secretary of the Confederate Navy Stephen R. Mallory was released from Fort Lafayette prison on "partial parole." He was ordered to remain in Bridgeport, Connecticut, at his daughter's home until given permission to move southward. Stephen Mallory walked out a free man although an oath of allegiance would be required before full rights of citizenship would be granted. The wanderer had returned to the bosom of his family and was held in their warm embrace.[49]

Part IV

THE LATER YEARS

15

Stephen and Angela

Stephen Russell Mallory and Angela Sylvania Moreno had disparate family backgrounds. Stephen's father and brother died when he was young and his mother, Ellen, reared him alone. She died in Key West on May 15, 1855.[1] On the other hand, a strong father, mother, and stepmother raised Angela within a large family structure.

Angela Moreno was born on June 20 (or 28), 1815, to Don Francisco Moreno and Josepha Lopez. Don Francisco Moreno, who was of Castilian stock, represented the Spanish government as vice consul in Pensacola for a half-century and was a prominent businessman. Angela had a brother, Francisco Moreno, Jr., and sister, Josefa Moreno. Her mother died in 1820 and her father remarried in 1821 to his first wife's sister, Margarita; they produced 13 children. Margarita died in 1851; in 1852 Mr. Moreno married his third wife, Mentoria Gonzalez; they had 12 children. Angela's father died November 19, 1883, in Pensacola, Florida. Thus Angela had a brother, sister, and 25 half-siblings.

Angela's family roots always were important to her and she consistently maintained close relationships with her father and many of her siblings. Stephen also came to embrace her family and, in turn, was welcomed by them.

After their marriage Stephen and Angela returned to Key West where they began producing their own family. They had four children that reached adulthood: Margaret "Maggie," born in 1839; Stephen Russell Mallory, Jr., "Buddy," born November 2, 1848; Atilla Fitzpatrick "Attie," born May 11, 1852; and Ruby Angela born April 18, 1855. Unhappily, they also gave birth to five other children who did not reach adulthood.[2]

From 1838 to 1858 the family resided in Key West and parental roles were well defined. Angela was busy giving birth to and nurturing babies while Stephen was engaged earning an income sufficient to support his growing family. He was a helpmate to his wife until he departed for the 32nd Congress in 1851.

As a new father, Stephen had a particularly close relationship with two of his sons, Francis Moreno (who was nicknamed "Frank" and died at age 11) and Stephen, Jr., ("Buddy"). Years later Stephen wrote to Buddy about what he and his brother meant to him:

> You and I and our dear Frank were very happy there [in Key West] my dear boy, for we were playmates, and I had scarcely a pleasure that you both did not share,

Angela Moreno Mallory Portrait c. 1838. This undated formal portrait of Angela Moreno, who married Stephen Mallory in July 1838 when she was 23 years of age, most likely was made prior to her marriage. Angela, who was of Castilian stock, was the daughter of the Spanish vice consul in Pensacola. She died in 1901, but Mallory Hall, a women's residence hall at the University of Florida, memorializes her. COURTESY OF PENSACOLA HISTORICAL SOCIETY.

and let me confess to you that the confidential intercourse, and free companionship between us, which I was ever anxious to maintain, constituted much of the happiness of my life. We were a devoted family, and you and Frank were ever with me. Teaching you boxing, swimming, shooting, boating, etc., telling you an instructive legend every evening nourished ever our mutual affection.[3]

Stephen added that his "rock of this earthly life" was love for his children and their mother and that his "heart swells with pleasure, with an enduring happiness at the reflection that I cannot tax myself with a needless harsh word, with any act or word not dictated by the purest affection toward my children."[4]

In the midst of national anxiety relative to the possible election of Abraham Lincoln for president, Mallory experienced his own turmoil when his married daughter, Maggie (Mrs. Henry Bishop), in Bridgeport, Connecticut, became ill in the fall of 1860. Congress was in recess at the time, so Stephen cared for the children in Pensacola while Angela went to Maggie's home to nurse her. The family had relocated to Pensacola from Key West in 1858. Stephen found himself somewhat insulated from all the national fuss because of his responsibilities for childcare that he seemed to thoroughly enjoy. He told stories about "bad Injuns," gave them lessons on geography, and explained the wonders of the telegraph to them. The latter subject provoked a squabble in which Ruby proclaimed that the words came through the middle of the wire and Attie declared that she "didn't know anything about it, nor himself either."[5] He helped the children build a doghouse, Attie was assigned jobs at whitewashing and gardening, and Ruby organized Angela's seashell collection. Stephen was content, the children were happy to have him with them, and Maggie regained her health.

Stephen longed for his wife and her comfort as he struggled with the loss of New

Orleans and other reverses. From Richmond he wrote to her on August 31, 1862, "I long my darling wife to be in your arms again; & but for the fatigue and endless trials of the journey, would ask you to come & see me for a sudden visit ... my affection for you becomes more & more the characteristic of my life."[6]

Being a prisoner in 1865 and 1866 sharpened the pain Stephen felt because of enforced separation from his loved ones. He wrote of devotion and angst for his family in a diary entry from Fort Lafayette prison on September 26, 1865:

> I am continually distressed by anxiety on account of my wife & children; my noble, pure souled Angela, my beloved Buddie & Attie & my darling little Ruby.— May God, in his infinite mercy, watch over them & shield them from harm, fill their hearts with obedience to him & love for mankind, and save their souls.— I have done for them as well as I could, & my love for them is indescribable. My children have in them every element of goodness, and will, with God's Grace, make good citizens.[7]

In fall 1865, Angela had been badly injured in a railroad accident when on her way to see him in prison; she was recuperating at Maggie's home in Bridgeport, Connecticut. Stephen's despair was nearly more than he could bear and he turned to God. He cried out in his diary on October 5, 1865:

> Have suffered mental distress beyond expression. To Reflect that my noble wife is suffering bodily pain from a rail-road accident. Confined to her bed & that I am not unable [able] to fly to her, I who have ever regarded kindness to her as my chief source of happiness in life. Oh My God! I feel this heavy misfortune. Oh enable me to overcome my murmuring & wretched spirit, & to regard this as a cross which tries my soul for his sanctification.— Lord Jesus, grant that she may be speedily restored, & that her heart may be cheered & purified by love of Thee.—

Additional remarks accentuate his despair:

> Walking this lonely cell to & fro, as I have seen wild beasts do in their cages, a thousand images of man's inhumanity to man crowd upon me & sicken me with life. Wrote twice to her. Her note of the 2d gave me a terrible shock, & my condition of health does not enable me to resist much. Have had a painful attack of gout.[8]

Five days later, Stephen again expressed his concern for Angela's fragile health occasioned by the railroad accident:

> May God give her his protection, & his Grace to endure this misfortune. I pray for her twice each day, & think of her constantly. True hearted, devoted, loving wife!— May the B. V. [Blessed Virgin] watch over you. Never can I forgive myself for unkind words to you; unkind, rude & unmanly, & all undeserved. If ever man was devoted to woman,— if ever man laid aside all thought of self, and looked to the happiness of his wife alone,- if ever man constantly kept his wife in his heart & loved her ever dearly & warmly, I have done so. However, even when angry & using most violent & reproachful words to her, have I ceased to love, honor & respect her; for I have felt my conscience denounce me even while angry. But I weakly gave way to passion, & did her wrong. God forgive me.[9]

Mallory wrote many letters to his children, but his most voluminous writing was reserved for his son, Stephen R. Mallory, Jr., usually referred to as "Buddy" but sometimes "Buddie." Mallory, the elder, afforded Stephen, Jr., much practical advice and guidance, obviously grooming him for important service in later life. Stephen wrote his son from prison, providing him with a lesson about respect for his parents:

> You are now at an age when, with an active, inquiring mind, thinking independently of all that crowds upon it, you will find yourself at times criticizing the conduct of others, ... [and] turn your thoughts to your parents.... A pure, undivided & confiding confidence & affection in & for your mother & father will serve you as an antidote against much of the poison of the world, & afford you relief, if not a cure for many a heart-ache.... I desire you to anchor your mothers image sacredly in your heart of hearts. A more truthful being ... I have never met in all my walks of life. She has, too, the genuine, trustful, hopeful spirit of piety & love of God. Her duty to God, & her love & devotion to her husband & her children have constituted all the mainsprings of her life. The approval of God first, the love of her husband & care of her family next, have ever been her guiding principles.[10]

Stephen also wrote Buddy about women:

> Cultivate the society of elevated minds, and particularly of high toned Catholic ladies. As your mind expands to the flood of light which constantly seeks to awaken man to his God, & your heart warms to the goodness of God & the beauty of all his creations, you will understand why I say Catholic ladies.... I know that there is that in the faith & worship of Catholic women which inevitably refines them, subdues & controls them, & gives a softness & a womanly delicacy, charity & kindness to their thoughts & manners, which is reflected upon, & is beneficial to their associates.... Cultivated, good women, refine & elevate a young man's nature. Avoid low & vulgar companions or pleasures my dear boy for you cannot descend to them without stains upon conscience & honor, & ever aim to preserve your self respect.[11]

Additionally, he wrote to Buddy of his love for Angela:

> We have been married twenty seven years.—On my part it was what the world would call a pure love match; but in fact, though I loved her beyond all the Earth beside, & would have invested her with ten thousand Earths if I had had them,—I was thus loving because she came up to the ideal which I had long cherished as the woman I would marry.—She was a good Catholic, was musical, spoke other languages than her own, & all about her & her family commanded respect.... My love for her has been the charm of my life, & it is, if possible more warm & holy today than it was upon the day of our wedding.[12]

Stephen's religion was most important to him. Ellen, his mother, was a Roman Catholic and Stephen adopted Catholicism at an early age. When he enrolled in the Moravian school at Nazareth, Pennsylvania, in 1826, he probably was the only student observing that religion. Nevertheless, he practiced his religion faithfully. Of this period in his life, he wrote, "To pray & bless myself was a habit; and I can never forget how boldly I could confront real or imaginary danger, that others frequently shrunk from, after blessing myself, & invoking Heaven's protection."[13]

While in prison, Stephen Mallory was often in the depth of despair because he was lonesome and isolated from his loved ones. He frequently returned to his faith for solace. Somehow, writing down his prayers brought him peace and comfort. Stephen composed this prayer on September 10, 1865:

> Oh God Eternal, Father of All, and thou Jesus, Savior of the world, grant me gracefully & implicitly to submit myself humble to thy dispensations, & to look upon them as justly due to my transgressions;—Humbly, Oh God, & with subdued & contrite spirit I beseech thee to pardon my sins, & to grant me grace to attain life with thee. Watch over me, Oh blessed spirit, assigned by God to attend upon my walk in life, & admonish me continually of my sins that my thoughts & words may not turn me aside from the path which leads to God, And there, Oh Blessed Trinity, Father Son, & Holy Ghost, I implore thee to watch over & protect my wife & children, to guide them by thy Holy precepts, to the end that they & I may enjoy bliss eternal with thee. Amen.[14]

Stephen's youngest child, Ruby, was never far from his mind and he wrote her a number of letters. From prison he penned a note telling her, "I sit here by the hour all alone, and let my thoughts wander to Bridgeport ... [and] I am there alongside of you, and I cannot make myself heard. You must act, however, just as if I were looking on all the time." He admonished her to "read and romp, practice and pray, my dear Ruby, and let each bring you something useful and new." Stephen closed by taking a wry rap at Atilla through Ruby inscribing, "Can you tell me why Atilla does not write to me? I know, of course, that he must be very busy, for all people who have nothing to do, are; but he might, I think, devote one day in the week, if necessary, to his correspondence."[15]

Of her love for her husband, 82-year-old Angela remarked on January 12, 1898:

> I grow young again when I think of him with whom so many years of my life were spent, whose strong hand held mine, and whose memory has never left my heart. He was the most devoted husband and father the world ever knew.... Never was there a truer or nobler man or one more determined to win where failure seemed assured.... He was tender and gentle as a woman to those he loved, and to any one in sorrow....[16]

Stephen Mallory had close personal relationships with his immediate family as well as his extended family. This was illustrated by his loyalty to his father-in-law, Don Francisco Moreno. Mr. Moreno, who was the Spanish vice consul in Pensacola, had been threatened with removal from office. He was accused of not maintaining his neutrality during the war and favoring the Confederate cause. This viewpoint most likely developed following an incident at Moreno's home that came to be known as the "Conflict at the Spanish Consulate."

This episode occurred in September 1863. Federal general Alexander Asboth had been assigned to the District of West Florida where he commanded Col. William C. Holbrook's First Brigade. In this brigade was Company H, Seventh Vermont Regiment, directed by Capt. Mahlon M. Young who was ordered to take a scouting party from Fort Barrancas at Warrington to the Pensacola area. At that time Federal forces controlled all forts and the Warrington Navy Yard but rebel patrols were scattered throughout the region. Around noon on September 8, Young's scouting party observed and covertly followed a small rebel force from the Fifth Alabama Calvary approaching Pensacola. The Alabama troops entered Moreno's home whereupon Young's Union force stormed the house, demanding that the Confederates surrender. They acquiesced and Captain Young took eight rebels as prisoners. To their astonishment, the Union army group also found that United States Navy captain Thomas F. Wade, from the U.S. bark *Arthur* that was blockading offshore, was part of the gathering. Wade and the Confederates apparently had been exchanging information and gossip. The naval officer was indignant and proclaimed that the army had no legal right to take the rebels as prisoners. Captain Wade amazed all present by demanding the prisoners be released or he would order 25 U.S. marines to protect them, adding that "if you take those men, you will have to do it over my dead body." Mr. Moreno claimed their capture was a "violation of the sanctity of the Spanish flag" and he told the rebels they should not leave because "they were under his official protection." He added that in his official capacity he knew "no distinction between Federals and Confederates; they are alike entitled to protection under my flag." Finally, all agreed to refer the legality of the arrests to higher authority and Moreno wrote a report to the Spanish ambassador at Washington. This may have been the genesis of a letter from the Spanish ambassador's office to Mr. Moreno.[17]

On May 19, 1866, Stephen Mallory was in Bridgeport, Connecticut, at Maggie's home when he wrote a letter in behalf of his father-in-law to Don Gabriel G. Tapara, a Spanish government official:

> I have learned this day that Don Francisco Moreno is to be removed from office. Believing that such removal could only result from misapprehension of his conduct ... I take the liberty of appealing ... in his behalf. I have never heard his official conduct questioned. He remained at his post in the abandoned and ruined town of Pensacola during the late war; &, though careful to avoid even the appearance of mingling in the strife, I fear that prejudice has been excited against him from the fact that his sons embarked in the Confederate Cause, & that I, his son in law, was Secretary of the Confederate Navy. Mr. Moreno maintained himself with that rectitude & neutrality which became an officer under just authority; & I am advised that officials & citizens of the U. States never vainly appealed to his kindness or hospitality. I pray that your Excellency will see that he is heard before he is degraded. I pledge myself that he will satisfactorily answer any complaints of his conduct so soon as they may be known to him.[18]

The outcome of this letter is unknown.

Stephen relocated his family from Key West to Pensacola, Florida, after his mother's death and established their permanent residence in Pensacola. Except for his government services in Washington and Richmond, Stephen lived in these two Florida towns throughout his adult life.[19]

During his service in the United States Senate, Mallory resided at the National hotel on Pennsylvania Avenue at Sixth Street in Washington. Apparently, he also lived in the suburbs on occasion.[20] On July 5, 1854, the Senate was debating a resolution for determining the time for its daily meeting; Senator Mallory stated, "If we meet at ten o'clock we cannot get there sooner than we do now, residing as we do, at a great distance from the Capital."[21]

One observer described our nation's capital during 1860:

> Washington was a mixture of Arlington grandeur, Jeffersonian simplicity, Dolly-Madisonism, Fillmore primness and the gracious chill of Miss Harriet Lane. Its society was a mosaic of elegance and pomp, of recklessness and parity, of culture and crudity.... It was a charming society and one much sought.... The leaders of

society were largely Southerners. Cultured, gracious, or brilliant women there were from North, East and West.[22]

The same observer noted changes taking place in the winter of 1860–1861 and said the capital social scene was the "most lavish and brilliant" as had ever been seen. It was also the "giddiest and most feverish" when "dull clouds of doubt and suspense began to press low on the horizon...." Sensing the approaching storm, the socialites continued their parties with a furor. This interval was followed by a dull silence when South Carolina seceded. "North and South were at last openly aligned against each other.... [A] dull, vague unrest brooded over Washington...." People said "this might be 'the end of the Old Wreck,' as slang began to call the capital."[23]

While Mallory was in Washington, Angela remained in Key West with the children because she found the capital's winter climate to be too cold. By spring 1854, Angela and the children were reunited with Stephen in the Washington suburbs, at least part of the year, where she entertained frequently and came to be known as a gracious hostess. In 1858 the Mallory family relocated to Pensacola where they built a house with the assistance of Angela's father. From time to time, Angela and the children would leave Pensacola to be with Stephen in Washington. The dates the family was together in Washington cannot be documented with two exceptions: their one- or two-year-old child (Nellie) is believed to have died in Washington on January 24, 1858, and 11-year-old Frank (Francis) died there on March 11, 1858. Because of these deaths, this could not have been a happy social season for the family. It is unlikely they could have been united in Washington earlier; beginning in 1850 children were born in Key West every year or two.

While Angela was in Washington, she attended social gatherings with Stephen. Of these occasions, Stephen wrote to her, "All your lady friends here inquire most affectionately for you, and no woman who ever came to Washington made more friends or a better impression than yourself." He continued, "You are greatly admired, and I am frequently congratulated on having the most delightful wife that can be found in the Senate."[24]

Mrs. Virginia Clay, the wife of Senator Clement C. Clay, was in Washington and became acquainted with the Mallory family. She had this to say of Angela: "Mrs. Mallory was particularly a favourite in the capital. The Mallorys were the owners of great orange groves in that lovely State, and were wont from time to time to distribute among their friends boxes of choicest fruit."[25] The diarist Mary Chesnut also mentions that Stephen Mallory presented her with "a splendid bunch of bananas" on May 3, 1861; on July 17–18, 1861, she wrote, "Mallory has just sent me the nicest peach."[26]

Scholar, Occie Clubbs, writes:

> Angela with her frank speech had caused a sensation in Washington society. Confronted with some impetuous remark, she would close the matter with, "I am sorry, but it is true"; the Castilians with perhaps a better knowledge of philology and therefore without the inhibitions of Anglo-Saxons in employing them, used at times, rather forcible words.... On one occasion, Mrs. Mallory was being driven by an Irish hackman, named Barie. Upon learning his name, she inquired if he were Irish. An affirmative reply led her to ask if he were a Catholic. "No," Barie answered. "Protestant?," pursued Mrs. Mallory. "No, atheist." "No," said Mrs. Mallory, "D--- Fool."[27]

Such statements might either engender contempt for her or provoke amusement and laughter. Her sharp wit did not go without comment.

Ms. Clubbs refers to Mrs. Mallory as being Castilian. Angela's origins were associated with the town of Castile in Spain since her paternal grandfather was born in that area. These folks are deemed to be a passionate people displaying great feeling in their music, their food, even their language. A Castilian is reputed to have a profound devotion to family, which is centered on the mother who brought children into the world. Castilian veneration for the maternal figure is profound and any disparaging remarks about her are to be avoided. This cultural feature is to be considered in all the positive remarks Stephen makes in his reference to his wife, mother of his children.

When the southern states seceded from the Union, southern social activity was transferred to the new capital cities, first Montgomery, Alabama, and then Richmond, Virginia. The two major hotels in Montgomery were the Montgomery Hall hotel and The Exchange hotel. Many lawmakers chose to establish their residence at the Montgomery Hall hotel although it was held to be somewhat unclean and expensive. The Exchange hotel was viewed as pretentious and a bit more comfortable; this is where President Davis and his family resided.[28] The president's office was in one of the parlors of the hotel. Cabinet members and other high officials came in without ceremony to discuss matters or to consult with the president's private secretary. An usher announced casual visitors when business did not prevent Davis from receiving them.[29]

While in Montgomery, Stephen Mallory boarded at the Montgomery Hall hotel and some of his companions there included James and Mary Chesnut and Benjamin Hill and his wife. They frequently dined together and engaged in lively conversations. Mrs. Chesnut wrote that although the stories told were "rather strongly spiced for my presence.[,] Mr. Mallory's were the best. 'Tho' they say his mother was a washer woman, he is the most refined in the group...."[30] "Mallory told the best stories," according to historian William C. Davis, "though sometimes rather too lurid for the ladies. Still his basic refinement left him second only to Chesnut in the wives' regards."[31] Other times the conversation would turn to plain gossip. Mallory would shock the ladies as he told stories about who had been sleeping with whom in Washington and he spoke (perhaps facetiously) of his own flirtatious relationship with a well-known Alabama lady who had been unfaithful to her husband.[32] Mary Chesnut had heard gossip about Mallory suggesting he was "notoriously dissolute" and that merely being with him could imperil a lady's character. Furthermore, those spreading rumors would suggest that Stephen's frequent attacks of gout were due to his drinking.[33] Mrs. Chesnut, on April 28, 1861, expressed her opinions about his gout and his daughter, Maggie, writing, "Saw Mr. Mallory a moment at his room door; he has gout, his daughter is not pretty & her husband is a Connecticut *Yankee* [emphasis in original]."[34]

Many observers of the social scenes in Washington, Montgomery, and Richmond have recorded their outward impressions of Stephen Mallory. "Most people liked the short, roly-poly Floridian," while he lived in the interim Confederate capital and "When he took a room at Montgomery Hall they met a pleasant, witty sort of fellow, definitely very pro-British, and even to some ears affecting an English accent. He pronounced 'clerk' as 'clark,' and the like, and dressed his chubby frame in the British fashion."[35]

Historian Virgil Carrington Jones had this to say of Stephen Mallory:

> He was a man of warm feelings, sometimes a bit naïve, but always sincere and in no sense a quitter.... He was fat of face and ruddy of complexion, and his hair sat out from the side of his head in bangs as though he had been careless with his

pillow.... He was a plodder with infinite patience, as well as the ability to remain cheerful in the face of great odds...."[36]

By early May 1861 Montgomery Hall had become the center of social activity for leaders of the Confederacy. Although Mrs. Mallory had originally remained in Florida when her husband journeyed to Montgomery in February, she had joined him in May at Montgomery Hall. Some Confederate officials gathering there for social events included the Memmingers, Alexander Stephens, Jefferson and Varina Davis, and Robert and Julia Toombs.[37]

Mary Chesnut was at some social functions in Montgomery that included Mr. and Mrs. Mallory. On May 7, 1861, she noted that Angela Mallory had arrived in Montgomery and "a nice woman she seems to be," but she qualified this view by indicating Angela was "so foreign and piquante [piquant]."[38] A month later Mrs. Chesnut observed that Mrs. Mallory was of Spanish heritage and noted, "one can see she has been a beauty. Now she is a grandmother pure and simple. Her name is Angela." The diarist wrote that most people pronounced her name "angelically" but "Mr. Mallory, who is very proud of her, gave the Spanish pronunciation — Anhla. We failed to reproduce the sound in his fashion ... because Mallory did it principally with his nose. Anhla."[39]

When the secretary of the Confederate navy moved with the rest of the Confederate government to the permanent capital at Richmond, Virginia, in June 1861, he was unknown, "But his quick perception, decided cultivation, and especially his wit, genial nature and frank courtesy, soon placed him high in the estimate of even the severest critics of men in position." He took genuine pleasure in "good cheer and a good joke." One noted the "twinkle in his eye and the placid curve of his full lips...."[40] Visitors to the Mallory house found they quickly felt at home due to the hosting abilities of husband and wife. Additionally, "Mr. Mallory brewed a punch as good as his stories and mots, and Mrs. Mallory knew tricks of Southern salads ... that made many Northern eyes wink and mouths water."[41]

The date family members joined Stephen in Richmond is unknown but a letter from Stephen to Angela indicates the family was together in Richmond around the time of the Battle of New Orleans on April 25, 1862; a draft letter from Angela to Varina Davis verifies she was in Richmond on September 12 through September 19, 1862.[42] Angela and remaining family members left Richmond prior to the evacuation of the city in April 1865 and sought safety in the Benjamin Hill's home in Georgia.

Angela recorded some observations of Richmond's social scene:

> Our home in Richmond, where we resided during the war, was the rendezvous of the cabinet officers, as were the homes of Mr. Davis and Mr. Semmes, who were our near neighbors. I knew General Lee, General Morgan, Judah F. Benjamin, Alexander H. Stephens and all the senators, and our home was their rendezvous. There they would come to consult with Mr. Mallory, and there, too, they would often come to receptions and parties, for Richmond was very gay, and though we heard the cannon booming all day and all night, we continued our parties, charades and receptions, even though often we could catch the flash of the guns as the shot and shell fell thick and fast. Those were stirring days and never to be forgotten.[43]

Mrs. Virginia Clay described informal dinners she and Senator Clay enjoyed in Richmond during the war. She wrote of dining in the Mallory home:

> The family of Mr. Mallory was a model one, every member seeming to have his or her share in rounding out the general attractiveness. An informal meal taken with that family was an experience long to be remembered, for the little children took each his turn in asking the blessing, which was never omitted, and which was especially impressive in those days, in which the shadows of growing privations soon grew to be recognized if not openly discussed or admitted. Our Secretary of the Navy, Mr. Mallory, was the merriest of hosts, with a wit as sudden and as brilliant as sheet-lightning, and a power of summing up, when he chose to exert it, both events and people, in the most amusing manner. A picture remains clearly in my mind of the evening [when] ... Ruby Mallory, then about thirteen years of age, recited for us Holmes's "The Punch-bowl," while our host, in hearty enjoyment of the verses, "Stirred the posses with his ladle," to the rhythm of his little daughter's speech.[44]

Mary Chesnut attended a Richmond party in 1863 and was treated to another elocution display by Ruby. "Ruby Mallory recited 'Bingen on the Rhine.' It was too appropriate. It brought a choking sensation to our throats."[45] The poem is about a soldier dying on the battlefield. The opening verse reads:

> A soldier of the Legion lay dying in Algiers,
> There was a lack of woman's nursing, there was dearth of woman's tears;
> But a comrade stood beside him, while his lifeblood ebbed away,
> And bent with pitying glances, to hear what he might say.
> The dying soldier faltered, and he took that comrade's hand,
> And he said, "I nevermore shall see my own, my native land:
> Take a message, and a token, to some distant friends of mine,
> For I was born at Bingen, — at Bingen on the Rhine.[46]

The emotional reaction of the guests suggests Ruby recited the poem dramatically and had struck a responsive chord.

Historian Rembert W. Patrick records some pithy observations of social activities in Richmond. He writes that Richmond was "a city of 40,000, a gleaming, urbane city with good hotels and fine private residences, many of them owned by wealthy planters who lived there in the winter. Davis and his wife first lived in the Spottswood hotel, which became the social center of the Confederate government. At social functions the presidential group usually included Judah P. Benjamin and Stephen R. Mallory and Mallory would hold a guest's amused attention with many a well-told anecdote."[47]

Patrick also noted:

> The Mallory home was a favorite with distinguished visitors in Richmond, as well as with the leaders in its society. Mallory and his Spanish wife were little known in Richmond prior to 1861, but his wit, his powers as a raconteur, his genial manners and frank courtesy soon won general esteem. Both he and his wife possessed in high degree the social graces which put guests at ease immediately upon entering their home. Mallory was somewhat of a gourmet and Mrs. Mallory was adept at preparing salads. Her husband was famous for his skill at mixing mint juleps with which even those of a Kentucky colonel could not compare, and his stories were as good as his juleps. He was known as the most adroit flatterer in Richmond and expressed his compliments in neatly turned phrases. The Mallory home was the rendezvous of Cabinet officers who frequently went there to consult with the Secretary of the Navy.[48]

Another observer of the social scene, Mrs. Burton Harrison, remembers attending a reception at the home of Raphael Semmes. "The drawing rooms were crowded with smart people, the President and Mrs. Davis, Mr. Benjamin, the silver-tongued Secretary of State, Mr. and Mrs. Mallory and their sparkling little Ruby with all the high world of the government."[49]

Angela Mallory and the president's wife, Varina Howell Davis, although necessarily thrown together in dinners and parties, did not always get along well together. Mrs. Davis may have viewed Mrs. Mallory as a challenger to her premier position. The first lady of the Confederacy wrote a letter to Mrs. Mallory and berated her for perceived slights and insulting remarks. Mrs. Mallory penciled a draft reply but we do not know if she actually sent a finished letter to Mrs. Davis. The two letters probably were written in October 1862. Both letters are valuable in that they provide insight into the personality and character of these two strong-willed ladies as they engaged in vitriolic communication. Their barely repressed fury is wrapped up in hoop skirts and orange blossoms as they take potshots at each other. The excerpted letters (with editorial comments) between Mrs. Davis and Mrs. Mallory follow.[50] First, the letter from Varina Davis to Angela Mallory:

Executive Mansion—
Richmond Oct 2nd

My dear Mrs Mallory,

In answer to your note of inquiry, I must frankly tell you that I felt very much insulted by your remarks during your evening visit before your departure from Richmond.

You had been in town two weeks or ten days, and had not offered to me the common courtesy of a call, usually considered due to the wife of the President, even where no official relations exist. I first met you in a candy shop, and with the disappointed affection of a friend, rallied you upon not caring to see me, or you would have called in the morning when an escort was not necessary....

However I concluded that you were conscious of not having been quite kind, to say nothing of the courtesy due to the official relations existing between our husbands, and cared for it only as an indication of changed feeling.

When you came in the evening I was unaffectedly pleased to see you, and gave you a cordial greeting. Upon your telling Mr. Mallory in the course of a conversation about Mr. Hawkins Wives that he had no acquaintance with them, I playfully remarked, Oh let him amplify, don't you always amplify when there is no member of the family by [nearby?] to check you—at which you took exceptions, and I explained that the 'you' was collective, not personal, and that the remark was a jest at best—to which you answered in a very excited manner, 'I am very glad it was so, for if *you* amplify *I* do not, if *you* do not tell the truth *I* do.[emphasis in original]' If you remember my only answer was, I could not be rude to you in my own house on any account. It was the only mode left to me by which I could express my appreciation of the insult and inability to answer it at that time, and that place—... [The reference to Mr. Hawkins' wives suggests that Mallory had some flirtations with them.]

Now having given you the plain—spoken explanation you justly expected of me if any were given, I will add that if no offense was intended I am perfectly willing to believe you spoke under the influence of a dyspeptic state of mind, and with no unkind intent.

My regard for you has been of the most sincere character, and I trust that years of acquaintance may tend only to its increase....

Varina Davis.

Mrs. Davis reminds Mrs. Mallory twice that she is the first lady. She appears to be "keeping score" of perceived insults, slights, and deficiencies in the respect owed her. She is aggressively critical of Mrs. Mallory, and finds it difficult to refrain from correcting her behavior in this rather astringent letter.

Varina Davis gives ample evidence of the importance to her of being first lady of the Confederacy and of the inherent power of that role. Noting this trait, some observers would somewhat derisively refer to her as "Queen Varina" and "Madame Presidentress."[51] Others would "call Mrs. Davis the Empress-Eugénie ..." [an allusion to the wife of Napoleon III][52] Another observer said Varina Davis was "naturally a frank though not a blunt woman, and her bent was to kindliness and charity. Sharp tongue she had, when set that way and the need came to use it."[53] An acquaintance said of her, "She frequently says strong things in strong words but, then, she has a strong mind."[54] As we shall see below, the same might be said of Mrs. Mallory.

Next is the draft letter of reply from Angela Mallory to Varina Davis that also is excerpted and includes editorial comments:

[?]—-/62

My DrMrs Davis

Your reply to my recent note came today & filled me with surprize [sic], regret, & pain; & it brings relief, because you have spoken as I desired & knew you would speak, with candor, & thus enable me to place myself right. [Mrs. Mallory almost always uses "&" for "and" as did her husband and others during this period.]

The sincere regard which, in the close of your ... note, you express for me, I have as sincerely confided in & as sincerely reciprocated; & having neither motive, feeling no purpose to do or say anything inconsistent with our mutual esteem, you can well understand my surprise & pain on learning your belief that I have done so. It is therefore eminently due to you as well as to myself to say ... that neither in my failure to call upon you, to which you refer, nor in word, thought or manner ... was I activated by any thought or feeling of unkindness, ... but I do deserve, my dear friend, to disclaim explicitly all design to offend you, or to treat you in any manner inconsistent with my personal regard for you....

I might stop here, and feel certain of being properly understood; but I am unwilling to admit that my language to you was "<u>if you do not tell the truth I do</u>"; [underlined in original]— nor do I plead guilty to "<u>an excited manner</u>," [underlined in original] for I assure you that, from several causes, I never felt more sad & depressed or freer from all excitement in my life—I said what I did so with such playfulness ... & without any special meaning or application.—nor must you suppose I "<u>was in town two weeks or ten days without offering to you the common courtesy of a call</u>"; [underlined in original] for I reached Richmond on the 12 Sept., called on you on the 16 & left on the 19, ... two of my seven days in Richmond I was ill.... This alone as I have before said, prevented me from calling to see you again....

Present me Kindly to the President ... in whose behalf my earnest prayers are offered—

Sincerely ... your friend
    <u>ASM</u>

Note: On the back of the last page, written in careful pen and ink script, is the following: "I admit that I said (in connection with ... what was being said about Mr. Mallory's knowing Judge Hawkin's wives that he did not tell the truth, anyway"

It should be noted that Angela's phrase, "If you do not tell the truth, I do," was a favorite aphorism that she used throughout her life. She spoke a variation of it when she first met Stephen and was not attracted to him. She also said it when she was pressed or contradicted on a point she had made when she would brusquely respond, "I'm sorry but it is true."[55]

It seems obvious that Varina Davis and Angela Mallory were two strong-willed, intelligent, and articulate ladies who were competitive with one another. They did not particularly care for each other but could maintain superficial friendliness.

Toward the end of war, not unmindful of the suffering and hunger of many Richmond citizens, Mr. and Mrs. Mallory would invite cabinet members to their house to enjoy "pea soup." However, this was a cover name for an evening of dining upon "oysters, champagne, and every delicacy of the epicure." While the cabinet members worked hard, "They were ever ready to avail themselves of the entertainment offered either within their own circle or by Richmond friends."[56]

Even as the Union army was closing in on Richmond, Stephen Mallory continued with his sense of humor and displayed his jocularity. In the fall of 1864 Union general Sherman had begun his march across Georgia and Mrs. Virginia Clay was living with Senator James H. Hammond's family in South Carolina while her husband was serving as a Confederate agent in Canada. Mallory was concerned about her safety and with his dry wit invited her to reside in the comparative safety of Richmond. He wrote, "Now that Sherman's barbarians are in unpleasant proximity to you, why not come to the front where security, sympathy, mint juleps, an admiring audience, the freshest gossip and the most unselfish regard, all combine with the boom and flash of guns to welcome your coming?"[57]

Angela Mallory was a complex person who could be gracious and compassionate as well as caustic and haughty. Additionally, she had a loving relationship with her husband, but experienced periods of unwarranted jealousy because of his contacts with certain females (as exhibited earlier in the reference to "Judge Hawkin's wives"). More serious than this were her occasional periods of moroseness and depression that worried Stephen greatly, and may have diverted him from important official tasks.

Angela's jealousy of other women who came into contact with her husband was infrequent, episodic, and usually of short duration. Stephen dealt with her unhappiness through use of humor and affirmation of his love for her. The root of Angela's negative feelings may have been her perception that she was trapped at home with her children and sometimes excluded from social activities available to Stephen. There is no documented evidence that he was unfaithful to her at any time. However, the diarist Mary Chesnut on June 28, 1861, did suggest playful flirtation between Stephen and Mrs. Margaret McLean when she wrote, "Mr. Mallory & Mrs. McLean were having queer jokes because Mrs. McLean's key was found in Mr. M's pocket."[58]

Through 1858 Stephen had received letters from Angela, who was in Pensacola, while he was staying at the National hotel in Washington. Apparently her letters generally consisted of complaints and trifles in which she reported most of the bad news from home and little of the good. Although they made him sad, Stephen was not unduly concerned until later in the year she began commenting about "an allegedly charming widow" whom she felt was attempting to steal the affections of her husband. Their physical separation, which was not helping the situation, served to stimulate her imagination. On January 1, 1859, he wrote to his "darling wife, my beloved Angela," and reported to her that he was amused as he read her suspicions about the widow. He said he had met the lady once and had mentioned her in a letter but that she was not to worry. The lady in question was "rickety frame of bone and muscles, ... an anatomical preparation whose dangling skinny arms tell of corresponding legs, and whose little pumkin [sic] belly gives the lie to the hips which crinoline would seek to impose upon us." Stephen assured Angela that his preferences were toward a "plump, pretty, charming, vivacious, bright and lovable bedfellow" such as his wife. He assured Angela of his "measureless and unswerving affection" for her and swore he had always been faithful to her and would continue to do so. He closed his missive by writing, "I wish you were with me and may the prayers of your ... husband for your happiness prevail, for he is nothing without you."[59]

Angela's deep depression was of more serious concern. She had been in Richmond at her husband's side when New Orleans fell and supported him in these dark hours. However, she left Richmond late in April 1862. On May 3 he wrote to her saying:

> You have been gone a week, and it already seems to me an age since I heard the voices of yourself and my dear children. Everything is quiet about the house as the grave. The table is so empty that I cannot endure to remain more than two minutes at it, and the bed is so large and desolate that I sit up reading nearly all night. We must endure much suffering, my dear wife, ere we win our independence; and we must present to the foe an undying resolve to conquer or to die.[60]

Angela wrote Stephen several gloomy letters in late May and "he had been 'greatly saddened' by the 'tone of complaint and distress' of one of her communications...."[61] In reply, he told her to have courage and stay the battle, while sharing amusing anecdotes with her. Stephen responded to more melancholy letters from Angela by teasing her about one of her old admirers who had appeared in Richmond. He suggested that the old beaux might want a lock of her hair. He also inquired what she might like him to get for her through ships running the blockade.

All this may have helped somewhat, but Angela was suffering personal tragedies that Stephen could not still in his correspondence. Her brother, Francisco Moreno, Jr., a lieutenant in the Confederate army, was wounded at the Battle of Shiloh on April 15, 1862, and died as a prisoner of war in Louisville, Kentucky, on May 4, 1862. His death was a severe blow to Angela since she and her "little brother" had been close. Adding to her anguish had been the death of her half-brother, Charles Albert Moreno, on August 4, 1861.[62] Angela's acute sense of loss was intensified by worry about two more half-brothers who were fighting for the Confederate cause and her husband's proximity to the front during McClellan's peninsular campaign.

Similar letters in summer 1862 began to test Stephen's patience and stamina for he had not only her problems to deal with, but also his responsibilities as navy chief. Reflecting an irritated state of mind, Stephen wrote Angela in August that he was "so depressed by her letters that [he] could do nothing.... I cannot argue with you, my Angela, upon your want of faith in God, your weakness, cowardice, and unpatriotism. I can only deplore them. My love for you is so unselfish, so pure and devoted ... that you could say and do nothing to me ... which I am not ever ready to forgive and forget...."[63] But Angela had suggested to Stephen that he did not want her to come back to him at Richmond. He retorted, "You do me injustice, Angela.... It is pitiable that you should thus be a prey to so mean a feeling. Come to me. I want to see you, to have you with me day and night."[64]

By 1864 Angela's gloomy letters had turned into epistles suggesting depression and death. Angela had been separated from her husband much of the time over the past 13 years; she missed him terribly when they were apart. "I know what the feeling is, to be left alone, for no matter whom I have with me, I feel all alone if my husband is absent. Oh! The tears that I have shed at being left!"[65] Then Mrs. Mallory learned that Varina Davis had lost her five-year-old son, Joe, who was killed in a fall from the second-floor porch at their home; she felt much compassion for the bereaved wife of the president. On May 6, 1864 she wrote to her friend, Mrs. Clay, about the incident and said, "He was a beautiful boy, and his parents' loss has been his gain, for he is now where the rumors of Wars never enter. *Oh, if I could only be there, too, with all those who are dear to me!* [emphasis added]."[66]

This clear death wish requires examination. Angela had experienced the death of so many relatives that it may have been extremely difficult for her to absorb these collective calamities. Her missives of complaint and bad news from home had begun in 1858. The catastrophes started for her on January 24, 1858, when her two-year-old baby Nellie died, and continued when two months later her 11-year-old son, Francis, also died. Throughout the marriage, five of her nine children had not lived to become adults. This loss would be difficult for any mother to fathom. By 1864 three of her brothers had been killed in the war and a fourth would die in 1865. Thirty-three years later she would speak to a newspaper reporter about these times: "Her voice grew tremulous with tears, and ... she said quietly, 'The war is always a painful theme to me; it strikes to my heart. I had six brothers who went out with their swords and determined to return ... and four were victims to the strife.'"[67] Considering her many losses, why would she not be depressed and express a death wish? Her husband tried to console her in various ways, but the pain was too deep.

16

The Declining Years and Quietus

Upon his release from prison on March 10, 1866, Stephen Russell Mallory immediately went to his family in Bridgeport, Connecticut. Angela, Attie, and Ruby were all staying with his daughter, Maggie, and her husband, Henry Bishop; Buddy was a student at Georgetown College in Washington. Angela was still recovering from her railroad accident and he feared "that her dancing [would] be seriously interrupted by it for some time to come."[1] Stephen was required to remain in Connecticut until given permission to return to Florida. His main concern was his impoverished condition and how he could support his family. He feared that he would have difficulty becoming licensed to practice law and that it might not be remunerative.

Stephen also had a host of other problems. His health had suffered because of the strains of war followed by imprisonment, and his gout was still bothering him. He had land investments in Missouri, but doubted that he could gain access to them because of his status as a paroled prisoner.

Also, he had received word that his house in Pensacola was in a sad state of disrepair because of damage done by Federal troops in 1862. In the prewar years, "the huge Mallory home [in Pensacola] like many others of the time was painted yellow, had green blinds and large white columns in front.... Among the high-ceilinged rooms were two parlors.... The garden outside [had] narrow walks outlining the beds of old-time violets, roses, narcissus, oleander, green-embossed snowdrops, crape myrtle, pink hemerocalis [daylily]— a charming mosaic of color."[2] The Mallory home had been purchased on October 2, 1858, for $1,200. The 192-foot by 192-foot lot was located on Garden Street, which was a northerly continuation of Palafox Street.[3]

The Confederates evacuated the Warrington Navy Yard on May 9, 1862, and set it ablaze that evening. From the roof of the Mallory home, a group of citizens viewed the "devastating display" as the "arcs of fire swept above the horizon."[4] Two days later, Federal forces took possession of the Pensacola area. From June to November 1862 Col. William Wilson, commander of the New York Sixth Regiment Infantry (Wilson's Zouaves), made his headquarters in the Mallory home. The fall of 1862 was cold and many vacant houses were damaged or destroyed by soldiers to get firewood. Since it had been occupied by Federal troops, the Mallory home was spared destruction. Throughout the Civil War Stephen's father-in-law, Francisco Moreno, vice consul of Spain for the Port of Pensacola, engaged in a unique tactic to protect his home — he secured immunity from attack by flying the Spanish flag and declaring that it rested on Spanish soil. Neither of the combatants cared to risk the wrath of the international community and did not disturb his property. Pensacola remained in Federal control throughout the rest of the war.[5]

After his release from prison, Mallory required a place to live since he could not rely for long upon the generosity of his daughter and her husband. He decided to return as soon as possible to Pensacola, make his home habitable, and then send for his family. In order to accomplish this goal, he needed permission from the Federal government to go to Pensacola and renovate his home. Stephen decided that he and his son Attie (who could be of great help in repairing the house) would go to Washington where Mallory would visit the president and secretary of war to thank them for his parole and obtain permission to return to Florida.

Father and son arrived in Washington early in June 1866. Stephen called upon President Johnson and Secretary Stanton, both of whom were cordial, and they gave him permission to return to Florida. While in the capital city, he conferred with old friends regarding legal matters and his Missouri land investments. Mallory also visited his son, Buddy, and wrote, "He went everywhere with me, and I presented him, with a great deal of pride, to all friends who saw me." Stephen wrote Angela that Buddy was playing on the Georgetown College baseball team and "is a fine fellow in all respects."[6]

Stephen and Attie visited Richmond so he could review business prospects there. The town was being rebuilt, but he was distressed at the state of its economy. Mallory was concerned about the status of the black man who was trying to adjust to being a free laborer. He found some slaves begging on the street because their former masters could no longer care for them. This stirred his anxiety about the status of his own free blacks in Pensacola.

Richmond offered him few business prospects but he and Attie enjoyed visiting old friends. He wrote to Angela that Attie was having fun with his old playmates shortly after their arrival, and that Ruby's old friends asked for her. Also, many adults were asking for "darling Ruby" and he wrote to her, "You cannot imagine, my dear child, how much I was gratified by their praises of you, because I know that they love you for your love, obedience, and kindness to your mother and for your general good conduct...."[7]

In late June Mallory decided it was time for him and Attie to continue on toward Florida. They were delayed for a few days because Stephen suffered from another attack of gout, but in the first week of July they were on the road again, reaching La Grange, Georgia, by July 6, 1866. They stayed for a while at the home of Mallory's old friend and former prison cellmate, Benjamin Hill. This served as a rest stop for them and while Stephen enjoyed socializing with the Hills it also gave him the opportunity to write letters to his family.

The first letter was to Angela; he referred to an earlier letter from her in which she complained of being unhappy. He acknowledged that her physical condition arising from the railroad accident might depress her, but he urged her to look at the blessings that had been bestowed on her by the mercy and goodness of God. He did not comment about any loneliness she might feel due to his separation from her.

Letters that Stephen wrote from Georgia reflected the continuing bitterness that

Mallory harbored toward northerners. This correspondence reveals how deep his wounds were and how divisive the war had been. He wrote Angela about Connecticut people of the opposite political party — the Republicans:

> There is some good in all classes of people, but the Republican ignorant women and men seem to me the least meritorious, if not the most despicable white people I have ever met with.... They are an inferior people to us in all respects, and they have cruelly wronged us....[8]

In a letter to his daughter Ruby, the father referred to a letter her mother had written to him saying Ruby was interested in a local boy in Bridgeport. He chastised his daughter:

> I trust that you will never allow yourself to make the slightest advance towards the acquaintance of any Republican in Bridgeport. As a well bred SOUTHERN [caps in the original] lady, I am unwilling for you to have any intimacies or any other than a formal intercourse with them. We are as different from them as oil is from water.... You are superior to ninety-nine in any hundred of them....[9]

His astringent remarks must have reflected the views of many southerners; numerous Yankees most likely uttered similar vitriolic criticism when speaking of rebels.

On July 16, Stephen and Attie traveled to Montgomery, Alabama, staying at the home of friends overnight, before leaving on the last leg of their journey home. Upon arrival in Pensacola, Stephen wrote another letter to "My Dear, Good Wife" on July 19 ("The Anniversary of My Marriage") announcing that the two of them had completed the trip. Stephen wrote that her family met them at the wharf "& your father seems very happy to have me." He ate at his host's house and said supper was served "in your father's time honored style, & embraced stewed chicken a la Creole, & a large dish of delicious figs which he had picked expressly for me." Stephen related that after sleeping he rose for "Breakfast at eight, of egg & tomato &c, with a second edition of figs, a dinner at two, came off in the old style, supper, with richly cooked dishes appeared at eight, and here I am, at half past twelve, in this little cooked [cocked?] hat of a room chatting with my darling wife over my first day in Pensacola." Stephen wrote of his walking over to their house and noting the specific items requiring repair. He closed saying, "Every body asks about you ... & all earnestly desire your return. With black as well as white you are a most popular woman...."[10]

On August 18, 1866, Stephen wrote Angela reporting progress in repairing their house:

> Masons (plasterers) & carpenters & glaziers are at work, but there are few good mechanics, a scarcity of materials, & work progresses very slow. All the rooms of the back building have their first coats of plaster ... there is extensive patching to be done to the plastering of the main building, & to its roof.... The parlours are done & look pretty well.... The only remaining mantle is in your room & I am having wooden mantles made ... all fences are up . . . the store room is in better order than ever.... Attie & I go there upon your father's old horse (riding double) every morning at 9 o'clock, work until one, go back at three and work until dark, doing more than any carpenter there.... He works cheerfully & faithfully....

Mallory moved to a discussion about free blacks and hiring servants. He opined that when she got to Pensacola, "I think if you can hire a good white woman at reasonable wages for a year, you had better do so, that you may be very sure of having one good servant.... Wages are very high, & Negros [sic] will not stay with their late owners, & all are unwilling to hire themselves by the month."

Stephen shared with his wife his concerns about supporting his family. "As Yet I have concluded upon nothing as to how I am to support my family. If I remain here, I will, of course, practice law.... I can work, & work hard at anything I may undertake; & with industry & integrity, will not starve.... If I could sell my house and your lands here, the money invested in U.S. stocks would yield you & Ruby ample support with what you already have, & my mind would be at ease."[11]

Stephen and Attie continued on a regular schedule to renovate the house with help from some hired men, but they had to slow down when the carpenters were laid up by yellow fever. Stephen wrote to his wife that he had been working in her bedroom and was disturbed by finding on the wall "drawings, and pencillings, and illustrations of Yankey brutality" that he had obliterated.[12]

During the month of August, Angela apparently had written several times complaining that she was not hearing from him frequently enough. Stephen replied that he could not write as often as she might like because of his morning-to-night work schedule. However, to mollify her he wrote her a number of long letters minutely detailing his daily work schedule as proof of how hard they were working.

By mid–September he wrote that the work was nearly done. The last task was reconstructing Angela's kitchen in accordance with her requirements. Stephen counseled his wife that "We are lucky, very lucky, to get our house even in the order it was. Thousands are mourning over the loss of everything."[13] Finally, at the end of September, Stephen wrote his wife that the house was finished, adding that she and Ruby should come home right away.[14]

The family reassembled in their renovated residence and tried to return to a life with some semblance of normalcy. Their main problem was paucity of money; they were nearly destitute. In resolving the problem of lack of available cash, Stephen's first step was to sell assets consisting of books, stocks, and land. On January 6, 1867, he wrote to Lloyd Book Exchange in New York asking them to exchange his library books saying, "Please do the best you can with them in exchanging them for law books, my law library having been annihilated in our late war...." A month later in a letter dated February 13, 1867, he wrote to his stock broker, Filer & Wood of New York, requesting they sell some of his "A.C." stock. On May 8, 1867, he wrote the same firm requesting they sell $5,000 North Carolina bonds at an appropriate time. On March 12, 1867, Mallory gave Rector and Snizer, a St. Louis law firm, power of attorney to sell some of his Missouri lands at $1 an acre although "this is considerably less than the first cost of the land many years ago." Around the same time, he took measures to sell some land he owned in Polk and Dade counties in Florida to pay taxes.[15] In order to produce income, Mallory established a law partnership in Pensacola with an old political ally, August E. Maxwell.[16]

The former Confederate navy secretary was able to supplement his income through speaking engagements since he was in demand to give his views on topics of the day. On January 1, 1867, he lectured on "Self Instruction" at the Young Man's Literary Association in Pensacola. An article in the *St. Augustine Examiner* dated January 19, 1867, says Mallory's lecture was "Chaste and elegant in diction, rich in metaphor, eloquent and logical in its conclusions...." On March 12, 1869, he presented a lecture in Key West on the subject "Woman and Her Rights."[17]

Another problem which Mallory addressed related to the economic burden of caring for his former 25 slaves who chose to stay with him even though they were free to leave. While in prison, he recognized and accepted his humanitarian obligation to them when he wrote to Florida's provisional governor, William Marvin, on July 15, 1865, indicating, "I could return home and provide for my servants ... who look to me for aid and advice."[18] He was anxious that they become independent and useful, but in the meantime they needed to be fed. He placed monthly orders for food beginning early in 1867 to feed his family and his ex-slaves. One typical order that was placed on February 19, 1867, was for "½ barrel of family beef; one tub of butter; ½ barrel of grits or hominy; 2 barrels best family flour; ½ barrel of white crushed sugar."[19]

Much of his career had been devoted to politics and Stephen Mallory had no intention of deserting internal affairs at this point in his life. He began writing and speaking to fellow citizens expressing where he stood on Reconstruction and reconciliation in Florida. He had previewed his stance in a letter he had written to his old friend and mentor, Judge (now provisional governor of Florida) William Marvin on July 15, 1865. Mallory said he fully accepted that slavery was gone forever and acknowledged that war had solidified the continuity of the Union. He wrote, "I desire in good faith to do all I can to conform our state to her new status, to put down agitations, restore quiet and develop her prosperity." The Floridian suggested that as a private citizen he could provide leadership to heal wounds for "I expect to live & die at the South. My heart is with Florida; & torn & bleeding as she is, she has my warmest affections & sympathies."[20]

The process of reorganizing former Confederate state governments and reintegrating them into the Union was a trying time for our nation and Florida. Upon Lincoln's assassination, Andrew Johnson assumed the presidency and inherited the responsibility for Reconstruction. He rejected black suffrage and political equality for former slaves; President Johnson believed in limited intrusion into state affairs by the Federal government. He strongly opposed any efforts to make black suffrage a condition of a state's readmission into the Union. Johnson's racial bias was apparent in his December 1867 annual message to Congress. The president said that blacks had less "capacity for government than any other race of people.... Wherever they have been left to their own devices they have shown a constant tendency to relapse into barbarism."[21]

President Johnson launched his plan of reconstruction with the release of two proclamations on May 28, 1865. They granted amnesty and pardon to most former Confederates who pledged loyalty to the Union and agreed to abolition of slavery. They also restored all property rights to former Confederates but freed slaves were excluded from this provision. Only whites were given the vote.[22] The impact of this policy was that the established white power structure — the planter society — could shape this transition from slavery to freedom and limit the civil status of their former slaves. After state elections of congressmen in 1865, it became clear that in the former Confederate states, Reconstruction had failed "to replace the prewar slaveocracy."[23]

When Stephen Mallory returned to Florida in the summer of 1866, he found the state undergoing constant change. Throughout the South, state legislatures began controlling and stabilizing black labor forces through creation of a series of black codes that limited economic opportunity for former slaves and severely restricted their civil rights. Black codes returned ex-slaves to a subordinate position to the white man. Many people in the North objected to what appeared to be reenslavement of these people and opined that the war was not won simply to relegate the free black to his original status.[24] The

Republican-controlled Congress convened in December 1865 and was determined to counter President Johnson's Reconstruction plan that essentially offered a return to the status quo. Presidential reconstruction was doomed to failure and congressional reconstruction was to follow.

Into this confusion stepped the radical wing of the Republican Party, the "Radical Republicans," who championed not only abolition of slavery but also full civil and political rights for ex-slaves. They were strong proponents of the black man's right to vote on the same basis as whites. President Johnson was vehemently opposed to their platform. This situation established a battleground where the president and the Congress would oppose one another. Congress passed bills to extend the life of the Freedmen's Bureau, as well as a Civil Rights Act, which extended citizenship to blacks. President Johnson vetoed both bills, and Congress enacted them over his veto.

As the split deepened, the Republican Congress developed a Reconstruction plan that consisted of two parts: the 14th Amendment to the Constitution and the Reconstruction Act. The constitutional amendment made it impermissible for a state to deny any person the equal protection of the laws. Its intent was to protect the rights of southern blacks. The amendment was passed in June 1866 and ratified in 1868.

Late in 1866, Congress passed a Reconstruction Act that was promptly vetoed by President Johnson, but Congress overrode his veto. This act or "Military Bill" became law on March 2, 1867, and "reduced the ten Southern states to military appendages...." It also abolished civil government except on a provisional basis. The act established a military commander who was responsible in his district for seeing that each state under his command wrote a constitution that provided for voting for all black and white adult males. When the state had ratified the constitution and the 14th Amendment, political reorganization would be complete; it would then be free to govern itself.[25]

As a result of these laws, Florida came under military control and had imposed upon it conditions by which it would be readmitted to the Union. According to author and historian William Watson Davis, the Reconstruction Act and supplemental laws, as implemented in Florida, "laid the foundation certainly for ruthless political reconstruction. That was their object, and the object was to be attained."[26] Into this chaos came "carpetbaggers" from the North who sought political office, opportunities for quick profit, or they simply were altruistic idealists trying to help former slaves. In Florida the carpetbaggers obtained "a major share of Reconstruction offices...."[27] Also prominent were "scalawags," southern whites who either "out of principle or pragmatism, supported the Reconstruction process."[28]

On March 28, 1867, a mass meeting of blacks and whites was held in Pensacola plaza. This was in anticipation of Pensacola city elections scheduled for April 1 in which former slaves would be participating. The three principal speakers were Hayes Satterlee, an aged Negro; J.D. Wolfe, an ex-officer of the Federal army; and Stephen Mallory. Skillfully assembled with the intent of presenting a harmonious concept were a freedman, a white newcomer from the North, and a former Confederate cabinet member.[29]

Stephen R. Mallory advised those assembled "to submit to recent Congressional legislation as further resistance was useless." He counseled the crowd to accept conditions as they were and said that the vote could not be kept from the Negro. Mallory added, "It was the interest of the state that he [the Negro] should be educated and enlightened, and made to comprehend the priceless value of the ballot, and the importance to himself and the State of its judicious use." Mallory told freedmen present that their goals blended with those of the white men because the two groups had similar political and economic aspirations. He continued by warning black men against joining secret political societies whose membership was based only on race or color since scheming men, who wished to take advantage of former slaves, had organized these groups. Regarding the upcoming city election, Mallory advised blacks in the crowd to get the best advice possible about local issues, and the merit of the candidates running for offices, then vote as wisely as they could. He proclaimed that freedom belongs equally to both races. Mallory added that it was in the interest of the white man to protect the black man and that the black man should make friends with the white man.[30]

Newspapers of the day, making calming remarks about changing times, urged people to accept the inevitable. The *Tallahassee Sentinel* opined, "Take it calmly, the memories of the past and the hopes of the future counsel a self-possessed, dignified, quiet acquiescence in the measure adopted for our humiliation and punishment." The *Quincy Commonwealth* suggested there was "Plenty of time for action by the Southern people."[31]

Mallory's comments were generally in line with the mood of these newspapers and others, but there is no record of how the crowd reacted to his exhortations. Given the times, his speech was quite remarkable since it urged submission to the new order engineered by the Republicans. These words reflect how Mallory could adapt to changing circumstances. After all, this was the same man who in July 1866 had told his wife that Republicans were the most despicable white people he had ever met, that they were inferior in all respects, and that they had wronged the South.[32] These feelings might still have been there but now they were submerged.

But Mallory would soon shift his stance because Republican Reconstruction was proceeding at breakneck speed and was intolerable to the South. Former Confederate states felt they were losing their self-respect and were being held in a subservient position. In face of these events, Mallory could not continue his admonition for cooperation and restraint. By 1868, he was participating in the counterattack of the Southern Democrats against "Republican Radicalism," by writing editorials for a local newspaper.[33] Once again he was flexible and in step with the changing mood of Floridians.

In late 1867 and 1868 unsigned editorials that are attributed to Mallory began appearing in the *West Florida Commercial* of Pensacola urging opposition to Negro suffrage and railing against the excesses of Reconstruction. Readers were reminded that black suffrage originally had not been part of the Republican creed and was not encompassed in the first Reconstruction Act. These columns proclaimed that through the 1866 Reconstruction Act the Negro had been given the right to vote and the power to hold office, but radical Republicans themselves admitted he was unfit for either of these duties. The editorialist added that there were Negroes capable of properly using the ballot, but there were ignorant blacks that had been driven to the polls by radical Republicans and voted with no comprehension of what they were voting for. The author asserted that no effort had been made to distinguish between these two groups by use of property or educational qualifications. The editorialist framed the voting rights conflict by declaring, "That this is a white man's government, and that the ascendancy of the white race must and shall be maintained."[34] The author contended that radicals were subjecting the South to tyrannical rule and predicted that eventually the North would be subjected to the same kind of despotism. The editorialist feared that the democratic form of government would perish from this onslaught.

Stephen Mallory supported the Democratic ticket of Horatio Seymour and Francis P. Blair in the presidential election of 1868. In September of that year, he addressed the

Seymour and Blair club in Milton, Florida, and provided a summary of events in the nation since Lee's surrender at Appomattox Court House. He said that at the surrender it was expected that the conquerors would treat the conquered in a fair way, but the Republicans, through Reconstruction, had turned away from fairness to an imposition of abhorrent conditions including giving the former slaves civil rights and the vote. He assured the crowd that the election of Seymour and Blair would return to government under the Constitution.[35] The radical Republican Party gained control of the Florida state government in June 1868; the Republican candidate for president, U.S. Grant, was elected a few months later.

In December 1868 after the Democrats were defeated in the election, Mallory wrote editorials asserting a negative view of the state of the nation. He claimed the rights of the states had been subverted and were under the dictates of Congress. He claimed that democracy was a failure and imperial government had taken its place. His remedy was to turn the government back to the Constitution and again embrace the doctrine of states' rights, but without the reenslavement of the Negro.[36]

Stephen Russell Mallory continued his involvement in business and politics in and around Pensacola. In addition, he continued corresponding with his friends and children. One of his more significant letters to his friends was that written on May 21, 1867, to James Henry Rochelle. It provides a glimpse of what Mallory thought he had accomplished as Confederate navy secretary. He wrote, "I am satisfied that, with the means at our control, and in view of the overwhelming force of the enemy at the outset of the struggle, our little navy accomplished more than could have been looked or hoped for; and," he continued, "if I have ever felt any surprise connected with its operations, it was that we accomplished so much." The former secretary amplified by saying, "Our Navy alone kept that of the U.S. from reaching Richmond by the James River, and from reaching Savannah and Charleston...." He concluded the letter with a postscript that gave his view of his life just a few years before his death. "I am just out of a sick bed, ... [and] I am here practicing law." Mallory the lawyer commented, "It is touch and go to make a living however."[37]

Stephen Mallory's last extant letters are those he wrote from Pensacola to his son Atilla who was matriculating at Georgetown College in 1868 and 1869. On October 3, 1868, he wrote Atilla and revealed a bit of himself when he said he was in pain from his gout. Apparently Atilla had written that he was having some academic shortcomings at college. Stephen expressed his expectations of Atilla when he wrote, "You must exert every faculty, my dear boy, to profit by your college course ... your companions and people generally will expect more from you than from others, from the fact that you are the son of S.R. Mallory." Stephen continued by stressing that people take it for granted that successful men may be more clever or able than themselves, and they expect the sons to exhibit the same qualities. He added that in doing this the world makes two mistakes: they overestimate the positive qualities of the father, and undervalue the son because he may not live up to their imaginary standards.[38]

In another letter Stephen revealed his standards when reminding Atilla that the boy had the opportunity to attend college, an opportunity that had been denied the father. In this context, the elder Mallory said, "Any failure of a son of mine would mortify me to the grave.... Aim not only at success, but at triumph; at being not only ahead of all others, but so far ahead that you may stand in a class by yourself.... Remember, my dear son, that as you conduct yourself now, you will walk and live hereafter. Be honest, frank, manly, and truthful as day. Be kind and gentle with women and aged people, and polite to all, and scorn rudeness, vulgarity and bad manners as you would some foul disease."[39]

About 10 months later Mallory again wrote Atilla in celebration of his 18th birthday. Stephen wrote that he and Angela had reminisced about Atilla's life and they had both laughed and cried, but these emotions were the result of their affection for him.[40]

In 1871 Atilla had told to his father that he was not making good academic progress at Georgetown and wished to leave school. Stephen took this news amazingly well considering his earlier views. He said it seemed clear that Atilla did not have a "special affinity" for Georgetown College and that perhaps a "separation, if not a divorce," was in order. Stephen suggested that if Atilla left college he might become a merchant. The father related to his son that failure had to be ruled out and that "There must be no such word as fail!" Stephen also shared with his son the news of his sister, 16-year-old Ruby. She had left for Paris, France, where she would attend a finishing school for young ladies operated by the Sisters of the Sacred Heart. He shared that he could not bear to part from Ruby but that he wanted the best education possible for her.[41]

During the winter of 1871–1872 Stephen's gout was causing him more pain than ever before and he complained about his heart. By spring he confessed that he was quite sick and in September 1872 Ruby had returned from school in France. No more was she his "little Ruby." She had matured into a fine young lady.

On the morning of November 8, 1873, Stephen played chess alone in his room as he had done in prison to pass the time. Angela was with him for a time, and noted that he was listless. That night he began to fail and the family gathered around him. Stephen Russell Mallory died in the early morning of November 9, 1873.[42] He was buried at St. Michael Cemetery in Pensacola and rests there today.[43]

> Now that I feel the tiredness of
> the day,
> my deep longing shall
> welcome the starlit night
> as a weary child does.
>
> Hands, cease your toiling,
> head, forget about thinking,
> for all my senses now
> are longing to sink themselves in
> slumber.
>
> And the unguarded spirit
> wants to float on free wings, so that
> in the magic circle of the night
> it may live deeply and a thousandfold.[44]

In his 60 years on earth, Stephen Russell Mallory lived a fruitful life as a son, husband, father, and public figure. He was raised in an isolated village in southwest Florida that lacked a school; his mother sent him to private schools in Alabama and Pennsylvania where he received the rudiments of an education that motivated him, upon his return home to Key West, to expand his knowledge base and discipline his mind through self-study. Stephen Mallory learned law under the tutelage of a knowledgeable judge, entered

Mallory Gravesite. Stephen Mallory, his wife, and other family members are entombed in a gravesite located at St. Michael Cemetery, Pensacola, Florida. A large Confederate flag, erected and maintained by the Sons of Confederate Veterans, Stephen R. Mallory Camp 1315, flies over the graves.

Mallory Headstone. Stephen Russell Mallory, Jr., wrote this inscription for his father's headstone. Mallory's term of service as a senator is shown to have begun in 1852, but he was sworn into office on December 1, 1851. The two lines at the bottom of the headstone are from a poem, "A Thought," by Father Abram Ryan, who was a Catholic priest and Confederate Army chaplain.

into private law practice, and plunged into public sector service through his appointments as inspector and collector with the United States Customs Service. The pinnacles of his public career were his service as United States senator and his selection as secretary of the Confederate States of America navy.

As Florida's senator, Stephen R. Mallory came upon the national scene little known and relatively unprepared when compared to many of his colleagues who had held elective state positions and were college graduates. By dint of continuing self-study, perseverance, and application of his native intelligence, Mallory progressed rapidly and earned the respect of his peers. Consequently he was appointed to the Senate Naval Affairs Committee, ultimately becoming its chairman. His prime contribution was strengthening the United States Navy. He resigned his seat when Florida seceded in 1861 and was appointed secretary of the Confederate navy.

Mallory was well known for his U.S. Senate activities and, arguably, was the best man available for the difficult job of building a Confederate navy fleet. He assembled a

Confederate Monument. This Confederate memorial was dedicated on June 17, 1891, and this photograph was taken about 10 years later. Angela Mallory was president of the organization that erected this 50-foot obelisk. The south face of the structure has an inscription memorializing Confederate navy chief Stephen Mallory. The monument still stands at Palafox Street and Lee Square in Pensacola, Florida. COURTESY OF LIBRARY OF CONGRESS, PRINTS AND PHOTOGRAPHS DIVISION, LC-D4-39610.

formidable force while faced with indomitable problems, especially those associated with the South's limited industrial resources. The Confederate navy secretary exhibited resourcefulness and creative thinking coupled with the courage to take chances and experience possible failure. In the end the North's superior resources overpowered his navy, but Mallory always believed he had done his best to further the southern cause. His Confederate career caused him to be imprisoned before he was allowed to return to Florida. After his arrival home in Pensacola, Mallory worked to foster Florida's return to a meaningful and respected place in the reconstructed United States of America.

Memorializing the Confederacy, a Confederate soldier stands atop a 50-foot obelisk on Palafox Hill in Pensacola, Florida. One face of the monument commemorates Stephen

R. Mallory. On it is inscribed a quotation from the play *Cato, a Tragedy* (act ii, scene 2) by Joseph Addison. In this scene Cato's son, Portius, is speaking to a senator named Sempronius:

> Tis not in mortals to command success,
> but we'll do more, Sempronius,
> we'll deserve it.

Mrs. Mallory selected this passage because Stephen, as a young man, had used the quotation at a gathering in Key West.[45]

Chapter Notes

Abbreviations Used in Notes

Cong. Globe   *Congressional Globe. Debates and Proceedings, 1833–1873*
Diary   *Stephen R. Mallory Diary and Reminiscences* (Typescript)
FHQ   *Florida Historical Quarterly*
JC   *Journal of the Congress of the Confederate States of America, 1861–1865*
MT   *Master's Thesis, Occie Clubbs, Stephen Russell Mallory, The Elder*
ORA   *The War of the Rebellion: A Compilation of the Official Records of the Union and Confederate Armies*
ORN   *Official Records of the Union and Confederate Navies in the War of the Rebellion*
SHC/UNC-CH   *Southern Historical Collection, University of North Carolina at Chapel Hill*

Chapter 1

1. Mark Twain, *A Connecticut Yankee in King Arthur's Court*. (Project Gutenberg eBook #86. Release date, July 7, 2004, n. pag.) Online. http://www.gutenberg.org/etxt/86. Internet, 10-28-04.

2. Occie Clubbs, "Stephen Russell Mallory, The Elder," Diss. U of Florida, 1936, 1, 6; Occie Clubbs, "Stephen Russell Mallory," FHQ 25.3 (January 1947): 222. It is difficult to be more precise with dates. See Clubbs, FHQ 25.3: 222 and 222n4.

3. Joseph T. Durkin, *Confederate Navy Chief: Stephen R. Mallory*, ed. William N. Still, Jr. (Columbia: University of South Carolina Press, 1987), 11, 11n43.

4. Clubbs on page 6 of her master's thesis says, "This stone was placed and the epitaph written by Stephen R. Mallory Jr." Later she indicates that Mallory's daughter Ruby placed his birth date as 1813.

5. The *Biographical Directory of the United States Congress* in the sketch on Stephen Russell Mallory gives his years of birth and death as "ca. 1813–1873." The *Civil War Desk Reference* says he was born in 1813, as do J. Thomas Scharf in *The Confederate States Navy*, and Burton J. Hendrick in *Statesmen of the Lost Cause*. The 1860 Federal Census of Escambia County, Florida, shows Mallory's age as 47, which would be consistent with an 1813 birth year. In the *Dictionary of American Biography* his date of birth is given as "ca. 1813" but in *American National Biography* his birth is established as "c. 1811." The *Rockbridge Citizen and Daily Dispatch* of Lexington, Virginia, in its November 24, 1873, issue gives Mallory's birth year as 1814.

6. Clubbs, MT, 5; Clubbs, "Stephen Russell Mallory," FHQ 25.3: 221.

7. J. Thomas Scharf, *History of the Confederate States Navy: From Its Organization to the Surrender of Its Last Vessel.* c. 1886. (New York: Gramercy-Random House, 1996) 29n1; Kathleen Bruce, "Mallory, Stephen Russell," *Dictionary of American Biography* (New York: Charles Scribner's Sons, c. 1996) 224; Burton J. Hendrick, *Statesmen of the Lost Cause: Jefferson Davis and His Cabinet* (1939. Boston: Little, Brown, 1944) 365.

8. Appleton's Cyclopaedia of American Biography, vol. 5, 1888, s.v. "Stephen Russell Mallory," 183–184.

9. Charles Burr Todd, History of Redding, CT, Online. "History of Redding," http://www.historyofredding.com/HRFamilies.htm#Mallory, Internet, 6-14-03.

10. Found at the University of West Florida Libraries, Special Collections Department, Cora Mallory Papers, M1947-07, Box 1, Folder 3.

11. FamilyOrigins.com, s.v. "Charles Mallory," Online. http://www.familyorigins.com/users/s/a/l/Thomas-W-Saltmarsh-jr/FAMO1-0001/d25.htm, Internet, 7-26-03.

12. Genealogy.com., "Stephen R. Mallory," *Mallory Family Genealogy Forum*, Online. http://genforum.genealogy.com/cgi-bin/pageload.cgi?charles,mallory,1780::mallory::1795.html. Internet, 1-18-04.

13. *The Barbour Collection of Connecticut Town Vital Records*, Wilma J. Standifer Moore, comp., Lorraine Cook White, ed. Baltimore: Genealogical Publishing, 2000. n.pag.

14. Stephen R. Wise, "Mallory, Stephen Russell." *American National Biography*. Ed. John A. Garraty and Mark C. Carnes. vol. 14 (New York: Oxford University Press, 1999) 380; Durkin, *Confederate Navy Chief*, 11, 11n44.

15. Raimondo Luraghi, *A History of the Confederate Navy*, trans. Paolo E. Coletta. (Annapolis: Naval Institute Press, 1996), 10.

16. Southern Historical Collection, Wilson Library, University of North Carolina at Chapel Hill. "Stephen R. Mallory Diary and Reminiscences." Mallory wrote two diaries and reminiscences that have been arbitrarily numbered 1 and 2. Diary #1 covers the period from 1861 to 1862 and diary #2 covers the period from 1865 to 1867. In the second diary he records some of his life experiences mainly for the edification and guidance of his family. Many of his entries provide advice and instruction to his children, especially to his eldest son Stephen R. Mallory, Jr., whose nickname was "Buddy." Mallory copied this excerpt from his second diary from a letter he wrote to Buddy from prison (Fort Lafayette, New York Harbor) on September 27, 1865. Both diaries currently reside in the Southern Historical Collection and are accompanied with a typescript. All citations are taken from Diary #2 unless indicated otherwise. Where reference to the typescript is used, page numbers are cited. Hereafter reference to the Southern Historical Collection is abbreviated as "SHC/UNC-CH" and reference to the Stephen R. Diary and Reminiscences is abbreviated as "Diary."

17. Geocities.com, "Port of Spain History," Online. http://www.geocities.com/caribisle_trinidad/history_of_port_of_spain.htm, Internet, 7-26-03.

18. Clubbs, MT, 5. In all sources, save one, the eldest child is named "John." In the Durkin, *Confederate Navy Chief* biography, this child is named "John Jr." which fits in nicely with his assertion that the father's name is John Mallory. The only reference to "John" in the Mallory diaries is to his brother, John.

19. Occie Clubbs, "Stephen Russell Mallory, Part II," FHQ 25.4 (April 1947): 297.

20. Dana Leslie Hughes's conversations with author in last quarter of 2003, and undated correspondence from Carmel Meehan to Ms. Hughes, in author's possession.

21. Letter from Stephen Mallory to his son Buddy dated July 28, 1865. (Quoted in Durkin, *Confederate Navy Chief*, 357n43.)

22. Samuel Eliot Morison, *The Oxford History of the American People* (New York: Oxford University Press, 1965), 400.

23. "History of the Seminole Wars," (Pamphlet), Dade City, Florida, Seminole Wars Historic Foundation, Inc., n.d., 1, 2.

24. Clubbs, MT, 7; Clubbs, "Stephen Russell Mallory," FHQ 25.3: 222–223; "Mortality Patterns: Then and Now," Alabama Department of Public Health, Health Statistics and Surveillance, vol. 8, no. 2, December 1999. Online. http://ph.state.al.us/Chs/HealthStatistics/Reports/lifeexpectancy2.PDF, Internet, 7-26-03, 1.

25. *A Guide to Key West* (New York: Hastings House, 1941) 31.

26. Durkin, *Confederate Navy Chief*, 3; Jefferson B. Browne, *Key West, the Old and the New* (St. Augustine: The Record Company, 1912, electronic version, State University System of Florida, 2001), 7–9.

27. Browne, 9, 11. William P. Duval was Florida's first territorial governor. President Monroe and Congress appointed him on March 30, 1822 (3 U.S. Statute 654). (Source: Florida Department of State, Bureau of Archives & Record Management, "Territorial Governor Duval's Message to Legislative Council, 1822.") Florida became the 27th state on March 3, 1845 (28th Congress, second session).

28. Walter C. Maloney, *A Sketch of the History of Key West, Florida*. 1876. Introd. Thelma Peters. Facsimile Reproduction. (Gainesville: University of Florida Press, 1968), 69, 70.

29. Browne, 173. It is noted that a number of the earlier settlers were from Connecticut. Since Charles was from the same state, perhaps he had acquaintances in Key West that served to encourage the family's migration there.

30. Maloney, 17n1.

31. Diary, SHC/UNC-CH, 163.

32. "The Village (La Aldea)," Tour of Olde Towne Daphne. Online. http://www.tourofdaphne.gulfpath.org/Pages/new_page_1.htm, Internet, 7-26-03; Maloney, 39.

33. Clubbs, "Stephen Russell Mallory," FHQ 25.3: 223–224; Diary, SHC/UNC-CH, 163–165. When Stephen fell out of the boat off Mobile Point, it is ironic that he was near the site of Fort Morgan (it was completed in 1834). This fort and others would try to destroy the fleet of Adm. David Farragut during the Battle of Mobile Bay on August 5, 1864. This fleet of 18 U.S. ships was largely the product of Mallory's work as chairman of the Senate Committee on Naval Affairs.

34. Tuberculosis was a common ailment in those days, but yellow fever was the most deadly and most feared cause of death.

35. Clubbs, MT, 12.

36. Clubbs, MT, 13; Clubbs, "Stephen Russell Mallory," FHQ 25.3: 224; Durkin, *Confederate Navy Chief*, 14. Some biographical sketches claim that Stephen Mallory was educated at the Jesuit College at Springhill, Mobile, Alabama (See "Stephen Russell Mallory," *The Catholic Encyclopedia*, vol. IX, at http://www.newadvent.org/cathen/09572a.htm.) However, this information is incorrect. Spring Hill College exists today and is located in Mobile at 4000 Dauphin Street. Its Web site makes no mention of Mallory and the "History of the College" segment reveals that the new college had its first class on May 1, 1830, formally opened for classes in November 1831, and was chartered by the State of Alabama in 1836. The author contacted Dr. Charles J. Boyle, archivist at the college, on July 29, 2003, and he could not verify that Mallory had been a student there. He added "The college was founded in 1830, as a diocesan college. The Jesuits took over in 1847." It is well documented elsewhere that Stephen was in Key West in and after 1847.

37. Uncommonwealth of Pennsylvania, "Historic

Nazareth." Online. http://webtrail.accu-find.com/map/areas/naz_8.cfm, Internet, 7-28-03.

38. However, Ellen apparently was taking no chances. She placed a small gold cross on a chain around his neck before he left for school and this may have helped to connect him both to his church and his mother. (Reference: Clubbs, "Stephen Russell Mallory," FHQ 25.3: 228.)

39. Comenius, "John Amos Comenius." Online. http://www.comenius.com/misc/comenius.php. Internet, 7-28-03; Clubbs, "Stephen Russell Mallory," FHQ 25.3: 226.

40. Clubbs, "Stephen Russell Mallory," FHQ 25.3: 227–228.

41. Diary, SHC/UNC-CH, 165–166.

42. Clubbs, "Stephen Russell Mallory," FHQ 25.3: 228.

43. Diary, SHC/UNC-CH, 165.

44. Diary, SHC/UNC-CH, 166.

45. Browne, 186, 187. Judge Marvin boarded in Ellen Mallory's home when he first arrived in Key West. He noted that her son Stephen "was a very pleasant and agreeable young man of about twenty years of age, bright and intelligent[.]" See "Autobiography of William Marvin," Kevin E. Kearney, ed., FHQ 36.3 (January 1958): 201.

46. Maloney, 61.

47. Clubbs, "Stephen Russell Mallory," FHQ 25.3: 229, 230.

48. Clubbs, MT, 35, 36, 38.

49. Durkin, *Confederate Navy Chief*, 20.

50. Kenneth Scott, "The City of Wreckers, Key West Letters of 1838," FHQ 25.2 (October 1946): 196, 197.

51. "Key West and Salvage in 1850," FHQ 8.1 (July 1929): 58, 59. The author of this piece most likely was a staff member of *Hunt's Merchants' Magazine* and it is thought that the accounts were accurate and objective.

52. Clubbs, "Stephen Russell Mallory," FHQ 25.3: 240.

53. Diary, SHC/UNC-CH, 217 (Quoted from "The Brave Wife of Stephen Mallory," *The Daily Picayune*, New Orleans, Louisiana, 1-12-98.).

54. Clubbs, "Stephen Russell Mallory," FHQ 25.3: 241.

55. Clubbs, MT, 39.

56. Browne, 12, 13. The person named Browne in this quotation is the author of this citation. Asa Tift, along with another brother, Nelson, would become prominent in the construction of ironclad vessels for the South during the Civil War.

57. Clubbs, "Stephen Russell Mallory," FHQ 25.3: 234; Durkin, *Confederate Navy Chief*, 20.

58. Browne, 202; Clubbs, "Stephen Russell Mallory," FHQ 25.3: 237, 238.

59. Clubbs, "Stephen Russell Mallory," FHQ 25.3: 238; Grolier Electronic Publishing, 1955, s.v. "Daniel Webster." Online. http://www.marshfield.net/History/webster.htm, Internet, 7-28-03.

60. Brown, 27, 34, 202; Maloney, 31, 32; Clubbs, "Stephen Russell Mallory," FHQ 25.3: 238.

61. William Marvin, "Autobiography of William Marvin," Kevin E. Kearney, ed., FHQ 36.3: 202.

62. Browne, 151; Clubbs, "Stephen Russell Mallory," FHQ 25.3: 238, 239.

63. Browne, 11.

64. *Ibid.*, 141, 157; Clubbs, "Stephen Russell Mallory," FHQ 25.3: 239.

65. "Key West and Salvage in 1850," FHQ 8.1: 53–55; Dorothy Dodd, "The Wrecking Business on the Florida Reef, 1822–1860," FHQ 22.4 (April 1944): 172, 173; Florida Maritime Heritage Trail, Florida Division of Historical Resources, "Key West." Online. http://dhr.dos.state.fl.us/maritime/ports/port.cfm?name-Key West, Internet, 7-28-03.

66. Scott, FHQ 25.2: 195.

67. *Ibid.*, 180.

68. Dodd, "The Wrecking Business on the Florida Reef, 1822–1860," FHQ 22.4: 184, 185.

69. *Ibid.*, 175, 176, 178, 179; "Key West"; "Key West and Salvage in 1850," FHQ 8.1: 50.

70. Browne, 12.

71. Clubbs, "Stephen Russell Mallory," FHQ 25.3: 235, 236. William Marvin's book is *A Treatise on the Law of Wreck and Salvage* (Boston: Little, Brown & Company, 1858). Of special interest is the section, "Salvage Serviced by Florida Wreckers," 211–221. He served as judge of the Superior Court from 1839 to 1863. In 1865 President Andrew Johnson appointed him provisional governor of Florida.

72. Clubbs, MT, 44.

73. Browne, 223; Maloney, 77; Clubbs, "Stephen Russell Mallory," FHQ 25.3: 235.

74. George E. Buker, *Swamp Sailors: Riverine Warfare in the Everglades*, (Gainesville, University Presses of Florida, 1975), 48. This would serve as a model for blockade activity during the Civil War.

75. George E. Buker, "Lieutenant Levin M. Powell, U.S.N., Pioneer of Riverine Warfare," FHQ 47.3 (January 1969): 254–265.

76. *Ibid.*, 268–275; Buker, *Swamp Sailors*, 55.

77. Diary, SHC/UNC-CH, 192, 193.

Chapter 2

1. Diary, SHC/UNC-CH, 192.

2. *Ibid.*, 217.

3. FamilyOrigins.com, "Moreno," Online. http://www.familyorigins.com/users/s/a/l/Thomas-W-Saltmarsh-jr/FAMO1-0001/d30.htm#P1234,P15, Internet, 9-5-03.

4. Diary, SHC/UNC-CH, 216.

5. *Ibid.*, 193.

6. *Ibid.*, 194.

7. *Ibid.*, 195.

8. *Ibid.*, 216. Angela was emotionally upset when she used the phrase "always speak the truth." This expression would reappear when she was involved in a tiff with Varina Davis in 1862.

9. *Ibid.*, 196, 216; Clubbs, MT, 72, 73.

10. Diary, SHC/UNC-CH, 197, 198, 216.

11. "Moreno," Online. However, the marriage date is given as July 21, 1838, in Occie Clubbs, "Stephen Russell Mallory, Part II," FHQ 25.4: 303.

12. Clubbs, "Stephen Russell Mallory, Part II," FHQ 25.4: 305.

13. Charles H. Mohr, "St. Francis Barracks, St. Augustine: The Franciscans in Florida," FHQ 7.3 (January 1929): 221–229.

14. Durkin, *Confederate Navy Chief*, 32, 33.

15. *Ibid.*, 34.

16. John Meador, "Florida and the Compromise of 1850," FHQ 39.1 (July 1960): 16.

17. Clubbs, "Stephen Russell Mallory, Part II," FHQ 25.4: 305.

18. *Ibid.*, 318.

19. *Ibid.*, 306, 307; Meador, "Florida and the Compromise of 1850," FHQ 39.1: 16; Dorothy Dodd, "The Secession Movement in Florida, 1850–1861. Part I," FHQ 12.1 (July 1933): 3–5.

20. *Britannica Concise Encyclopedia*, 2003, s.v. "Nashville Convention," Online. Encyclopaedia Britannica Premium Service, http://www.britannica.com/ebc/article?eu=398357, Internet, 9-9-03.

21. Dodd, "The Secession Movement in Florida, 1850–1861, Part I," FHQ 12.1: 7, 8.

22. William Watson Davis, *The Civil War and Reconstruction in Florida*, 1913. Introd. Fletcher M. Green (Gainesville: University of Florida Press, 1964), 35, 36.

23. Clubbs, "Stephen Russell Mallory, Part II," FHQ 25.4: 307, 308.

24. Meador, "Florida and the Compromise of 1850," FHQ 39.1: 19; *The Handbook of Texas Online*. s.v. "Nashville Convention," Online. http:www.tsha.utexas.edu/handbook/online/articles/view/NN/vbn2.html, Internet, 9-9-03.

25. Gorrell Clinton Prim, Jr., "History and Confederate Leadership: A Study in the Intellectual History of the Civil War" (Diss., Appalachian State University, 1974), 30.

26. Article I, Section 3 of the United States Constitution provided that senators were to be selected by their state legislature. This procedure was amended by ratification of Article XVII in 1913 that provides for election of senators by direct vote of the people.

27. Arthur W. Thompson, "The Railroad Background of the Florida Senatorial Election of 1851," FHQ 31.3 (January 1953): 189.

28. Stephen R. Mallory, "Reply of Mr. Mallory of Florida...." *Contested U.S. Senate Election — 1852*, University of Florida, Special Collections Department, F324 M255r. 4,5.

29. *Ibid.*, Appendix, 66.

30. Thompson, "Railroad Background": 182–186, 189–194; Meador, "Florida and the Compromise of 1850," 22; Dodd, "The Secession Movement in Florida, 1850–1861, Part I," 14, 15, 19; Clubbs, "Stephen Russell Mallory, Part II," 309, 310; Stephen R. Mallory, Reply of Mr. Mallory....," 4, 5. In 1854 Yulee would be returned to the United States Senate when he succeeded Jackson Morton.

31. Quoted in Clubbs, "Stephen Russell Mallory, Part II," FHQ 25.4: 310, 311.

32. Dodd, "The Secession Movement in Florida, 1850–1861. Part I," 15. The April 8, 1851, edition of the *Florida Sentinel* stated, "We understand that Mr. Mallory happened to be in Havana during Mr. Clay's late visit to the island...." Apparently Mallory intimated to Clay that he supported the Union and Clay suggested he could see no reason why Mallory should not be confirmed to the Senate seat, and would stand by him.

33. Cong. Globe, 32nd Cong., 1st Sess., 2–4 (1851).

34. *Ibid.*

35. Quoted in Clubbs, "Stephen Russell Mallory, Part II," 312, 313; Edwin M. Stanton, "Argument Before the Select Committee...." *Contested U.S. Senate Election — 1852*, University of Florida, Special Collections Department, F324 M255s.

36. Statement of Mr. S.R. Mallory.... *Contested U.S. Senate Election — 1852*, 4, 16.

37. Cong. Globe, 32nd Cong., 1st Sess., 2390 (1852).

38. Quoted in "Key West and Salvage in 1850," 61.

Chapter 3

1. Wise, "Mallory, Stephen Russell," 380.
2. *The Columbia Encyclopedia, Sixth Edition, 2001*, s.v. "Kossuth, Louis," Online. http://www.bartleby.com/65/ko/Kossuth.html, Internet, 9-16-03.

3. Cong. Globe, 32nd Cong., 1st Sess., 82 (1851). This is the earliest reference found relating to Mallory's health problems that are referred to throughout this book.

4. The word "impersonation" sounds awkward and incorrect. Today's reader might think Mallory had intended to use the word "personification." However, in that era the word "impersonation" was defined "to embody or personify." (Source: *The American Heritage Dictionary of the English Language*, Fourth Edition.)

5. Cong. Globe, 32nd Cong., 1st Sess., 82, 83, 90 (1851). Interestingly, the *Budapest* (Hungary) *Sun* Online published an article titled "Hungary's Founding Fathers" on March 18, 2004, vol. XII, issue 12. At that time Kossuth was honored as one of the liberals involved in the 1848 revolution that produced an independent republic. The revolution in neighboring Germany in the same year produced a large migration of Germans to Texas. They were involved in the Union Loyal League in Texas and were the subject of my study in *Death on the Nueces* (Austin: Eakin Press, 2000).

6. Morison, *Oxford History*, 577.

7. Cong. Globe, 32nd Cong., 1st Sess., 199 (1852).

8. Cong. Globe, 35th Cong., 1st Sess., 1704, 1705, 1782, 1999, 2546, 2591 (1858); Prim, "History and Conderate Ledership," 11.

9. Cong. Globe, 32nd Cong., 1st Sess., 145 (1851).

10. *Ibid.*, 556–561, 952–960 (1852).

11. *Ibid.*, 618 (1852).

12. *Ibid.*, 1024 (1852).

13. *Ibid.*, 1152(1852).

14. *Ibid.*, 2461 (1852).

15. *Ibid.*, 2433 (1852).

16. James M. McPherson, *Battle Cry of Freedom: The Civil War Era* (New York: Oxford University Press-Ballantine Books, 1988), 118–120.

17. Cong. Globe, 33rd Cong., 1st Sess., 1550 (1854).

18. *Ibid.*, 1551 (1854).

19. *Ibid.*, 1553, 1554 (1854).

20. McPherson, *Battle Cry of Freedom*, 122.

21. Cong. Globe, 33rd Cong., 1st Sess., 775 (1854).

22. Prim, "History and Confederate Leadership," 22, 22n68.

23. McPherson, *Battle Cry of Freedom*, 121.

24. *Ibid.*, 163–167.

25. Cong. Globe, 35th Cong., 1st Sess., 919–927, 1120–1124 (1858); McPherson, *Battle Cry of Freedom*, 122, 123.

26. Cong. Globe, 35th Cong., 1st Sess., 1133–1136 (1858).

27. *American College of Rheumatology Fact Sheet*, "Gout," Online. http://www.rheumatology.org/patients/factsheet/gout.html, Internet, 10-22-23. Gout is one kind of arthritis and the favorite targets for a gout attack are the base of the big toe and the knee. The standard treatment for gout was the use of a drug named colchicines. While this was effective it could cause nausea, vomiting, and other adverse events.

28. Cong. Globe, 35th Cong., 1st Sess., 1137, 1138 (1858). Mallory himself noted the state of his health in the Senate chambers on March 1, 1859. During a long debate the question was called and Senator Mallory remarked, "I know very well that the Senate are impatient for a vote. I have myself voted three times for an adjournment. I came here ill this morning, and shall probably be so tomorrow, and be unfit for business then, if we stay here much longer to-night." (Source: Cong. Globe, 35th Cong., 2nd Sess., 1529 [1859].)

29. The remarks delivered in the Senate Chamber are found in Cong. Globe, 35th Cong., 1st Sess., 1136–1140 (1858); the revised and published speech is found in Cong. Globe, 35th Cong., 1st Sess., Appendix, 214–218 (1858).
30. Letter from Abraham Lincoln to Albert G. Hodges quoted in David Donald, *Lincoln* (New York: Simon & Schuster-Touchstone, 1995), 15.
31. McPherson, *Battle Cry of Freedom*, 168, 169.
32. Underwood, *Death on the Nueces*, 22; McPherson, *Battle Cry of Freedom*, 102–104.
33. Thomas Jefferson, "Cuba, Acquisition by United States," *The Jeffersonian Cyclopedia*. Online. Thomas Jefferson Collection, Electronic Text Center, University of Virginia Library, Charlottesville, Virginia. Internet, http://etext.lib.virginia.edu/, 4-19-04.
34. Hugh Thomas, *The Slave Trade: The Story of the Atlantic Slave Trade: 1440–1870* (New York: Simon & Schuster, 1997), 748.
35. Cong. Globe, 32nd Cong., 2nd Sess., Appendix, 130 (1853).
36. Ibid.
37. Ibid., 1199 (1854).
38. Ibid., 1259 (1854).
39. Ibid., 1259 (1854).
40. Ibid., 1260 (1854).
41. Ibid., 1298 (1854); Robert Douthat Meade, *Judah P. Benjamin: Confederate Statesman* (New York: Oxford University Press, 1943), 92.
42. Thomas, *The Slave Trade*, 758.
43. Morison, *Oxford History*, 599.
44. Cong. Globe, 35th Cong., 2nd Sess., Appendix, 295 (1859). Apparently Mallory had been "hoist with his own petard" (with apologies to Shakespeare and *Hamlet*, Act 3, Scene 4).
45. Ibid. The February 21 portion of the speech is found on pages 294–299 while the portion of the speech delivered on February 25 is found on pages 300–302. The record of the speech as delivered on the floor of the Senate is found in Cong. Globe, 35th Cong., 2nd Sess., 1188–1192 (for the February 21, 1859 session) and 1327–1332 (for the February 25 session). The published speech found in the Appendix has minor alterations but the substance is the same as the delivered speech.
46. Ibid., 296 (1859). A close reading of this segment suggests that portions of it were taken from reports by Commodore David Porter and others that were written in 1822 and 1823. For example, on November 19, 1823, Porter wrote, "I venture to predict, that the first important naval contest in which this country shall be engaged will be in the neighborhood of this very island [referring to Key West]." (Source: Maloney, *History of Key West*, 71–75.)
47. Cong. Globe, 35th Cong., 2nd Sess., Appendix, 296 (1859).
48. Ibid., 297, 299 (1859).
49. Ibid., 299 (1859).
50. Ibid., 301 (1859).
51. Ibid., 302 (1859). Frederick II, King of Prussia, invaded Silesia without warning in 1740 while offering aid to the ruler if she would cede a portion of that country to him. (Source: *The Columbia Encyclopedia*, Sixth Edition, 2001.) The tone of this quotation is reminiscent of language contained in the Ostend Manifesto.
52. Cong. Globe, 35th Cong., 2nd Sess., Appendix, 302 (1859).
53. Durkin, *Confederate Navy Chief*, 108n93.
54. W.E.F. Ward, *The Royal Navy and the Slavers: The Supression of the Atlantic Slave Trade* (New York: Random House-Pantheon Books, 1969), 77, 161.
55. Suzanne Miers, *Britain and the Ending of the Slave Trade* (New York: Africana, 1975), 20n62.
56. Ibid., 19, 20.
57. Morison, *Oxford History*, 597.
58. Thomas, *The Slave Trade*, 764; Miers, *Britain and the Ending*, 19, 20.
59. Cong. Globe, 35th Cong., 1st Sess., 2530 (1858).
60. Ibid., 2531 (1858).
61. Ibid., 3061 (1858); Thomas, *The Slave Trade*, 764; Miers, *Britain and the Ending*, 20. The United States signed the Treaty of Washington with Britain on April 7, 1862, granting her the right to search suspected slave ships flying the American flag. This, along with measures taken by Cuba, nearly ended the Atlantic slave trade (Miers, 20n67).
62. Cong. Globe, 32nd Cong., 2nd Sess., 799–803 (1853).
63. Cong. Globe, 35th Cong., 1st Sess., 2783 (1858).
64. Ibid., 2789 (1858).
65. Clubbs, "Stephen Russell Mallory, Part III," FHQ 26.1 (July 1947): 72; Durkin, *Confederate Navy Chief*, 106.
66. Cong. Globe, 33rd Cong., 1st Sess., 1094 (1854).
67. Ibid., 1095 (1854).
68. Ibid., 1096 (1854).
69. Ibid., 1097 (1854).
70. Ibid., 1194, 1195 (1854); Clubbs, "Stephen Russell Mallory, Part III," 63.
71. Cong. Globe, 33rd Cong., 1st Sess., 1911 (1854).
72. Ibid., Index, 1190, 1208 (1854); Ibid., 1160, 1197–1199 (1854).
73. Durkin, *Confederate Navy Chief*, 87; Cong. Globe, 34th Cong., 1st Sess., Index, 175 (1856).
74. Cong. Globe, 34th Cong., 1st Sess., Index, 175–177 (1856).
75. Ibid., 2227–2229 (1856).
76. Ibid., 515–518 (1856).
77. McPherson, *Battle Cry of Freedom*, 162.
78. Clubbs, "Stephen Russell Mallory, Part III," 71.
79. Cong. Globe, 36th Cong., 1st Sess., 2538, 2540 (1860).
80. Mark M. Boatner III, *The Civil War Dictionary*, rev. ed. (New York: Random House–Vintage Books, 1988), 91; McPherson, *Battle Cry of Freedom*, 206.
81. Cong. Globe, 36th Cong., 1st Sess., 27, 28 (1859).

Chapter 4

1. Charles A. Malin, "Flogging," *Ratings and Evolution of Jobs in the Navy, Navy Historical Center, Department of the Navy.* Online. http://www.history.navy.mil/faqs/faq78-1.htm #anchor95620. Internet, 7-24-04.
2. Cong. Globe, 32nd Cong., 1st Sess., Appendix, 108 (1852); Durkin, *Confederate Navy Chief*, 52.
3. Cong. Globe, 32nd Cong., 1st Sess., Appendix, 108 (1852).
4. Ibid
5. Ibid., 108–119 (1852). Captain Franklin Buchanan was a disciplinarian from the old school who favored flogging. Eleven years later he wrote, "If we could use the lash we should have no trials for desertion or thefts—I never knew solitary confinement to have any effect upon a crew." In 1863 Buchanan told Mallory that he strongly disapproved of the regulations against corporal punishment in the Confederate navy. (Source:

William N. Still, Jr., *Iron Afloat: The Story of the Confederate Armorclads* [n.p. Vanderbilt University Press, 1971], 197.)

6. Cong. Globe, 32nd Cong., 1st Sess., 1265 (1852).

7. *Ibid.*, 1576–1578 (1852); *Navy Historical Center, Department of the Navy*, "The Stevens Battery," Online. http://www.history.navy.mil/photos/sh-usn/usnsh-s/stevns-b.htm. Internet, 7-24-04.

8. Cong. Globe, 33rd Cong., 1st Sess., 1437 (1854).

9. *Ibid.*, 1456, 1457 (1854). This concept of designing one's naval power to counter the strength of the opponent would guide Mallory during the Civil War in developing the Confederate navy.

10. *Ibid.*, 1457 (1854).

11. *Ibid.*, 1437, 1438 (1854).

12. *Ibid.*, 1458, 1459 (1854).

13. *Ibid.*, 1462 (1854).

14. Cong. Globe, 33rd Cong., 2nd Sess., 990 (1855).

15. Durkin, *Confederate Navy Chief*, 70; Boatner, *The Civil War Dictionary*, 520.

16. Luraghi, *History Confederate Navy*, 238.

17. Cong. Globe, 34th Cong., 1st Sess., 1638 (1856).

18. Cong. Globe, 34th Cong., 3rd Sess., 399 (1857).

19. For further discussion of this point see Durkin, *Confederate Navy Chief*, 83 and n82–85.

20. Cong. Globe, 33rd Cong., 1st Sess., 2155 (1854).

21. *Ibid.*, 2156 (1854).

22. *Ibid.*, 2156–2158 (1854).

23. Cong. Globe, 35th Cong., 1st Sess., 2729–2731 (1858).

24. Mallory would use the same phrase ("we have a navy to build") on April 26, 1861, when he delivered his first Report of the Secretary of the Navy to Confederate President Davis.

25. These amendments covered such things as pay for pursers at navy yards, purchase of tools and fitting out the machine shop and foundry at Norfolk Navy Yard, improvements at the Brooklyn Navy Yard, appointing a judge advocate general for the navy, deferring expenses and compensation for a commissioner to Paraguay, and other similar matters.

26. Cong. Globe, 35th Cong., 1st Sess., 2731–2754, 2982 (1858).

27. Cong. Globe, 35th Cong., 2nd Sess., 1526–1531 (1859).

28. Clubbs, "Stephen Russell Mallory, Part III," *FHQ* 26.1: 71; Clubbs, MT, 176, 177; Durkin, *Confederate Navy Chief*, 108. It is ironic that in April 1861 the *Pensacola* led the attack by the U.S. Navy on the city of New Orleans, Louisiana.

29. Cong. Globe, 32nd Cong., 1st Sess., 933, 935 (1852).

30. Cong. Globe, 33rd Cong., 2nd Sess., Index, 354 (1855).

31. Cong. Globe, 33rd Cong., 2nd Sess., Appendix, 355 (1855).

32. Cong. Globe, 36th Cong., 1st Sess., 1400 (1860).

33. *Ibid.*, 2268 (1860).

34. Cong. Globe, 36th Cong., 1st Sess., 3063, 3108, 3205 (1860).

35. Scharf, *History Confederate States Navy*, 30n1.

Chapter 5

1. Dorothy Dodd, "The Secession Movement in Florida, 1850–1861. Part II," *FHQ* 12.2 (October 1933): 45.

2. *Ibid.*, 45, 46.

3. David B. Chesebrough, *God Ordained This War: Sermons on the Sectional Crisis, 1830–1865* (Columbia: University of South Carolina Press, 1991), 195; Dodd, "The Secession Movement in Florida," 45, 46.

4. William Watson Davis, *Civil War and Reconstruction*, 43.

5. *Ibid.*, 53.

6. *Ibid.*, 53, 54.

7. *Ibid.*, 55.

8. George F. Pearce, *Pensacola During the Civil War: A Thorn in the Side of the Confederacy* (Gainesville: University Press of Florida, 2000), 4, 5, 7.

9. Lewis N. Wynne and Robert A. Taylor, *Florida in the Civil War* (Charleston: Tempus-Arcadia, 2002), 9, 10.

10. Dodd, "The Secession Movement in Florida," 51–55; Wynne and Taylor, *Florida in the Civil War*, 18.

11. Charles B. Dew, *Apostles of Disunion: Southern Secession Commissioners and the Causes of the Civil War* (Charlottesville: University Press of Virginia, 2001), 38, 39.

12. *Ibid.*, 42–44.

13. *Ibid.*, 42, 43.

14. *Ibid.*, 43, 44.

15. Robert Manning Strozier Library, Florida State University, "Ordinance of Secession — State of Florida," Special Collections, MSS 0:197; *Ibid.*, "George T. Ward Secession Broadside," MSS O:256; Dodd, "The Secession Movement in Florida," 60, 61; William Watson Davis, *Civil War and Reconstruction*, 64; Florida State Archives, Tallassee, FL, Florida Memory Project, "Ordinance of Secession," Constitution of 1861 (Preamble). Online. http://www.floridamemory.com/Collections/, Internet, 3-25-04.

16. Increasingly, Stephen R. Mallory was addressed as "S. R. Mallory" and as time passed much of his official and personal correspondence was so signed.

17. Durkin, *Confederate Navy Chief*, 119.

18. ORA, ser. I, vol. 1: 348–351. "The War of the Rebellion: A Compilation of the Official Records of the Union and Confederate Armies." (128 vols.) (*The Civil War CD-ROM*) CD-ROM v.1.0. Carmel, Indiana: Guild Press of Indiana, 1996. (Yulee to Floyd, December 21, 1860; Floyd to Yulee, December 28, 1860; Yulee and Mallory to Floyd, January 2, 1861; Floyd to Yulee and Mallory, January 3, 1861; Holt to Yulee and Mallory, January 9, 1861); Boatner, *The Civil War Dictionary*, 286, 406; Bruce Catton, *The Coming Fury* (New York: Doubleday & Co, 1961), 173.

19. Winfield Scott, "Letter to President-Elect Lincoln, copy to Secretary of War Floyd, 12-28-60," *The Abraham Lincoln Papers at the Library of Congress*. Online. http://www.memory.loc.gov/cgi-bin/query/P?mal:292:./temp/~ ammem_KpDU::@@/md... Internet, 6-19-04; Boatner, *The Civil War Dictionary*, 728, 729.

20. ORA, ser. I, vol. 1: 442, 443 (Yulee to Finegan, 1-5-61).

21. *Ibid.* (1-7-61).

22. Wynne and Taylor, *Florida in the Civil War*, 13.

23. ORA, ser. I, vol. 1: 444 (Mallory to Chase, 1-10-61); Scharf, *History Confederate States Navy*, 30n1. Forts Pickens and McRee were across from one another at the entrance to Pensacola Bay.

24. Pearce, *Pensacola During the Civil War*, 2, 4; Luraghi, *History Confederate Navy*, 4. William M. Chase had retired from the U.S. Army in 1856 with the rank of major and became president of the Alabama and Florida Railroad. In January 1861 he joined the Confederate cause and was appointed to the rank of colonel. In the literature he is referred to by both ranks.

25. ORA, ser. I, vol. 52, pt. 2: 6 (Crittenden et al to Magoffin, 1-12-61).
26. ORA, ser. I, vol. 52, pt. 2: 8 (Yulee and Mallory to Perry, 1-15-61).
27. ORA, ser. I, vol. 1, 445. Mallory and eight senators to Perry, January 18, 1861. (The southern senators backing Mallory were Slidell, Benjamin, Iverson, Hemphill, Wigfall, Clay, Fitzpatrick, and Davis); Senators Fitzpatrick and Clay to Governor Moore (Alabama), January 19, 1861; Yulee and Mallory to Perry, January 20, 1861.
28. Clubbs, MT, 194, 195.
29. William C. Davis, *"A Government of Our Own:" The Making of the Confederacy* (New York: Macmillan–The Free Press, 1994), 306.
30. McPherson, *Battle Cry of Freedom*, 254–257.
31. Virginia Clay-Clopton, *A Belle of the Fifties* (Electronic Edition), ed. Ada Sterling (New York: Doubleday, Page, 1904). Online. http://docsouth.unc.edu/clay/clay.html#clay19, Internet, 2-7-04, 147, 148.
32. Clubbs, MT, 218n2.
33. Cong. Globe, 36th Cong., 2nd Sess., 485–486 (1861).
34. William Watson Davis, *Civil War and Reconstruction*, 79.
35. Boatner, *The Civil War Dictionary*, 641.
36. ORA, ser. I, vol. 1: 445, 446 (Moore to Chase, 1-18-61). Presumably the officer referred to is Samuel Barron.
37. ORA, ser. I, vol. 1: 354 (Mallory to Slidell, 1-28-61).
38. ORA, ser. I, vol. 1: 355, 356 (Holt to Slemmer, 1-29-61; Holt and Toucey to Slemmer, 1-29-61).
39. Ernest F. Dibble, "War Averters: Seward, Mallory, and Fort Pickens," FHQ 49.3 (January 1971): 233.
40. Ibid., 234, 235.
41. Ibid., 234–236; Clubbs, MT, 219; Cong. Globe, 36th Cong., 2nd Sess., 501 (1861); Pearce, 33–37.
42. Dibble, *War Averters*, 241
43. Prim, "History and Confederate Leadership," 68; Letter, Mallory to Governor Milton, 11-2-61. (John Milton Letter book and Correspondence, MSS 92-1, Florida Historical Society, Alma Clyde Field Library of Florida History, Cocoa Village, Florida.) Milton, who had taken the oath of office for governor on October 5, 1861, maintained a positive relationship with President Davis and Mallory throughout the war and he was an advocate of Confederate nationalism. On April 1, 1865, as the southern cause was collapsing, Milton took his own life. He believed that death was preferable to reunion.
44. Letter, Mallory to Milton, 10-13-61.
45. Mallory gives a full explanation of his actions in this matter in a letter he wrote that is excerpted in Clubbs, MT, 193–197.
46. Clubbs, MT, 198, 199.

Chapter 6

1. *Journal of the Congress of the Confederate States of America, 1861–1865*. S.Doc.No.234, 58th Cong., 2nd Sess. (1904–1905, seven vols.). Online. http://memory.loc.gov.ammen/amlaw/lwcc.html, Internet, 2003, 2004.
2. JC I: 851–896.
3. McPherson, *Battle Cry of Freedom*, 259; Catton, *The Coming Fury*, 214; Boatner, *The Civil War Dictionary*, 225. Jefferson Davis was inaugurated as president of the permanent government on February 22, 1862, at Richmond.
4. JC I: 901 (Section 6, Item 13).
5. Ibid., 42, 44, 48, 51.
6. William C. Davis, *"A Government of Our Own,"* 180, 181.
7. Durkin, *Confederate Navy Chief*, 134.
8. William C. Davis, *"A Government of Our Own,"* 12, 181; *Mary Chesnut's Civil War*, ed. C Vann Woodward (New York: Quality Paperback Book Club, 1981), 14.
9. ORA, ser. I, vol. 53: 200 (Joint Resolution, 12-16-61).
10. JC II: 74.
11. T.C. DeLeon, *"Four Years in Rebel Capitals: An Inside View of Life in the Southern Confederacy, from Birth to Death; From Original Notes, Collated in the Years 1861 to 1865"* (1892. Spartanburg, S.C.: The Reprint Co., 1975), 34.
12. *Mary Chesnut's Civil War*, 16.
13. Boatner, *The Civil War Dictionary*, 225, 226; *Civil War@Smithsonian*, s.v. "Jefferson Davis," Online. http://www.civilwar.si.edu/leaders_davis.html, Internet, 6-18-03; William C. Davis, *Look Away! A History of the Confederate States of America*. (New York: Simon & Schuster–The Free Press, 2002), 83; Rembert W. Patrick, *Jefferson Davis and his Cabinet* (Baton Rouge: Louisiana State University Press, 1944), 244–246; Frank E. Vandiver, *Rebel Brass: The Confederate Command System*. Introd. T. Harry Williams (Baton Rouge: Louisiana State University Press, 1956), 40–42.
14. Boatner, *The Civil War Dictionary*, 795.
15. Vandiver, *Rebel Brass*, 42, 43.
16. Boatner, *The Civil War Dictionary*, 885; Vandiver, *Rebel Brass*, 43.
17. Boatner, *The Civil War Dictionary*, 841, 842; William C. Davis, *Look Away!*, 372; Patrick, *Jefferson Davis Cabinet*, 77, 86, 87, 89.
18. Boatner, *The Civil War Dictionary*, 542; Patrick, *Jefferson Davis Cabinet*, 206, 227, 228, 231, 233.
19. Vandiver, *Rebel Brass*, 45.
20. Boatner, *The Civil War Dictionary*, 59.
21. Boatner, *The Civil War Dictionary*, 682, 683; *The Handbook of Texas Online*, s.v. "Reagan, John Henninger." Online. http://www.tsha.utexas.edu/handbook/online/articles/view/RR/fre2.html, Internet, 11-20-03; Patrick, *Jefferson Davis Cabinet*, 293, 296, 297.
22. Royce Lee Smith. "Union and Confederate Secretaries of the Navy: A Comparative Study of the Secretaries During the Civil War" (Diss. U.S. Army Command and General Staff College, 1995): 45.
23. Smith, "Comparative Study," 44, 45; Diary #1, 21, 22.
24. John H. Reagan, *Memoirs: With Special Reference to Secession and the Civil War*. Ed. Walter Flavious McCaleb. Introd. George P. Garrison (New York: Neale, 1906), 182, 183.
25. Luraghi, *History Confederate Navy*, 17–22; Durkin, *Confederate Navy Chief*, 145, 146.
26. Luraghi, *History Confederate Navy*, 18–20.
27. Smith, "Comparative Study," 41.
28. ORN, ser. II, vol. 1: 714 (Mallory to Davis, 3-8-62).
29. Durkin, *Confederate Navy Chief*, 146.
30. V.C. Jones, "How the South Created a Navy," *Civil War Times Illustrated*. (Gettysburg, PA. vol. VIII, no. 4, July 1969), 8, 9; Raphael Semmes, *Memoirs of Service Afloat During the War Between the States*, 1868 (Baton Rouge: Louisiana State University Press, 1996), 368, 369; Smith, 67.
31. Smith, "Comparative Study," 67–71.

32. *Ibid.*, 71, 72; Luraghi, *History Confederate Navy*, 104, 159, 246.
33. Smith, "Comparative Study," 68.
34. *Ibid.*, 68, 69.
35. Luraghi, *History Confederate Navy*, 30; Smith, "Comparative Study," 73.
36. *Ibid.*
37. William C. Davis, *Look Away!*, 92.
38. Luraghi, *History Confederate Navy*, 5; William C. Davis, *Look Away!*, 92; Boatner, *The Civil War Dictionary*, 54, 55.
39. JC III: 552.
40. Luraghi, *History Confederate Navy*, 12–15; Durkin, *Confederate Navy Chief*, 136–144.
41. Luraghi, *History Confederate Navy*, 15.
42. *Ibid.*, 96, 114.
43. *The Stranger's Guide and Official Directory for the City of Richmond. Showing the Location of the Public Buildings and Offices of the Confederate, State and City Governments, Residences of the Principal Officers, etc.* Electronic Edition, Online. http://docsouth.unc.edu/imls/stranger/stranger.html, Internet, 1-8-04, 14.
44. Luraghi, *History Confederate Navy*, 13; Durkin, *Confederate Navy Chief*, 137–139; *The Stranger's Guide*, 14; V.C. Jones, "South Created Navy," 7.
45. Luraghi, *History Confederate Navy*, 13; Durkin, *Confederate Navy Chief*, 140, 141. *The Stranger's* Guide, 14; V.C. Jones, "South Created Navy," 7, 8; Still, *Iron Afloat*, 7, 8.
46. ORN ser. II, vol. 2: 643 (De Bree to Mallory, 4-28-64); Luraghi, *History Confederate Navy*, 13, 14, 28, 29; Durkin, *Confederate Navy Chief*, 141, 142; V.C. Jones, "South Created Navy," 8; JCI: 124, 125.
47. Luraghi, *History Confederate Navy*, 30; Durkin, *Confederate Navy Chief*, 142–144; V.C. Jones, "South Created Navy," 8.
48. Luraghi, *History Confederate Navy*, 27; Durkin, *Confederate Navy Chief*, 145; *The Straight Dope*, "What did the U.S. Marines do during the Civil War?" Online. http://www.straightdope.com/mailbag.mmarines.html, Internet, 6-12-03; V.C. Jones, 8.
49. Still, *Iron Afloat*, 8.
50. Luraghi, *History Confederate Navy*, 13, 14; Durkin, *Confederate Navy Chief*, 145; V.C. Jones, "South Created Navy," 8.
51. Luraghi, *History Confederate Navy*, 14.
52. V.C. Jones, "South Created Navy," 6.
53. William C. Davis, "*A Government of Our Own*," 218, 219; Still, *Iron Afloat*, 7.
54. Scharf, *History Confederate States Navy*, 41.
55. Patrick, *Jefferson Davis Cabinet*, 244.
56. *Ibid.*, 246–248.
57. *Confederate States Navy Research Center, Mobile, Alabama*, "Report of the Secretary of the Navy, April 26, 1861," Online. http://www.csnavy.org/mallory,apr61.htm, Internet, 6-6-03.
58. John M. Belohlavek, "'I Have Done My Duty': Stephen Mallory and the Failure of the Confederate Navy." *Divided We Fall: Essays on Confederate Nation Building*, ed. John M. Belohlavek and Lewis N. Wynne (Saint Leo, FL: Saint Leo College Press, 1991), 12; Scharf, *History Confederate States Navy*, 32.
59. Luraghi, *History Confederate Navy*, 356n55; Semmes, *Memoirs*, 82–84, 87, 88; Scharf, *History Confederate States Navy*, 28, 28n1; Boatner, *The Civil War Dictionary*, 731.
60. Luraghi, *History Confederate Navy*, 33, 78.
61. Luraghi, *History Confederate Navy*, 78; Semmes, *Memoirs*, 92, 93.
62. Csa-dixie.com, "James Dunwoody Bulloch." Online. http://www.csa-dixie.com/Liverpool_Dixie/bulloch.htm, Internet, 6-8-03; Ted Fisher, "James Dunwoody Bulloch: Covert Confederate," *Bits of Blue and Gray*, Online. http://www.bitsofblueandgray.com/june2002.htm, Internet. 6-1-03; Csa-dixie.com, "Obituary to James Dunwoody Bulloch," Online. http://www.csa-dixie.com/Liverpool_Dixie/obit.htm, Internet, 6-1-03.
63. James D. Bulloch, *The Secret Service of the Confederate States in Europe or How the Confederate Cruisers Were Equipped.* New ed., 2 vols. (New York: Thomas Yoseloff–Sagamore, 1959), I: 38.
64. *Ibid.*, I: 36–41.
65. *Ibid.*, I: 46.
66. *Ibid.*, I: 47, 48.
67. ORN, ser. II, vol. 2: 64 (Mallory to Bulloch, 5-9-61).
68. *Ibid.*, 64, 65 (Mallory to Bulloch, 5-9-61); Luraghi, *History Confederate Navy*, 76.
69. Bulloch, *Secret Service*, I: 48–54.
70. ORN, ser. II, vol. 2: 67–69 (Mallory to Conrad, 5-10-61).
71. *Ibid.*, 70–72 (Mallory to North, 5-17-61).
72. *Ibid.*, 72 ("Estimate of the Amount Required...." Mallory, Approved by Davis, 5-20-61).
73. Luraghi, *History Confederate Navy*, 92.
74. McPherson, *Battle Cry of Freedom*, 280; Luraghi, *History Confederate Navy*, 16, 17; William C. Davis, "*A Government of Our Own*," 399.
75. *The Stranger's Guide*, 14.
76. ORA, ser. II, vol. 2: 166 (Barnum to Cameron, 11-29-61; F.W. Seward to Dix, 12-3-61). The famous small circus performer and Bridgeport native Tom Thumb was said to have met his future small wife, Lavinia Stratton, at Lindencroft. (Source: Bassick High School History, Bridgeport, Connecticut, Online. http://bridgeport.ct.schoolwebpages.com/education/school/schoolhistory.php?sectiondetailid=2752, Internet, 2-9-04.)
77. Diary, SHC/UNC-CH, 219. (Originally published as "The Brave Wife of Stephen Mallory," *The Daily Picayune–New Orleans*, Wednesday, January 12, 1898.)

Chapter 7

1. ORN, ser. II, vol. 2: 76–79 (Mallory to Davis, Report of Operations, 7-18-61).
2. Still, *Iron Afloat*, 12–15.
3. *Ibid.*, 18, 19; Kathleen Bruce, *Virginia: Iron Manufacture in the Slave Era.* 1930 (New York: Augustus M. Kelley, 1968), 350–356, passim.
4. Luraghi, *History Confederate Navy*, 93–96.
5. ORN, ser. II, vol. 2: 174, 175 (Mallory to Davis, 3-29-61).
6. *Ibid.*, 186 (Mallory to Bulloch, 4-30-62); Luraghi, *History Confederate Navy*, 98, 99, 386n72.
7. Luraghi, *History Confederate Navy*, 182, 183.
8. Jay W. Simson, *Naval Strategies of the Civil War: Confederate Innovations and Federal Opportunism* (Nashville: Cumberland House Publishing, 2001), 65, 66; Bruce, *Virginia: Iron Manufacture in the Slave Era*, 351, 352.
9. Luraghi, *History Confederate Navy*, 183, 184; Simson, *Naval Strategies*, 66–69.
10. Luraghi, *History Confederate Navy*, 184– 185; ORN, ser. I, vol. 6: 112–146, 612ff, 664.
11. ORA, ser. I, vol. 6: 309 (Withers, Assistant Adju-

tant General for Secretary of War, Special Orders No. 206); Luraghi, *History Confederate Navy*, 186, 187.

12. Simson, *Naval Strategies*, 77, 78, 150; McPherson, *Battle Cry of Freedom*, 245.

13. Luraghi, *History Confederate Navy*, 95–99; Still, *Iron Afloat*, 20.

14. Luraghi, *History Confederate Navy*, 117; Scharf, *History Confederate States Navy*, 152, 153.

15. ORN, ser. I, vol. 6: 776, 777 (Mallory to Buchanan, 2-24-62).

16. Simson, *Naval Strategies*, 60.

17. ORN, ser. I, vol. 6: 780, 781 (Mallory to Buchanan, 3-7-62).

18. Luraghi, *History Confederate Navy*, 146, 401n88, 89.

19. ORN, ser. I, vol. 3: 356. (Mallory to Hogg, 5-7-64).

20. *Ibid.*, 352–367. However, Durkin in *Confederate Navy Chief*, on pages 167 and 168, states that the project "was a complete success" without documenting his sources.

21. Luraghi, *History Confederate Navy*, 115.

22. ORN, ser. I, vol. 6: 659 (Welles to Worden, 2-20-62).

23. Luraghi, *History Confederate Navy*, 137.

24. Luraghi, *History Confederate Navy*, 139, 140–143; John R. Eggleston, "Captain Eggleston's Narrative of the Battle of the *Merrimac*," *Blue & Gray At Sea: Naval Memoirs of the Civil War*, ed. Brian M. Thomsen (New York: Doherty, 2003), 395–401.

25. Luraghi, *History Confederate Navy*, 143.

26. "Captain Eggleston's Narrative," 402– 404; Dinwiddie B. Phillips, "Notes on the Monitor-Merrimac Fight," *Blue & Gray At Sea: Naval Memoirs of the Civil War*, ed. Brian M. Thomsen (New York: Doherty, 2003), 405–407.

27. The *Patrick Henry* was stationed in the upper James River throughout the war and became the training ship for the Confederate States Naval Academy. Mallory's son, Stephen, Jr., had originally enlisted in the Confederate army but was transferred to the school ship as a midshipman in March 1863. (Sources: Clubbs, MT, 331–347; Belohlavek, "I Have Done My Duty," 27.)

28. Luraghi, *History Confederate Navy*, 145, Still *Iron Afloat*, 34, Simson, *Naval Strategies*, 87, 150.

29. ORN, ser. II, vol. 2: 122 (Mallory, Undated Memorandum); ORN, ser. II, vol. 1: 148, 149.

30. ORN, ser. II, vol. 1: 546, 547 (Testimony of Nelson Tift, 9–62); 571ff (Letters from Nelson and Asa Tift to Mallory).

31. *Ibid.*, 601, 602 (Two letters from Mallory to Tift Brothers, 8-28-61 and 9-5-61).

32. *Ibid.*, 575, 576 (Two letters from Tift Brothers to Mallory, 10-9-61 and 10-13-61); Luraghi, *History Confederate Navy*, 108, 109; Bruce, *Virginia: Iron Manufacture in the Slave Era*, 366–368.

33. *Ibid.*, 757 (Testimony of Murray, 2-20-63); Luraghi, *History Confederate Navy*, 109.

34. Luraghi, *History Confederate Navy*, 107.

35. ORN, ser. II, vol. 1: 780 (Testimony of Shirley, 2-26-63).

36. *Ibid.*

37. ORN, ser. I, vol. 22: 811 (Mallory to Polk, 12-24-61).

38. ORN, ser. II, vol. 1: 782 (Testimony of Shirley, 2-26-63).

39. Still, *Iron Afloat*, 45, 54, 54n29.

40. ORN, ser. II, vol. 1: 754, 760 (Testimony of Murray, 2-20-63); Luraghi, *History Confederate Navy*, 120, 121, 394n65.

41. ORN, ser. II, vol. 1: 466 (Mallory to Mitchell, 2-24-62).

42. *Ibid.*, 466, 467 (Mallory to Mitchell, 3-15-62).

43. Luraghi, *History Confederate Navy*, 120–123; ORN, ser. II, vol. 1: 534–537 (Testimony of Nelson Tift, 9-22-62).

44. Luraghi, *History Confederate Navy*, 122.

45. *Ibid.*; ORN, ser. II, vol. 1: 577 (Tift Brothers to Mallory, 10-20-61, 10-22-61).

46. ORN, ser. II, vol. 1: 589–590 (Tift Brothers to Mallory, various dates).

47. Luraghi, *History Confederate Navy*, 125; Durkin, *Confederate Navy Chief*, 203.

48. Durkin, *Confederate Navy Chief*, 203, 204.

49. ORN, ser. II, vol. 1: 606 (Mallory to Tift Brothers, 3-11-62).

50. ORN, ser. I, vol. 7: 773, 774 (Mallory to S.S. Lee, 4-24-62).

51. Luraghi, *History Confederate Navy*, 128, 129.

52. ORN, ser. II, vol. 1: 605 (Telegram, Mallory to Tift Brothers, 3-15-62).

53. *Ibid.*, 606 (Telegram, Mallory to Tift Brothers, 3-22-62).

54. *Ibid.*, 512 (Mallory to Sinclair, 3-21-62); Luraghi, *History Confederate Navy*, 130.

55. Luraghi, *History Confederate Navy*, 131.

56. *Confederate Navy Research Center, Mobile, Alabama*, s.v. "C.S.S. Manassas." Online. http://www.csnavy.org/ships,area.htm. Internet, 5-25-04; Hern, 270. A carronade is a short cannon designed to throw a large projectile with low velocity. It was fixed on the bow and could be aimed only by maneuvering the ship into firing position; Spencer Tucker, *A Short History of the Civil War at Sea* (Wilmington, DE: SR Books–Scholarly Resources, 2002), 22.

57. Chester G. Hearn, *The Capture of New Orleans, 1862* (Baton Rouge: Louisiana State University Press, 1955), 234–236; George Hamilton Perkins, "Commodore Farragut Captures New Orleans," *The Blue and the Gray: The Story of the Civil War as Told by Participants*. 2 vols. Ed. Henry Steele Commager (New York: Bobbs-Merrill, 1950), II: 807–810.

58. Luraghi, *History Confederate Navy*, 156–163.

59. Luraghi, *History Confederate Navy*, 126–128; Simson, *Naval Strategies*, 99, 100, 107; Hearn, *Capture of New Orleans*, 2–4.

60. Simson, *Naval Strategies*, 54, 55; Luraghi, *History Confederate Navy*, 124, 125.

61. Luraghi, *History Confederate Navy*, 125, 126.

62. Still, *Iron Afloat*, 61.

63. *Ibid.*, 41, 43, 43n3, 60n45.

64. Luraghi, *History Confederate Navy*, 129, 130, 170.

65. *Ibid.*, 170, 171.

66. *Ibid.*; 169; McPherson, *Battle Cry of Freedom*, 418.

67. Luraghi, *History Confederate Navy*, *History Confederate Navy*, 171–177.

68. *Ibid.*, 175.

69. ORN, ser. I, vol. 18: 650 (Van Dogs to Ruggles, 6-24-62).

70. Luraghi, *History Confederate Navy*, 176–180; Still, *Iron Afloat*, 62–78; ORN, ser. I, vol. 19: 64–75 (Various reports on action involving the *Arkansas*).

71. Simson, *Naval Strategies*, 121.

72. ORN, ser. I, vol. 7: 787, 788 (Mallory, Finding of the Court of Inquiry, 6-11-62); Durkin, *Confederate Navy Chief*, 212, 213.

73. Durkin, *Confederate Navy Chief*, 187, 188.

74. ORN, ser II, vol. 2: 187 (Mallory to Bulloch, 4-30-62).
75. Still, *Iron Afloat*, 78.
76. Diary #1, SHC/UNC-CH, 19.
77. Quoted in Durkin, *Confederate Navy Chief*, 208. The reference to the medicine he had taken is probably related to his gout that had been bothering him as early as his U.S. Senate years.
78. Quoted in Belohlavek, "I Have Done My Duty," 23.
79. Diary #1, SHC/UNC-CH, 21.
80. JC, 5: 303; Luraghi, *History Confederate Navy*, 181.
81. Quoted in Durkin, *Confederate Navy Chief*, 225 (Mallory to his wife, 8-31-62).
82. ORN, ser. II, vol. 1: 430, 431 (Joint Select Committee, 8-27-62); Luraghi, *History Confederate Navy*, 182; Durkin, *Confederate Navy Chief*, 230, 231.
83. ORN, ser. II, vol. 1: 431–434.
84. *Ibid.*, 435–500.
85. *Ibid.*, 723–753.
86. *Ibid.*, 809 (Committee Adjournment, 3-24-63).
87. Quoted in Smith, "Comparative Study," 51.
88. Luraghi, *History Confederate Navy*, 182.
89. Hearn, *Capture of New Orleans*, 260, 261.

Chapter 8

1. ORN, ser. I, vol. 1: 612 (Mallory to Semmes, 4-18-61).
2. *Ibid.*, 613, 614 (Semmes to Mallory, 4-22-61).
3. Luraghi, *History Confederate Navy*, 80–83.
4. ORN, ser. I, vol. 1: 615 (Semmes to Mallory, 6-14-61); Luraghi, *History Confederate Navy*, 83.
5. *Ibid.*, 616 (Semmes to Chief Pilot, 6-22-61).
6. Luraghi, *History Confederate Navy*, 83–84; Boatner, *The Civil War Dictionary*, 731.
7. Luraghi, *History Confederate Navy*, 85.
8. *Ibid.*, 380n84.
9. *Rare Book Collection*, William Stanley Hoole Special Collections Library, Tuscaloosa, Alabama, The University of Alabama, "Letter from Captain Semmes, C.S. Navy, commanding C.S.S. Alabama, to Lieutenant Low, C. S. Navy, commanding C. S. bark Tuscaloosa, giving instructions regarding the cruise of that vessel, dated June 21, 1863." Online. http://www.lib.ua.edu/libraries/hoole/digital/cssala/main.shtml, Internet, 12-13-03.
10. Luraghi, *History Confederate Navy*, 86, 87, 380n85; ORN, ser. I, vol. 1, 653, 659. The ransom bond was valid only if the CSA won the war but it was questionable legally since it was a device that emanated from the era of privateering; CSA cruisers or raiders were not considered to be privateers.
11. ORN, ser. I, vol. 1: 659–686 (Various letters and reports from Semmes); Lurgahi, 85–88.
12. *Confederate State Navy Research Center, Mobile, Alabama*, s.v. "List of Ships." Online. http://www.csnavy.org/ships,area.htm, Internet, 6-6-03.
13. Luraghi, *History Confederate Navy*, 161, 406n29.
14. Not to be confused with the identically named armor-clad that gained fame at Mobile Bay in 1864. In Jay W. Simson's *Naval Strategies of the Civil War*, the armor-clad is referred to as *Nashville II*.
15. Simson, *Naval Strategies*, 40, 41; Confederate Navy Research Center, Mobile, Alabama, s.v. "C.S.S. Nashville." Online. http://www.csnavy.org/Ships,area.htm, Internet, 6-8-03, n. pag.; Luraghi, *History Confederate Navy*, 87, 88; Philip Van Doren Stern, *When the Guns Roared: World Aspects of the American Civil War* (Garden City, NY: Doubleday, 1965), 87–91.

16. Luraghi, *History Confederate Navy*, 76.
17. Bulloch, *Secret Service*, I: 3, 21, 67; Smith, "Comparative Study," 408; Jim Dan Hill, *Sea Dogs of the Sixties: Farragut and Seven Contemporaries* (New York: Barnes, 1935 [Perpetua Edition, 1961]), 67. French Emperor Napoleon III issued a similar Proclamation of Neutrality on June 1, 1861.
18. Bulloch, *Secret Service*, I: 62; Luraghi, *History Confederate Navy*, 76, 77.
19. Luraghi, *History Confederate Navy*, 200, 415n8; Bulloch, *Secret Service*, I: 112.
20. Luraghi, *History Confederate Navy*, 200, 201, 415n15; Dean B. Mahin, *One War at a Time: The International Dimensions of the American Civil War* (Washington, D.C.: Brassey's, 1999), 60, 68; ORN, ser. II, vol. 2: 113, 114 (Mallory to Bulloch, 11-30-61).
21. ORN, ser. II, vol. 2: 129 (Mallory to Bulloch, 1-11-62).
22. Luraghi, *History Confederate Navy*, 201.
23. Mahin, *One War at a Time*, 145. In correspondence dated August 8, 1862, from Mallory to Bulloch, the secretary suggests that earlier letters from Bulloch to Mallory had been intercepted and intelligence from these documents probably was being used in the admiralty court in Nassau. Mallory urged Bulloch to use a previously agreed-upon cipher code to transmit information about sensitive matters. (Source: ORN, ser. II, vol. 2: 234.)
24. Luraghi, *History Confederate Navy*, 217–223.
25. ORN, ser. I, vol. 1: 762, 763 (Mallory to Maffitt, 10-25-62). There is no indication that this rather simple encoding was ever broken by the Union.
26. ORN, ser. 1, vol. 2: 644, 645 (Two letters to and from Maffitt and Read, both dated 5-6-63); Luraghi, *History Confederate Navy*, 222. The Union vessel *Sumpter* is not to be confused with the rebel commerce raider *Sumter*.
27. Hill, *Sea Dogs*, 182; Underwood, *Death on the Nueces*, vii, 18; Underwood, *Waters of Discord: The Union Blockade of Texas During the Civil War* (Jefferson, NC: McFarland, 2003), 130–132.
28. ORN, ser. 1, vol. 2: 654 (Read to Mallory, 7-30-63).
29. *Ibid*.
30. *Ibid*.; Robert H. Woods, "Cruise of the (CSS) Clarence, Tacony-Archer" (Taken from the Southern Historical Society Papers, Vol. XXIII, January–December 1895) *Confederate Navy Research Center, Mobile, Alabama*, Online. http://www.csnavy.org/shsp/shsp,clar-tac-arch,v23,p274.htm. Internet, 6-8-03.
31. Hill, *Sea Dogs*, 185.
32. ORN, ser. I, vol. 2: 274 (Welles to Lee, 6-13-63).
33. *Ibid.*, 274–278.
34. Luraghi, *History Confederate Navy*, 329, 330.
35. ORN, ser. II, vol. 2: 183, 184 (Bulloch to Mallory, 4-11-62).
36. Warren F. Spencer, "Ships for the South: James D. Bulloch, Confederate Agent in Europe." *Divided We Fall: Essays on Confederate Nation Building*, ed. John M. Belohlavek and Lewis N. Wynne (Saint Leo, FL: Saint Leo College Press, 1991), 49.
37. C.S.S. Alabama Digital Collection, *Rare Book Collection*, William Stanley Hoole Special Collections Library, Tuscaloosa, Alabama, The University of Alabama, "Documents." Online. http://www.lib.ua.edu/libraries/hoole/digital/cssala/main.shtml, Internet, 12-13-03.
38. Luraghi, *History Confederate Navy*, 224–226.
39. John McIntosh Kell, *Recollections of a Naval Life Including the Cruises of the Confederate State Steamers "Sumter" and "Alabama"* (Electronic Edition). Online.

http://docsouth.unc.edu/kell/kell.html. Internet, 1-4-04. The *Alabama* was active for nearly two years during which time she sank, burned, or captured 69 ships (Boatner, *The Civil War Dictionary*, 4).

40. Luraghi, *History Confederate Navy*, 242.

41. Peter Cliffe, "Vigilant Envoy Finally Stops Ship After Attacks End," *The Washington Times*. Online. http://dynamic.washtimes.com/print_story.cfm?StoryID=20031024-075917-1020r. Internet, 10-28-03; Luraghi, *History Confederate Navy*, 231, 232; "List of Ships," C.S. Cruiser *Georgia*; James Morris Morgan, *Recollections of a Rebel Reefer* (Electronic Edition). Online. http://docsouth.unc.edu/morganjames/morgan.html#morgan89. Internet, 2-04-04.

42. Frank Lawrence Owsley, Jr., *The C.S.S. Florida: Her Building and Operations* (New Edition), 1965 (Tuscaloosa: University of Alabama Press, 1987), 161; V.C. Jones, 42.

43. ORN, ser. II, vol. 2: 708 (Mallory to Bulloch, 8-19-64).

44. *Ibid.*, 687 (Mallory to Bulloch, 7-18-64).

45. Luraghi, *History Confederate Navy*, 341.

46. ORN, ser. I, vol. 3: 759–755 (Bulloch to Waddell, 10-5-64).

47. James Waddell, "Documents of CSS *Shenandoah*." *Blue & Gray At Sea: Naval Memoirs of the Civil War*, ed. Brian M. Thomsen (New York: Doherty, 2003), 339–344; Robert F. Jones, "Rebel Without A War: The *Shenandoah*," *With My Face To The Enemy: Perspectives on the Civil War*, ed. Robert Cowley (New York: Putnam, 2001), 507, 508; ORN, ser. I, vol. 3: 783–784 (Waddell to Lord Russell, 11-6-85); Luraghi, *History Confederate Navy*, 344; University of Hawaii, "CSS *Shenandoah*." Online. http://www.skaggs.org/html/u_of_hawaii.html. Internet, 3-9-04. Mallory had memorized the sailing directions of *Shenandoah* and provided this information to his captors at Fort Lafayette prison in 1865 to facilitate his release from prison.

Chapter 9

1. Luraghi, *History Confederate Navy*, 148.
2. ORN, ser. I, vol. 7: 772 (Mallory to S.S. Lee, 4-22-62). Mallory sent several other communications to Captain Lee around this time to the same effect.
3. Luraghi, *History Confederate Navy*, 208.
4. ORA, ser. I, vol. 28, pt. 2: 503 (Beauregard to Wm. Porcher Miles, 11-14-63).
5. ORN, ser. I, vol. 15: 700 (Mallory to Congressman Wm. Porcher Miles, 12-19-63).
6. Luraghi, *History Confederate Navy*, 208–210; Still, *Iron Afloat*, 112–115, 117–125; Simson, *Naval Strategies*, 206.
7. Hill, *Sea Dogs*, 178ff; Luraghi, *History Confederate Navy*, 210.
8. Luraghi, *History Confederate Navy*, 211.
9. *Ibid.*, 212.
10. ORN, ser. I, vol. 14: 710, 711 (Webb to Mallory, 6-10-63).
11. Simson, *Naval Strategies*, 149.
12. ORN, ser. I, vol. 14: 263–270 (Capture of CSS *Atlanta* 6-17-63); Luraghi, *History Confederate Navy*, 213–215; Still, *Iron Afloat*, 128–138.
13. ORN, ser. I, vol. 14: 270 (Telegram Lee to Welles, 6-22-63).
14. "List of Ships," CSS Floating Battery *Georgia*; Luraghi, *History Confederate Navy*, 215, 216. (Luraghi reports that *Georgia* is still at Savannah, at the bottom of the Savannah River, where she was scuttled.)
15. Luraghi, *History Confederate Navy*, 280; Still, *Iron Afloat*, 80.
16. ORN, ser. I, vol. 21: 886 (Simms to Jones, 3-20-64).
17. Simson, *Naval Strategies*, 208.
18. Still, *Iron Afloat*, 204, 212.
19. ORN, ser. I, vol. 19: 788, 789 (Mallory to Randolph 9-24-62).
20. Luraghi, *History Confederate Navy*, 272, 273.
21. *Ibid.*, 273.
22. *Ibid.*, 274; Still, *Iron Afloat*, 140–148.
23. Still, *Iron Afloat*, 148, 149, 226.
24. Underwood, *Waters of Discord*, 29, 42, 43; ORN, ser. I, vol. 16: 759–761 (Hunter to Hebert, 11-8-61 and 11-11-61); *Ibid.*, 761, 762 (Hunter to Mallory, 11-13-61 and 1-4-62).
25. ORN, ser. I, vol. 19: 789, 790 (Hunter to Mallory, 9-28-62); 811 (Magruder, by E.P. Turner, to Hunter, 12-8-62); 813–817 (Journal of Commander Hunter, 12-18-62 to 4-24-63).
26. ORN, ser. II, vol. 2: 72, 73 (Mallory to Ingraham, 5-20-61).
27. *Ibid.*, 73 (Ingraham to Mallory, 5-23-61).
28. Luraghi, *History Confederate Navy*, 41.
29. ORN, ser. II, vol. 2: 73, 74 ("Statement of contracts made by the Navy Department").
30. George H. Daniels, "The Confederate Government and Industrialization: Joseph R. Anderson and the Tredegar Iron Works," *Divided We Fall: Essays on Confederate Nation Building*, ed. John M. Belohlavek and Lewis N. Wynne (Saint Leo, FL: Saint Leo College Press, 1991), 139; Tucker, *Civil War at Sea*, 34; Leslie S. Bright, William H. Rowland, and James C. Bardon, *C.S.S. Neuse: A Question of Iron and Time* (Raleigh, NC: Division of Archives and History, North Carolina Department of Cultural Resources, 1981), 5, 6; Bruce, *Virginia: Iron Manufacture in the Slave Era*, map between 452, 453, 325–380 passim.
31. ORA, ser. I, vol. 51, pt. 2: 638 (Mallory to Randolph, 10-28-62).
32. ORA, ser. I, vol. 18: 766 (Mallory to Vance, 11-4-62). Captain Lynch appears to have had difficulties in his relationships with more than one important Confederate figure. His troubles with North Carolina Governor Vance have been chronicled. Lynch also had ongoing conflict with Commander James W. Cooke who supervised the construction of the ironclad Albemarle and later led her into battle. For a detailed discussion of this contentiousness, see *Ironclad of the Roanoke* by Robert G. Elliott.
33. NOR, ser. I, vol. 8: 849 (Vance to Mallory, 11-21-62).
34. ORA, ser. I, vol. 18: 875 (Mallory to Vance, 2-13-63).
35. *Ibid.*, 912 (Vance to Mallory, 3-7-63).
36. *Ibid.*, 919 (Mallory to Hill, 3-13-63).
37. Luraghi, *History Confederate Navy*, 174, 274; Durkin, *Confederate Navy Chief*, 171n55. Mallory would again get into a squabble with Vance over the matter of coal in February 1865 (reference: Durkin, *Confederate Navy Chief*, 315n79, 316n80).
38. Luraghi, *History Confederate Navy*, 38–42; Durkin, *Confederate Navy Chief*, 150.
39. Luraghi, *History Confederate Navy*, 42, 43; Bruce, *Virginia: Iron Manufacture in the Slave Era*, 325–380 passim.
40. Luraghi, *History Confederate Navy*, 47, 49. However, another historian, William N. Still, Jr., contends

that "The marine engines and boilers used on the ironclads built within the Confederacy were notoriously inadequate and constantly in need of repair. The absence of qualified machinists and insufficient tools and materials were the principal reasons." (Source: Still, *Iron Afloat*, 101.)

41. Luraghi, *History Confederate Navy*, 49, 50.
42. ORA, ser. I, vol. 52, pt. 2: 286, 287 (Mallory to Benjamin, 7-1-64).
43. ORA, ser. 4, vol. 3: 520–523 (Mallory to Davis, 7-1-64).
44. Luraghi, *History Confederate Navy*, 50–52.
45. Gen. William S. Walker was a Confederate division commander who had lost his leg at Petersburg. Years after the war a fellow Southron commented to him, "General, the blockade whipped us." Walker shifted the stump of his leg across his crutch, blew rings of cigar smoke through the air, and answered slowly: "Well, that ... and the fact that the mothers of the South did not bear all male children!" (Source: T.C. De Leon, *Belles Beaux and Brains of the 60's* [New York: Billingham, 1907], 395, 396.)
46. Letters, Mallory to Milton, 10-20-61, 11-2-61, 11-19-61.
47. Confederate States Navy Research Center, Mobile, Alabama, s.v. "Confederate Navy Shipyards." Online. http://www.csnavy.org/index-assorted.htm, Internet, 1-12-04. (Much of the discussion about these shipyards is attributed to this site.)
48. Still, *Iron Afloat*, 91, 92.
49. Dan L. Morrill, *The Civil War In Charlotte-Mecklenburg, Chapter Five.* (University of North Carolina at Charlotte) Online. http://www.danandmary.com/historyofcharch5.htm, Internet, 1-12-04. (Most of the discussion concerning Charlotte, North Carolina, is attributed to this site.)
50. Luraghi, *History Confederate Navy*, 36, 37, 53.
51. Luraghi, *History Confederate Navy*, 33–35; Underwood, *Waters of Discord*, 28, 29.
52. Stephen R. Mallory, "Letter, 10 January 1862," *Department of the Navy, Naval Historical Center, Washington, DC*, Online. http://www.history.navy.mil/biblio/biblio3/mallory.htm, Internet, 11-5-03.
53. ORA, ser. IV, vol. 2: 90 (Mallory to Randolph, 9-20-62).
54. *Ibid.*, 705 (Mallory to Seddon, 8-11-63).
55. Luraghi, *History Confederate Navy*, 274, 275. For a classification of all Confederate ironclads into major classes and types, refer to: "DANFS," *The Dictionary of American Naval Fighting Ships* (Confederate States Navy, List of Major Classes and Types). Online. http://www.hazegray.org/danfs/csn/classes.
56. ORA, ser. I, vol. 18: 69 (Garrard to Mix, 12-17-62); Bright, 8, 9.
57. ORA, ser. I, vol. 33: 1101, 1102 (Lee to Davis, 1-20-64); Luraghi, *History Confederate Navy*, 277.
58. Luraghi, *History Confederate Navy*, 277, 278.
59. ORN, ser. I, vol. 15: 709 (Tattnall to Conrad, 2-3-64); Luraghi, *History Confederate Navy*, 279, 280.
60. Luraghi, *History Confederate Navy*, 278, 279, 438n96.
61. *Ibid.*, 280.
62. *Ibid.*, 281–283, 439n122. *Tennessee* is the name commonly used to designate the vessel built at Selma because the ship of the same name that was built at Memphis in 1861 was never commissioned.
63. "Report of the Secretary of the Navy, April 26, 1861."
64. Luraghi, *History Confederate Navy*, 40, 44.
65. *Ibid.*, 44, 45.
66. ORA, ser. IV, vol. 3: 523 (Jones to Brooke, May 14, 1864).
67. *Ibid.*, 521 (Mallory to Davis, July 1, 1864).

Chapter 10

1. Tucker, *Civil War at Sea*, 1, 2.
2. ORN, ser. II, vol. 2: 131 (Mallory to Bulloch, 5-10-61).
3. Frank Merli, "The South on the Seas," *Civil War Times Illustrated*, vol. XI, no. 7 (Gettysburg, PA: November 1972), 7; Mahin, *One War at a Time*, 177.
4. ORN, ser. II, vol. 2: 270 (Mallory to Bulloch, 9-20-62).
5. *Ibid.*, 212 (Bulloch to Mallory, 7-4-62).
6. Spencer, "Ships for the South," 60, 61; Mahin, *One War at a Time*, 176, 177; Rick Gage, "The Laird Rams for the Confederacy," *ACWS Archives*. Online. http://www.acws.co.uk/archives/history/laird.htm. Internet, 6-1-04; Hendrick, 380–386.
7. Luraghi, *History Confederate Navy*, 205.
8. ORN, ser. II, vol. 2: 235 (Mallory to Bulloch, 8-8-62).
9. *Ibid.*, 270 (Mallory to Bulloch, 9-20-62).
10. *Ibid.*, 264 (Bulloch to Mallory, 9-10-62).
11. *Ibid.*, 292, 293 (Bulloch to Mallory, 11-7-62).
12. ORN, ser. II, vol. 3: 529–533 (Mason to Benjamin, 9-18-62, Mason to Mallory, 9-18-62).
13. Luraghi, *History Confederate Navy*, 206.
14. ORN, ser. II, vol. 2: 345, 346 (Bulloch to Mallory, 1-23-63).
15. Stern, *When the Guns Roared*, 193–195.
16. Luraghi, *History Confederate Navy*, 268.
17. ORN, ser. II, vol. 2: 455, 456 (Bulloch to Mallory, 7-9-63).
18. *Ibid.*, 485; Luraghi, *History Confederate Navy*, 268.
19. Quoted in Luraghi, *History Confederate Navy*, 271. See also Mahin, *One War at a Time*, 178–184.
20. Luraghi, *History Confederate Navy*, 271; Stern, *When the Guns Roared*, 265, 266.
21. Luraghi, *History Confederate Navy*, 266, 267, 287, 288, 343; ORN, ser. II, vol. 2: 588 (Bulloch to Mallory, 2-18-64). *Cheops* ultimately was commissioned in the Prussian navy. (Source: Luraghi, *History Confederate Navy*, 457n47.)
22. ORN, ser. II, vol. 2: 795 (Barron to Mallory, 2-1-65, quoting Captain Page's letter to him).
23. David G. Surdam, "The Confederate Naval Buildup: Could More Have Been Accomplished?" (*Naval War College Review* [Newport, RI], vol. LIV, no. 1, Winter 2001, n. pag.) Online. http://www.nwc.navy.mil/press/Review/2001/Winter/art7-w01.htm. Internet, 5-20-03; Luraghi, *History Confederate Navy*, 344.
24. Quoted in Durkin, *Confederate Navy Chief*, 294. According to *Webster's Revised Unabridged Dictionary* (1998) "Jeremy Diddler" is a character in a play called "Raising the Wind." This colloquial expression is applied to a confidence man. See also Reagan, *Memoirs: With Special Reference to Secession and the Civil War*, 154, 155.
25. Semmes, *Memoirs*, 413.
26. Stern, *When the Guns Roared*, 250.
27. ORN, ser. II, vol. 2: 368.
28. Luraghi, *History Confederate Navy*, 285; Simson, *Naval Strategies*, 161; Stern, *When the Guns Roared*, 251; *Dictionary of American Fighting Ships*, Vol. II, Appen-

dix II, Confederate Forces Afloat, s.v. "Coquette." DANFS Online. http://www.hazegray.org/danfs/csn/c.txt. Internet, 6-7-04; Stephen R. Wise, *Lifeline of the Confederacy: Blockade Running During the Civil War* (Columbia: University of South Carolina Press, 1988), 238. This is the first documentation of the *Coquette* arriving in the Confederacy. Naval clothing may have been delivered prior to loading the marine engines and ordnance.

29. The proper name for this ship most likely was *Advance*. See Wise, *Lifeline of the Confederacy*, 286 and 344n37.

30. Luraghi, *History Confederate Navy*, 285, 286; Wise, *Lifeline of the Confederacy*, 145, 146.

31. Wise, *Lifeline of the Confederacy*, 147; ORN, ser. II, vol. 2: 617, 618 (Memminger to Mallory, 3-39-64).

32. Simson, *Naval Strategies*, 161; Wise, *Lifeline of the Confederacy*, 148, 149.

33. Wise, *Lifeline of the Confederacy*, 151–154.

34. *Ibid.*, 213, 240; ORN, ser. II, vol. 2: 804, 805 (Mallory to Maffitt, 2-24-65).

35. Wise, *Lifeline of the Confederacy*, 214, 219.

36. ORN, ser. II, vol. 2: 588–590 (Bulloch to Mallory 2-18-64).

37. *Ibid.*, 613 (Mallory to Bulloch, 3-21-64).

38. *Ibid.*, 618, 619 (Mallory to Barron, 4-6-64).

39. *Ibid.*, 622 (Mallory to Bulloch, 4-7-64).

Chapter 11

1. Luraghi, *History Confederate Navy*, 234, 235.
2. *Ibid.*, 238, 239.
3. Belohlavek, "I Have Done My Duty," 30–32; Tucker, *Civil War at Sea*, 104, 105.
4. ORN, ser.I, vol. 4: 566, 567 (Rowan to Welles, 7-7-61); Luraghi, *History Confederate Navy*, 239.
5. Luraghi, *History Confederate Navy*, 242, 243; Belohlavek, "I Have Done My Duty," 30.
6. Luraghi, *History Confederate Navy*, 244.
7. ORN, ser. I, vol. 23: 545 (Porter to Welles, 12-17-62); Luraghi, *History Confederate Navy*, 246, 247.
8. ORN, ser. I, vol. 13: 699, 700 (Worden to DuPont, 3-3-63).
9. ORN, ser. I, vol. 25: 282 (Porter to Welles, 7-14-63).
10. Luraghi, *History Confederate Navy*, 248; V.C. Jones, "How the South Created a Navy," 48. Jones reports the loss to be 75 of her crew of 120 men; Tucker, *Civil War at Sea*, 106.
11. Luraghi, *History Confederate Navy*, 249, 429n114; Tucker, *Civil War at Sea*, 106.
12. ORA, ser. I, vol. 42, pt. 3: 1219 (Rains to Seddon, 11-18-64).
13. ORN, ser. I, vol. 10: 279 (Lamson to S.P. Lee, 5-25-64). Furthermore, Lieutenant Lamson reported, "These torpedoes [galvanic] are constructed with great ingenuity and scientific skill, and when taken from the water were in as good a state of preservation as when first put down...."
14. Luraghi, *History Confederate Navy*, 234, 235.
15. *Ibid.*, 250–255.
16. *Ibid.*, 258; Tucker, *Civil War at Sea*, 108, 109. The *Hunley* was located and raised from her watery grave off Charleston Harbor and a funeral service was conducted for her eight-man crew in Charleston, South Carolina, on April 17, 2004.
17. ORN, ser. I, vol. 15: 330 (Dahlgren to Welles, 2-19-64).
18. ORA, ser. I, vol. 14: 648, 649 (F.D. Lee to Jordan, 10-22-62); Luraghi, *History Confederate Navy*, 259.
19. ORN, ser. I, vol. 15: 20, 21 (Tomb to Tucker, 10-6-63); Luraghi, *History Confederate Navy*, 259–264; Tucker, *Civil War at Sea*, 106, 107.
20. ORN, ser I, vol. 15: 14 (Dahlgren to Fox, 10-7-63).
21. ORA, ser. I, vol. 35, pt. 1: 548, 549 (Rives to F. D. Lee, 1-27-64); Luraghi, *History Confederate Navy*, 262, 263.
22. ORN, ser. II, vol. 2: 627, 628 (Mallory to Bulloch, 4-16-64); Luraghi, *History Confederate Navy*, 262, 263.
23. ORN, ser. I, vol. 15: 329, 330 (Dahlgren to Welles, 2-19-64).

Chapter 12

1. ORN, ser. I, vol. 9: 801, 802 (Forrest [for Mallory] to Pegram, 3-3-64); Mallory to Stevens, 3-10-64); Luraghi, *History Confederate Navy*, 288. (It was common to refer to the *Virginia II* as the *Virginia*.)
2. ORN, ser. I, vol. 15: 697. (Extract from Report of the Secretary of the Navy, dated 11-30-63, regarding vessels completed and under construction.)
3. Luraghi, *History Confederate Navy*, 289.
4. *Ibid.*, 289, 290.
5. ORN, ser. I, vol. 21: 879 (Seddon to Maury [Telegram] 2-23-64); 889–890 (Buchanan to Polk 4-1-64 enclosing a letter from Mitchell); Luraghi, *History Confederate Navy*, 290.
6. Luraghi, *History Confederate Navy*, 291.
7. *Ibid.*, 321–329; Simson, *Naval Strategies*, 215–221.
8. Luraghi, *History Confederate Navy*, 338, 339; Ludwell H. Johnson, *Red River Campaign: Politics and Cotton in the Civil War*. 1958 (Kent, Ohio: Kent State University Press, 1993), 277–279.
9. Simson, *Naval Strategies*, 206.
10. ORA, ser. I, vol. 33: 1061 (Lee to Davis, 1-2-64).
11. ORN, ser. I, vol. 9: 799, 800 (Mallory to Cook, 1-15-64).
12. Luraghi, *History Confederate Navy*, 291, 292.
13. ORN, ser. I, vol. 9: 634–658. (Union and Confederate Accounts of Battle of Plymouth, especially Cooke to Mallory, 4-23-63, pp. 656, 657.)
14. Luraghi, *History Confederate Navy*, 295.
15. ORN, ser. I, vol. 9: 658 (Resolution of Thanks by Confederate Congress, 5-17-64).
16. ORN, ser. I, vol. 9: 658 (Extract from the report of the Secretary of the Navy of the Confederate States, dated 4-30-64).
17. Luraghi, *History Confederate Navy*, 296.
18. ORN, ser. I, vol. 9: 768, 769 (Statement of John B. Patrick, 6-27-64); 770, 771 (Report of Commander Cooke, 5-7-64); 733–752 (Report of Acting Rear Admiral S.P. Lee to Welles, with enclosures, 5-14-64)
19. Luraghi, *History Confederate Navy*, 298.
20. ORN, ser. I, vol. 10: 24 (Report of the court of enquiry, 6-6-64); 18–24 (Attack upon United States Vessels, enclosing battle reports, 5-7-64); 77 (Cushing to Welles, Plan for Capture of Raleigh, 5-21-64).
21. Luraghi, *History Confederate Navy*, 298.
22. *Ibid.*, 299.
23. ORN, ser. I, vol. 5: 18 (Ives to Magaw, 10-8-62); 119 (Harwood to Magaw, 10-25-62).
24. *Ibid.*, 137–140 (Various Federal reports of the raid, 10-29-62 to 11-9-62).
25. *Ibid.*, 344, 345 (Wood to Mallory, 9-7-63); 344

(McCabe to Welles, 9-28-63); ser. I, vol. 9: 180 (Mallory to Hoge, 9-21-63); ORA, ser. I, vol. 39, pt. 1: 76, 77 (Rosser to Henry C. Lee, 9-5-63); Luraghi, *History Confederate Navy*, 300–303. This U.S. merchantman named *Coquette* is not to be confused with the Southern blockade runner of the same name.
  26. ORA, ser. I, vol. 39, pt. 1: 77 (Joint Resolution No. 32, 2-15-64).
  27. Luraghi, *History Confederate Navy*, 303.
  28. ORA, ser. I, vol. 29, pt. 1: 639 (Lockwood to Schenck, telegram, 11-15-63).
  29. ORA, ser. I, vol. 29, pt. 1: 639, 640 (Lockwood to Chesebrough, 11-16-63).
  30. ORA, ser. I, vol. 29, pt. 1: 640 (Chesebrough to Lockwood, 11-21-63).
  31. Luraghi, *History Confederate Navy*, 303.
  32. ORN, ser. I, vol. 9: 439–456 (Various Federal and Confederate Reports of the Capture and Destruction of U.S.S *Underwriter*, 2-3-64 to 3-25-64); ORN, ser. I, vol. 9: 451, 452 (Detailed Report of Commander Wood, 2-11-64); ORN, ser. I, vol. 9: 454 (Extract from Report of the Secretary of the Navy of the Confederate States, 4-30-64); ORN, ser I, vol. 9: 451 (Wood to Davis and Mallory, Report of Commander Wood, 2-4-64); Luraghi, *History Confederate Navy*, 304–308.
  33. ORN, ser. I, vol. 9: 589 (Fox to S.P. Lee, 4-8-64). Speaking of the Confederate commando raids, Fox wrote, "I have been reading this new English naval history, and I find their wars abounded in rash coast attacks and cutting-out expeditions of all kinds; they were encouraged and formed a bright page of naval history. You may be very sure that the Department will not find any fault with any dashing expeditions that give reasonable hope of a result injurious to the enemy, even though they fail occasionally." Perhaps S.R. Mallory had been reading the same book?
  34. ORN, ser. II, vol. 2: 707–709 (Mallory to Bulloch, 8-19-64); *Dictionary of American Fighting Ships*, Vol. II, Appendix II, Confederate Forces Afloat, s.v. "Tallahassee." DANFS Online. http://www.hazegray.org/danfs/csn/t.txt. Internet, 6-7-04. The cruiser and blockade runner, *Atalanta*, is frequently confused in the literature with the ram *Atlanta*. In fact, *Atalanta* is incorrectly named *Atlanta* in the Mallory letter cited above. The second ship Mallory had in mind was the *Sea King* that would become the *Shenandoah*.
  35. Luraghi, *History Confederate Navy*, 310.
  36. Ibid., 311; *Dictionary of American Fighting Ships*, s.v. "Tallahassee," n.pag.
  37. Ibid.
  38. Luraghi, *History Confederate Navy*, 311, 312.
  39. Quoted in McPherson, *Battle Cry of Freedom*, 775.
  40. ORN, ser. II, vol. 2: 635, 636 (Mallory to the President, 4-30-64).
  41. ORN, ser. I, vol. 3: 649–651 (Semmes to Barron, 6-21-84).
  42. Ibid., 631–633 (Morris to Barron, 10-13-64).
  43. ORN, ser. I, vol. 10: 611–612 (Cushing to Porter, 10-30-64); Simson, *Naval Strategies*, 192–197; W.B. Cushing, "Lieutenant Cushing Torpedoes the *Albemarle*," *The Blue and the Gray: The Story of the Civil War as Told by Participants*. 2 vols. Ed. Henry Steele Commager (New York: Bobbs-Merrill, 1950), II: 836–838.
  44. Still, *Iron Afloat*, 214, 227n3. The ships commissioned were the *Albemarle, Arkansas, Atlanta, Baltic, Chicora, Charleston, Fredericksburg, Georgia, Huntsville, Manassas, Missouri, Nashville, Neuse, North Carolina, Palmetto State, Raleigh, Richmond, Savannah, Tennessee, Tuscaloosa, Virginia,* and *Virginia II* (Still, *Iron Afloat*, 227n3); Bright, vii. But compare the fate of *Albemarle* with that of *Manassas* as discussed on page 106.
  45. T.C. DeLeon, *Belles Beaux and Brains of the 60's* (New York: Dillingham, 1907), 415, 416. A slightly different version of this story is found in his other cited book, "Four Years in Rebel Capitals," 309.
  46. ORN, ser. I, vol. 16: 465 (Hardee to Hunter, 11-27-64 and Hunter to Kennard, 11-27-64). *Macon* then participated in the defense of Augusta.
  47. Ibid., 466ff; Luraghi, *History Confederate Navy*, 331–333.
  48. ORN, ser. I, vol. 11: 797–798 (Mallory to Mitchell, 1-15-1864[5]).
  49. Ibid., 803 (Mallory to Mitchell, 1-21-65).
  50. Ibid., 804 (Telegram Mallory to Mitchell, 1-21-65, sent at 9:00 P.M., received at 10:30 P.M.).
  51. Luraghi, *History Confederate Navy*, 335, 336.
  52. Ibid., 336, 337.
  53. ORN, ser. I, vol. 16: 171–179 (Union battle reports, 1-16-65 to 1-24-65).
  54. Ibid., 283 (Dahlgren to Welles, 3-1-65).
  55. Underwood, *Waters of Discord*, 139.

Chapter 13

  1. James M. McPherson, "Failed Southern Strategies," *With My Face To The Enemy: Perspectives on the Civil War*, ed. Robert Cowley (New York: Putnam, 2001), 75.
  2. Quoted in McPherson, "Failed Southern Strategies," 77.
  3. Bulloch, *Secret Service* II: 197, 198.
  4. ORN, ser. II, vol. 1: 742 (Mallory to Conrad, 5-8-61).
  5. Bulloch, *Secret Service* II: 202.
  6. Durkin, *Confederate Navy Chief*, 153, 154.
  7. Bright, *C.S.S. Neuse*, title page.
  8. These strategic concepts were adapted from material occurring passim in Luraghi, *A History of the Confederate Navy*.
  9. Bulloch (quoting Scharf), *Secret Service*, 445nII: 185.
  10. Simson, *Naval Strategies*, 187, 188.
  11. George W. Dalzell, *The Flight from the Flag: The Continuing Effect of the Civil War upon the American Carrying Trade* (Chapel Hill: University of North Carolina Press, 1940), 233–265; Mahin, *One War at a Time*, 293–300.
  12. Dalzell, *Flight from the Flag*, 237–239, 242, 247, 248.
  13. Merli, "The South on the Seas," 41.
  14. Luraghi, *History Confederate Navy*, 204, 268.
  15. Merli, "The South on the Seas," 40.

Chapter 14

  1. McPherson, *Battle Cry of Freedom*, 846; Reagan, *Memoirs: With Special Reference to Secession and the Civil War*, 196, 197; Bruce, *Virginia: Iron Manufacture in the Slave Era*, 426.
  2. ORN, ser. I, vol. 12: 191 (Mallory to Semmes, 4-2-65).
  3. William C. Davis, *An Honorable Defeat*, 59, 85; William H. Parker, "The Gold and Silver in the Confederate States Treasury: What Became of It?" (Reprint from *Richmond* [Virginia] *Dispatch*, July 16, 1893). Con-

federate Navy Research Center, Mobile, Alabama, Online. http://www.csnavy.org/parker,w,h,treas.htm. Internet, 6-8-03.
 4. Luraghi, *History Confederate Navy,* 337.
 5. Quoted in Durkin, *Confederate Navy Chief,* 339; Robert Douthat Meade, *Judah P. Benjamin: Confederate Statesman* (New York: Oxford University Press, 1943), 312.
 6. Quoted in Durkin, *Confederate Navy Chief,* 339.
 7. Meade, *Judah P. Benjamin,* 315.
 8. Shelby Foote, *The Civil War, A Narrative, Red River to Appomattox* (New York: Vintage-Random, 1974), 989–993.
 9. ORA, ser. I, vol. 47, pt. 3: 832–834 (Mallory to Davis, 4-24-65).
 10. Parker, "Gold and Silver," n.pag.
 11. William C. Davis, *An Honorable Defeat,* 236.
 12. Quoted in Joseph T. Durkin, *Armorer of the Confederacy, Secretary Mallory* (New York: Benziger, 1960), 130.
 13. Quoted in Durkin, *Armorer of the Confederacy,* 130, 131.
 14. William C. Davis, *An Honorable Defeat,* 258; Underwood, *Waters of Discord,* 103, 104; Clubbs, "Stephen Russell Mallory, Part III," FHQ 26.1: 75.
 15. Clubbs, MT, 255, 255n2, 256.
 16. ORA, ser. II, vol. 8: 844 (Stanton to President Johnson, 1-4-66).
 17. Clubbs, MT, 256, 257. Clubbs suggests the reason for the midnight arrest was to avoid any resistance by citizens of La Grange (Clubbs, MT, 257, 258).
 18. Clubbs, MT, 257.
 19. ORA, ser. I, vol. 49, pt. 2: 883, 884 (Special Orders No. 87 from E.A. Beaumont, Assistant Adjutant-General, Military Division of the Mississippi, 5-23-65).
 20. Speer, *Portals to Hell.* Online [excerpt at http://www.correctionhistory.org/html/chronicl/cw_pows/html/cwpows3.html], Internet, 2-3-04.
 21. ORA, ser. I, vol. 49, pt. 2: 901, 902 (Wilson to Stanton, 5-25-65).
 22. ORA, ser. II, vol. 8: 640 (Van Buren to Burke, 6-5-65). Clubbs contends that Mallory and Hill were confined together in a cell at 1:00 P.M. on June 4, 1865. (Source: Clubbs, "Stephen Russell Mallory, Part III," FHQ 26.1: 75n47.)
 23. ORA, ser. II, vol. 8: 652 (Townsend to Burke, 6-13-65).
 24. Stephen R. Mallory Papers #1186, SHC/UNC-CH (Mallory to his wife, 6-17-65).
 25. Eric Foner, *A Short History of Reconstruction, 1863–1877* (New York: Perennial Library–Harper & Row, 1990), 86–92.
 26. ORA, ser. II, vol. 8: 865 (Holt to Stanton, 11-23-65).
 27. ORA, ser. II, vol. 8: 833 (Asboth to Stanton, 12-10-65). General Asboth, a Hungarian and close associate of Louis Kossuth, served with him in the 1848 Hungarian revolution. He and Kossuth were imprisoned and upon release they arrived together in 1851 in the United States.
 28. Diary, SHC/UNC-CH, 81–86 (Mallory to President Johnson, 6-21-65).
 29. Diary, SHC/UNC-CH, 2, 3 (Entry, 7-17-65).
 30. *New Hampshire Division of Historical Resources,* "Zachariah Chandler." Online. http://www.state.nh.us/nhdhr/warheroes/chandlerz.html, Internet, 2-4-04; Durkin, *Confederate Navy Chief,* 69n23, 357–358.
 31. ORA, ser. II, vol. 8: 737, 738 (Mallory to Chandler, 7-2-65). In this self-serving statement, Mallory clearly was leaning toward the right to vote for black men with qualifications. He would continue with this moderating influence after his release from prison as he spoke and wrote on the subject in Florida.
 32. ORA, ser. II, vol. 8: 738 (Chandler to Mallory, 7-29-65).
 33. *Ibid.,* 736 (Chandler to Johnson, 9-1-65).
 34. *Ibid.,* 729 (Burke to Seward, 8-28-65).
 35. *Ibid.,* 713, 714 (Boyce to Seward, 7-29-65); *Confederate Military History,* "South Carolina Quick Facts." Online. http://www.confederatemilitaryhistory.com/reference/states/southcarolina/index.shtml, Internet, 2-05-04; *Biographical Directory of the United States Congress,* "Boyce, William Waters, 1818–1890." Online. http://bioguide.Congress.gov/scripts/biodisplay.pl?index=B000713, Internet, 2-05-04.
 36. Diary, SHC/UNC-CH, 7, 8 (Entry, 9-11-65).
 37. Reagan, *Memoirs: With Special Reference to Secession and the Civil War,* 228.
 38. Durkin, *Confederate Navy Chief,* 363 n58, 365.
 39. Quoted in Durkin, *Confederate Navy Chief,* 365 (Mallory to Johnson, 9-27-65).
 40. ORA, ser. II, vol. 8: 769 (Marvin to Johnson, 10-22-65).
 41. Angela S. Mallory to President Johnson, 11-14-65.
 42. Quoted in Durkin, *Confederate Navy Chief,* 373. In footnote 95 Durkin states "the chances that Mallory would be kept in prison much longer or indicted for treason were very slim ... [because] such punishment would have been permitted neither by Northern public opinion nor by constitutional lawyers."
 43. Quoted in Durkin, *Confederate Navy Chief,* 379 (Angela to Mrs. Caroline Tunstall Clay, 2-7-66).
 44. Quoted in Durkin, *Confederate Navy Chief,* 378, 379 (Angela to Mrs. Caroline Tunstall Clay, 2-7-66).
 45. Edward Steers, Jr., *Blood on the Moon: The Assassination of Abraham Lincoln* (Lexington, KY: University Press of Kentucky, 2001), 223–225. The Federal Government eventually dropped all conspiracy charges against Confederate officials and agents.
 46. Foner, *A Short History of Reconstruction,* 83.
 47. *Ibid.,* 89.
 48. William C. Davis, *An Honorable Defeat,* 12.
 49. Durkin, *Confederate Navy Chief,* 379, 380; William C. Davis, *An Honorable Defeat,* 385.

Chapter 15

 1. Clubbs, "Stephen Russell Mallory, Part II," FHQ 25.4: 297; Maloney, *History of Key West,* 62.
 2. Source of genealogical data was *FamilyOrigins.com,* Online. http://www.familyorigins.com/users/s/a/l/Thomas-W-Saltmarsh-jr/FAMO1-0001/d31.htm#P15; http://www.familyorigins.com/users/s/a/l/Thomas-W-Saltmarsh-jr/FAMO1-0001/d25,d26.htm, n.pag. Internet, 2003.
 3. Diary, SHC/UNC-CH, 191 (Mallory to Buddy, 9-27-65).
 4. Clubbs, "Stephen Russell Mallory, Part II," FHQ 25.4: 305; Diary, SHC/UNC-CH, 191 (Mallory to Buddy, 9-27-65).
 5. Quoted in Durkin, *Confederate Navy Chief,* 116.
 6. Stephen R. Mallory Papers #1186, SHC/UNC-CH (Mallory to his wife, 8-31-62).
 7. Diary, SHC/UNC-CH, 14, 15.
 8. *Ibid.,* 15.
 9. *Ibid.,* 16.
 10. *Ibid.,* 164, 165.

11. *Ibid.*, 166, 167.
12. *Ibid.*, 174, 175.
13. *Ibid.*, 165, 166.
14. *Ibid.*, 4.
15. Mallory to Ruby, 8-3-65.
16. Diary, SHC/UNC-CH, 215 (Originally published as "The Brave Wife of Stephen Mallory," *The Daily Picayune–New Orleans*, Wednesday, January 12, 1898).
17. Boatner, *The Civil War Dictionary*, 27–28 (Asboth, Alexander Sandor); "Conflict at the Spanish Consulate," excerpted by Laura Lee Scott from *Florida Footprints, West Florida Genealogical Society*. Online. http://www.rootsweb.com/~flescamb/civwar.htm. Internet, 11-26-04 (n.pag); ORA, ser. I, vol. 26, part 1: 743–748 (Colonel W. C. Holbrook to General Charles P. Stone, 9-30-63; Morino [Moreno] to Holbrook, 9-22-63; Holbrook to Morino [Moreno], 9-17-63; General Dabney H. Maury to Holbrook, 9-21-63; Holbrook to Maury, 9-30-63; Captain Mahlon M. Young to Holbrook with Inclosures G, H, I, 9-9-63.)
18. Diary, SHC/UNC-CH, 118, 119.
19. Clubbs, "Stephen Russell Mallory, Part III," FHQ 26.1: 74.
20. *Ibid.*, 64, 65. Clubbs points out that 40 years later Mallory's son, Stephen Russell Mallory, Jr., who was also a senator, occupied the same room at the National hotel as had his father. She adds that the building was constructed in 1827 and in 1933 became a District of Columbia armory.
21. *Ibid.*, 65; Cong. Globe, 33rd Cong., 1st Sess., 1606.
22. DeLeon, *"Belles Beaux and Brains of the 60's,"* 33–35.
23. *Ibid.*, 35–38.
24. "Stephen R. Mallory, Secretary of the Navy, Confederate States of America" (Pamphlet), Pensacola Home & Savings Association, Pensacola, Florida. n.d., n.pag.
25. Clay-Clopton, *A Belle of the Fifties*, 55.
26. *The Private Mary Chesnut: The Unpublished Civil War Diaries*, ed. C. Vann Woodward, Elisabeth Muhlenfeld (New York: Oxford University Press, 1984), 65, 98.
27. Clubbs, MT, 328n1.
28. DeLeon, *"Belles Beaux and Brains of the 60's,"* 48.
29. DeLeon, *"Four Years in Rebel Capitals,"* 25.
30. *The Private Mary Chesnut*, 21.
31. William C. Davis, *"A Government of Our Own,"* 265, 266.
32. *Ibid.*, 271.
33. *Ibid.*, 181.
34. *The Private Mary Chesnut*, 63.
35. William C. Davis, *"A Government of Our Own,"* 180, 181.
36. V.C. Jones, "How the South Created a Navy," 4, 6.
37. William C. Davis, *"A Government of Our Own,"* 376.
38. *The Private Mary Chesnut* 67, 68.
39. *Mary Chesnut's Civil War*, 68.
40. DeLeon, *"Belles Beaux and Brains of the 60's,"* 85. Many persons had a positive impression of Secretary Mallory, but one vehement faultfinder of Mallory and the Confederate Navy was Catherine Ann Devereux Edmondston whose husband was a prominent planter in Halifax County, North Carolina. In her diary entry dated October 24, 1863, she wrote, "I have seen this Secy Mallory, seen & heard him, & he is just the man to be blinded by a dose of flattery skillfully administered. He is emphatically ... 'a bag of wind.'" On November 2, 1864, Mrs. Edmondston inferred in her diary that Mallory's staff consisted of numbskulls who get drunk and neglect their duty. (Source: Quoted from *"Journal of a Secesh Lady"* in *Ironclad of the Roanoke*, pp. 120, 261.)
41. *Ibid.*, 86.
42. Referred to in Durkin, *Confederate Navy Chief*, 213 (Mallory to his wife, 5-3-62); Pensacola Historical Society, Box 1, Folder 2, Letters of Angela S. Mallory and Mrs. Jefferson Davis, draft letter from ASM [Angela S. Mallory] to Mrs. Davis, ?/62 [Probably October].
43. Diary, SHC/UNC-CH, 218. (Originally published as "The Brave Wife of Stephen Mallory," *The Daily Picayune–New Orleans*, Wednesday, January 12, 1898.)
44. Clay-Clopton, *A Belle of the Fifties*, 170. The reference to the "Punch-bowl" pertains to Oliver Wendell Holmes' poem, "On Lending a Punch-Bowl."
45. *Mary Chesnut's Civil War*, 431.
46. Caroline Norton, "Bingen on the Rhine," *Poet's Corner*, Online. http://www.theotherpages.org/poems/norton01.html. Internet, 11-6-04.
47. Patrick, *Jefferson David Cabinet*, 328.
48. *Ibid.*, 333.
49. Quoted in Meade, *Judah P. Benjamin*, 278.
50. Varina Davis to Angela Mallory, Executive Mansion—Richmond Oct 2nd [probably 1862]; Draft letter from ASM [Angela S. Mallory] to Mrs. Davis, ?/62 [Probably October]. Both original documents were viewed on 7-9-03 at the Pensacola Historical Society, Pensacola, Florida, and were located in Box 1, Folder 2, "Letters of Angela S. Mallory and Mrs. Jefferson Davis." To my knowledge these documents have not been published previously. Editorial comments, which are intended to clarify, are enclosed in brackets.
51. William C. Davis, *"A Government of Our Own,"* 378.
52. *Mary Chesnut's Civil War*, 85, 85n9; *The Private Mary Chesnut*, 97.
53. DeLeon, *"Belles Beaux and Brains of the 60's,"* 67.
54. William C. Davis, *"A Government of Our Own,"* 275.
55. Durkin, *Confederate Navy Chief*, 45.
56. Patrick, *Jefferson David Cabinet*, 337.
57. Clay-Clopton, *A Belle of the Fifties*, 230.
58. *The Private Mary Chesnut*, 87, 68n7. Mrs. McLean was the wife of Lt. Eugene McLean of Maryland.
59. Durkin, *Confederate Navy Chief*, 100, 110, 111; Quoted in Durkin, 110 (Mallory to his wife, 1-1-59).
60. Quoted in Durkin, *Confederate Navy Chief*, 213 (Mallory to his wife, 5-3-62).
61. Durkin, *Confederate Navy Chief*, 216, 217.
62. *FamilyOrigins.com*, Online. http://www.familyorigins.com/, n.pag.
63. Stephen R. Mallory Papers #1186, SHC/UNC-CH (Mallory to his wife, 8-31-62).
64. *Ibid*.
65. Angela S. Mallory to Mrs. Clay, 5-6-64 (Quoted in Durkin, *Confederate Navy Chief*, 308).
66. Angela S. Mallory to Mrs. Clay, 5-6-64 (Quoted in Durkin, *Confederate Navy Chief*, 309); *The Private Mary Chesnut*, xxii.
67. Diary, SHC/UNC-CH, 217. (Originally published as "The Brave Wife of Stephen Mallory," *The Daily Picayune–New Orleans*, Wednesday, January 12, 1898.)

Chapter 16

1. Quoted in Durkin, *Confederate Navy Chief*, 382.
2. Clubbs, MT, 309.
3. Clubbs, MT, 312. According to Clubbs, the house was razed in 1928 for commercial development. (As an aside, "Palafox," refers to a Spanish general, Francisco

de Palafox y Melci, who won distinction opposing Napoleon's forces in Spain.)

4. Clubbs, MT, 314.

5. Clubbs, MT, 315, 328–330, 329n2, 333, 334; Boatner, *The Civil War Dictionary*, 634, 931; "Union Regimental Histories, New York." *The Civil War Archives*, Online. http://www.civilwararchive.com/Unreghst/unnyinf1.htm# 14. Internet, 7-16-03; William Watson Davis, 166–169.

6. Pensacola Historical Society, Box 1, Folder 3, S. R. Mallory Letters (Mallory to his wife, 6-22-66).

7. Quoted in Durkin, *Confederate Navy Chief*, 384, 385.

8. Quoted in Durkin, *Confederate Navy Chief*, 388 (Mallory to his wife, 7-6-66).

9. Quoted in Durkin, *Confederate Navy Chief*, 389 (Mallory to Ruby, 7-6-66).

10. Cora Mallory Papers, Box 1, File 7, University of West Florida (Mallory to his wife, 7-19-66).

11. Cora Mallory Papers, Box 1, File 7, University of West Florida (Mallory to his wife, 8-18-66).

12. Quoted in Durkin, *Confederate Navy Chief*, 393.

13. Quoted in Durkin, *Confederate Navy Chief*, 396 (Mallory to his wife, 9-3-66).

14. Referenced in Durkin, *Confederate Navy Chief*, 397 (Mallory to his wife, 9-28-66).

15. Clubbs, MT, 316, 317n1. Earlier note has been made of the Mallorys giving gifts of oranges to their friends in Richmond. These probably came from their properties in Dade and Polk counties.

16. Durkin, *Confederate Navy Chief*, 397, 397n61, 230, 231, 242.

17. Clubbs, MT, 319, 319n2 and n3.

18. Clubbs, MT, 317, 318n1.

19. Clubbs, MT, 317n2,n3.

20. Mallory to Marvin, 7-15-65.

21. Quoted in Foner, *A Short History of Reconstruction*, 84.

22. Foner, *A Short History of Reconstruction*, 85.

23. *Ibid.*, 92.

24. William Watson Davis, *Civil War and Reconstruction*, 422–425.

25. *Ibid.*, 446; Wynne and Taylor, *Florida in the Civil War*, 146, 147; Peter Kolchin, *Stanford University*, "Reconstruction." Online. http://www.stanford.edu/~paherman/reconstruction.htm. Internet, 7-28-04.

26. William Watson Davis, 447.

27. Foner, *A Short History of Reconstruction*, 130.

28. Kolchin, "Reconstruction," n.pag.

29. William Watson Davis, *Civil War and Reconstruction*, 456.

30. Clubbs, MT, 320; Durkin, *Confederate Navy Chief*, 400.

31. William Watson Davis, *Civil War and Reconstruction*, 447.

32. Refer to page 204.

33. Durkin, *Confederate Navy Chief*, 401.

34. *Ibid.*, 401, 402 404, 405. Durkin makes persuasive arguments to support his belief that the editorials were written by Mallory.

35. The address was summarized in the September 8, 1868, edition of the *West Florida Commercial* and was signed by "Escambia" (Reference, Durkin, *Confederate Navy Chief*, 407n95).

36. Durkin, *Confederate Navy Chief*, 405– 409.

37. Quoted in Durkin, *Confederate Navy Chief*, 409, 410.

38. Quoted in Durkin, *Confederate Navy Chief*, 411 (Mallory to Atilla, 10-3-68).

39. Quoted in Durkin, *Confederate Navy Chief*, 411, 412 (Mallory to Atilla, 7-18-69).

40. Referenced in Durkin, *Confederate Navy Chief*, 412, 413 (Mallory to Atilla, 5-11-70).

41. Quoted in Durkin, *Confederate Navy Chief*, 412–414. Atilla did not follow his father's advice. Ultimately he became a supervisor with the Louisville and Nashville Railroad.

42. According to an article in the *Pensacola News–Journal* dated May 29, 1999, Stephen Russell Mallory died on November 9, 1873. The author viewed Mallory's grave and monument at St. Michael Cemetery on July 10, 2003, and the inscription gives his date of death as November 9, 1873. Occie Clubbs in her masters' thesis (page 323) also gives the date of his death as November 9, 1873. Mrs. Mallory says her husband died on November 9, 1873 (Scharf, *History Confederate States Navy*, 29n1). Durkin, in his biography, *Confederate Navy Chief* (page 414) reports Mallory's date of death as November 12, 1873. The date of Mallory's death as reported by Durkin is in error.

43. St. Michael Parish, "St. Michael Cemetery." Online. http://stmichael.ptdiocese.org/cemetery.htm. Internet, 11-05-04. The Mallory burial plot contains other notable family members including Angela Mallory (died March 26, 1901) and the eldest son, Stephen Russell Mallory, Jr. (died December 23, 1907). This son followed his father into the United States Congress where he served as Florida's senator from May 15, 1897, until his death. The graves of Angela's father, Don Francisco Moreno, and many of his other children are found elsewhere in the cemetery.

44. Richard Strauss, "Vier Letzte Lieder (Four Last Songs)," lyrics from a poem by Herman Hesse, "Beim Schlafengehen (Going to Sleep)." *Program Notes* by Jason Sundram. Online. http://jsundram.freeshell.org/ProgramNotes/Strauss_Leider.html. Internet, 11-6-04.

45. Clubbs, MT, 325n2.

Bibliography

PRIMARY SOURCES

Manuscripts and Letters

Barron, Samuel. Papers. MSS 10134. University of Virginia Libraries, Special Collections Library, Charlottesville, VA.
Florida State University, Tallahassee, FL. Special Collections, Robert Manning Stozier Library. Manuscripts. Mss1 Ay445 b 359–374 *and* b 332–345, Ordinance of Secession — State of Florida, MSS 0:197; Edward M. Tidball Civil War Papers 1859–1865, MSS 0:245; George T. Ward Secession Broadside, MSS 0:256.
John Milton Letterbook and Correspondence, MSS 92–1, Photocopies of Correspondence from Stephen Mallory to Governor John Milton, Box 4, Folder 3. Florida Historical Society, Alma Clyde Field Library of Florida History, Cocoa Village, FL.
Mallory, Cora. Papers. Box 1, Folders 3 and 7. Accession number M1974-07. University of West Florida Libraries, Special Collections Department, Pensacola, FL.
Mallory Manuscripts. Folders 1, 2, 3 and 7. Pensacola Historical Society, Resource Learning Center and Library, Pensacola, FL.
Scott, Winfield. "Letter to President-Elect Lincoln, copy to Secretary of War Floyd, 12-28-60." *The Abraham Lincoln Papers at the Library of Congress.* Online. http://www.memory.loc.gov/cgi-bin/query/P?mal:292:./temp/~ammem_KpDU::@@@md.... Internet, 6-19-04.
University of Florida, Gainesville, FL. George A. Smathers Libraries, Department of Special & Area Studies Collections. Four Letters Addressed to Jefferson Davis, F.07 V452f; Stephen Russell Mallory, Jr., Memorial Addresses, 60th Congress, First Session, FB M255u; Stephen Mallory Letter (60 pieces), FL. Misc. Ms. Box 27, File 28; Stephen Mallory, Three Senate Speeches, K4750.M35 1852, FB M255s, FB M255e; Contested U.S. Senate Election 1852 — S.R. Mallory and D. L. Yulee, F324 M255u, F324 M255s, F324 M255m, F324 M255y, F324 M255r, F324 M255ye.
University of North Carolina at Chapel Hill, NC. Wilson Library, Southern Historical Collection. Kate Simpson Letter, #1187; Stephen R. Mallory Papers, #1186; Stephen R. Mallory Diary and Reminiscences (Diary #1 and Diary #2), #2229.
Virginia Historical Society, Research Library, Richmond, VA. Manuscripts. Mss1 Ay445 b 359–374 *and* b 332–345, *Aylett family*; Mss5:7 B2473:3, *Barksdale, George Ainsley*, 1835–1910, comp.; Mss2 2787 a 2–7 *Barron family*; Mss1 W4597 e 63 *and* e 64, *Confederate States of America, Navy*; Mss2 D3537 b, *DeBree, John*; Mss1 M6663 a 399–409, *Minor family*; Mss1 P3496 c 59–79, *Pegram family*; Mss2 Q4495 a 1, *Quinn, William*; Mss5:7 B2473:3, *Stuart, Jeb*, 1833–1864; Mss3 T1425 a 71–75, *Talbott & Brother (Richmond, Va.)*.

Published Documents

"An Act for the Reorganization of the Navy." *Confederate States Navy Research Center*, Mobile, Alabama; n. pag. Online. http://www.csnavy.org/mallory,apr61.htm. Internet, 6-2-03.

Buchanan, James. "Inaugural Address." *The Avalon Project at Yale Law School*. Online. http://www.yale.edu/lawweb/avalon/presiden/inaug/buchanan.htm. Internet, 10-21-03.

Bulloch, James D. *The Secret Service of the Confederate States in Europe or How the Confederate Cruisers Were Equipped*. New ed. 2 vols. New York: Thomas Yoseloff Publisher-Sagamore Press, Inc., 1959.

Clay-Clopton, Virginia. *A Belle of the Fifties* (electronic edition). Ada Sterling, ed. New York: Doubleday, Page & Company, 1904. Online. http://docsouth.unc.edu/clay/clay.html#clay19. Internet, 2-7-04.

Congressional Globe. Debates and Proceedings, 1833–1873. Online. http://memory.loc.gov.ammen/amlaw/wcglink.html. Internet, 2003, 2004.

Cushing, W. B. "Lieutenant Cushing Torpedoes the *Albemarle*." *The Blue and the Gray: The Story of the Civil War as Told by Participants*. 2 vols. Henry Steele Commager, ed. New York: Bobbs-Merrill Company, 1950. Vol. II: 836–838.

Davis, Jefferson. "Inaugural Address." *The Papers of Jefferson Davis*. Reprinted in *C.S.A. Congressional Journal* 1:64–66, Lynda L. Crist and Mary S. Dix, eds. Baton Rouge: Louisiana State University Press, 1992. Online. http://sunsite.utk.edu/civil-war/jdinaug.html. Internet, 6-21-04.

"Documents." C.S.S. *Alabama* Digital Collection, *Rare Book Collection*, William Stanley Hoole Special Collections Library, The University of Alabama, Tuscaloosa. Online. http://www.lib.ua.edu/libraries/hoole/digital/cssala/main.shtml. Internet, 12-13-03.

Eggleston, John R. "Captain Eggleston's Narrative of the Battle of the *Merrimac*." *Blue & Gray At Sea: Naval Memoirs of the Civil War*. Brian M. Thomsen, ed. New York: Tom Doherty Associates, 2003. 395–404.

Ford, Arthur P. "A Confederate Submarine Sinks the *Housatonic*." *The Blue and the Gray: The Story of the Civil War as Told by Participants*. 2 vols. Henry Steele Commager, ed. New York: Bobbs-Merrill Company, 1950. Vol. II: 827–829.

Jefferson, Thomas. "Cuba, Acquisition by United States." *The Jeffersonian Cyclopedia*. Online. Thomas Jefferson Collection, Electronic Text Center, University of Virginia Library, Charlottesville, Virginia. http://etext.lib.virginia.edu/. Internet, 4-19-04.

Jones, J.B. (John Beauchamp). *A Rebel Clerk's Diary at the Confederate States Capital*. Vol. II. Philadelphia: Lippincott 1866. n.p. Time-Life Books, 1981.

"Journal of a Secesh Lady": The Diary of Catherine Ann Devereux Edmondston, 1860–1866. Ed. Beth G. Crabtree, James W. Patton. Raleigh: North Carolina Division of Archives, 1979.

Journal of the Congress of the Confederate States of America, 1861–1865. S. Doc. No. 234, 58th Cong., 2nd Sess. (1904–1905). Seven vols. Online. http://memory.loc.gov.ammen/amlaw/lwcc.html, Internet, 2003, 2004.

Kell, John McIntosh. *Recollections of a Naval Life Including the Cruises of the Confederate State Steamers "Sumter" and "Alabama"* (electronic edition). Online. http://docsouth.unc.edu/kell/kell.html. Internet, 1-04-04.

"Letter from Captain Semmes, C. S. Navy, commanding C.S.S. *Alabama*, to Lieutenant Low, C. S. Navy, commanding C. S. bark *Tuscaloosa*, giving instructions regarding the cruise of that vessel, dated June 21, 1863." Rare Book Collection, William Stanley Hoole Special Collections Library, Tuscaloosa, Alabama. The University of Alabama, Online. http://www.lib.ua.edu/libraries/hoole/digital/cssala/main.shtml. Internet, 12-13-03.

The Library of Congress, Congressional Globe. Online. http://memory.loc.gov/ammem/amlaw/lwcg.html. Internet, 2003, 2004.

Mallory, Stephen R. "Letter, 10 January 1862." Naval Historical Center, Department of the Navy. Online. http://www.history.navy.mil/biblio/biblio3/mallory.htm. Internet, 11-5-03.

___. "Reply of Mr. Mallory of Florida..." *Contested U.S. Senate Election—1852*, University of Florida, Special Collections Department, F324 M255r.

___. "Statement of Mr. S.R. Mallory..." *Contested U.S. Senate Election—1852*, University of Florida, Special Collections Department, F324 M255m.

Maloney, Walter C. *A Sketch of the History of Key West, Florida*. 1876. Introd. Thelma Peters. Facsimile Reproduction. Gainesville: University of Florida Press, 1968.

Marvin, William. "Autobiography of William Marvin." Kevin E. Kearney, ed. *Florida Historical Quarterly* 36.3 (January 1958): 179–222.

_____. *A Treatise on the Law of Wreck and Salvage*. Boston: Little, Brown, & Company, 1858.

Mary Chesnut's Civil War. C. Vann Woodward, ed. New York: Quality Paperback Book Club, 1981.
Morgan, James Morris. *Recollections of a Rebel Reefer* (electronic edition). Online. http://docsouth.unc.edu/morganjames/morgan.html#morgan89. Internet, 1-04-04.
"Official Records of the Union and Confederate Navies in the War of the Rebellion." 30 vols. *The Civil War CD-ROM II.* CD-ROM. Carmel, Guild Press of Indiana, Inc., 1999.
"Ordinance of Secession." Florida State Archives, Tallassee, FL, Florida Memory Project, Constitution of 1861 (Preamble). Online. http://www.floridamemory.com/Collections/. Internet, 3-25-04.
Parker, William H. "The Gold and Silver in the Confederate States Treasury: What Became of It?" Reprint from Richmond, Va. *Dispatch*, July 16, 1893. Confederate Navy Research Center, Mobile, Alabama. Online. http://www.csnavy.org/parker,w,h,treas.htm. Internet, 6-8-03, n. pag.
Perkins, George Hamilton. "Commodore Farragut Captures New Orleans." *The Blue and the Gray: The Story of the Civil War as Told by Participants.* 2 vols. Henry Steele Commager, ed. New York: Bobbs-Merrill Company, 1950. Vol. II: 807–810.
Phillips, Dinwiddie B. "Notes on the *Monitor-Merrimac* Fight." *Blue & Gray at Sea: Naval Memoirs of the Civil War.* Brian M. Thomsen, ed. New York: Tom Doherty Associates, 2003. 405–407.
The Private Mary Chesnut: The Unpublished Civil War Diaries. C. Vann Woodward and Elisabeth Muhlenfeld, eds. New York: Oxford University Press, 1984.
Reagan, John H. *Memoirs: With Special Reference to Secession and the Civil War.* Walter Flavius McCaleb, ed. Introd. George P. Garrison. New York: The Neale Publishing Company, 1906.
"Report of the Secretary of the Navy, April 26, 1861." Confederate State Navy Research Center, Mobile, Alabama. Online. http://www.csnavy.org/mallory,apr61.htm. Internet, 6-6-03.
Semmes, Raphael. *Memoirs of Service Afloat During the War Between the States.* 1868. Baton Rouge: Louisiana State University Press, 1996.
Sinclair, Arthur. "The Campaign in the Gulf of Mexico and Southward." (From Two Years on the *Alabama.*) *Blue & Gray at Sea: Naval Memoirs of the Civil War.* Brian M. Thomsen, ed. New York: Tom Doherty Associates, 2003. 193–245.
The Stranger's Guide and Official Directory for the City of Richmond. Showing the Location of the Public Buildings and Offices of the Confederate, State and City Governments, Residences of the Principal Officers, etc. (electronic edition). Online. http://docsouth.unc.edu/imls/stranger/stranger.html. Internet, 1-8-04.
"Territorial Governor Duval's Message to Legislative Council, 1822," Florida Department of State, Bureau of Archives & Record Management. Online. http://www.floridamemory.com/FloridaHighlights/s876/s876TerrLeg.cfm. Internet, 7-27-03.
Waddell, James. "Documents of CSS *Shenandoah*." *Blue & Gray at Sea: Naval Memoirs of the Civil War.* Brian M. Thomsen, ed. New York: Tom Doherty Associates, 2003. 279–344.
Wait, Horatio L. "The United States Navy Blockades the Confederacy." *The Blue and the Gray: The Story of the Civil War as Told by Participants.* 2 vols. Henry Steele Commager, ed. New York: Bobbs-Merrill Company, 1950. Vol. II: 848–859.
"The War of the Rebellion: A Compilation of the Official Records of the Union and Confederate Armies." 128 vols. *The Civil War CD-ROM.* CD-ROM v.1.0. Carmel: Guild Press of Indiana, Inc., 1996.

Secondary Sources

Adamiak, Stanley J. "A Naval Depot and Dockyard on the Western Waters: The Rise and Fall of the Memphis Naval Yard, 1844–1854." *International Journal of Naval History* 1.1 (2002), n. pag. Online. http://www.ijnhonline.org/volume1_number1_Apr02/article_adamiak_memphis_navyyard.doc.htm. Internet, 4-11-04.
Alabama Department of Public Health, Health Statistics and Surveillance, vol. 8, no. 2, December 1999. "Mortality Patterns: Then and Now." Online. http://ph.state.al.us/Chs/HealthStatistics/Reports/life-expectancy2. PDF. Internet, 7-26-03, 1.
American College of Rheumatology Fact Sheet. "Gout." Online. http://www.rheumatology.org/patients/factsheet/gout.html. Internet, 10-22-23.
Anderson, Bern. *By Sea and by River: The Naval History of the Civil War.* New York: Alfred A. Knopf–Borzoi, 1962.
Appleton's Cyclopaedia of American Biography. vol. 5. s.v. "Stephen Russell Mallory." New York, 1888.
Barbour Collection of Connecticut Town Vital Records. Wilma J. Standifer Moore, comp., Lorraine Cook White, ed. Baltimore: Genealogical Publishing Company, Indiana, 2000.
Belohlavek, John M. "'I Have Done My Duty': Stephen Mallory and the Failure of the Confederate

Navy." *Divided We Fall: Essays on Confederate Nation Building.* Ed. John M. Belohlavek and Lewis N. Wynne. St. Leo, FL: St. Leo College Press, 1991. 11–38.

Bergeron, Arthur W., Jr. "Stephen R. Mallory." *Encyclopedia of the Confederacy*, vol. 3. Ed. Richard N. Current. New York: Simon & Schuster, 1993. 991–994.

Beringer, Richard E., Herman Hattaway, Archer Jones, and William N. Still, Jr. *Why the South Lost the Civil War.* Athens: University of Georgia Press, 1986.

Biographical Directory of the United States Congress. s.v. "Boyce, William Waters, 1818–1890." Online. http://bioguide.congress.gov/scripts/biodisplay.pl?index=B000713. Internet, 2-05-04.

_____. s.v. "Stephen Russell Mallory." Online. http://bioguide.congress.gov/. Internet, 7-23-03.

Boatner, Mark M., III. *The Civil War Dictionary.* Rev. ed. New York: Random House–Vintage Books, 1988.

Bradlee, Francis B.C. *Blockade Running During the Civil War, and the Effect of Land and Water Transportation on the Confederacy.* 1925. Philadelphia: Porcupine Press, 1974.

Bright, Leslie S., William H. Rowland, and James C. Bardon. *C.S.S. Neuse: A Question of Iron and Time.* Raleigh: Division of Archives and History, North Carolina Department of Cultural Resources, 1981.

Britannica Concise Encyclopedia, 2003. s.v. "Nashville Convention." Encyclopaedia Britannica Premium Service. Online. http://www.britannica.com/ebc/article?eu=398357. Internet, 9-9-03.

Browne, Jefferson B. *Key West, the Old and the New.* St. Augustine: Record, 1912.

Bruce, Kathleen. "Mallory, Stephen Russell." *Dictionary of American Biography.* New York: Scribner, c. 1996. 224–226.

_____. *Virginia: Iron Manufacture in the Slave Era.* 1930. New York: Kelley, 1968.

Buker, George. "Lieutenant Levin M. Powell, U.S.N., Pioneer of Riverine Warfare." *Florida Historical Quarterly* 47.3 (January 1969): 254–265.

_____. *Swamp Sailors: Riverine Warfare in the Everglades.* Gainesville: University Presses of Florida, 1975.

Campbell, R. Thomas. *Gray Thunder: Exploits of the Confederate States Navy.* Shippensburg: White Mane Publishing-Burd Street Press, 1996.

Catholic Encyclopedia. vol. IX. s.v. "St. Stephen." Online. http://www.newadvent.org/cathen/14286b.htm. Internet, 6-27-03.

Catton, Bruce. *The Coming Fury.* New York: Doubleday, 1961.

Chesebrough, David B. *God Ordained This War: Sermons on the Sectional Crisis, 1830–1865.* Columbia: University of South Carolina Press, 1991.

Civil War Archives. "Union Regimental Histories, New York." Online. http://www.civilwararchive.com/Unreghst/unnyinf1.htm#14. Internet, 7-16-03.

Civil War@Smithsonian. "Jefferson Davis." Online. http://www.civilwar.si.edu/leaders_davis.html. Internet, 6-18-03.

Cliffe, Peter. "Vigilant Envoy Finally Stops Ship After Attacks End." *The Washington Times.* Online. http://dynamic.washtimes.com/print_story.cfm?StoryID=20031024-075917-1020r. Internet, 10-28-03.

Clubbs, Occie. "Stephen Russell Mallory." *Florida Historical Quarterly* 25.3, January 1947. 221–245.

_____. "Stephen Russell Mallory, Part II." *Florida Historical Quarterly* 25.4, April 1947. 295–318.

_____. "Stephen Russell Mallory, Part III." *Florida Historical Quarterly* 26.1, July 1947. 56–76.

_____. "Stephen Russell Mallory, The Elder." Diss., University of Florida, 1936.

Columbia Encyclopedia, Sixth Edition, 2001. s.v. "Kossuth, Louis." Online. http://www.bartleby.com/65/ko/Kossuth.html. Internet, 9-16-03.

Comenius. "John Amos Comenius." Online. http://www.comenius.com/misc/comenius.php. Internet, 7-28-03.

Confederate Military History. s.v. "South Carolina Quick Facts." Online. http://www.confederatemilitaryhistory.com/reference/states/southcarolina/index.shtml. Internet, 2-05-04.

Confederate States Navy Research Center, Mobile, Alabama. s.v. "Confederate Navy Shipyards." Online. http://www.csnavy.org/index-assorted.htm. Internet, 1-12-04.

_____. s.v. "C.S.S. Manassas." Online. http://www.csnavy.org/ships,area.htm. Internet, 5-25-04. n. pag.

_____. s.v. "C.S.S. *Nashville,*" Online. http://www.csnavy.org/Ships,area.htm, Internet, 6-8-03. n. pag.

_____. s.v. "List of Ships." Online. http://www.csnavy.org/ships,area.htm. Internet, 6-6-03.

Cooper, William. Review of *Hunters in the Shallows: A History of the PT Boat*, by Curtis L. Nelson, and *PT Boats at War: World War II to Vietnam*, by Norman Polmar and Samuel Loring Morison. "Fast Torpedo Boats," Naval War College Press, Spring 2000: 238–240. Online. http://www.nwc.navy.mil/press/Review/bkrevind%202000.htm. Internet, 6-25-04.

Crook, David Paul. *The North, the South, and the Powers, 1861–1865.* New York: Wiley, 1974.

CSA-dixie.com. "James Dunwoody Bulloch." Online. http://www.csa-dixie.com/Liverpool_Dixie/bulloch.htm. Internet, 6-8-03.

_____. "Obituary to James Dunwoody Bulloch." Online. http://www.csa-dixie.com/Liverpool_Dixie/obit.htm. Internet, 6-1-03.

_____. "Rebel with a Cause." (Bulloch Exhibition in Liverpool, August 6, 2001.) *When Liverpool Was Dixie.* Online. http://www.csa-dixie.com/exhib.htm, Internet, 6-15-04.

Daily Picayune. "The Brave Wife of Stephen Mallory." New Orleans, Louisiana, January 12, 1898. (Found in Mallory Diary and Reminiscences, SHC-UNC, 214–219).

Dalzell, George W. *The Flight from the Flag: The Continuing Effect of the Civil War upon the American Carrying Trade.* Chapel Hill: University of North Carolina Press, 1940.

"DANFS." *The Dictionary of American Naval Fighting Ships.* (Confederate States Navy, List of Major Classes and Types.) Online. http://www.hazegray.org/danfs/csn/classes.txt. Internet, 6-11-04. Vol. II, 490–492.

Daniels, George H. "The Confederate Government and Industrialization: Joseph R. Anderson and the Tredegar Iron Works." *Divided We Fall: Essays on Confederate Nation Building.* Ed. John M. Belohlavek and Lewis N. Wynne. St. Leo, FL: St. Leo College Press, 1991. 129–150.

Davis, William C. *"A Government of Our Own": The Making of the Confederacy.* New York: Macmillan–The Free Press, 1994.

_____. *An Honorable Defeat: The Last Days of the Confederate Government.* New York: Harcourt, 2001.

_____. *Look Away! A History of the Confederate States of America.* New York: Simon & Schuster–The Free Press, 2002.

Davis, William Watson. *The Civil War and Reconstruction in Florida.* 1913. Introd. Fletcher M. Green. Gainesville: University of Florida Press, 1964.

DeLeon, T. C. *Belles Beaux and Brains of the 60's.* New York: Dillingham, 1907.

_____. *Four Years in Rebel Capitals: An Inside View of Life in the Southern Confederacy, from Birth to Death; From Original Notes, Collated in the Years 1861 to 1865.* 1892. Spartanburg, S.C.: The Reprint Co., Publishers, 1975.

Dew, Charles B. *Apostles of Disunion: Southern Secession Commissioners and the Causes of the Civil War.* Charlottesville: University Press of Virginia, 2001.

Dibble, Ernest F. "War Averters: Seward, Mallory, and Fort Pickens." *Florida Historical Quarterly* 49.3 (January 1971): 232–244.

Dictionary of American Fighting Ships. Vol. II, Appendix II, Confederate Forces Afloat. "Coquette." DANFS Online. http://www.hazegray.org/danfs/csn/c.txt. Internet, 6-7-04.

_____. "Tallahassee." http://www.hazegray.org/danfs/csn/t.txt. Internet, 6-7-04.

Dodd, Dorothy. "The Secession Movement in Florida, 1850–1861. Part I." *Florida Historical Quarterly* 12.1 (July 1933): 3–25.

_____. "The Secession Movement in Florida, 1850–1861. Part II." *Florida Historical Quarterly* 12.2 (October 1933): 45–66.

_____. "The Wrecking Business on the Florida Reef, 1822–1860." *Florida Historical Quarterly* 22.4 (April 1944): 171–199.

Donald, David Herbert. "Died of Democracy." *Why the North Won the Civil War.* David Herbert Donald, ed. New York: Simon & Schuster-Touchstone, 1996. 81–92.

_____. *Lincoln.* New York: Simon & Schuster-Touchstone, 1995.

Durkin, Joseph T. *Armorer of the Confederacy, Secretary Mallory.* New York: Benziger, 1960.

_____. *Confederate Navy Chief: Stephen R. Mallory.* Ed. William N. Still, Jr., Columbia: U. of South Carolina Press, 1987. Reprint of *Stephen R. Mallory.* 1954.

Eaton, Clement. *A History of the Southern Confederacy.* New York: Macmillan, 1954.

Elliott, Robert G. *Ironclad of the Roanoke: Gilbert Elliott's Albemarle.* Shippensburg, PA: White Mane Publishing Co., Inc., 1999.

Family Origins. s.v. "Charles Mallory." http://www.familyorigins.com/users/s/a/l/Thomas-W-Saltmarsh-jr/FAMO1-0001/d25.htm. Internet, 7-26-03.

_____. s.v. "Thomas W. Saltmarsh, Jr." Online. http://www.familyorigins.com/users/s/a/l/Thomas-W-Saltmarsh-jr/FAMO1-0001/d30.htm#P1234,P15; http://www.familyorigins.com/users/s/a/l/Thomas-W-Saltmarsh-jr/FAMO1-0001/d25,d26.htm. Internet, 2003.

Fisher, Ted. "James Dunwoody Bulloch: Covert Confederate." *Bits of Blue and Gray.* Online. http://www.bitsofblueandgray.com/june2002.htm. Internet, 6-1-03.

Florida Footprints, West Florida Genealogical Society. "Conflict at the Spanish Consulate," excerpted by Laura Lee Scott. Online. http://www.rootsweb.com/~flescamb/civwar.htm. Internet, 11-26-04.

Florida Maritime Heritage Trail, Florida Division of Historical Resources. "Key West." Online. http://dhr.dos.state.fl.us/maritime/ports/port.cfm?name-KeyWest. Internet, 7-28-03.

Foner, Eric. *A Short History of Reconstruction, 1863–1877*. New York: Perennial Library-Harper & Row, 1990.

Foote, Shelby. *The Civil War: A Narrative, Red River to Appomattox*. New York: Vintage-Random, 1974.

Fuller, Howard J. "John Ericsson, the Monitors, and Union Naval Strategy." *International Journal of Naval History*. vol. 2, no. 3 (December 2003). n. pag. Online. http://www.ijnhonline.org/volume2_number 3_Dec03/article_fuller_ericsson_dec03.htm. Internet, 6-25-04.

Gage, Rick. "The Laird Rams for the Confederacy." *ACWS Archives*. Online. http://www.acws.co.uk/archives/history/laird.htm. Internet, 6-1-04.

Genealogy.com. *Mallory Family Genealogy Forum*, s.v. "Stephen R. Mallory." Online. http://genforum.genealogy.com/cgibin/pageload.cgi?charles,mallory,1780::mallory::1795.html. Internet, 1-18-04. (By independent Genealogist Dana Leslie Hughes, Clearwater, Florida.)

Geocities. "Port of Spain History." Online. http://www.geocities.com/caribisle_trinidad/history_of_port_of_spain.htm. Internet, 7-26-03.

Grolier Electronic Publishing. s.v. "Daniel Webster." 1955. Online. http://www.marshfield.net/History/webster.htm. Internet, 7-28-03.

A Guide to Key West. New York: Hastings House, 1941.

Hammond, E. Ashby. "Notes on the Medical History of Key West, 1822–1832." *Florida Historical Quarterly* 46.2 (October 1967): 93–110.

Handbook of Texas Online. s.v. "Nashville Convention." Online. http:www.tsha.utexas.edu/handbook/online/articles/view/NN/vbn2.html. Internet, 9-9-03.

_____. s.v. "Reagan, John Henninger." http://www.tsha.utexas.edu/handbook/online/articles/view/RR/fre2.html. Internet, 11-20-03.

Hearn, Chester G. *The Capture of New Orleans, 1862*. Baton Rouge: Louisiana State University Press, 1955.

Hendrick, Burton J. *Statesmen of the Lost Cause: Jefferson Davis and His Cabinet*. 1939. Boston: Little, Brown, 1944.

Hill, Jim Dan. *Sea Dogs of the Sixties: Farragut and Seven Contemporaries*. New York: Barnes, 1935. (Perpetua Edition, 1961).

"History of the Seminole Wars" (pamphlet). Dade City: Florida, Seminole Wars Historic Foundation, Inc. n.d.

Johnson, Ludwell H. *Red River Campaign: Politics and Cotton in the Civil War*. 1958. Kent, OH: Kent State University Press, 1993.

Jones, Robert F. "Rebel Without a War: The *Shenandoah*." *With My Face to the Enemy: Perspectives on the Civil War*. Ed. Robert Cowley. New York: Putnam, 2001. 498–510.

Jones, V.C. "How the South Created a Navy." *Civil War Times Illustrated* 8, no. 4 (July 1969): 4–9, 42–48.

Jones, Virgil Carrington. *The Civil War at Sea, January 1861–March 1862: The Blockaders*. vol. I. New York: Holt, Rinehart, Winston, 1960.

_____. *The Civil War at Sea, March 1862–July 1863: The River War*. vol. II. 1961. Wilmington, NC: Broadfoot, 1990.

_____. *The Civil War at Sea, July 1863–November 1865: The Final Effort*. vol. III. 1962. Wilmington, NC: Broadfoot, 1990.

"Key West and Salvage in 1850." *Florida Historical Quarterly* 8.1 (July 1929): 47–64. (Reprinted from *Hunt's Merchants' Magazine*, January 1852, from *Harper's Magazine*, 1859, and from several other sources.)

Kolchin, Peter. "Reconstruction." *Stanford University*. Online. http://www.stanford.edu/~paherman/reconstruction.htm. Internet, 7-28-04.

Luraghi, Raimondo. *A History of the Confederate Navy*. Trans. Paolo E. Coletta. Annapolis: Naval Institute Press, 1996.

Mahan, Alfred Thayer. *The Influence of Sea Power Upon History 1660–1805*. Englewood Cliffs, NJ: Prentice-Hall, 1980.

Mahin, Dean B. *One War at a Time: The International Dimensions of the American Civil War*. Washington: Brassey's, 1999.

Mahon, John K. *History of the Second Seminole War 1835–1842*. Rev. ed. Gainesville: University of Florida Press, 1967.

Malin, Charles A. "Flogging." *Ratings and Evolution of Jobs in the Navy, Navy Historical Center, Department of the Navy*. Online. http://www.history.navy.mil/faqs/faq78-1.htm# anchor95620. Internet, 7-24-04.

McPherson, James M. *Battle Cry of Freedom: The Civil War Era*. New York: Oxford University Press–Ballantine Books, 1988.
_____. "Failed Southern Strategies." *With My Face to the Enemy: Perspectives on the Civil War*. Ed. Robert Cowley. New York: Putnam, 2001. 72–86.
Meade, Robert Douthat. *Judah P. Benjamin: Confederate Statesman*. New York: Oxford University Press, 1943.
Meador, John. "Florida and the Compromise of 1850." *Florida Historical Quarterly* 39.1 (July 1960): 16–34.
Merli, Frank. "The South on the Seas." *Civil War Times Illustrated* 11, no. 7 (November 1972): 4–8, 39–45.
Merrill, James M. *Battle Flags South: The Story of the Civil War Navies on Western Waters*. Cranbury, NJ: Associated University Presses, 1970.
Miers, Suzanne. *Britain and the Ending of the Slave Trade*. New York: Africana, 1975.
Mohr, Charles H. "St. Francis Barracks, St. Augustine: The Franciscans in Florida." *Florida Historical Quarterly* 7.3 (January 1929): 214–233.
Morison, Samuel Eliot. *The Oxford History of the American People*. New York: Oxford University Press, 1965.
Morrill, Dan L. *The Civil War in Charlotte-Mecklenburg, Chapter Five*. (University of North Carolina at Charlotte.) Online. http://www.danandmary.com/historyofcharch5.htm. Internet, 6-09-03.
Murphy, David J. *Naval Strategy During the American Civil War*. (Research Report, Air War College, Air University, Maxwell Air Force Base, Alabama, April 1999). Online. http://papers.maxwell.af.mil/projects/ay1999/awc/99-175.pdf. Internet, 9-5-02.
Musicant, Ivan. *Divided Waters: The Naval History of the Civil War*. New York: Harper Collins, 1995.
Nash, Howard P., Jr. *A Naval History of the Civil War*. South Brunswick, NJ: Barnes, and London: Thomas Yesloff, 1972.
Navy Historical Center, Department of the Navy. s.v. "The Stevens Battery." Online. http://www.history.navy.mil/photos/sh-usn/usnsh-s/stevns-b.htm. Internet, 7-24-04
New Hampshire Division of Historical Resources. s.v. "Zachariah Chandler." Online. http://www.state.nh.us/nhdhr/warheroes/chandlerz.html. Internet, 2-4-04.
Owsley, Frank Lawrence. *The C.S.S. Florida: Her Building and Operations*. New Edition. 1965. Tuscaloosa: University of Alabama Press, 1987.
_____. *King Cotton Diplomacy: Foreign Relations of the Confederate States of America*. 2nd ed., revised by Harriet Chappell Owsley). Chicago: University of Chicago Press, 1959.
Patrick, Rembert W. *Jefferson Davis and His Cabinet*. Baton Rouge: Louisiana State University Press. 1944.
Pearce, George F. *Pensacola during the Civil War: A Thorn in the Side of the Confederacy*. Gainesville: University Press of Florida, 2000.
Pensacola Home & Savings Association, Pensacola, Florida. "Stephen R. Mallory, Secretary of the Navy, Confederate States of America" (pamphlet), n.d., n. pag.
Potter, David M. "Jefferson Davis and the Political Factors in Confederate Defeat." *Why the North Won the Civil War*. David Herbert Donald, ed. New York: Simon & Schuster–Touchstone, 1996. 93–113.
Prim, Gorrell Clinton, Jr. "History and Confederate Leadership: A Study in the Intellectual History of the Civil War." Diss., Appalachian State University, 1974.
Reed, Rowena. *Combined Operations in the Civil War*. Annapolis: Naval Institute Press, 1978.
St. Michael Parish. "St. Michael Cemetery." Online. http://stmichael.ptdiocese.org/cemetery.htm. Internet, 11-05-04.
Sandgren, Andreas, and Spyken Lund. "Causes of the Civil War in America (1861–1865)." Online. (Attributed to Jordan, Winthrop D. *The Americans* (Evanston, IL: McDougal, Littell, 310–311). http://www.student.lu.se/~svp95asa/Civwar/Civil.htm. Internet, 5-5-99.
Scharf, J. Thomas. *History of the Confederate States Navy: From Its Organization to the Surrender of Its Last Vessel*. c. 1886. New York: Gramercy-Random House, 1996.
Scott, Kenneth. "The City of Wreckers, Key West Letters of 1838." *Florida Historical Quarterly* 25.2 (October 1946): 191–202.
_____. "Secession in Florida-Pensacola on its Own, Documents, Letters and other Papers," *Florida Historical Quarterly* 26.4 (April 1949): 284–300.
Shaughnessy, Edward L. "The Iceman Melteth: O'Neill's Return to Cultural Origins." *The Eugene O'Neill Newsletter*, Suffolk University, 1979. Online. http:www.eoneill.com/library/on/shaughnessy/newsletter79.htm. Internet, 12-17-03.

Silverstone, Paul H. *Warships of the Civil War Navies.* Annapolis: Naval Institute Press, 1989.
Simson, Jay W. *Naval Strategies of the Civil War: Confederate Innovations and Federal Opportunism.* Nashville: Cumberland House, 2001.
Smith, Royce Lee. "Union and Confederate Secretaries of the Navy: A Comparative Study of the Secretaries During the Civil War." Diss. U.S. Army Command and General Staff College, 1995.
Speer, Lonnie R. *Portals to Hell: Military Prisons of the Civil War.* Mechanicsburg, PA: Stackpole Books, 1997. Online. (Excerpt at http://www.correctionhistory.org/html/chronicl/cw_pows/html/cwpows3.html.) Internet, 2-3-04.
Spencer, Warren F. "Ships for the South: James D. Bulloch, Confederate Agent in Europe." *Divided We Fall: Essays on Confederate Nation Building.* Ed. John M. Belohlavek and Lewis N. Wynne. St. Leo, FL: St. Leo College Press, 1991. 39–69.
Stackpole, Edouard A. Introduction. *Mystic Seaport and the Origins of Freedom,* by Phillip R. Mallory. New York: The Newcomen Society in North America, 1954. n. pag.
Steers, Edward, Jr. *Blood on the Moon: The Assassination of Abraham Lincoln.* Lexington, KY: University Press of Kentucky, 2001.
Stern, Philip Van Doren. *When the Guns Roared: World Aspects of the American Civil War.* Garden City, NY: Doubleday, 1965.
Still, William N., Jr. *Iron Afloat: The Story of the Confederate Armorclads.* n.p. Vanderbilt University Press, 1971.
The Straight Dope. "What Did the U.S. Marines Do During the Civil War?" Online. http://www.straightdope.com/mailbag.mmarines.html. Internet, 6-12-03.
Surdam, David G. "The Confederate Naval Buildup: Could More Have Been Accomplished?" *Naval War College Review* 54, no. 1 (Winter 2001): 107–128. Online. http://www.nwc.navy.mil/press/Review/2001/Winter/art7-w01.htm. Internet, 5-20-03.
_____. "The Union Navy's Blockade Reconsidered." *Naval War College Review* 51, no. 4, sequence 364, (Autumn 1998): 105–127. Online. http://www.nwc.navy.mil/press/Review/1998/autumn/art5-a98.htm. Internet, 5-14-03.
Taylor, John M. *Confederate Raider: Raphael Semmes of the Alabama.* Washington: Brassey's, 1994.
_____. "The Fiery Trail of the *Alabama.*" *With My Face to the Enemy: Perspectives on the Civil War.* Ed. Robert Cowley. New York: Putnam, 2001. 429–442.
Theberge, Albert E. *The Coast Survey in the Civil War 1861–1865, Volume I of the History of the Commissioned Corps of the National Oceanic and Atmospheric Administration,* "The Strategic Contribution." Online. http://www.lib.noaa.gov/edocs/TITLE.htm#TITLE. Internet, 9-9-02.
Thomas, Hugh. *The Slave Trade: The Story of the Atlantic Slave Trade: 1440–1870.* New York: Simon & Schuster, 1997.
Thompson, Arthur W. "The Railroad Background of the Florida Senatorial Election of 1851." *Florida Historical Quarterly* 31.3 (January 1953): 181–195.
Todd, Charles Burr. *History of Redding, CT.* Online. "History of Redding." http://www.historyofredding.com/HRFamilies.htm#Mallory. Internet, 7-14-03.
Tour of Olde Towne Daphne. "The Village (La Aldea)." Online. http://www.tourofdaphne.gulfpath.org/Pages/new_page_1.htm. Internet, 7-26-03.
Tucker, Spencer. *A Short History of the Civil War at Sea.* SR Books-Scholarly Resources, 2002.
Twain, Mark. *A Connecticut Yankee in King Arthur's Court.* Project Gutenberg eBook #86. Release date, July 7, 2004, n. pag. http://www.gutenberg.org/etxt/86. Internet, 10-28-04.
Uncommonwealth of Pennsylvania. "Historic Nazareth." Online. http://webtrail.accu-find.com/map/areas/naz_8.cfm. Internet, 7-28-03.
Underwood, Rodman L. *Death on the Nueces.* Austin: Eakin Press, 2000.
_____. *Waters of Discord: The Union Blockade of Texas During the Civil War.* Jefferson, NC: McFarland, 2003.
University of Hawaii. "CSS *Shenandoah.*" Online. http://www.skaggs.org/html/u_of_hawaii.html. Internet, 3-9-04.
Vandiver, Frank E. *Rebel Brass: The Confederate Command System.* Introd. T. Harry Williams. Baton Rouge: Louisiana State University Press, 1956.
Wagner, Margaret E., Gary W. Gallagher, and Paul Finkelman, eds. *Library of Congress Civil War Desk Reference.* s.v. "Stephen R. Mallory." New York: Simon & Schuster, c.2002. 185.
Ward, W.E.F. *The Royal Navy and the Slavers: The Suppression of the Atlantic Slave Trade.* New York: Random House-Pantheon Books, 1969.
Weddle, Kevin J. "There Should Be No Bungling About the Blockade: The Blockade Board of 1861 and

the Making of Union Naval Strategy," *International Journal of Naval History*, from the U.S. Army War College, Princeton University. Online. http://www.ijnhonline.org/volume1_number1_Apr02/article_weddle_blockade_board.doc.htm#_ednref24. Internet, 9-9-02.

Weeks, Gregory. Review of *Hunters in the Shallows: A History of the PT Boat*, by Curtis L. Nelson. *International Journal of Naval History* 2, no. 3 (December 2003). Online. http://www.ijnhonline.org/volume2_number3_Dec03/review_nelson_weeks_Dec03.htm. Internet, 6-25-04.

Wise, Stephen R. *Lifeline of the Confederacy: Blockade Running During the Civil War*. Columbia: University of South Carolina Press, 1988.

_____. "Mallory, Stephen Russell." *American National Biography*. Ed. John A. Garraty and Mark C. Carnes. vol. 14. New York: Oxford University Press, 1999. 380.

Woods, Robert H. "Cruise of the (CSS) Clarence, Tacony-Archer" (taken from the Southern Historical Society Papers, Vol. XXIII, January-December 1895.) *Confederate Navy Research Center, Mobile, Alabama*. Online. http://www.csnavy.org/shsp/shsp,clar-tac-arch,v23,p274.htm. Internet, 6-8-03.

Wynne, Lewis N., and Robert A. Taylor. *Florida in the Civil War*. Charleston: Tempus-Arcadia, 2002.

Index

Abbeville, SC 174
abolitionists 62, 63
Adams, Charles Francis 118, 143
Adams, John Quincy 44
Addison, Joseph 214
Ad-Vance 145
African slave trade *see* slavery
Alabama (state) 7, 33, 65, 66, 68, 70, 72, 77, 79, 84, 135, 136, 194, 210
Alabama, CSS 117, 118, 122–125, 164
Albatross, CSS 146
Albemarle, CSS 138, 158, 159, 164
Albemarle Sound 158
Alexander (maritime commerce) 161
Alfred H. Partridge (maritime commerce) 119
Alleghanian (maritime commerce) 160
Alliance (maritime commerce) 161
America, USS 121
anaconda plan 105
Anderson, Joseph R. 133
Appomattox Court House 159
Archer (maritime commerce) 120
Arkansas (state) 45, 77
Arkansas, CSS 100, 102, 108, 109
Arman, Lucien 142
Armstrong, James (USN) 72
Army of Northern Virginia 166
Army of the Potomac 166
Arthur, USS 192
Asboth, Alexander Sandor USA 180, 191
Atalanta, CSS 163; see also *Tallahassee*

Atlanta, CSS 129, 130
Atlanta Rolling Mill 132

Bahama Banks 8
Bahia, Brazil 121, 164
Baltic, CSS 130
Baltimore, MD 93
Banks, Nathaniel USA 120
Barnum, P. T. 93
Baron De Kalb, USS 150
Barracouta (British bark) 126
Barron, Samuel (CSN) 72, 96, 143, 144, 147
Barvay and Company 143
Bat (blockade runner) 146
Baton Rouge, LA 109
Battle of New Orleans 106–108; *see also* specific vessels involved
Battle of Shiloh 107, 200
Battle of the Wilderness 159
Bayne, Thomas L. (CSA) 145
Beall, John Yates (CSN) 161
Beall, Lloyd (CSN–Marines) 87
Beaufort, SC 49, 96
Beauregard, Pierre G. T. (CSA) 85, 107, 128, 129, 152, 153, 157, 159, 165, 175
Bell, John 63
Bellona Foundry 134
Benjamin, Judah P. 41, 70, 80, 81, 90, 135, 175, 195–197
Bering Sea 126
Bienville (mail steamer) 90
Bishop, Henry R. 92, 188, 202
Boarding School for Young Gentlemen 9, 16
Boyce, William Waters 181, 182
Brady, Mathew B. 65
Bridgeport, CT 5–7, 16, 46, 92, 93, 182, 184, 188, 189, 191, 192, 202, 204

Brooke, John Mercer 86, 94, 95, 139
Brooke rifle (gun) 102, 105, 138, 139, 156, 158
Brooklyn, USS 72, 106, 115
Broome, James E. 62
Brown, Isaac N. (CSN) 108
Brown, John 49, 50, 62
Brown, Joseph E. 68
Brown, Thomas 21
Browne, Jefferson 10, 11
Bruce, Kathleen 6
Buchanan, Franklin (CSN) 82–84, 97–99, 156
Buchanan, James 35, 41, 46, 49, 68–70, 72
Bulloch, James Dunwoody (CSN) 83, 84, 90–92, 95, 110, 117–119, 121, 122, 125, 126, 140–147, 153, 162, 167, 168, 170, 171
Bureau for the Defense of Coastal Waters and Rivers 149
Bureau of Details and Orders 83
Bureau of Medicine and Surgery 86, 87
Bureau of Orders and Detail 86
Bureau of Ordnance and Hydrography 86, 87
Bureau of Provisions and Clothing 86
Burke, Martin (CSA) 179, 181
Bushnell, David 148
Butcher, Matthew J. 122

Cabell, Edward Carrington 21
Cairo, IL 102
Cairo, USS 150, 151
Caleb Cushing (US revenue cutter) 120
Calhoun, John C. 12, 21, 22
California (state) 32

Cameron, Simon 93
Cape Fear River 164
Carrick-on-Suir, Ireland 5
Carter, Jonathan (CSN) 131
Carter, Robert R. CSN 145
Cato, a Tragedy 214
Chameleon, CSS 163; see also *Tallahassee*
Chandler, Zachariah 181
Charleston, CSS 138, 155, 165
Charleston, SC 70, 85, 87, 96, 100, 107, 115, 116, 118, 128, 129, 136, 138, 147, 150, 152, 153, 165, 209
Charleston & Savannah railroad 164
Charleston Harbor 66, 151, 153, 155, 157, 173
Charleston Mercury (newspaper) 110
Charlotte, NC 136, 137, 175
Charlotte Navy Yard 137
Chase, Salmon P. 121
Chase, William H. 68–70
Cheops (cover name) 144
Chesapeake Bay 160, 161
Chesnut, James 194
Chesnut, James, Jr. 78
Chesnut, Mary Boykin (wife of James) 78, 193, 194, 195
Chickamauga, CSS (formerly blockade runner *Edith*) 163
Chicora, CSS 128, 129, 165
Cincinnati (USN) 108
City of Richmond, CSS 144
City Point, VA 165
Clarence (maritime commerce) 119
Clay, Clement C., Jr. 70, 111, 113
Clay, Henry 21, 22, 24, 31–34, 40
Clay, Virginia (wife of Clement C.) 183, 193, 195, 201
Clinch, Duncan L. USA 15
Cobb, Howell (CSA) 178
Collins Steamship Line 52, 59, 60
Columbiad guns 69
Columbus, GA 136, 138
Columbus, KY 104
Columbus Naval Iron Works 134
Comenius, John Amos 9
Commodore Barney, USS 150
Commodore Jones, USS 150
Company G, 1st U.S. Artillery 72
Company H, Seventh Vermont Regiment 191
Compromise of 1850 20, 22, 24, 32, 33
Confederate Committee on Naval Affairs 85
Confederate Naval Foundry and Iron Works 136
Confederate Navy Yard, Rocketts Landing 136
Confederate State Acid Works 137
Confederate States of America 5,
65, 74, 77–80, 92, 114, 158, 173, 174, 212
Confederate water battery 69
Congress, USS 99
A Connecticut Yankee in King Arthur's Court 5
Conrad, Charles M. 77, 85, 91, 111, 112
Cooke, James W. (CSN) 158, 159
Coquette, CSS 145, 146
Coquette, USS 161
Courtenay, Thomas E. (CSN) 150
Crenshaw, Edward (CSN) 163
Crimean War 91
Cromwell Steamship Line 90
Crow, CSS 161
Cuba 11, 13, 39–44, 46, 48, 49, 115, 118, 144
Cumberland, USS 99
Cunard Line 59
Cushing, William B. (USN) 164

Dahlgren, J.A. (USN) 166
Danville, VA 175
Dauphin Island 156
Davenport, H. K. (USN) 98
David, CSS 153
Davidson, Hunter 149
Davis, Jefferson 46, 67, 68, 70, 74; as CSA president 77–81, 83, 85, 90, 92, 105, 107, 109, 111, 134, 135, 138, 139, 167, 169, 171, 174–176, 194
Davis, Varina Howell 197–199
Davis, William C. 194
De Bree, Paymaster John (CSN) 86
Deer (blockade runner) 146
Delaware, USS 150
Democratic Party 20, 22, 23, 35, 37, 49
Department of Steam Engineering 87
Dismal Swamp Canal 96
District of West Florida 191
Dix, John A. USA 93
Dobbin, James C. 53, 55, 56
Dodge, CSS 131
Douglas, Stephen A. 33
Drewry's Bluff 100, 163
Duke, Basil (CSA) 176
Duncan, Johnson Kelly (CSA) 107
Durkin, Joseph T. 5, 6, 83

Edith, CSS 163
Edwards Ferry 138
Elizabeth City, NC 96
Elizabeth River 99
Enoch Train see *Manassas*
Enrica 122
Episcopal bishop of Florida 63
Erlanger and Company 142
Essex, USS 109
Farragut, David G. (USN) 106, 109, 156, 157
Fernandina, FL 96
Fifth Alabama Cavalry 191
Fifth Virginia Cavalry Regiment 160
Finegan, Joseph 67
Fingal, CSS 118, 129
First Texas Cavalry 120
Fitzpatrick, Benjamin 70
Florida (state) 5–8, 11, 13–15, 18–25, 29–31, 39, 40, 42, 45, 47–52, 54, 57–59, 61–63, 65–72, 77–79, 91, 96, 103, 117, 118, 133, 136, 145, 146, 170, 176, 180, 182, 187, 188, 191, 192, 195, 202, 203, 205–207, 209–213
Florida (territory) 8, 12, 14, 19
Florida, CSS 117–121, 164
Florida Baptist state convention 63
Floridian and Journal (newspaper) 43
Floyd, John B. 66, 67
Foote, Andrew Hull (USN) 107
Forrest, French (CSN) 86
Fort Advanced Redoubt 69
Fort Alcatraz 99
Fort Barrancas 66, 69, 191
Fort Clark 96
Fort Donelson 104, 107
Fort Fisher 164
Fort Gaines 156
Fort Hatteras 96
Fort Henry 107
Fort Jackson 106
Fort Jefferson 49, 67
Fort Lafayette 178, 179, 182–184, 189
Fort McRae 66, 72
Fort Morgan 156
Fort Pickens 66–70
Fort Pulaski 96, 129
Fort St. Phillip 106
Fort Sumter 173
Fort Taylor 67
Fort Williams 158
Fourth Indiana Cavalry 178
Fox, Gustavus Vasa 141, 162
Francis Elmore maritime commerce 160
Fraser, Trenholm and Company 91, 146
Fredericksburg, CSS 100, 175
Fulton, CSS 88

Gaines, CSS 156
Georgetown College 203
Georgia (state) 12, 45, 48, 49, 65–68, 76, 79, 80, 85, 90, 95, 96, 118, 129, 132–134, 136, 138, 150, 163, 164, 176, 178, 195, 199, 203
Georgia, CSS (commerce raider, formerly *Japan*) 124

Index

Georgia, CSS (ironclad classified as floating battery) 130, 164
Gloire (French frigate) 91, 140
Golden Rocket (maritime commerce) 115
Golden Rod, USS 161
Gosport Navy Yard, VA 86, 94, 96, 104, 110, 114, 127, 135, 136, 145, 169
Grant, Ulysses S (USA) 107
Graves, William A. (CSN) 158
Graves Shipyard 136
Great Britain and the Foreign Enlistment Act 91, 117; and laws of neutrality 91, 116; and the Proclamation of Neutrality 91, 117
Great Pee Dee River 136
Greyhound, USS 150
Guinard, S. Y. 19

Halifax, Nova Scotia, Canada 163
Hammond, John Hays 44, 66
Hardee, William J. (CSA) 164
Harpers Ferry, VA 49, 50, 62
Harrison, Mrs. Burton 197
Harvest Moon, USS 166
Harvey Birch maritime commerce 117
Hatteras Inlet 96
Havana, Cuba 8, 24, 49, 144–146, 172
Hawkins, George S. 68, 197
Hearn, Chester 113
Hebert, P.O. (CSA) 131
Hendrick, Burton J. 6
Hill, Benjamin H. 78, 178, 194
Hill, Benjamin H., Jr. 178
Hill, D.H. (CSA) 133
Hoge, Francis L. (CSN) 160, 161
Hogg, Thomas E. (CSN) 98
Hoke, Robert F. (CSA) 158
Holbrook, William C. USA 191
Hollins, George N. (CSN) 107, 108
Holt, Joseph 67, 72, 179, 180
Horseman (maritime commerce) 161
Howell, William F. 86
Hughes, Dana Leslie 7
Hull, F.S. 117
Hunley, CSS 151, 152
Hunter, William W. (CSN) 131, 164
Huntsville, CSS 138

Ingomar (river steamer purchased to scavenge) 103
Ingraham, Duncan M. CSN 86, 129, 131, 132, 157
Investigator maritime commerce 116
Ironsides, USS 152
Isabel (mail steamer) 49
Island No. 10 104

Jackson, Andrew 7, 45
Jackson, CSS (formerly *Muscogee*) 138
Jacksonville, FL 96
Jacob Bell maritime commerce 120
James River 100
James River Squadron 83, 97
Jamestown 100; see also *Thomas Jefferson*
Japan (Scottish brig) 124
John Hughes and Company 100
Johnson, Andrew 180
Johnston, James D. (CSN) 130
Johnston, Joseph E. (CSA) 175
Jones, Catesby ap R. (CSN) 139
Jones, Virgil Carrington 194

Kansas-Nebraska Act 34
Kearsarge, USS 125, 164
Kell, John McIntosh (CSN) 100, 114, 123
Kennard, J.S. (CSN) 164
Kennon, Beverly (CSN) 84, 85
Key West 5–8, 10–14, 16, 18, 22, 23, 29, 31, 39, 43, 46, 61, 210, 214
Key West Inquirer (*Enquirer*) (newspaper) 13
Kinston, NC 161
Kneeland, G.H. USA 178
Knights of the Golden Circle 39

Lafayette Fire Department 12, 13
La Grange, GA 178
Lancaster, USS 98
La Palata River 30
Lark (blockade runner) 146
Lawrenceburg, NC 133
Lecompton Constitution 34, 35
Lee, Francis D. (CSN) 152
Lee, Robert E. (CSA) 49, 96, 104, 107, 126, 137, 138, 143, 155, 157–159, 161, 163, 164, 166, 169, 171, 174, 175, 195, 209
Lee, S.S. (CSN) 104
Lincoln, Abraham 38, 62, 63, 66, 67, 70, 72, 73, 90, 121, 183, 188
Liverpool, England 91, 126
Lockwood, Henry H. USA 161
Louisiana (state) 31, 42, 67, 77, 84, 107, 109, 115, 118, 130, 136, 137
Louisiana, CSS 102, 103, 105, 106
Louisiana Purchase 7, 31, 42
Lovell, Mansfield (CSA) 107, 108
Low, John (CSN) 118
Loyall, Benjamin P. (CSN) 162
Luraghi, Raimondo 6, 87, 92, 100, 104, 150
Lynch, William F. (CSN) 133

Macon, CSS 164
Madeira, Portugal 126
Madrid, Spain 7, 40, 46

Maffitt, John Newland (CSN) 118, 146
Magruder, John 99
Maine 31
Mallory, Angela Moreno (Stephen's wife) 17, 19, 187, 201
Mallory, Atilla "Attie" Fitzpatrick (Stephen's daughter) 187–189, 191, 202–205, 209, 210
Mallory, Charles (Stephen Mallory's father) 6–8
Mallory, Cora S. (Stephen Mallory's granddaughter) 6
Mallory, Ellen (Stephen Mallory' mother) 8–12; *see also* Russell, Ellen
Mallory, Francis "Frankie" (Stephen's son) 35, 187, 193, 201
Mallory, John (Stephen Mallory's alleged father) 6
Mallory, John (Stephen Mallory's older brother) 5, 7
Mallory, Margaret "Maggie" (Mrs. Henry Bishop) (Stephen's daughter) 59, 92, 93, 187, 188, 194, 202
Mallory, Nellie (Stephen's daughter) 193, 201
Mallory, Ruby Angela (Stephen's daughter) 187–189, 191, 196, 197, 202–205, 210
Mallory, Stephen "Buddy" Russell, Jr. 6, 179, 187, 189, 190, 202, 203, 212
Mallory, Stephen Russell: early life 5–7, 11–23, 35, 182, 183, 189, 194, 202, 203, 209, 210; later years 202–214; as Navy secretary 77, 78, 80–92, 94–139, 141–146, 148–178; as prisoner 178–184, 187–192; as senator 20–25, 29, 30–62, 63, 65–73, 77–80, 92, 111, 180, 182
Maloney, Walter C. (early Key West settler) 8, 10
Manassas, CSS (formerly *Enoch Train*) 105, 106
Marcy, William 40
Mare Island Navy Yard 99
Marine Corps 87
Marion, USS 121
Marvin, William 10–14, 18, 19, 182–184, 206
Mary Anne maritime commerce 161
Maury, Matthew Fontaine CSN 55, 84, 95, 124, 149
Maury, William Lowndes (CSN) 124
McBlair, Charles H. (CSN) 108
McIntosh, Charles F. (CSN) 105
McIntosh, James 16
McIntosh, Lydia (wife of James, Stephen Mallory's cousin) 16–18

McPherson, James M. 167
McRae, CSS 114, 116
Mecklenburg Gun Factory 137
Mecklenburg Iron Works 136
Memminger, Christopher G. 80, 81
Memphis, TN 102, 108
Merrimack, USS 94, 97, 129; see also *Virginia*
Miami, USS 158
Milledgeville, CSS 138
Milton, John 73, 74
Minnesota, USS 99
Minor, George (CSN) 86
Mississippi (state) 7, 21, 31, 66, 67, 77
Mississippi, CSS 101, 102–106
Mississippi, USS 106
Mississippi River 67, 85, 100, 102, 104–113, 115, 116, 127, 128, 131, 169, 171
Mississippi River Squadron (Union) 107
Missouri, CSS 130, 131
Missouri Compromise of 1820 20, 31, 33
Mitchell, John K. (CSN) 86, 103, 107, 165
Mobile, AL 8, 9, 12, 84, 85, 87, 102, 109, 119, 130, 138, 150, 151, 153, 155, 157
Mobile, CSS 130
Mobile Bay 155, 157
Monitor, USS 98, 99
Montauk, USS 150
Montgomery, AL 67–70
Montgomery Hall hotel 194, 195
Montmorenci maritime commerce 116
Moore, A.B. 72
Moreno, Don Francisco 19, 187, 191, 192, 203
Morgan, CSS 156
Morton, Jackson 20, 21, 24, 57, 65, 77, 78
"Mosquito Fleet" (Hollins) 106
"Mosquito Fleet" (Maury) 95, 96
Mound City, USS 108
Murray, E.C. 102
Muscogee, CSS (later named the *Jackson*) 138

Nashville, TN 104
Nashville, CSS (cruiser converted to blockade runner *Thomas L. Wragg*, then became privateer *Rattlesnake*) 116, 117
Nashville, CSS (ironclad, iron unavailable, not completed) 130, 138, 139, 155
Nashville Convention 21, 22
Nassau 118
Naval Ordnance Works 135
Naval reform act 55. 56
Naval Retiring Board 55, 56, 83, 95

Naval Station, Charlotte, NC 135
Nebraska, organization of territory 33, 34
Neuse, CSS 137, 138, 159, 165
Neuse River 96, 133, 137, 138, 157, 159, 162
New Bern, NC 96, 159, 161, 162
New Ironsides, USS 153
New Mexico (state) 32, 70
New Orleans, LA 59, 77, 84, 85, 90, 100, 102–114, 116, 119, 120, 127, 130, 133, 135, 136, 141, 145, 151, 169, 195, 200; see also Battle of New Orleans
New York Sixth Regiment Infantry 202
Norfolk, VA 94, 96
North Carolina (state) 29, 47, 52, 77, 95–97, 133–138, 143, 153, 155, 157–159, 161, 164, 169, 171, 174–176, 205
North Carolina, CSS 137, 155
North Carolina Powder Manufacturing Company 137
Northwest Ordinance 31
Noyes, A.B. (CSN) 145

Ocracoke Inlet 96
Office of Naval Constructor 87
Office of navy secretary 86
Office of Ordnance and Hydrography 139, 149
Okhotsk Sea 126
Olustee, CSS 163; see also *Tallahassee*
Onondaga, USS 165
Order of Franciscans 20
Ostend Manifesto 41
Otero (cover name) 117
Owl (blockade runner) 146
Owsley, Frank Lawrence, Jr. 125

Page, Thomas Jefferson (CSN) 144
Palmetto State, CSS 128, 129, 165
Pamlico Sound 96, 159
Parker, William H. (CSN) 174
Patapsco, USS 165
Patrick, Rembert W. 196
Patrick Henry, CSS (school ship, formerly *Yorktown*) 100, 163, 174
Pearsall (maritime commerce) 161
Pearson, Bird M. 21
Penguin (blockade runner) 146
Pensacola, FL 5, 7, 15–19, 21, 22, 30, 46, 49, 57–59, 62, 63, 66–72, 74, 88, 92, 187, 188, 191–193, 199, 202–205, 207–211, 213
Pensacola, USS 59
Pensacola Bay, Florida 66, 69, 74, 85, 88
Pensacola Navy Yard 72, 74; see also Warrington Navy Yard
Perry, Madison Starke 62, 63, 68

Pickett, George E. (CSA) 162
Pierce, Franklin 34, 41, 55, 79
Plymouth, NC 158, 159, 161, 164
Port of Spain, Trinidad 7
Port Royal, SC 96, 130
Porter, David D. (USN) 109, 150
Porter, John Luke (CSN) 87, 94, 137
Powell, Levin M. (USA) 15, 17, 18
Powhatan, USS 115
Prim, Gorrell, Jr. 34
Prioleau, Charles K. 91

Quincy Commonwealth (newspaper) 208

Raines, G.J. (CSA) 149
Raleigh, CSS 137, 159, 160
"ram fever" 106
Randolph, Victor (CSN) 84
ransom bond 114, 116, 119
Rappahannock River 160
Rattlesnake (privateer) 117; see also *Nashville*
Read, Charles W. (CSN) 119–121
Reagan, John H. 80, 81
Redding see Bridgeport, CT
Reliance, USS 160
Republican Party 39, 49, 62, 73, 207, 209
Richmond, VA 81, 84, 87, 92, 95, 100, 103, 104, 118, 128, 131–134, 136, 142, 149, 152, 161, 163, 166, 174, 177, 182, 189, 192, 194–200, 203, 209
Richmond, CSS 100, 104
Rio Grande expedition 120
River Defense Fleet (CSA) 107, 108
Roanoke Island, NC 96
Roanoke River 137, 138, 158, 159, 164
Rochelle, James Henry 209
Rosser, Thomas L. (CSN) 160
Rousseau, Lawrence (CSN) 86, 100, 107
Russell, Ellen 5–7; see also Mallory, Ellen
Russell, Lord John 116, 143
Russell, Stephen 7
Russell, Stephen (Jr.?) 7

Sabine, USS 121
St. Augustine, FL 19, 30, 96
St. Augustine Examiner (newspaper) 205
St. John's Church, Tallahassee, FL 62
St. Marks, FL 136
St. Michael Catholic Church, Pensacola, FL 19
St. Michael Cemetery, Pensacola, FL 5, 210, 211
St. Paul's Episcopal Church, Key West, FL 12

San Domingo revolution 40
San Jacinto (USN) 118
San Salvador maritime commerce 98
Santa Rosa Island 66, 69
Sarah A. Boyce (maritime commerce) 163
Satellite, USS 160
Satterlee, Hayes 207
Savannah, GA 12, 49, 84, 85, 87, 90, 96, 100, 117, 118, 129, 130, 136, 138, 150, 164
Savannah, CSS 138, 164
Scharf, J. Thomas 6, 61, 88
Scott, Winfield (USA) 67, 73, 105
Sea King see Shenandoah
Second Seminole war 15, 45, 46
Secret Service Corps (CSN) 150
Selma, CSS 156
Selma Cannon Factory 135
Selma Navy Yard and Ordnance Works 136
Seminole, USS 59
Seminole Indians 7, 15, 17, 39, 44
Semmes, Raphael (CSN) 83, 84, 90, 114–116, 123, 145, 165, 174, 195, 197
Semple, James A. (CSN) 86
Seward, F. W. 93
Seward, William H. 34, 35, 73, 93, 181, 184
Seymour and Blair Club, Milton, FL 209
Shark, USS 14
Shelby Iron Company 134
Shenandoah, CSS (commerce raider, formerly *Sea King*) 125, 126, 181
The Shepherd of the Valley (newspaper) 47
Sherman, William T. (USA) 164, 175
Shirley, John T. 102
Simms, Charles C. (CSN) 130
Simson, Jay W. 98
Sinclair, Arthur (CSN) 105
Sisters of the Sacred Heart 210
slavery 20–22, 31–44
Slemmer, Adam J. USA 72
Slidell, John 67, 68, 72
Smith, Kirby (CSA) 176
South Carolina (state) 44, 49, 65, 66, 77, 78, 80, 95, 96, 116, 128–130, 136, 165, 166, 173, 174, 176, 181, 193, 199
Southfield, USS 158
Sphinx (cover name) 144
Spotswood, Dr. W. A. (CSN) 86
Spratt, Leonidas W. 65
Squib, CSS 153
Stag (blockade runner) 146
Stanton, Edwin M. 178
Star of the West (maritime commerce) 173

Stephens, Alexander H. 79, 81
Stepping Stones, USS 150
Stern, Philip Van Doren 145
Stevens, Henry Kennedy (CSN) 108
Stevens Battery 53, 88
Still, William N. 164
Stockton, Robert F. 51, 52
Stonewall, CSS 144, 172
Submarine Battery Service (CSN) 149
Sumter, CSS 114–116
Supply, USS 72
Swan, CSS 161

Tacony maritime commerce 120
Tallahassee, CSS (formerly *Atalanta*, renamed *Olustee*, renamed *Chameleon*) 163
Tallahassee Sentinel (newspaper) 208
Tampico, Mexico 59
Tar River 137, 138
Tattnall, Josiah (CSN) 84
Tecumseh, USS 157
Tennessee (state) 21, 63, 77, 102, 104, 109, 111, 133, 135, 179
Tennessee, CSS 138, 156, 157
Tennessee, CSS (destroyed on slip, never commissioned) 102, 106, 108
Texas, CSS 100
Texas (state) 32, 39, 45, 77, 100, 119, 120, 130, 131, 166, 175, 178
Texas Marine Department 131
Thomas, John Henry 117
Thomas Jefferson, CSS (formerly *Jamestown*) 100
Thomas L. Wragg, CSS 117; see also *Nashville*
Tiddball, Edward M. (CSN) 86
Tift, Amos 11
Tift, Asa 11–13, 20, 100, 104
Tift, Nelson 100–102, 105, 129
Tift brothers 100, 101 102–105, 108, 112
Toombs, Robert 80, 81
Torpedo Bureau (CSA) 149
Torpedo Bureau (CSN) 87
Toucy, Isaac 72
Trans-Mississippi Department 109, 176, 178
Treaty of 1819 7
Treaty of Guadalupe Hidalgo 20, 32
Tredegar Iron Works 95, 97, 104, 105, 132–134, 136
Trent (British mail packet) 118
Trent crisis 118
Trinidad, West Indies 5–7
Tritonio, USS 150
Tucker, Spencer C. 150
Turner, Nat 40

Tuscaloosa, CSS 138
Tuscarora, USS 116, 122
Twain, Mark 5
Two Brothers, USS 161

Underwriter, USS 162
Utah 32

Vance, Zebulon B. 133
Van Dorn, Earl (CSA) 109
Vera Cruz, Mexico 59
Vicksburg, MS 108, 109
"The Village" (present-day Daphne, Alabama) 8, 9
Virginia (state) 34, 49, 50, 52, 53, 57, 58, 72, 77, 86, 92, 96, 99, 105, 133–137, 143, 152, 155, 160, 164, 174, 175, 177, 194
Virginia, CSS 82, 95–101, 108–110, 113, 124, 127–129, 133, 168, 171, 173
Virginia, USS 121
Virginia II, CSS 100, 175

Wachusett, USS 121, 164
Waddell, James I. (CSN) 106, 126
Wade, Thomas F. (USN) 192
Walker, Leroy P. 79–81
Wall, William H. 12
War Department building 92
War of 1812 7
Ward, George T. 65
Ward, William H. (CSN) 163
Warner, James W. (CSN) 104
Warrington, FL 69, 191
Warrington Navy Yard 191; see also Pensacola Navy Yard
Warrior (British ironclad warship) 140
Washington, DC 21, 24, 31, 46, 48, 65, 66, 69–73, 93, 97, 98, 143, 182, 183, 192–194, 199, 202, 203
Washington, GA 176, 178
Water Witch, USS 30
Webb, James 14
Webb, William H. (CSN) 129
Webster, Daniel 12
Welles, Gideon 99, 107
West Florida Commercial (newspaper) 208
Whig Party 20–23, 57, 65
Whistling Wing maritime commerce 119
Whitehead, John 8
Whitehead, William A. 8, 14, 18
Whiting, Samuel 118
Whittle, William C. (CSN) 107
Wigfall, Louis T. (CSA) 178
Williamson, William P. (CSN) 87, 94
Wilmington Journal (newspaper) 111

Wilmington, NC 96, 159, 164–166, 169
Wilson, William (USA) 202, 203
Wilson's Zouaves *see* New York Sixth Regiment Infantry
Wise, Stephen R. 6
Wolfe, J.D. 207

Wood, John Taylor (CSN) 160, 161
Worden, John L. (USN) 99
Wren (blockade runner) 146

Yazoo City 108
Yazoo River 108

yellow fever 8, 10, 119, 205
Yorktown see *Patrick Henry*
Young, Mahlon M. (USA) 191
Young Man's Literary Association 205
Yulee, David Levy 21–24, 34, 49, 66–68, 70, 182

www.ingramcontent.com/pod-product-compliance
Ingram Content Group UK Ltd.
Pitfield, Milton Keynes, MK11 3LW, UK
UKHW050535150426
5217IPUK00026B/1947